# THE BIG BIG BOOK OF PAPER PLANES

AMAZING PAPER AIRPLANES THAT REALLY FLY!

**Thang Yang**

Winner Great International Paper Airplane Contest

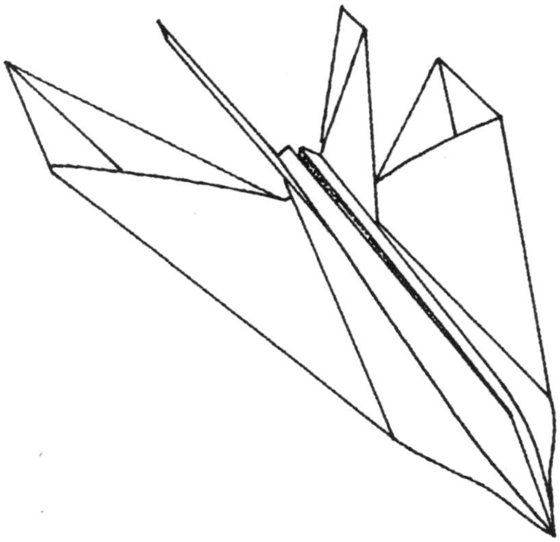

MUD PUDDLE BOOKS, INC.
New York, New York

Big Big Book of Paper Planes

This edition published in 2004 by:

Mud Puddle Books, Inc.
54 W. 21st Street
Suite 601
New York, NY 10010

info@mudpuddlebooks.com

ISBN: 1-59412-053-6



Cover designed by Elizabeth Elsas

Printed in the United States of America

Special thanks to

Say Yang and Vun Yang

# A Note from the Author

It gives me great pleasure to offer you these fourteen marvelous aircraft for folding and flying. For some time I've dreamed of sharing the Asian art of paper folding as applied to both simple and sophisticated airplanes as a way of demonstrating the magical uses of paper.

Paper that is neither written on nor read from can still educate and entertain you. In the hands of a clever student, the folding and flying of exotic paper airplanes can teach you about aeronautic principles while inspiring your creative imagination to soar.

# Contents



**THE PLANES**

# Introduction

Beginning with the Wright Brothers' first flight, airplanes have revolutionized the world. Planes of different types with very different purposes began appearing in and being tested by nations around the globe. Planes such as the U.S. F-14 Tomcat, the F-18 Hornet, Stealth fighters and other military planes are high performance descendants of the early dreams of flight.

The industrialized nations of the world have a variety of defensive aircraft, including both fighters and bombers, with individualized style and appearance. All have made a significant impact on world power. Many youngsters dream about flying such aircraft, and, if they are industrious and study hard, they may someday realize their dream.

Right now, young and old alike can learn a great deal about aeronautics while enjoying the challenge of creating modern fighting aircraft through the secret of folding paper airplanes. Never before have such compact and perfect paper airplanes been made. With only one sheet of paper, without knife or scissors, you will be able to create actual replicas of the world's fastest and most powerful planes. If you have ever dreamed of folding exotic paper airplanes, your dream is about to come true.

Once you have mastered the steps that are fully covered in the first two chapters (the Concord and the Jet), creating the rest of the planes should be easy.

In this book, you will find clear diagrams and easy-to-follow instructions to fold these marvelous planes with a single sheet of paper. No cutting is required. No previous book has ever offered techniques for constructing paper aircraft which did not involve cutting (although I offer optional cutting techniques) or the use of more than one piece of paper. No previous book offers this much realism in appearance as well as flight.

I urge you to fold each plane in sequence. You will need to learn the simple folding techniques in the first planes to master the more complex planes at the book's end.

While I hope that you will have fun with the book, you can also learn from it. After you have folded these planes several times, I think you'll want to experiment: change the shape, combine different techniques, learn to create other airplanes. That's what happened to me. If you are patient and let your creativity and imagination soar, it will happen to you as well.

# Glossary

**Aileron (or flap)** ▪ the hinged, movable trailing edge of a wing used to alter wing shape (camber), and therefore lift and drag, especially during landing.

**Crease** ▪ the result of a fold

**Elevator** ▪ a horizontal control surface at the trailing edge of the plane that can be bent up or down to control or cause climbing or diving.

**Fin** ▪ the upright part of the tail.

**Fuselage** ▪ the body of the airplane.

**Rudder** ▪ a vertical control surface at the trailing edge of the plane that can be moved to initiate a right or left turn.

**Stabilizer** ▪ the fixed horizontal part at the tail of the plane.

**Trim** ▪ fold or bend to control turning, climbing or diving.

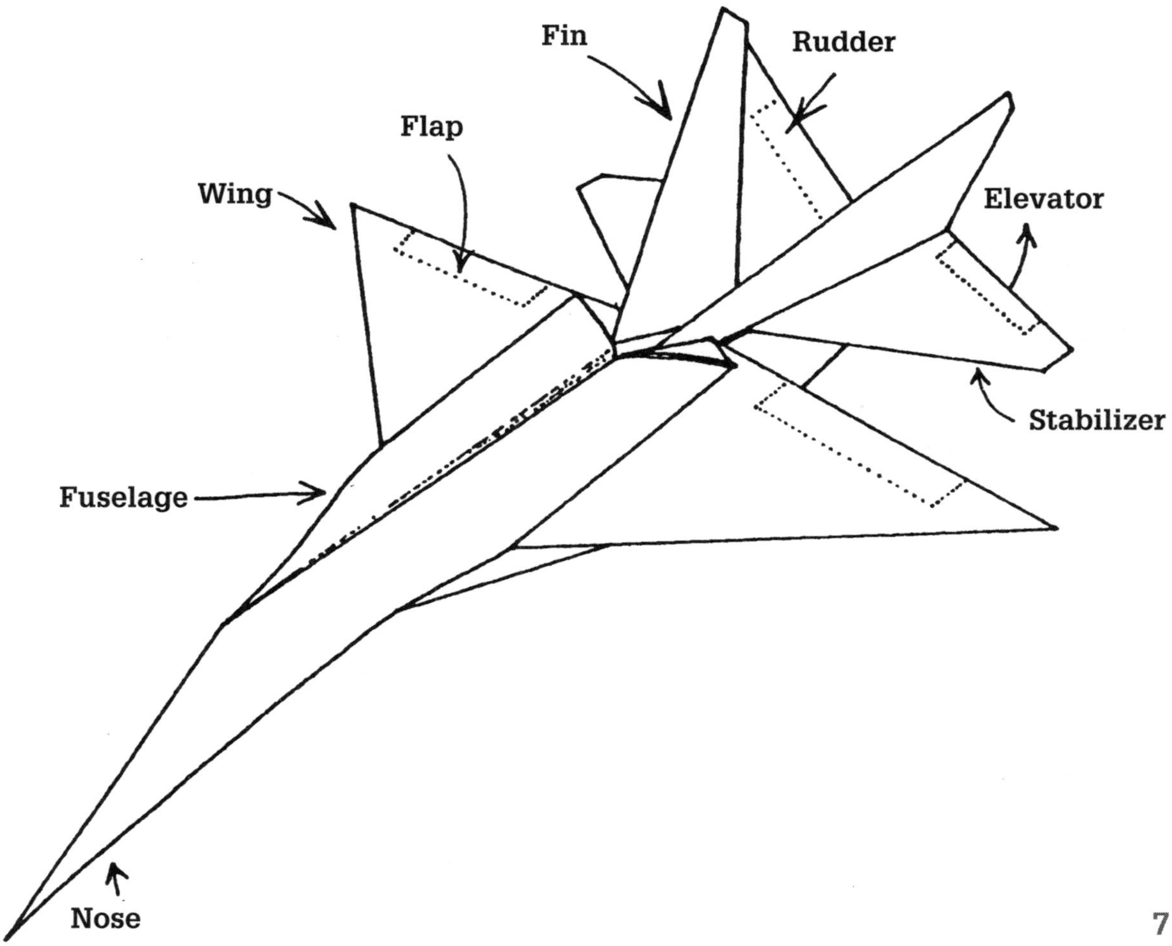

# Flying Tips for Paper Airplanes

**1)** Fold paper evenly. A firm sturdy shape flies best.

**2)** Fold the tail fin straight up.

**3)** Use pressure when folding to ensure crisp points.

**4)** Throw straight.

**5)** If plane loops, add weight (e.g., a paperclip) to the nose.

**6)** To climb, trim the elevators up. To dive, trim the elevators down.

**7)** Trim rudders to the right for right turns and to the left for left turns.

**8)** For stunts, trim one aileron down and the other up. This will make the plane spin and roll as it flies.

# Guide to Symbols

Indication of a hidden fold 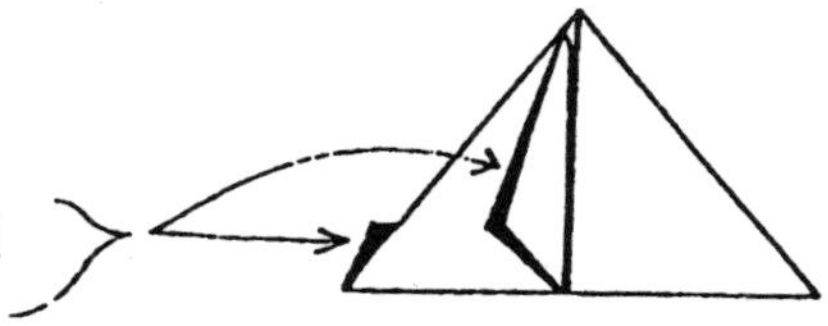

Fold line ----------------

Crease line ........................

Distance 

Inches = "

Fold direction 

Fold back & forth (or side to side) 

Fold behind 

Fold then unfold 

Turn model over 

Unfold 

Where to press your thumb & index finger 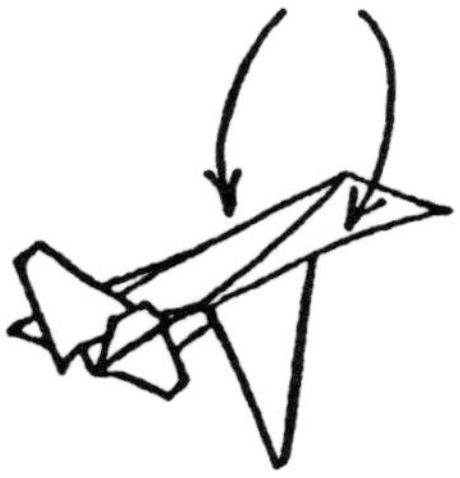

# Practice Fold #1:
# Inside-Reverse Fold

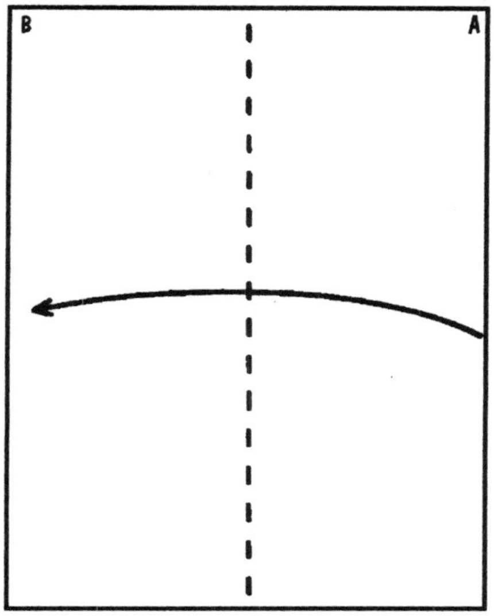


1) Fold the paper in half.

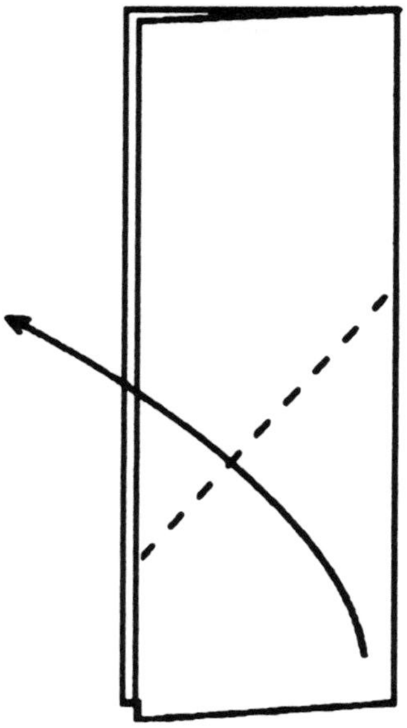

2) Fold the bottom half diagonally to the left side.

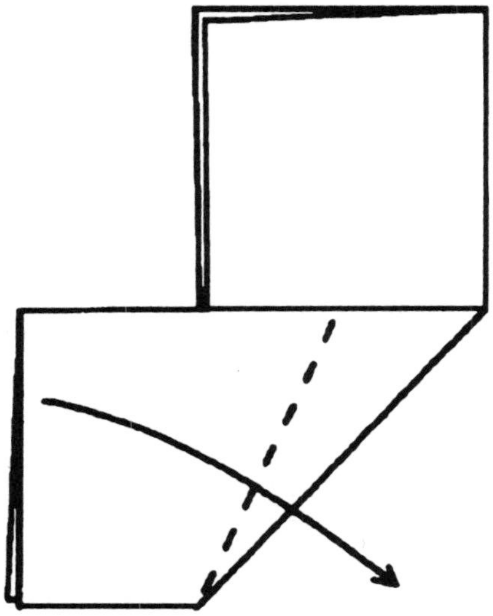

3) Fold diagonally back down.

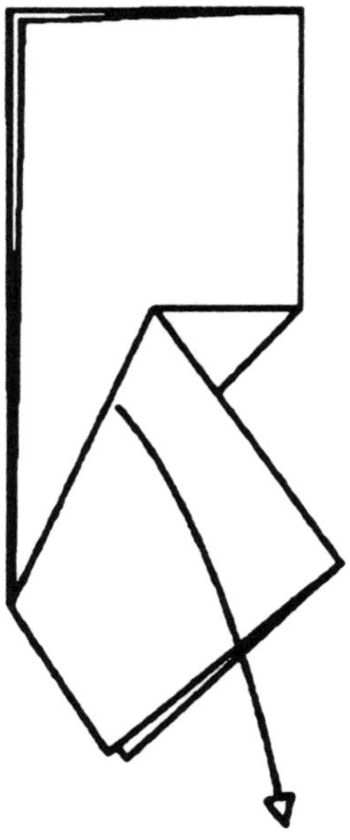

4) Unfold completely.

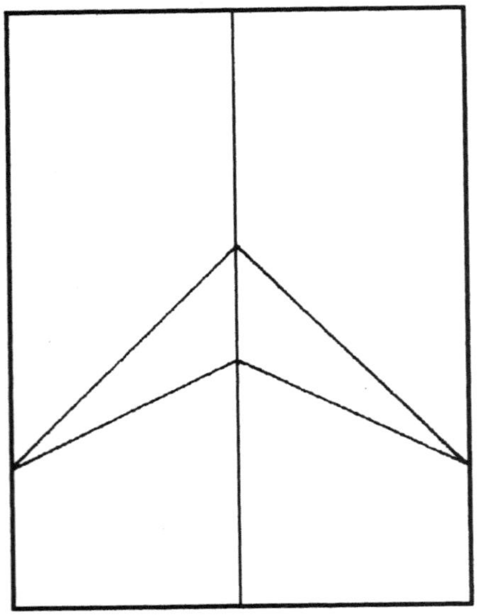

5) This is what the paper should look like with crease lines.

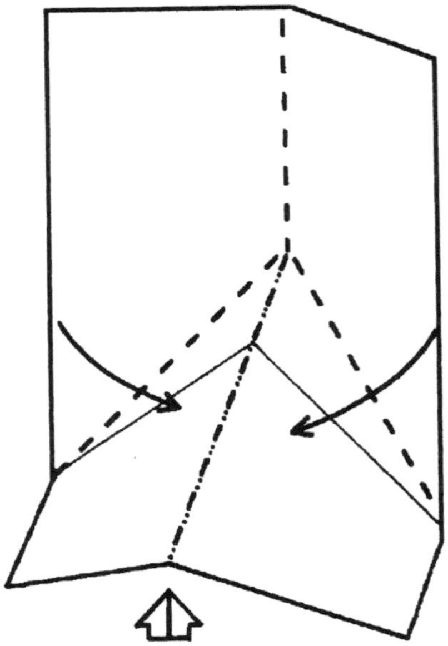

6) Fold the two sides together and raise up the center fold.

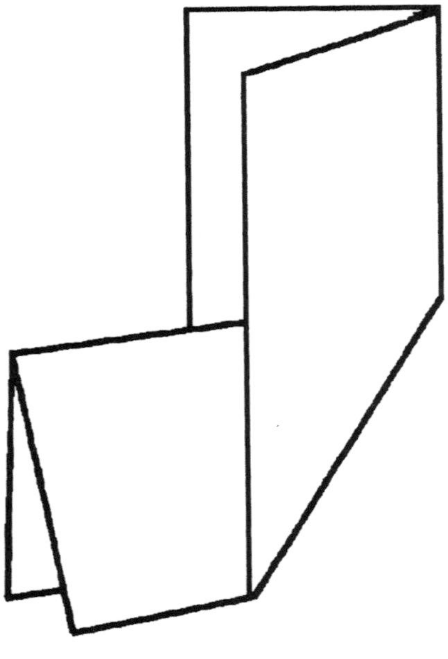

7) The fold looks like this.

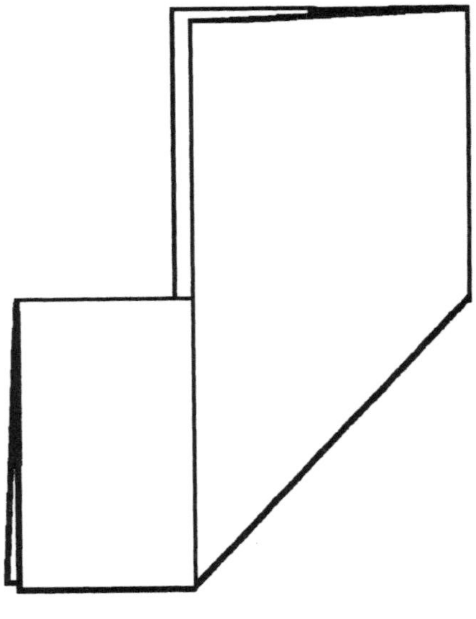

8) Push flat.

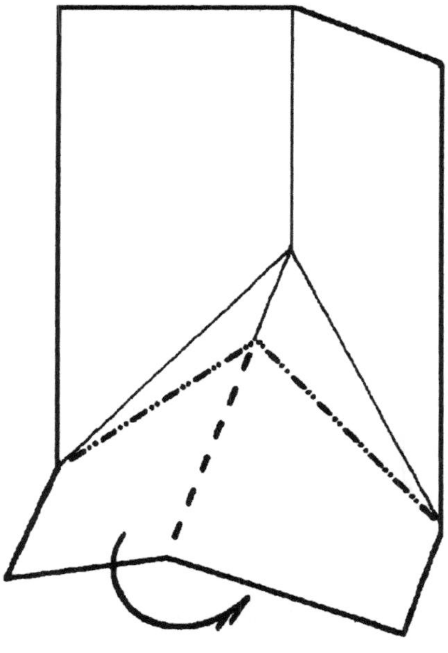

9) Open the paper half way and fold inward on the marked crease lines.

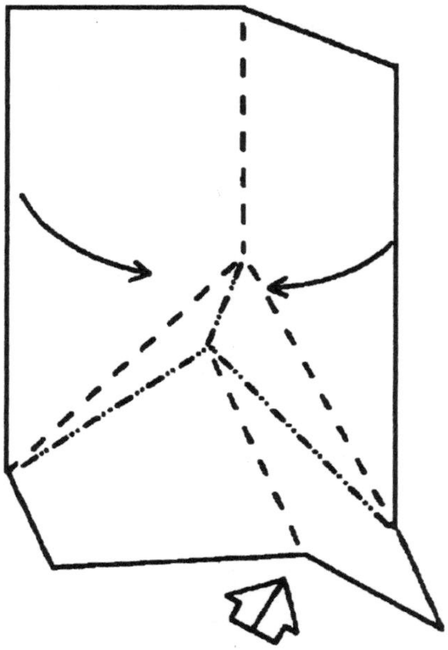

10) Fold the two sides of the paper together again with the bottom part of the paper folding away to the back side.

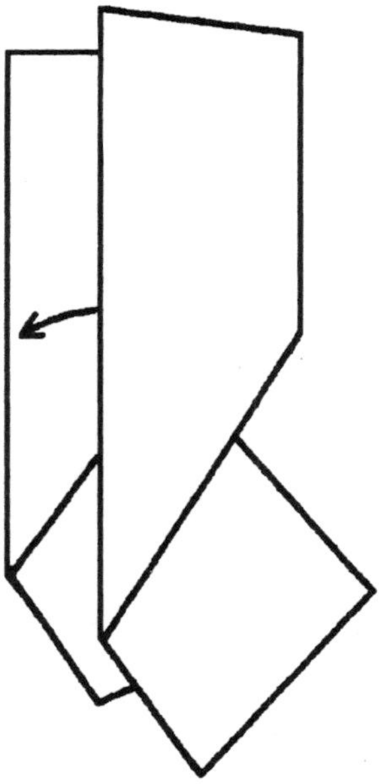

11) Close the paper tightly together.

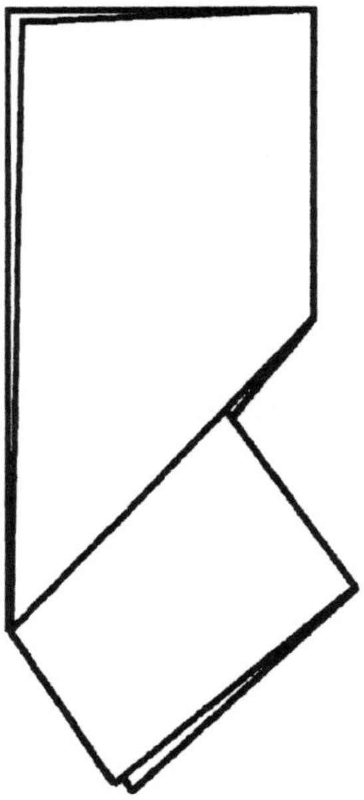

12) Completion of inside-reverse fold. This is a vital folding technique, so try it a few times before moving on.

# Practice Fold #2: The Fuselage Fold

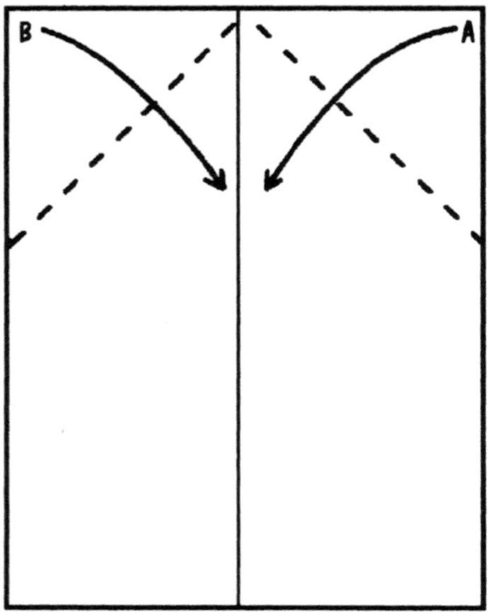


1) Begin with a center line. Fold corners A and B down to the center crease line.

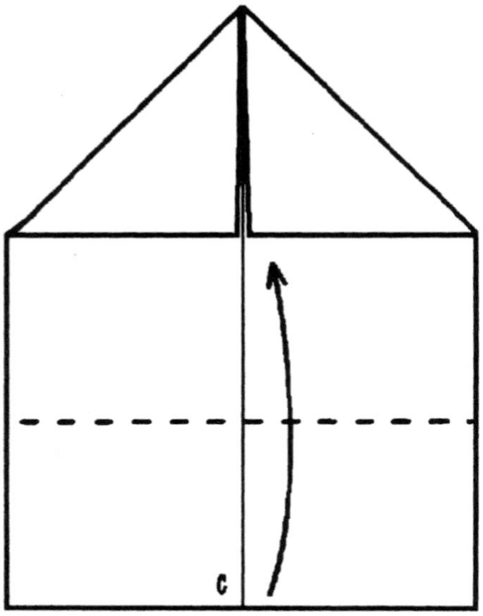


2) Fold C up to meet with the horizontal bottom edge of A and B.

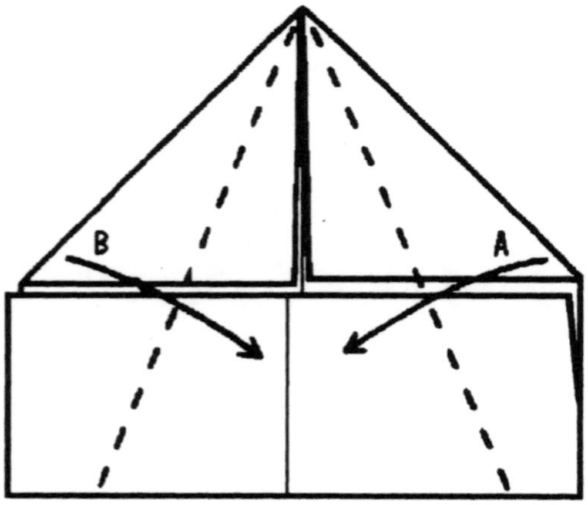


3) Fold A & B to the center line.

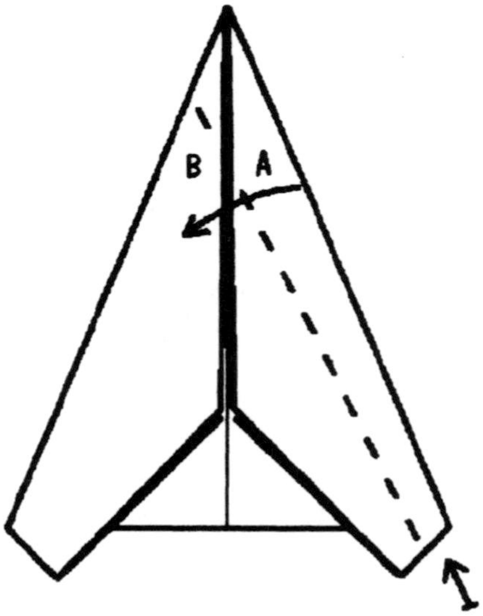


4) The coordinates for this fold are 2" down and 1/2" at the pivot point indicated by the small arrow). Fold side A.

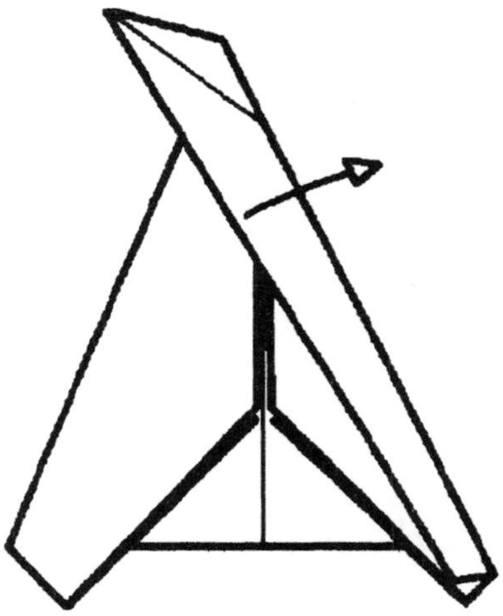

5) unfold.

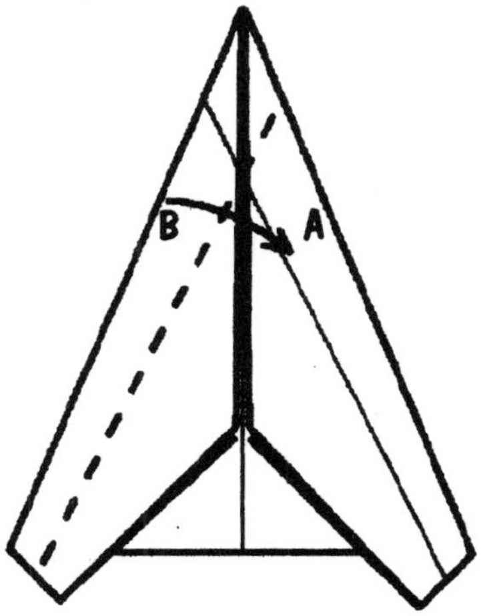


6) Fold side B.

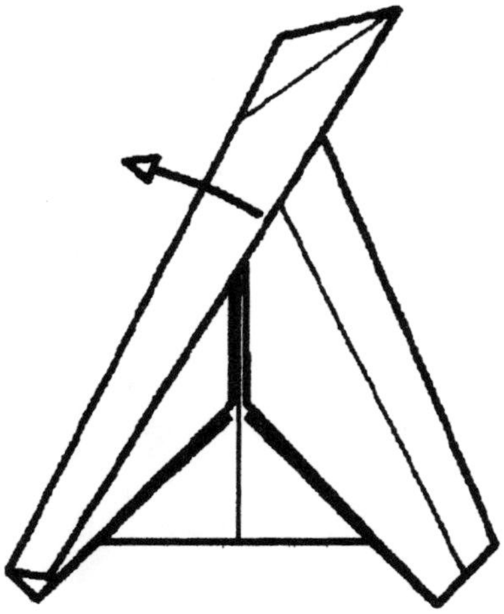

7) Unfold

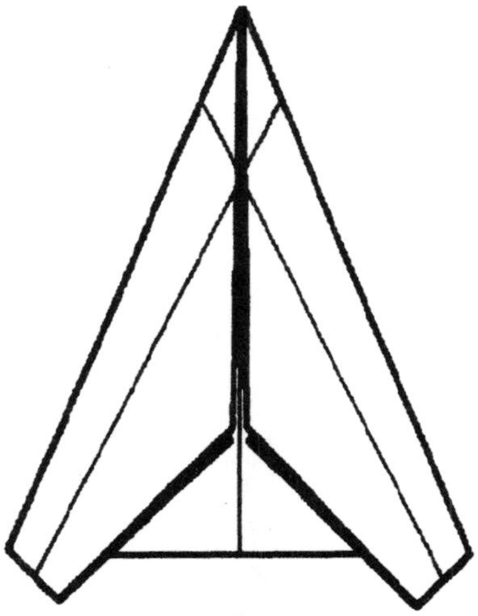

8) This diagram shows the two resulting crease lines crossing.

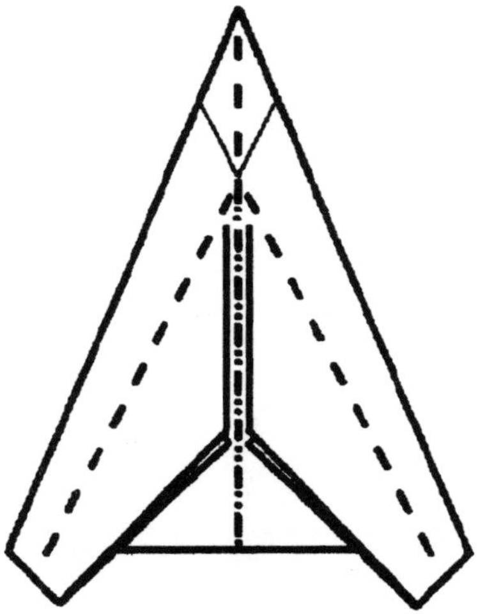

9) Make an inside-reverse fold using the existing creases. The mountain crease rises up between the two outside edges.

NOTE: This is the fuselage reverse fold. The fuselage folds for the planes in this book have similar diagrams but different coordinates.

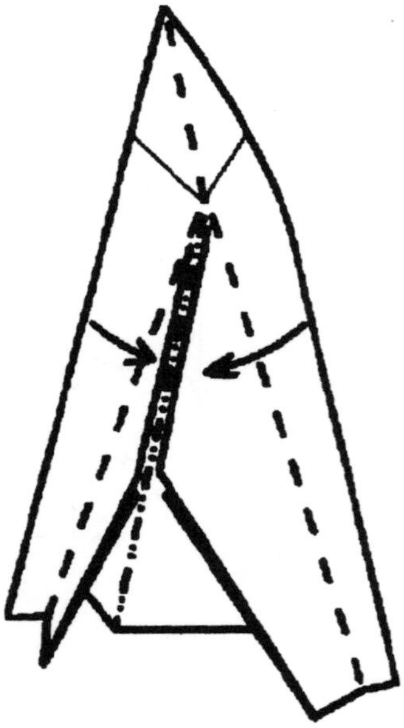

10) Proceed through the fold.

11) Flatten loosely.

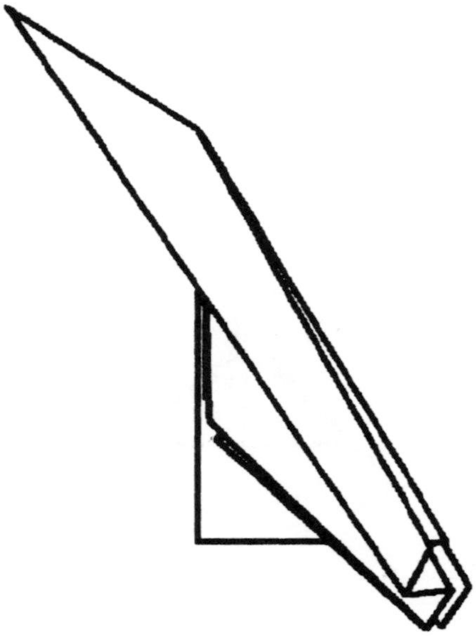

12) Fuselage fold completed.

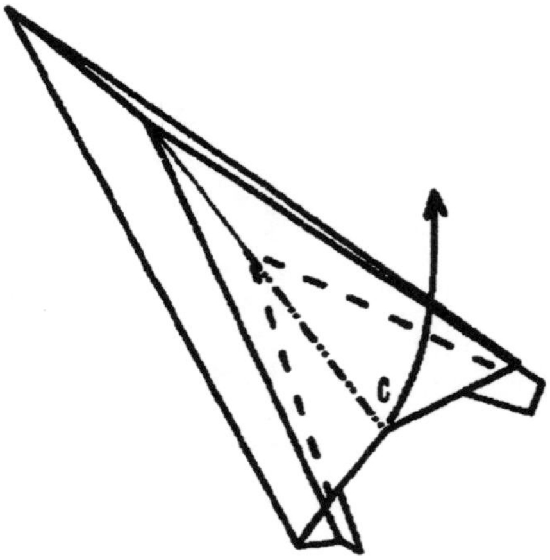

13) The tail fin of the plane. Here the inside-reverse fold is going up.

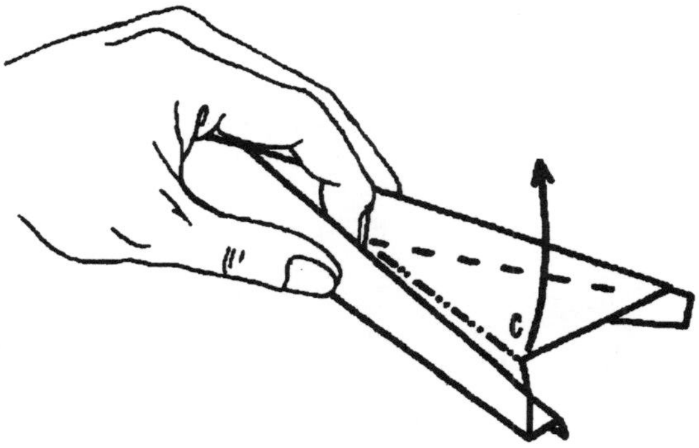


14) To make this reversal, hold the nose end of the plane with your left hand. Place your index finger in the center crease line as shown here. Hold the plane tightly at the nose end, and control the size of the tail fin by sliding your index finger up or down the center crease line. At the lowest point of the belly, reverse it straight up the center with your right hand.

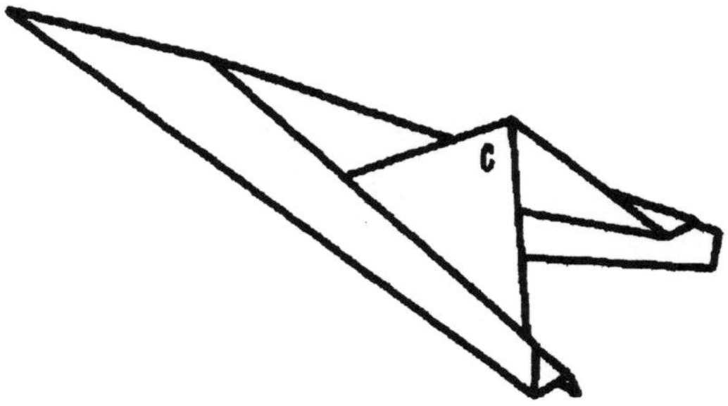


15) The inside-reverse fold looks like this.

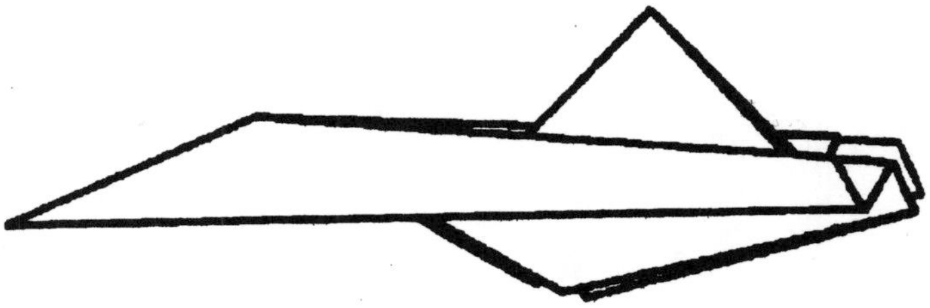

16) Completed tail fin fold.

Practice these important folds a few times until you are confident. Now you're ready to start folding real planes. You've earned your wings!

# CONCORD SST

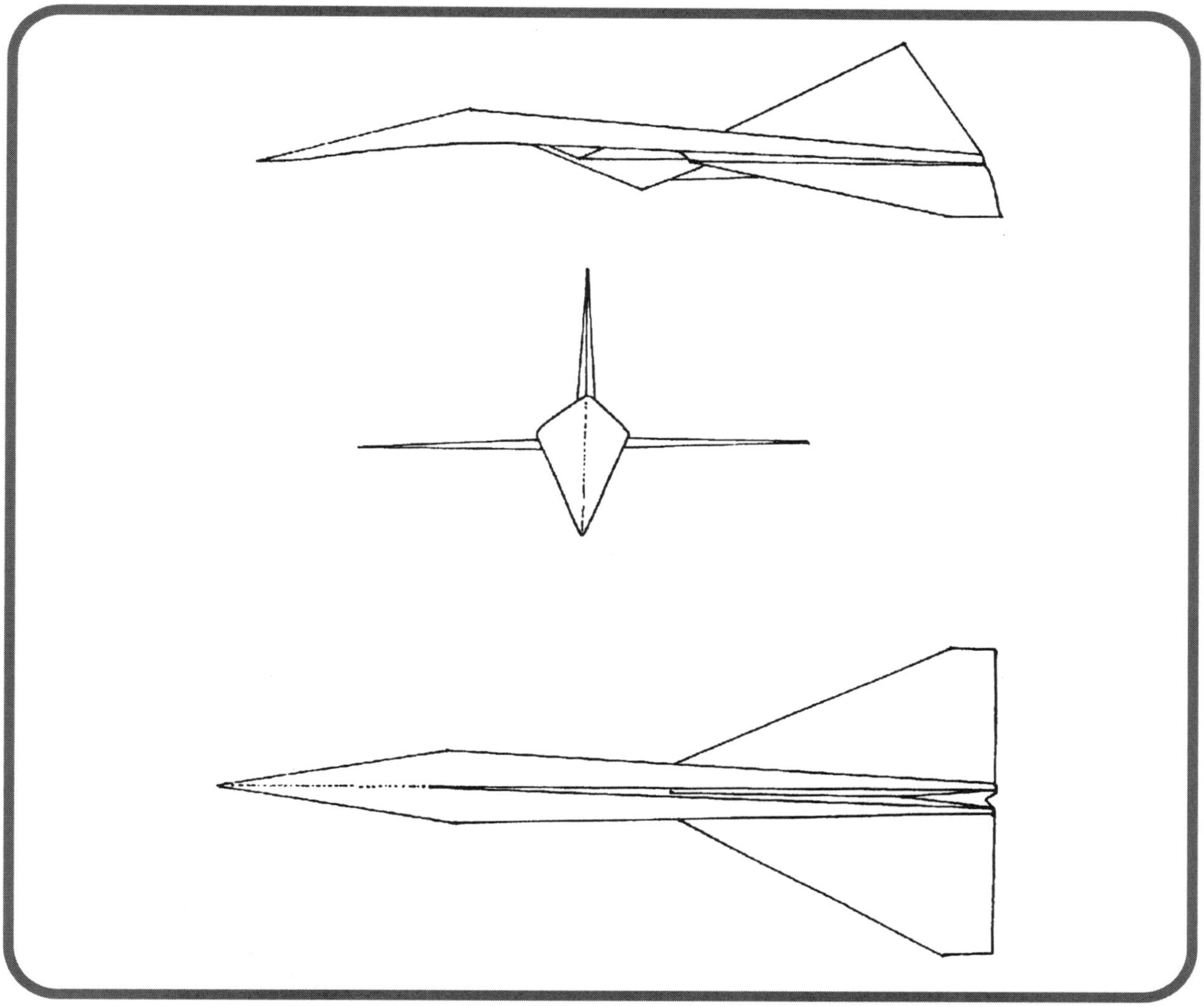

This plane is the simplest to fold of all the planes in this book. It uses basic folding techniques employed throughout the rest of the book. To be successful, follow the steps carefully and precisely. The most important element is to pull up the nose of the plane, and carefully press and align the back, as shown in the drawings. Also, make sure both sides are folded evenly on every fold throughout the plane assembly. Mastering the steps displayed in drawings 16 through 22 in the Concord will greatly improve your future foldings.

NOTE: I suggest that you fold this plane at least five times before going on to other planes.

**1**

Lay an ordinary piece of 8½" x 11" paper on a flat surface.

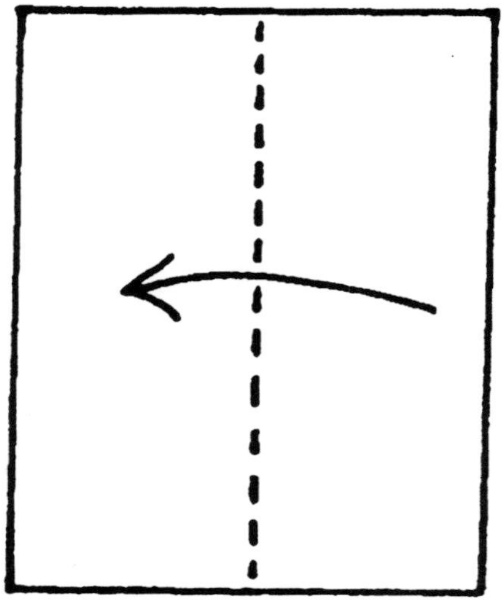

**2**

Fold the paper in half.

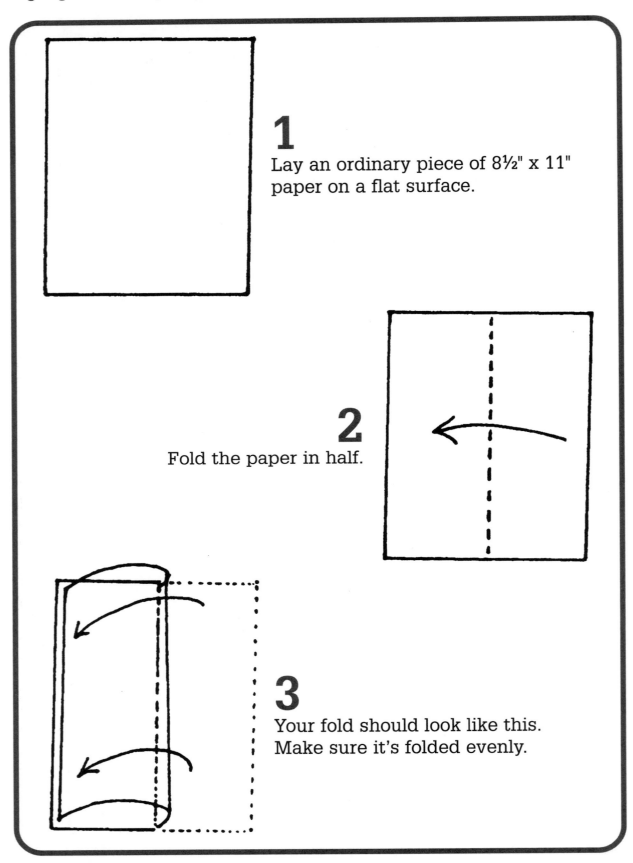

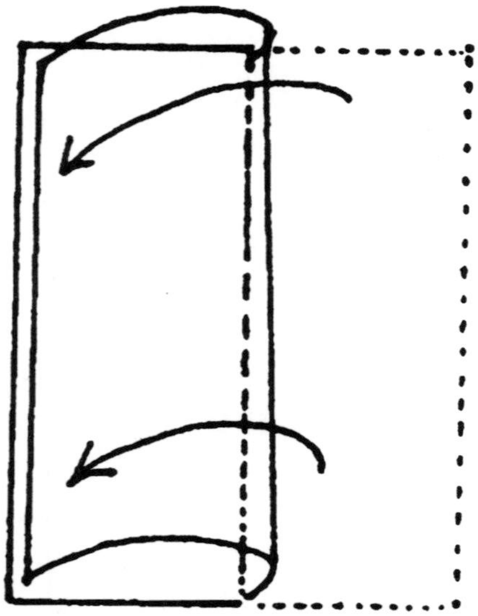

**3**

Your fold should look like this. Make sure it's folded evenly.

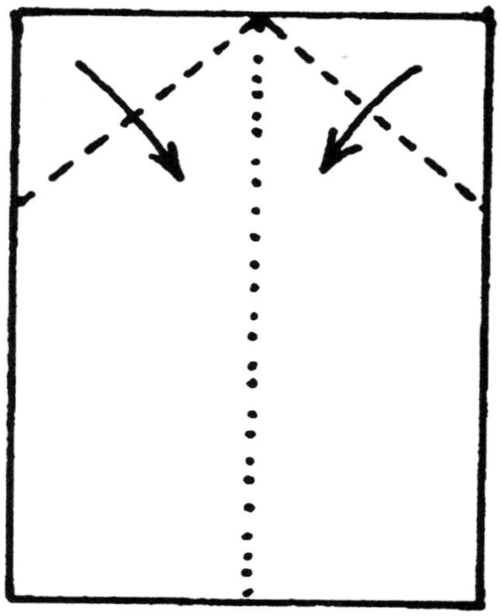

# 4

Now, unfold the paper and fold down the top corners as indicated by the arrows.

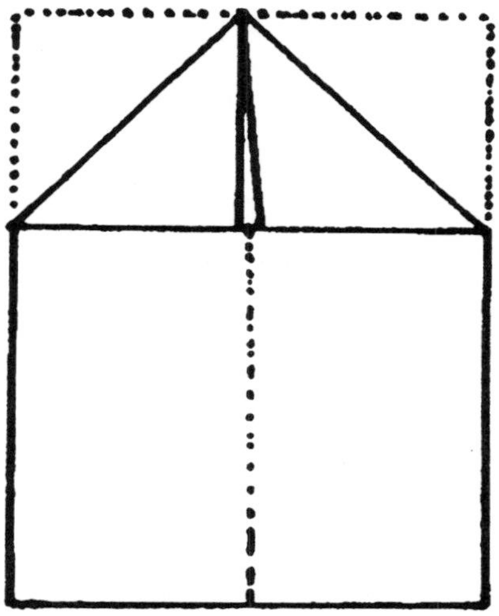

# 5

Your fold should look like this.

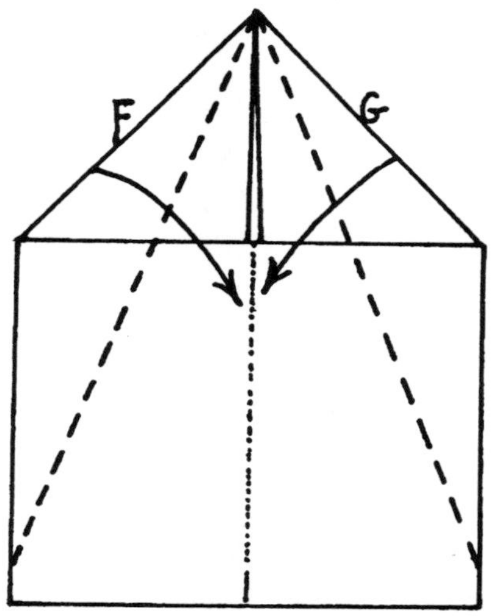


# 6

Fold the two edges, F & G, toward the centerline, as indicated.

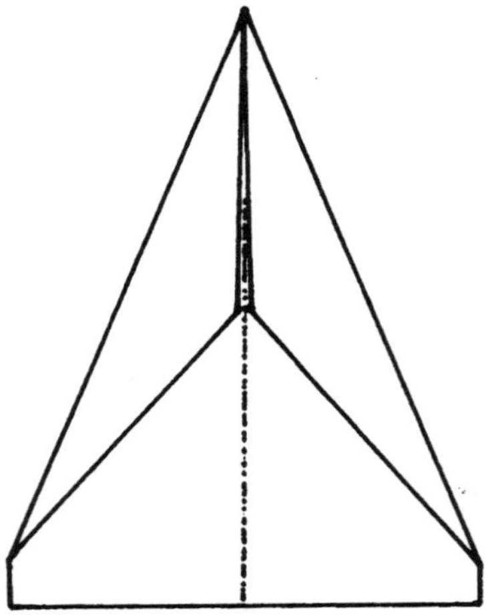

# 7

It should now look like this.

# 8

Now, fold the two sides, B & C, in toward the centerline.

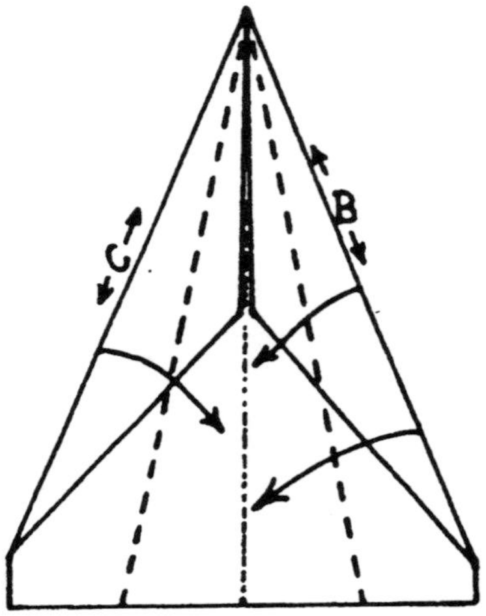


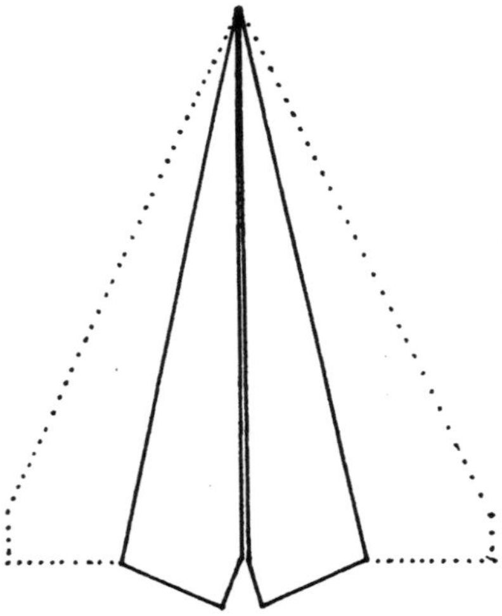

# 9

After folding toward the centerline, the paper should look like this.

# 10

Fold the wings out 2½" from the tip as shown by the two big arrows.

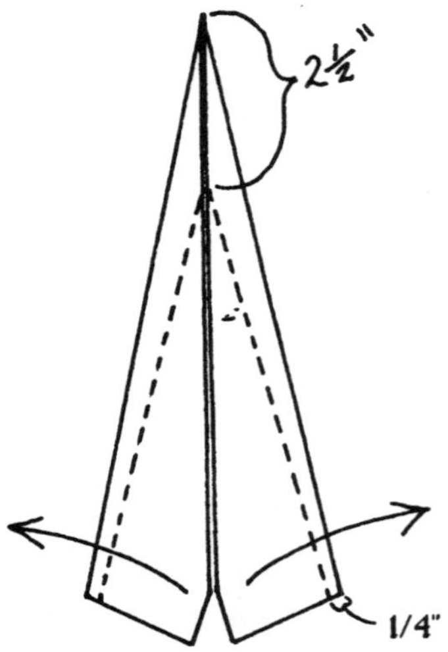

## 11

Your folded wings should look like this.

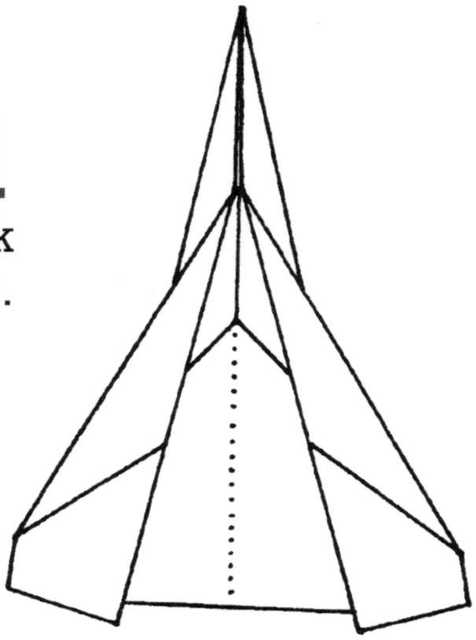

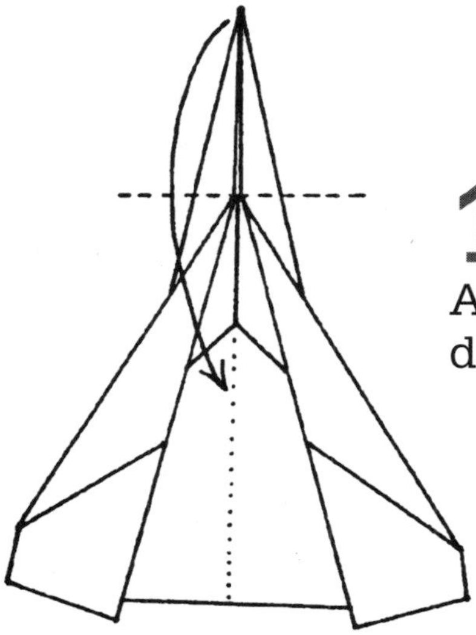

## 12

About 2" from the top, fold down on the dotted line.

## 13

Your fold should look like this.

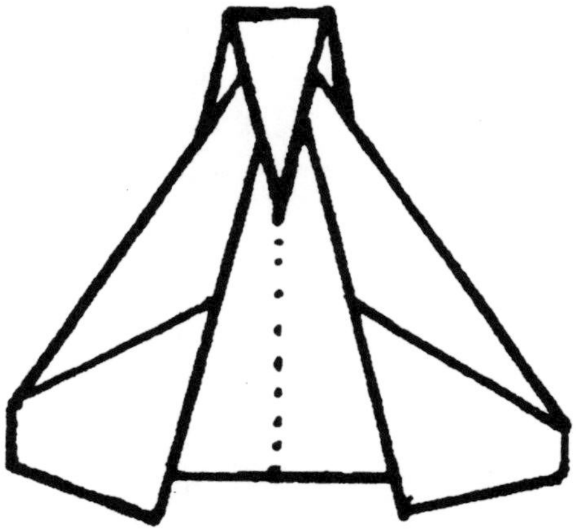

## 14

After you have folded the nose down, fold the two sides of the plane toward the back as indicated, along the centerline.

## 15

It should look like this from the side. Pull up the nose as shown by the arrows.

## 16

After you have pulled up the nose of the plane, position your hands as indicated here.

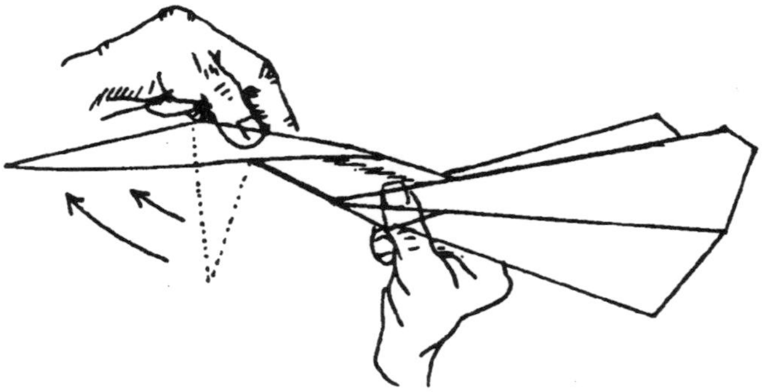

## 17

Now, place the plane upside down on a flat surface.

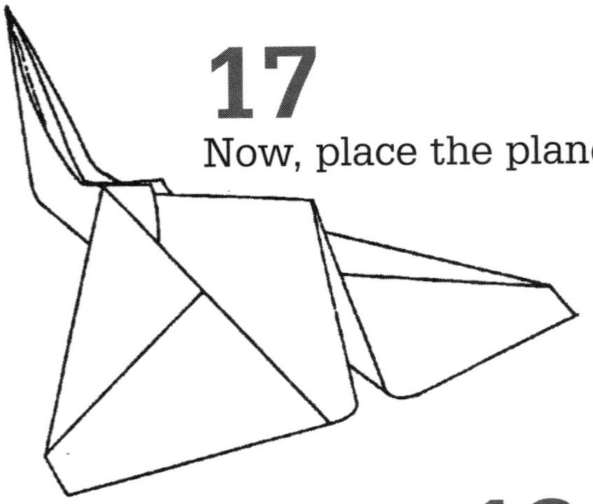

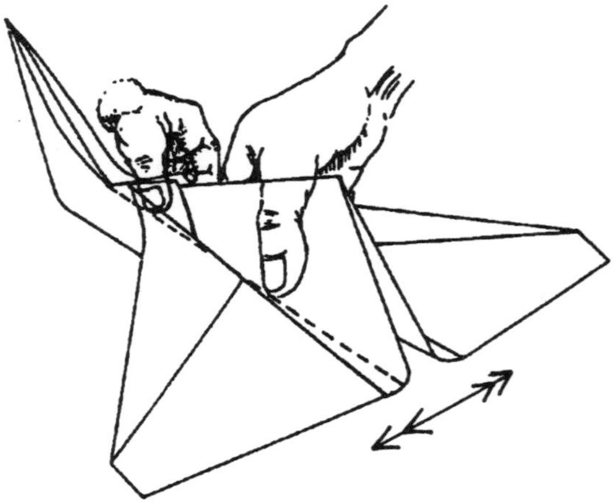

## 18

Place both of your hands exactly as shown here and hold the plane tightly. Fold back and forth on the dotted line three times on each side.

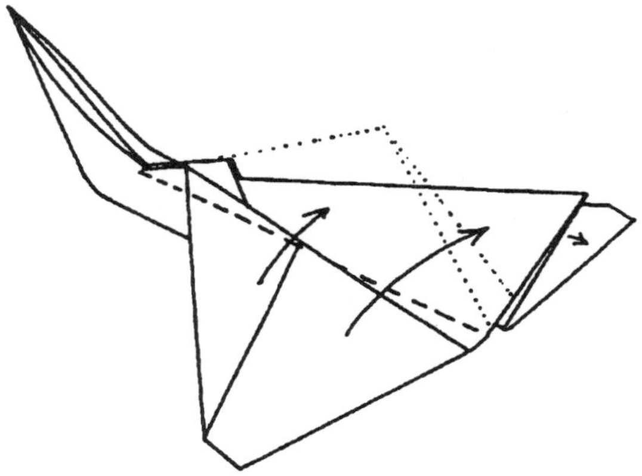

## 19

Fold it to the right as shown here, and then to the left.

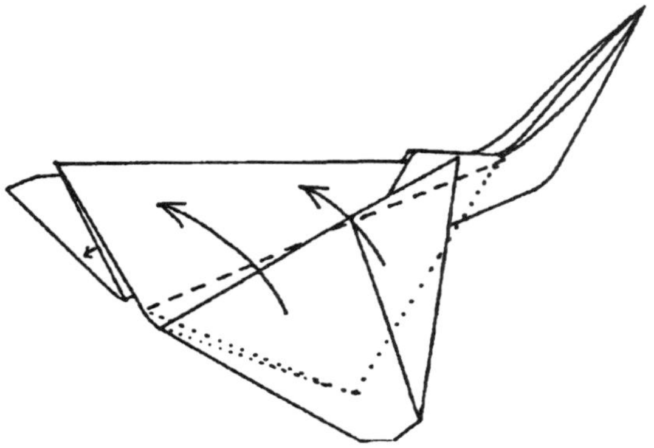

## 20

Fold it to the left as shown, then to the right. This sets the back into position.

NOTE: Steps 17 to 20 here should be used for all planes in this book.

## 21

Now, flip the plane upright again and press the back down and together as indicated by the arrows.

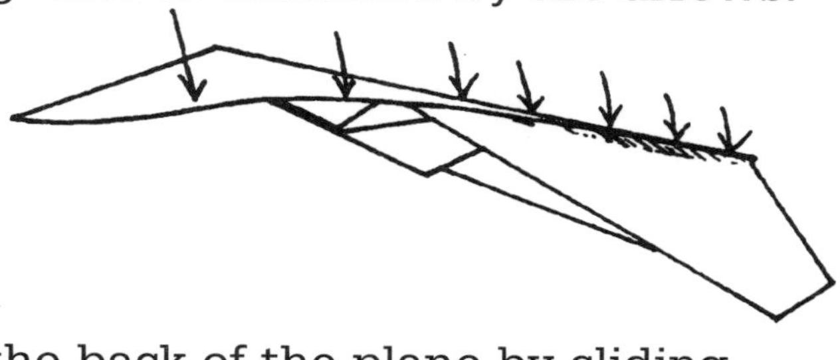

## 22

Now, carefully line up the back of the plane by sliding your left hand back and forth as shown here. Then fold the wings up on the dotted line.

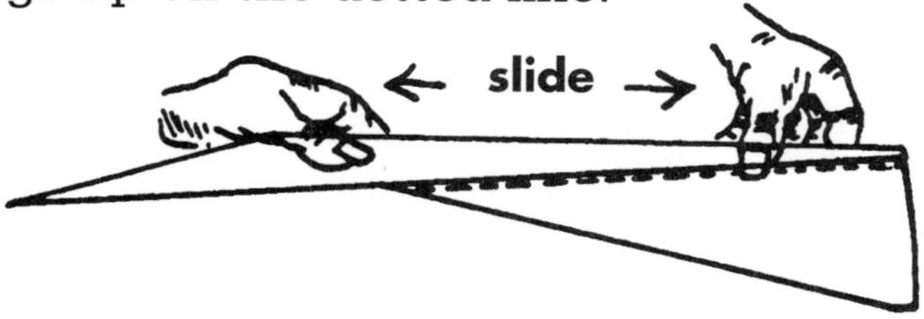

## 23

Your folded wings should look like this.

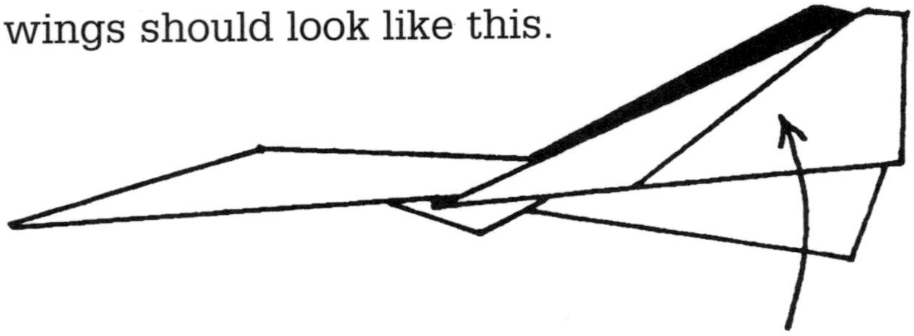

## 24

To make a tail fin, fold the tail back and forth three or four times at the dotted line.

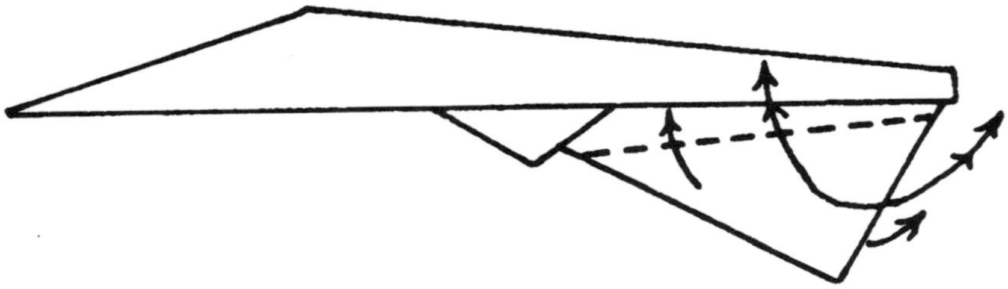

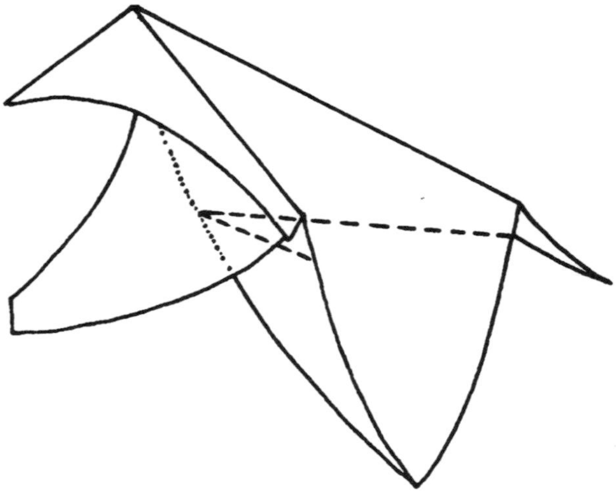

## 25

After folding the tail back and forth a few times, it should look like this from the rear.

## 26

Now, carefully lift the tail (fin upward) on the dotted line as indicated here from the rear view.

NOTE: Once you know how to pull up the tail fin, you won't need to fold it back and forth first.

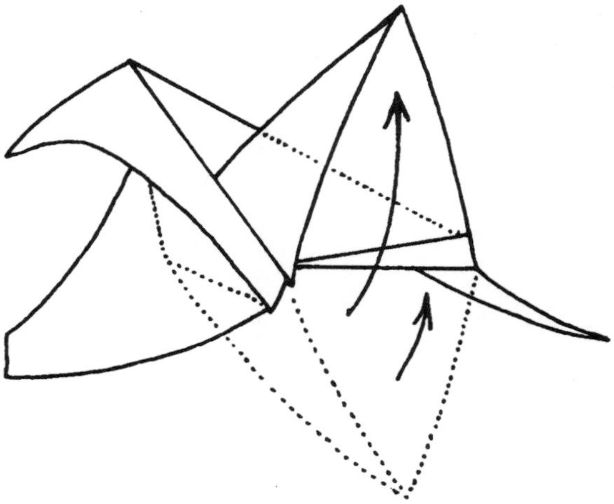

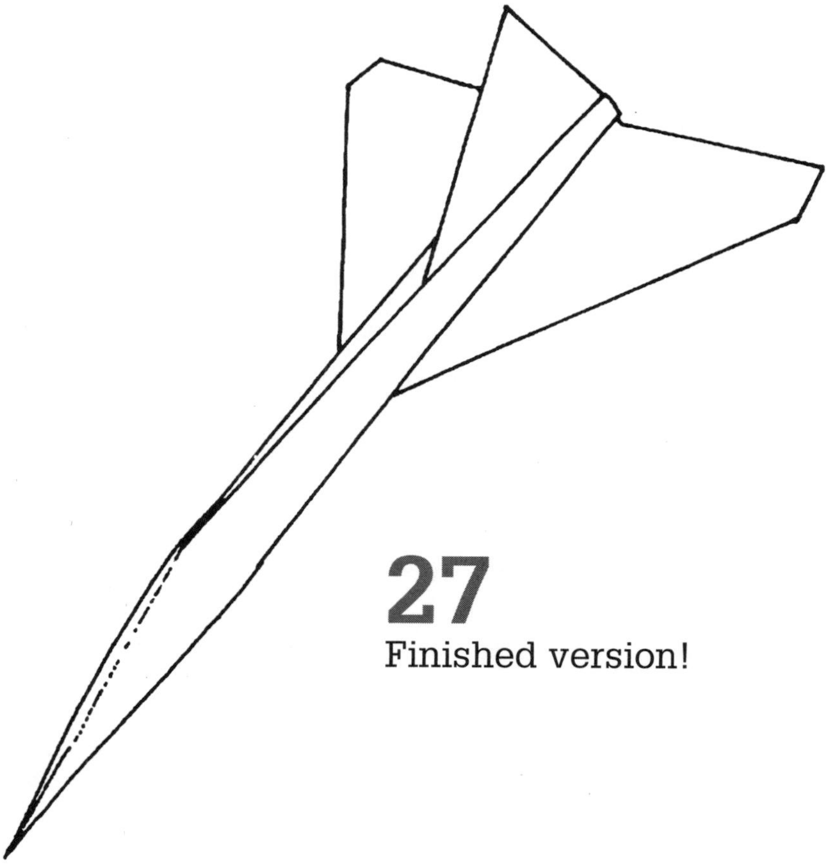

## 27

Finished version!

# CONCORD SST

# JET

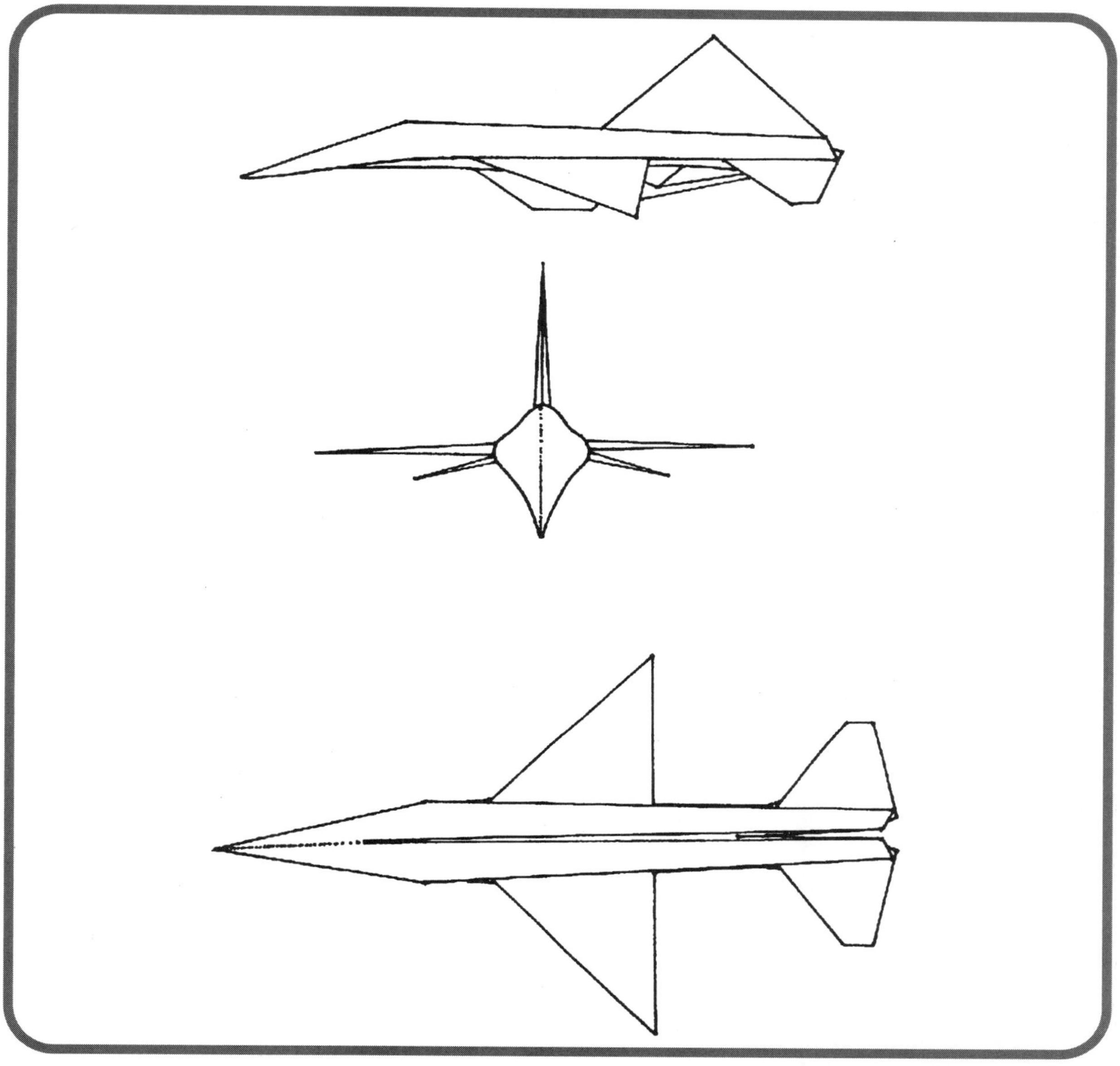

The Jet is the second primary plane that you must know how to fold before going on to other planes. Carefully follow all the steps and diagrams. Remember, always make sure that all folds are even. Use the techniques you learned from the Concord to help you align the back.

NOTE: Many of the steps you learn in this section will also be used on the planes ahead.

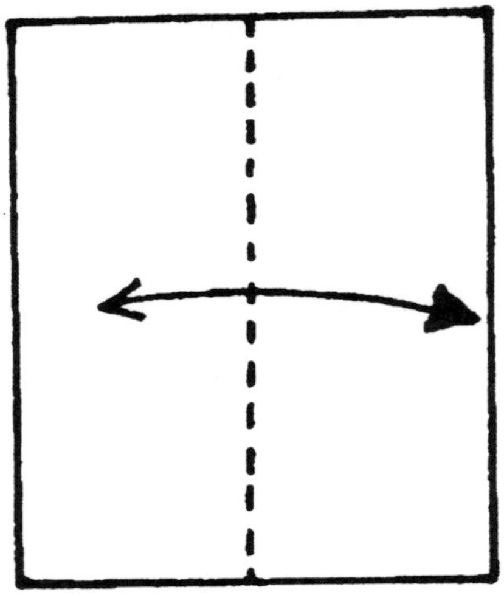

**1**

Fold paper in half, then unfold.

**2**

Fold diagonally at dotted lines, then unfold.

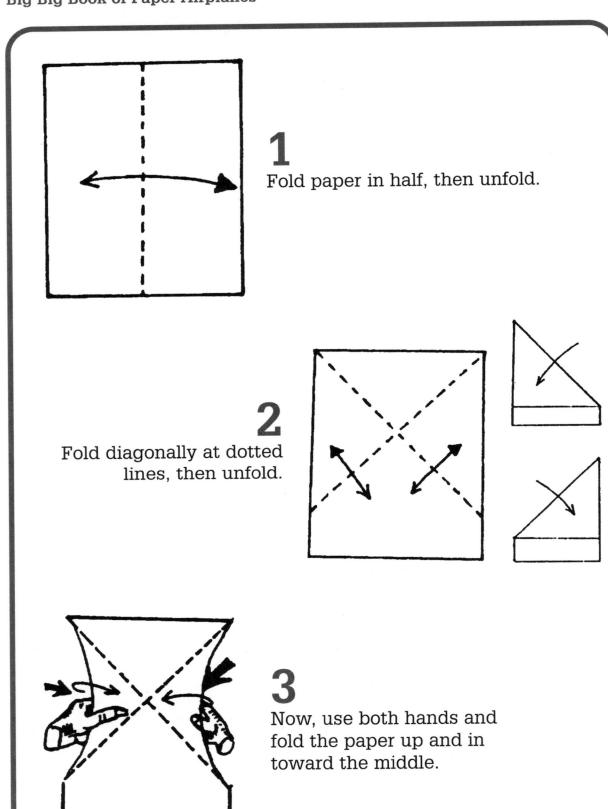

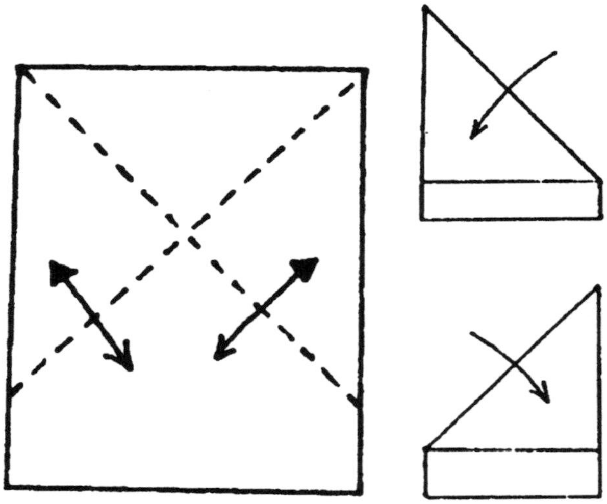

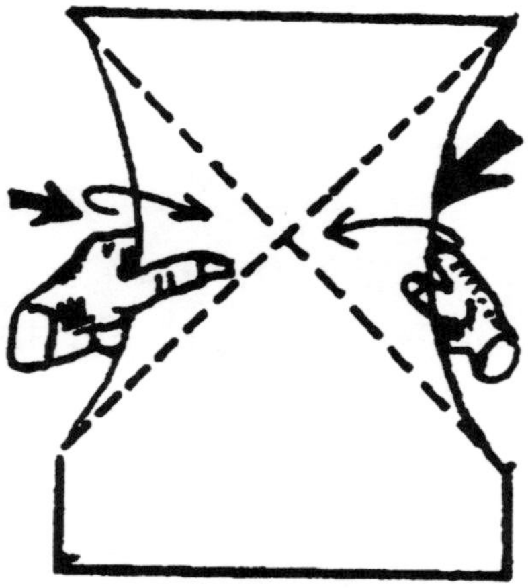

**3**

Now, use both hands and fold the paper up and in toward the middle.

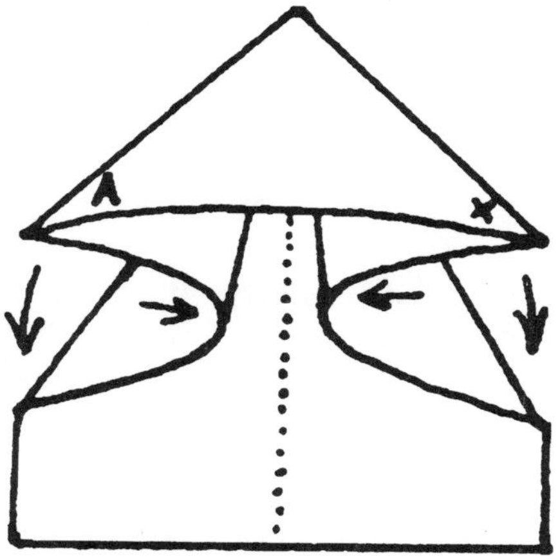


## 4

This is how the paper should look. Gently press down from the top.

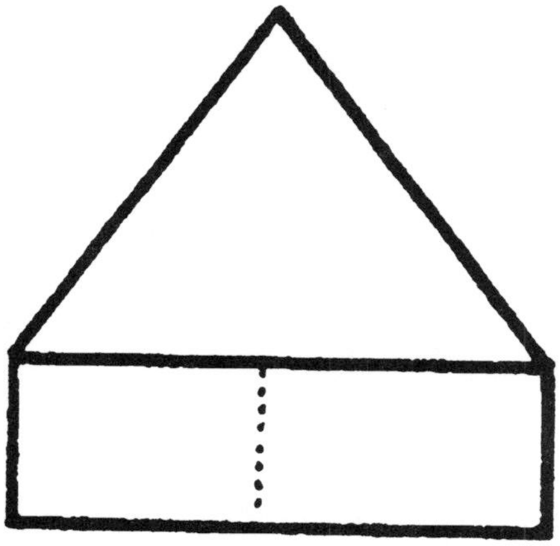

## 5

Now, it should look like this.

## 6

Slide your right hand under Flap X as shown here.

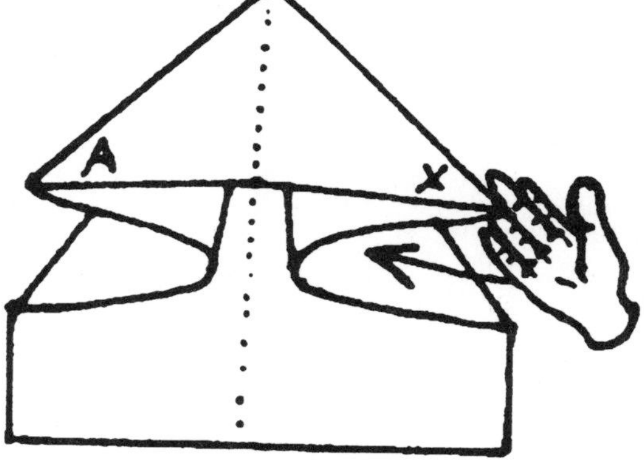

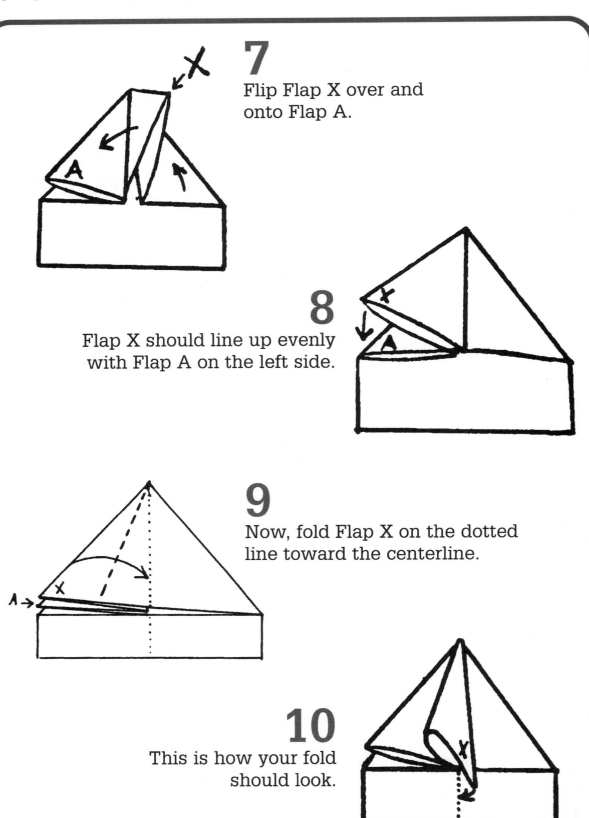

## 7

Flip Flap X over and onto Flap A.

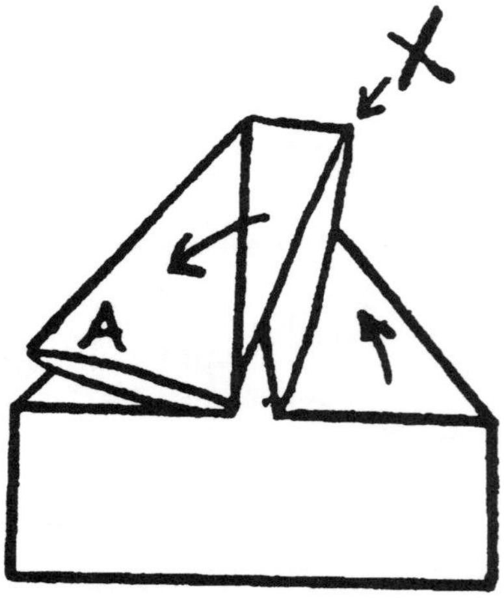


## 8

Flap X should line up evenly with Flap A on the left side.

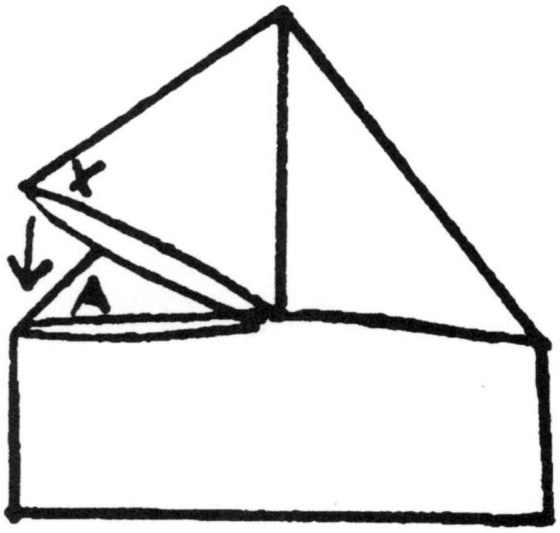


## 9

Now, fold Flap X on the dotted line toward the centerline.

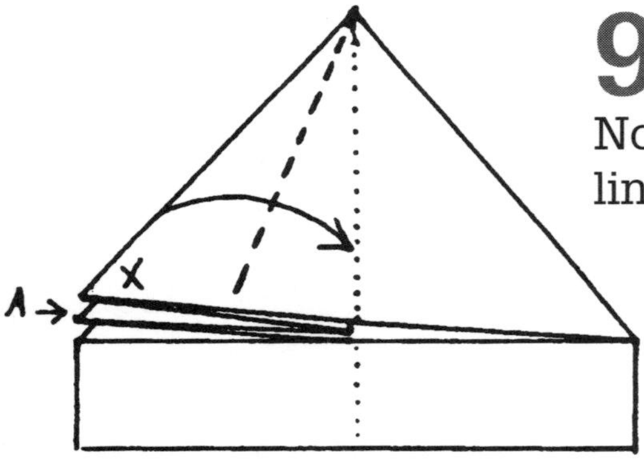


## 10

This is how your fold should look.

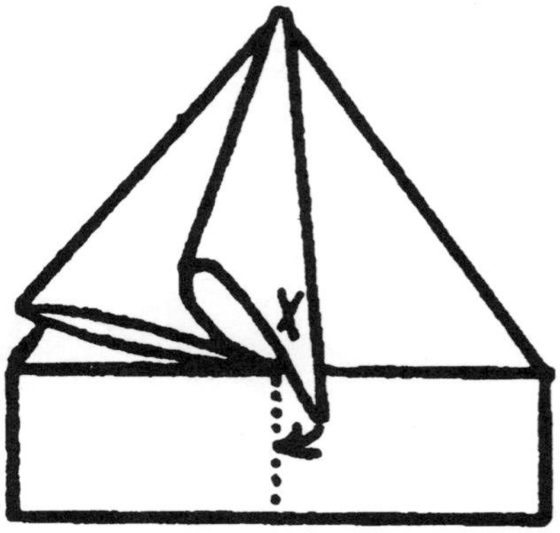

## 11

After you have folded Flap X toward the middle flap, flip it to the right side. Notice the B Edge.

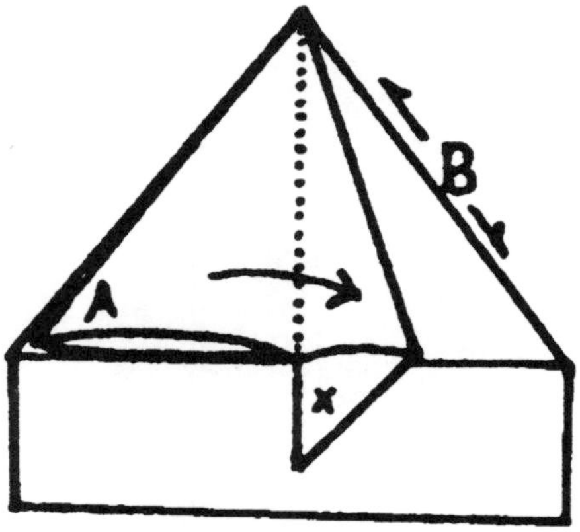


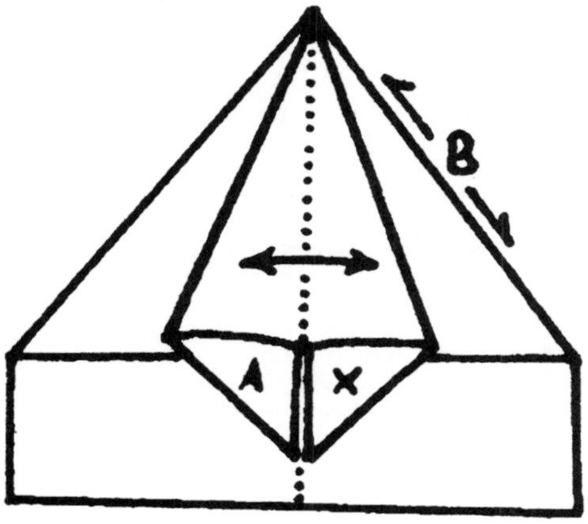


## 12

Now, repeat Steps 9–11 for the left side, and open the flaps to look like this.

## 13

Now, flip Flap X to the left, over Flap A again.

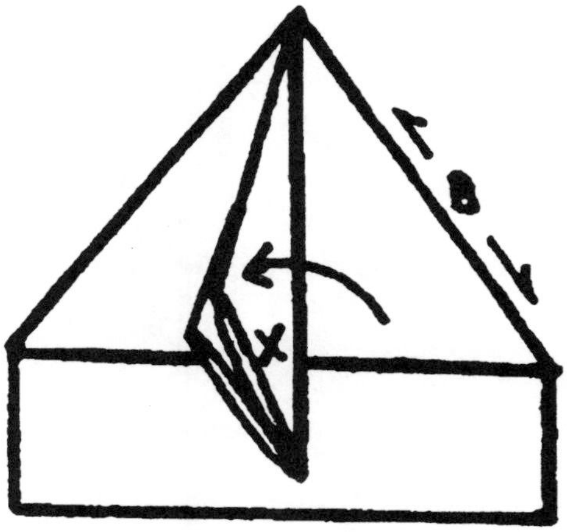


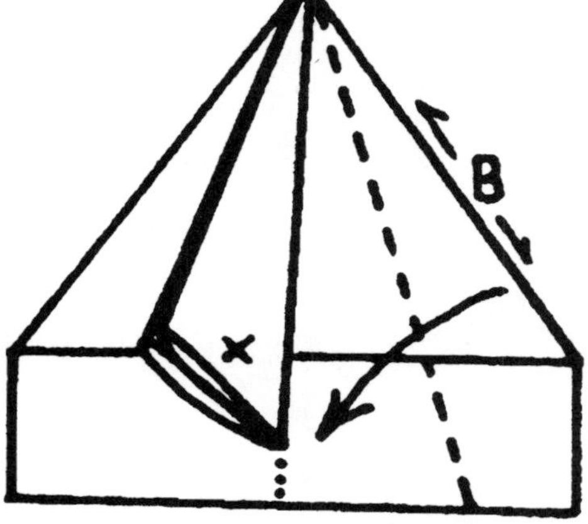


## 14

Then fold Side B on the dotted line to the centerline.

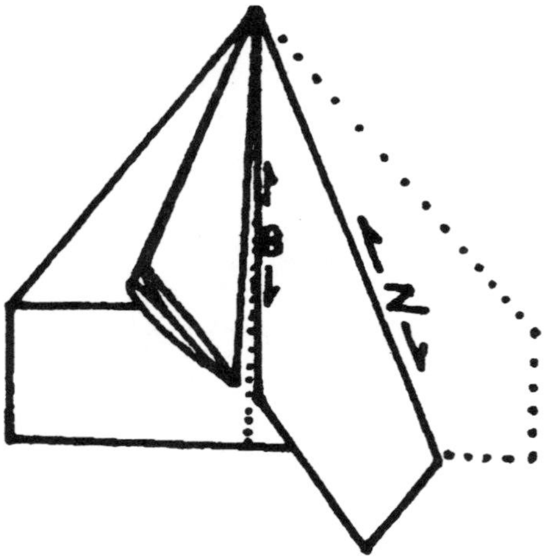


## 15

Now it should look like this.

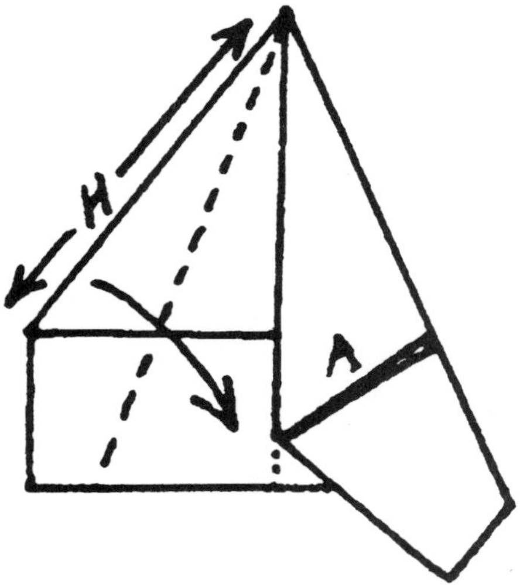


## 16

Now, flip both Flaps A & X to the right side. Repeat Step 14 for the left side.

## 17

Spread Flaps A & X apart like this.

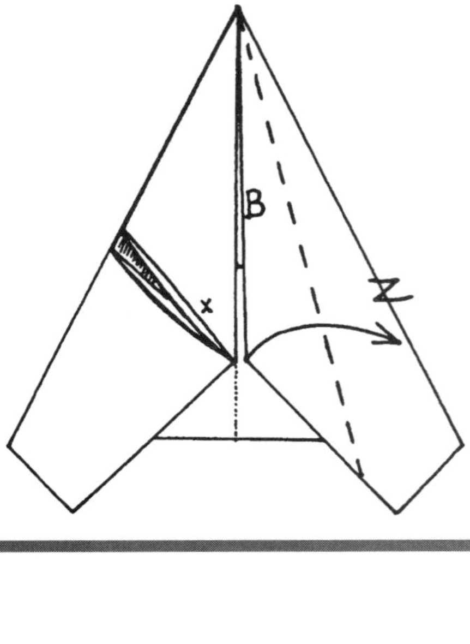


## 18

Now, flip Flap X to the left side. Then fold Edge B on the dotted line and match it evenly with Edge Z.

## 19

This is how the fold should look.

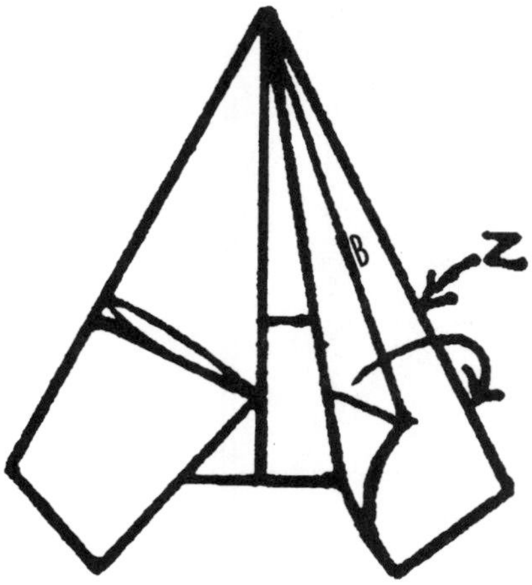


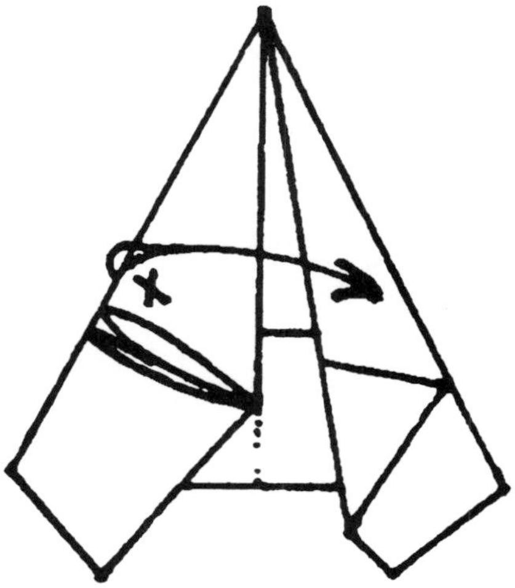


## 20

Now, flip Flaps A & X to the right.

## 21

Repeat Step 18 on the left side.

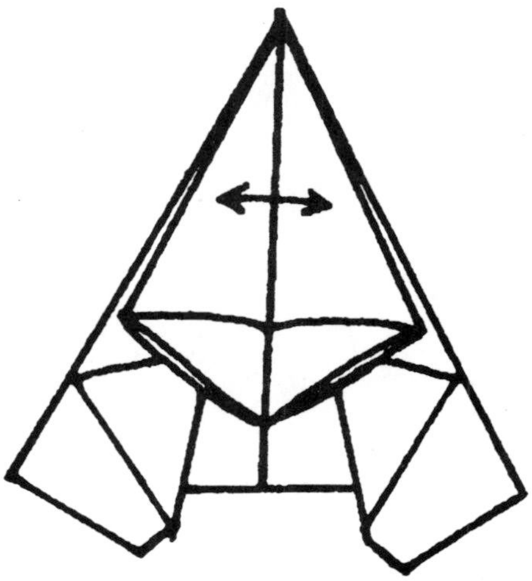

## 22

Then spread the flaps as shown here.

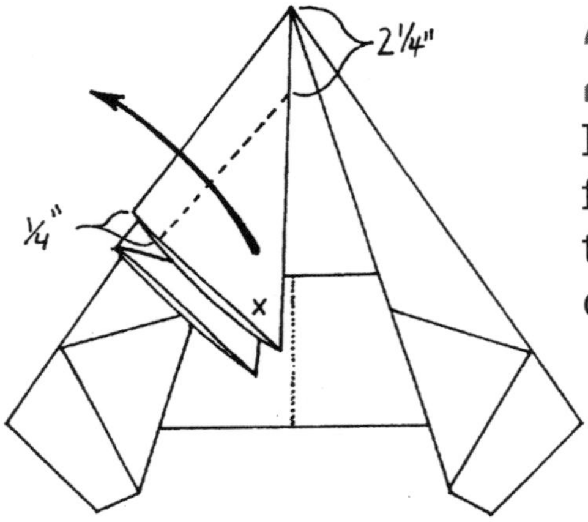


## 23

Now, you're going to carefully fold the wings out. Fold Flap X to the left side on the dotted line.

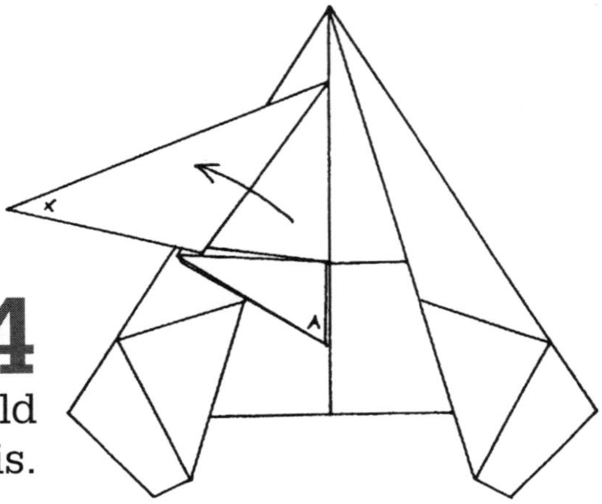


## 24

Your folded wing should look like this.

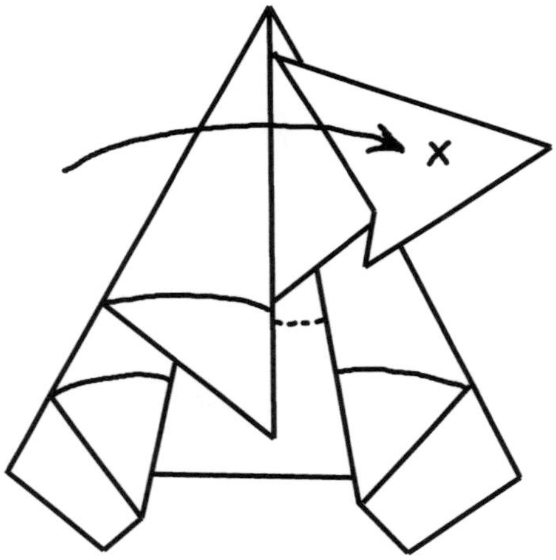


## 25

Now, flip Flap X to the right side.

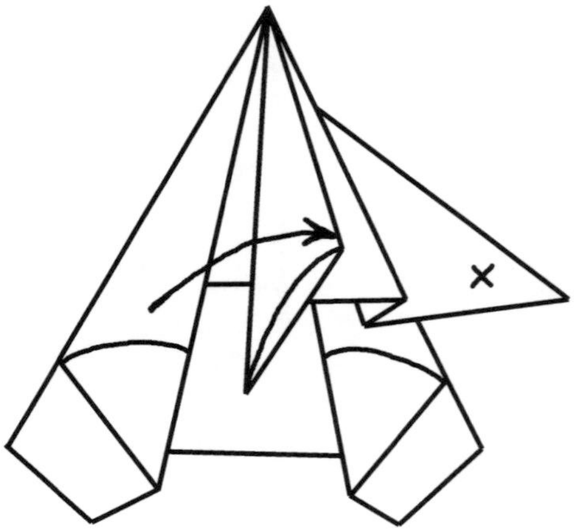


## 26

Also flip Flap A to the right. Fold Flap A so it matches up evenly with Flap X on the right side.

## 27

Now, move Flap A back to the left so it looks like this. Label A's and C's if you wish.

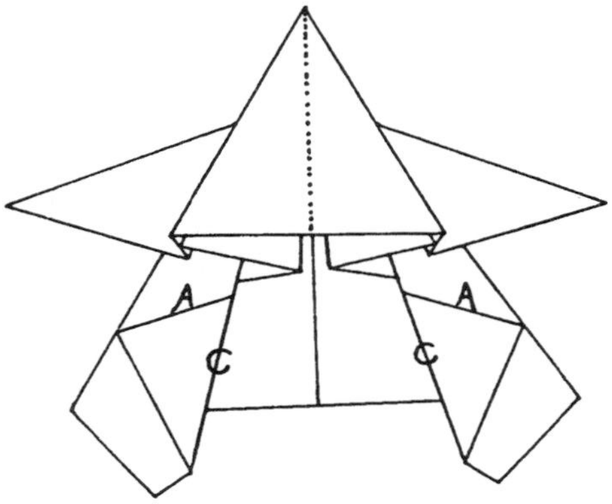


## 28

Now you're going to fold the stabilizers. Fold Edge C evenly toward Line A.

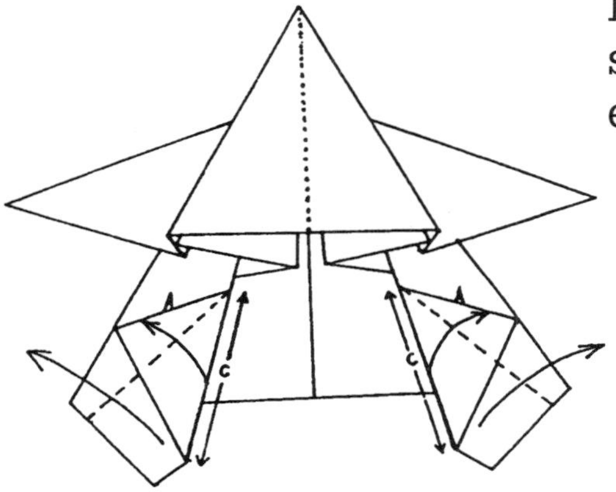


## 29

Make sure your folds are even.

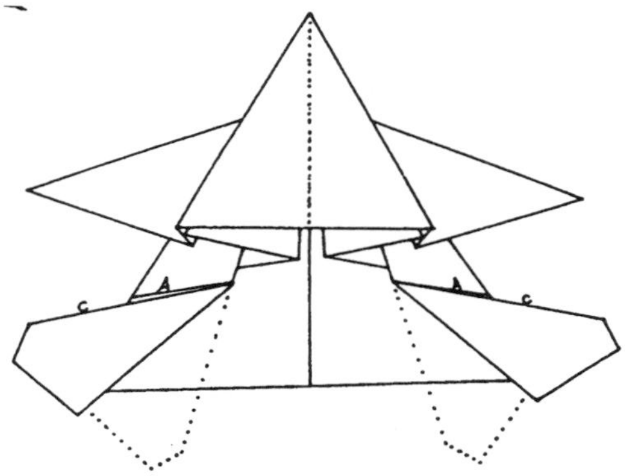


## 30

Now, unfold the stabilizers and flip Wing X to the left side.

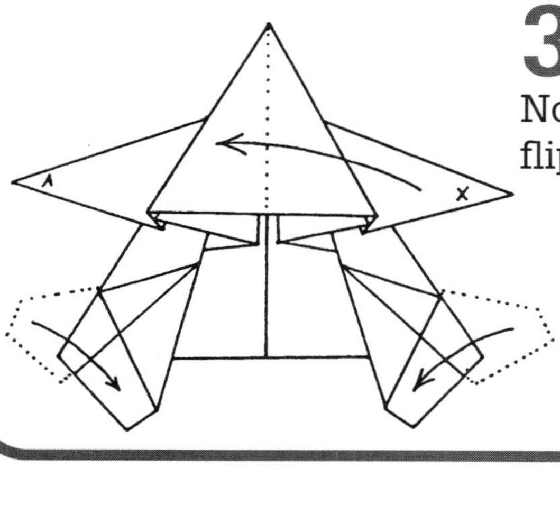

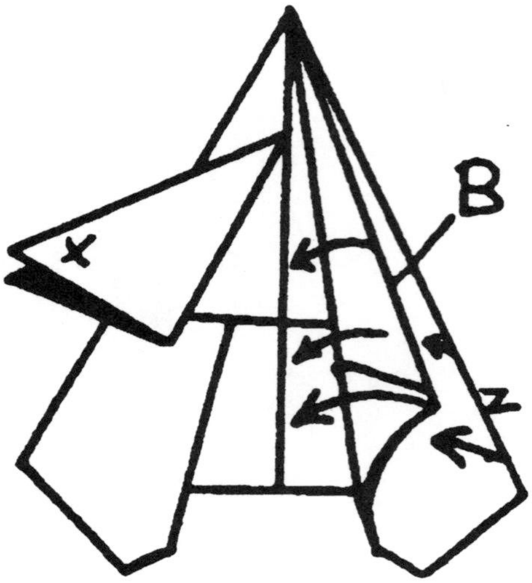


## 31

Flip Edge B to the middle.

## 32

You should have three crease lines as shown here.

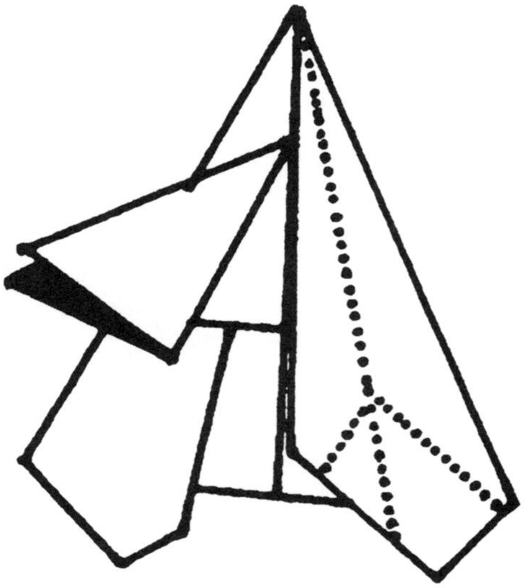

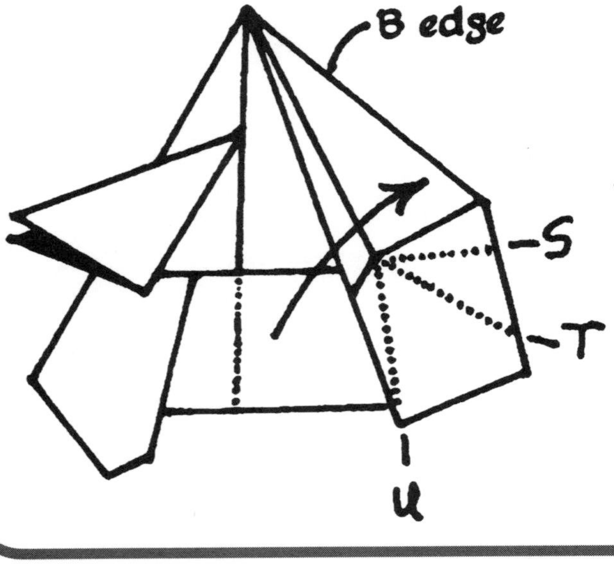


## 33

Unfold the B Edge further and you should see the crease lines—S, T & U.

## 34

Put your index finger on the middle of Line T and push it outward while pushing Lines S & U inward as indicated by the arrows.

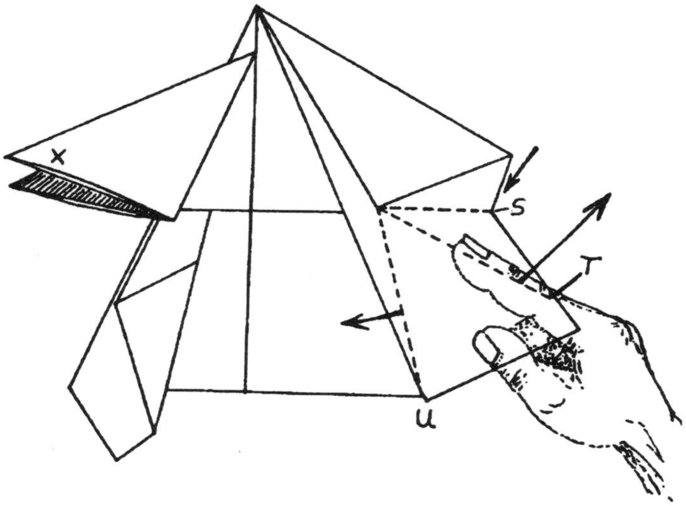


## 35

Your plane should look like this after you push out Line T. Press down on Point A. Repeat Steps 32–35 on the left side.

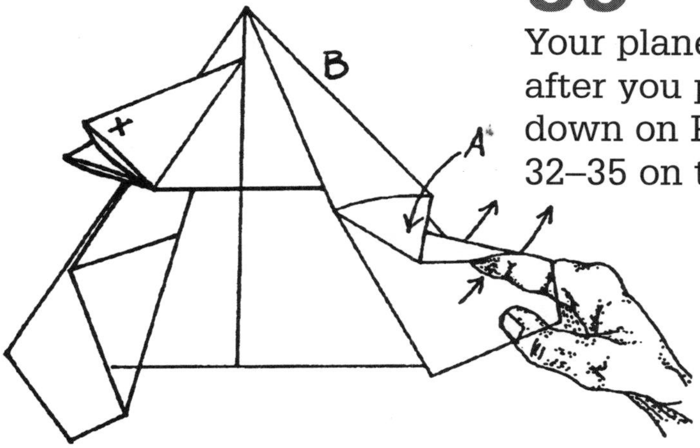


## 36

Open Side A to the left side so the plane looks like this.

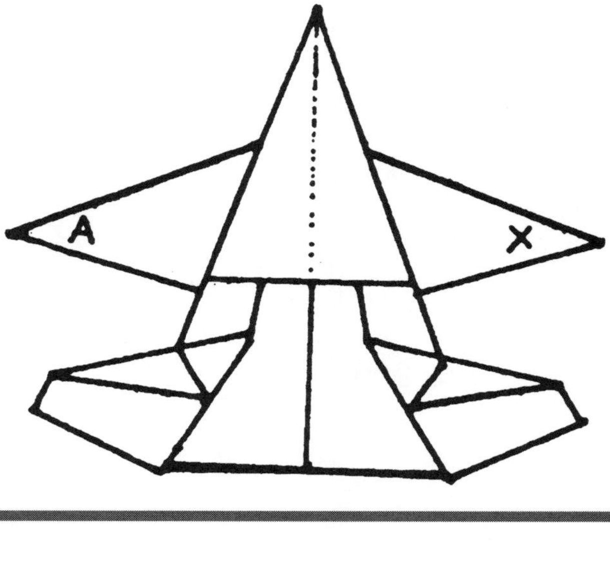

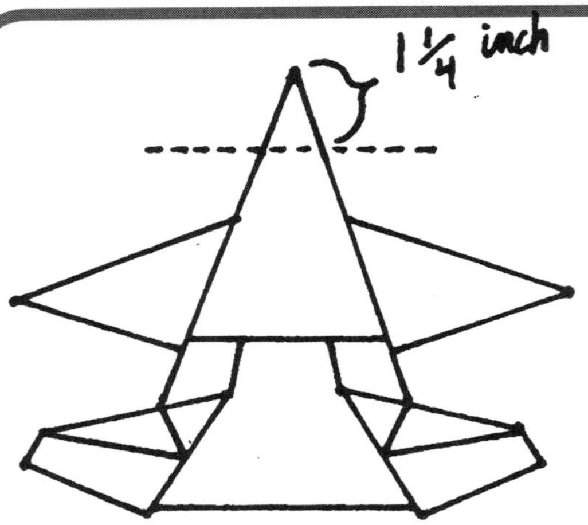


## 37

Measure about 1¼ inches from the end of the nose. Fold down the nose along the dotted line.

## 38

Your fold should look like this.

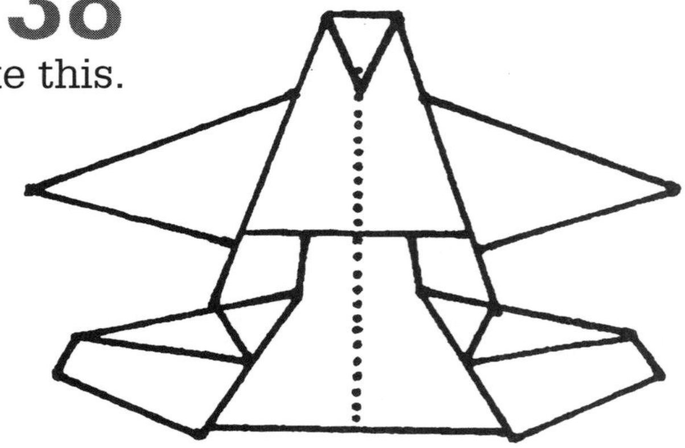

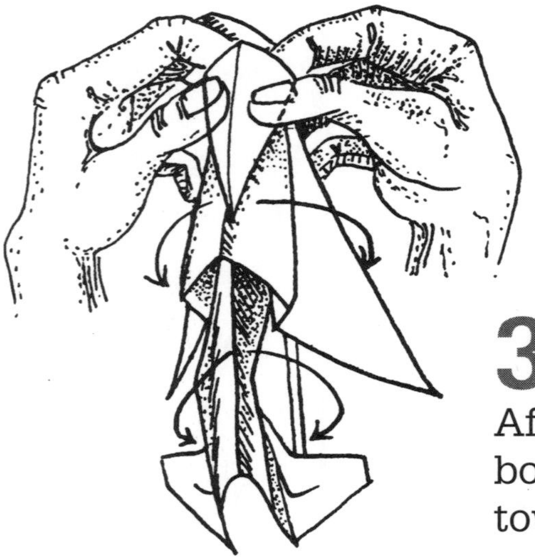

## 39

After folding down the nose, fold both sides of the plane's body toward the back as shown.

# 40

From the side, your plane should look like this. Now, hold the body with your left hand, and, with the other, pull up the nose. Then, as you did on the Concord (Steps 17–20), lay the plane, upside down, on a flat surface and fold the under fuselage back and forth. (This method is used on all the planes in this book.) Notice the 2-inch depth.

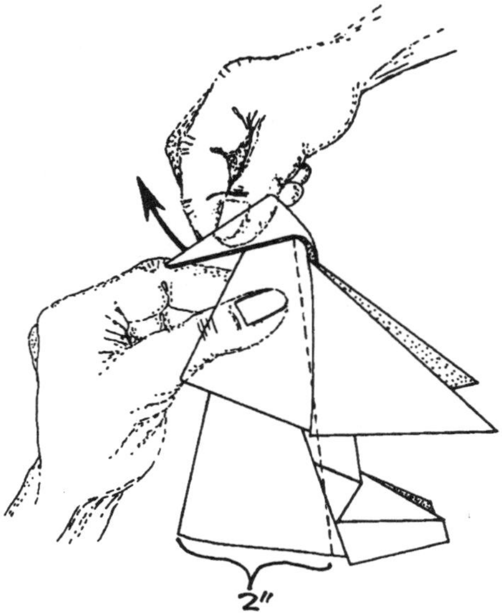


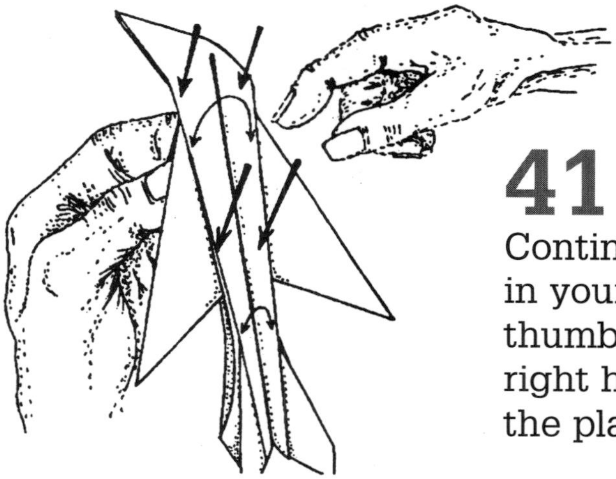

# 41

Continue to grip the plane firmly in your left hand while using the thumb and index finger of your right hand to press hard along the plane's body, as shown here.

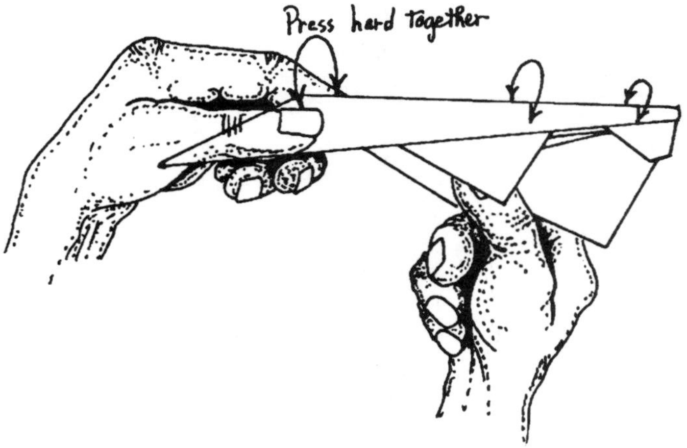


# 42

Move your right hand under the wings.

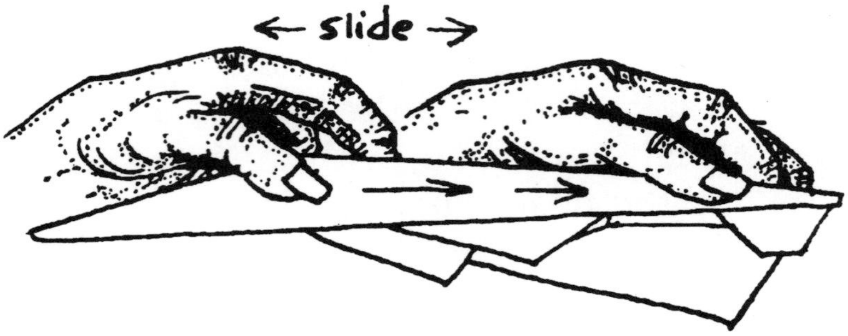


# 43

Carefully apply pressure while sliding your left hand along the back of the plane.

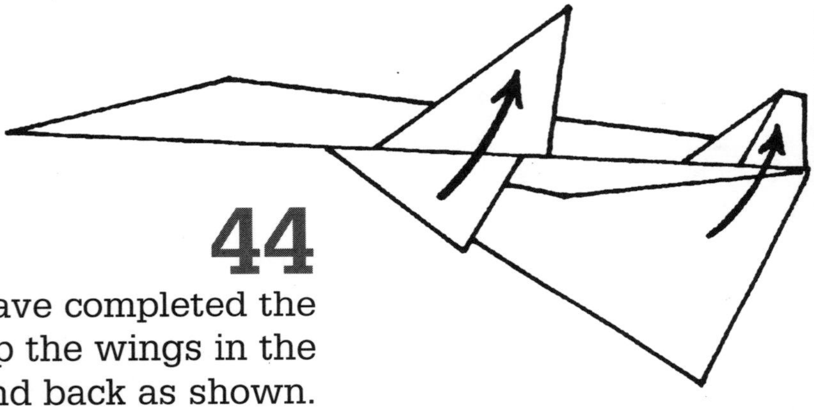

# 44

After you have completed the back, fold up the wings in the front and back as shown.

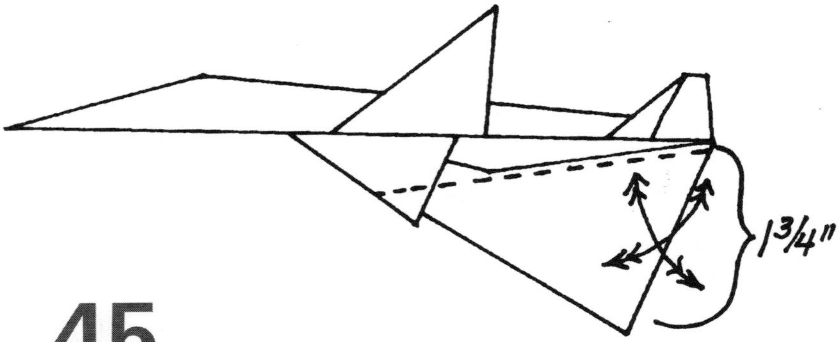


# 45

Fold along the dotted line four times from side to side.

## 46

This is the rear view of the plane. Lift the tail inward & up as indicated by the arrows.

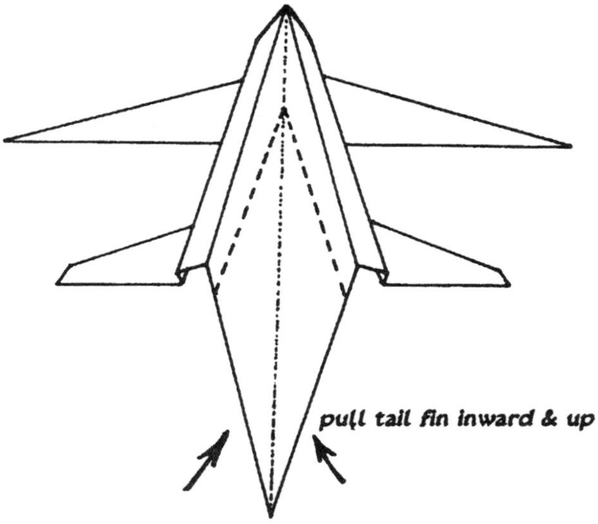


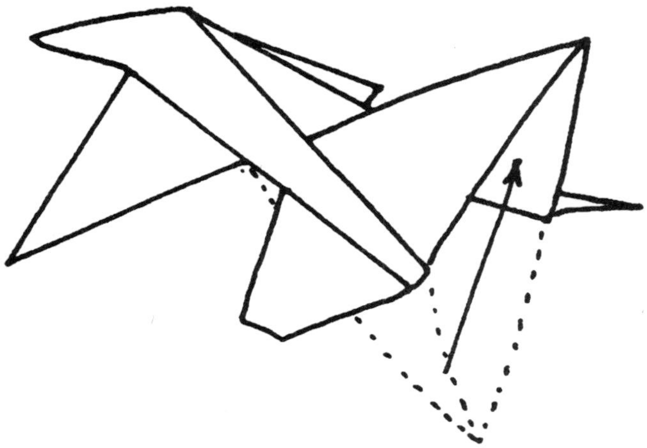

## 47

Your tail fin should come up like this.

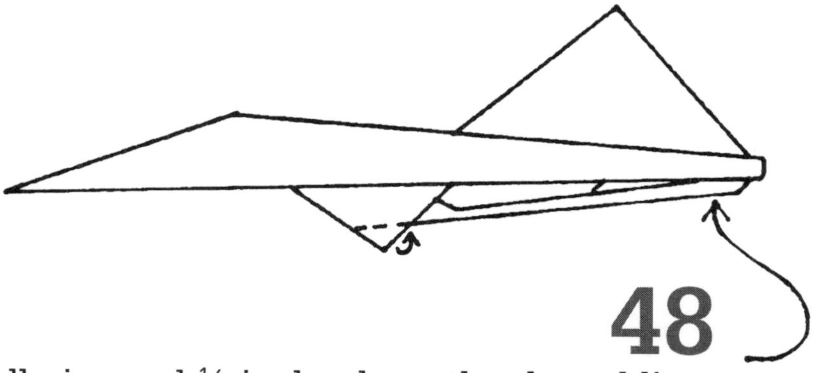

## 48

Fold the belly inward ½ inch, along the dotted line. You can tape here to bond the two sides together. Taping improves flight performance. You can tape all other planes, except the Hornet, in the same place.

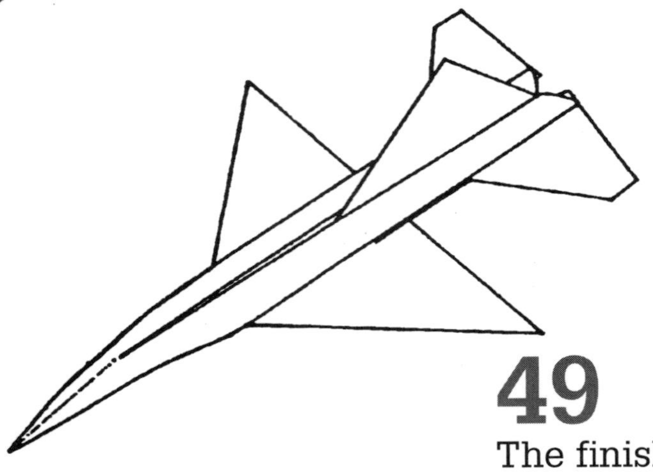

# 49

The finished version of the Jet.

# 50

Curve the side of the nose for a nice, round, clean, front end like the one in Diagram B.

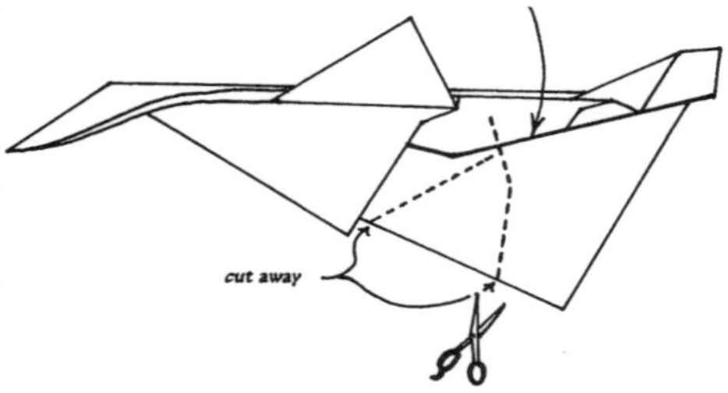


# 51

You are now finished with the Jet, a highly original plane. If you want the tail to look more realistic, pull it down the way it was before you raised it, then cut along the dotted lines and push it up again. Make sure that it's even with the body.

NOTE: This tail-cut technique may also be used on the MIG-27.

## 52

Bring the tail up like this.

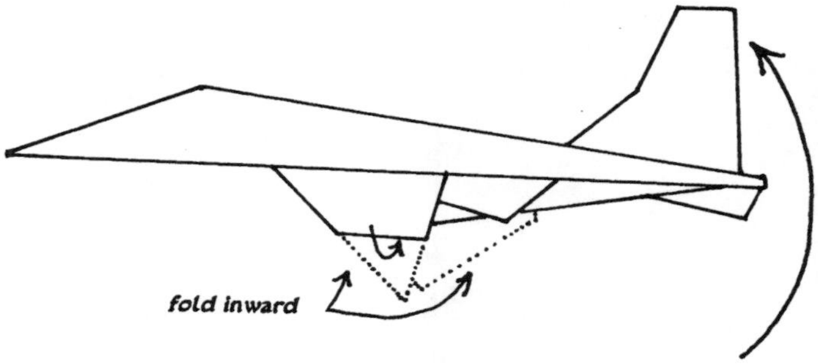


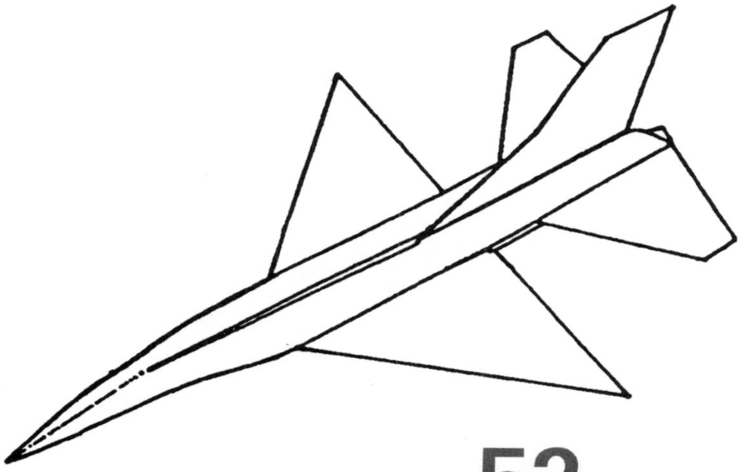

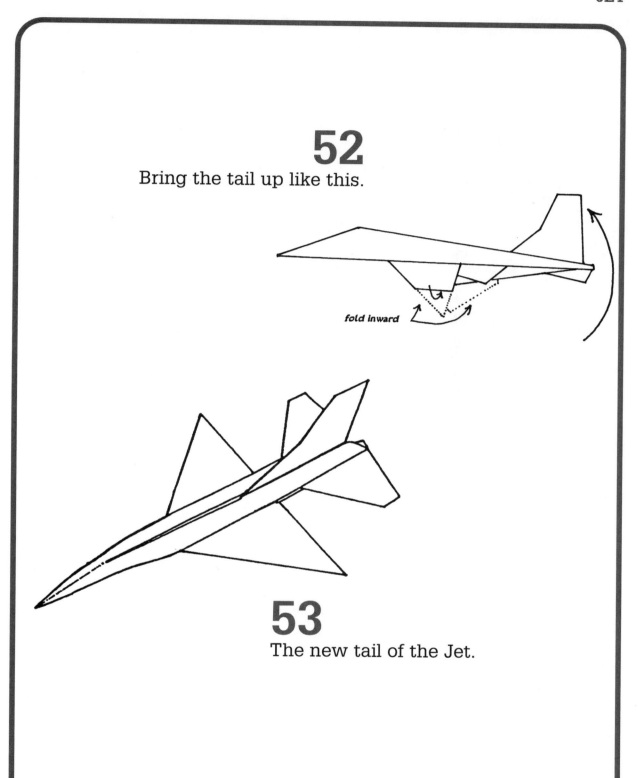

## 53

The new tail of the Jet.

# JET

# SPACE SHUTTLE

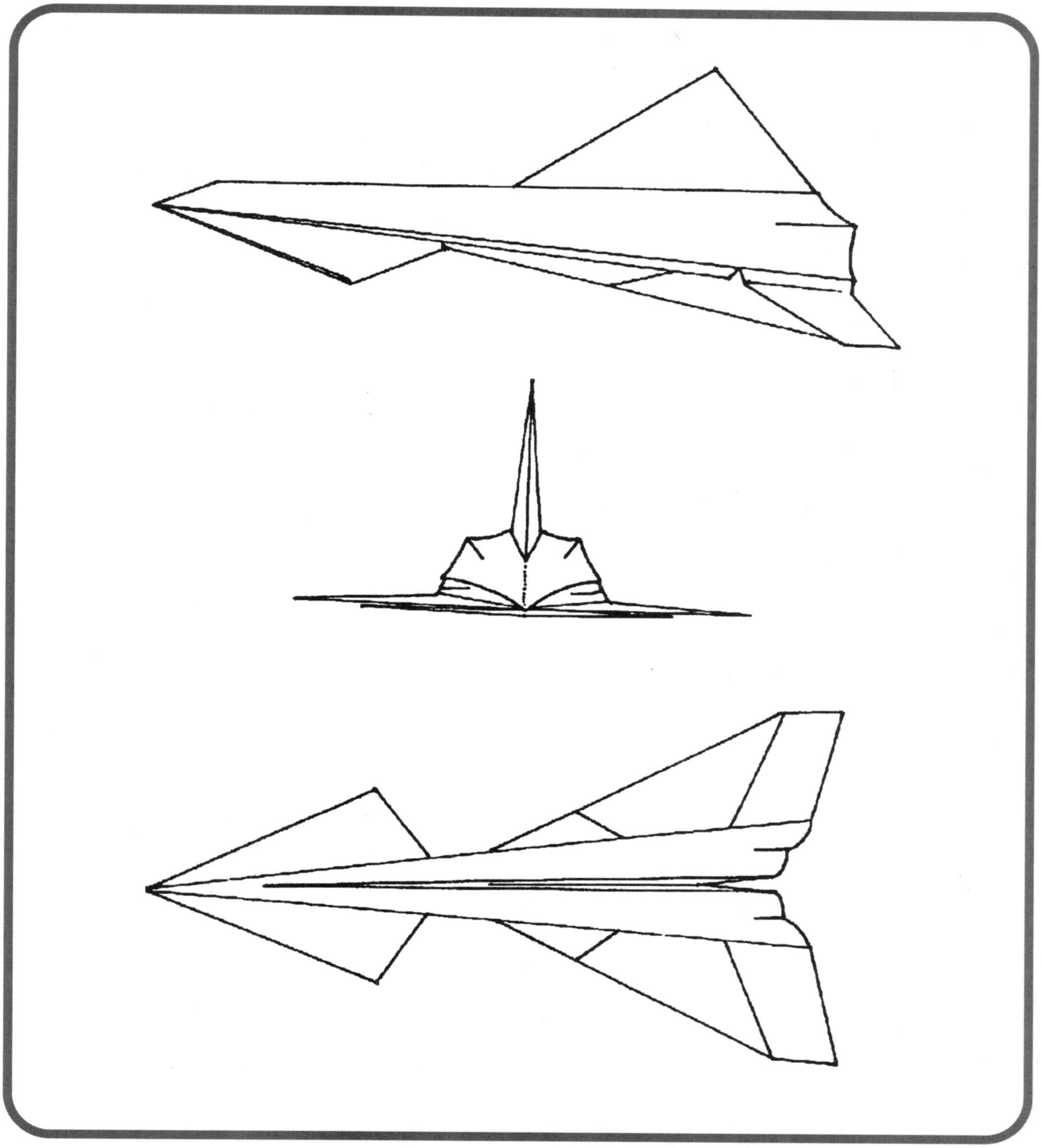

In making the Shuttle, the first few folds are exactly the same as the Jet's.

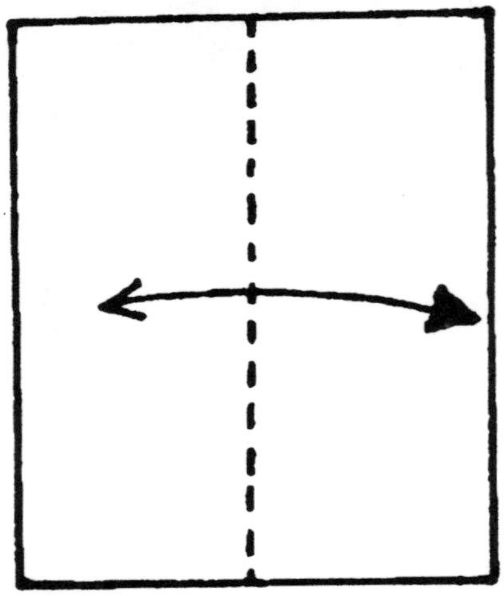

## 1

Fold paper in half, then unfold.

## 2

Fold diagonally at dotted lines, then unfold.

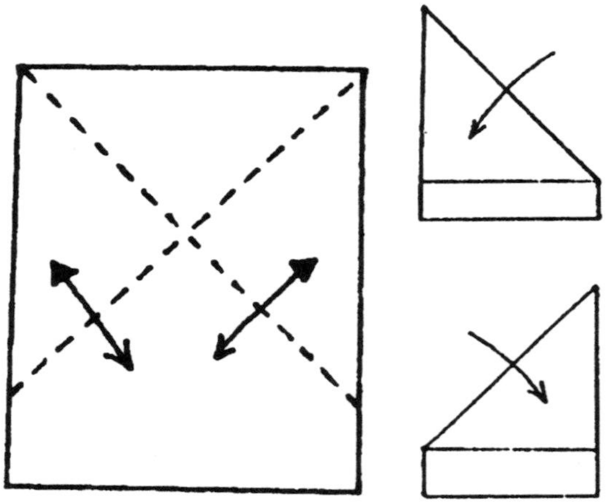

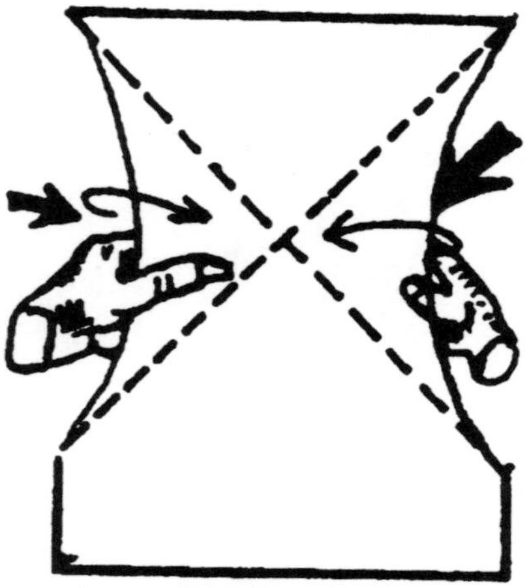

## 3

Now, use both hands and fold the paper up and in toward the middle.

# 4

This is how the paper should look. Gently press down from the top.

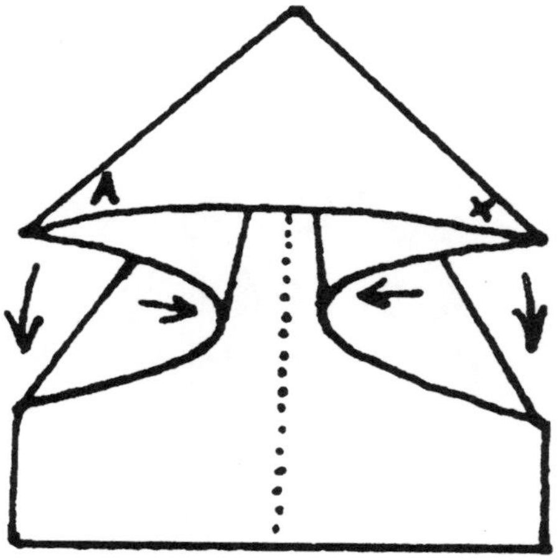


# 5

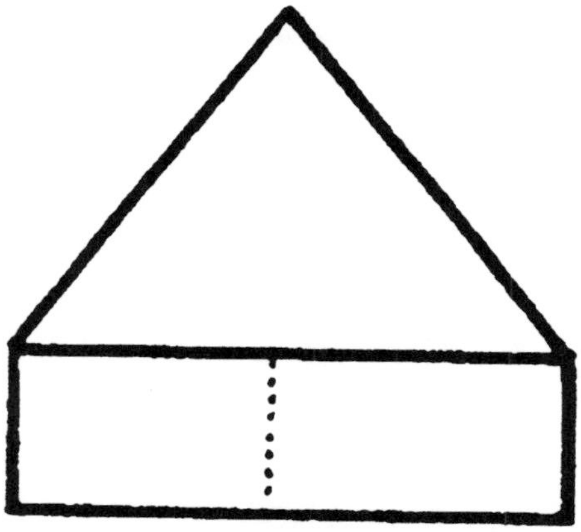

Now, it should look like this.

# 6

Slide your right hand under Flap X as shown here.

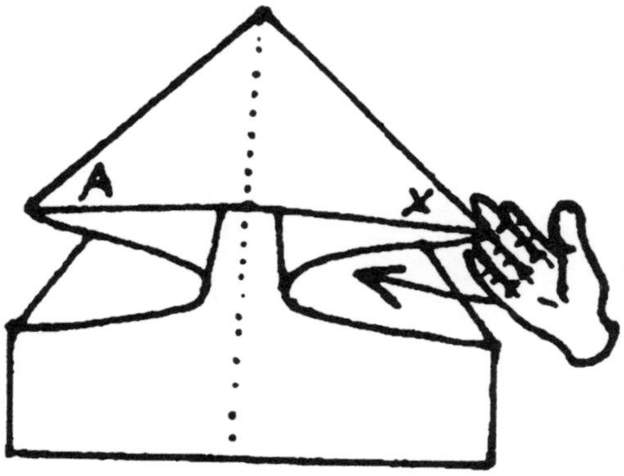

# 7

Flip Flap X over and onto Flap A.

# 8

Flap X should line up evenly with Flap A on the left side.

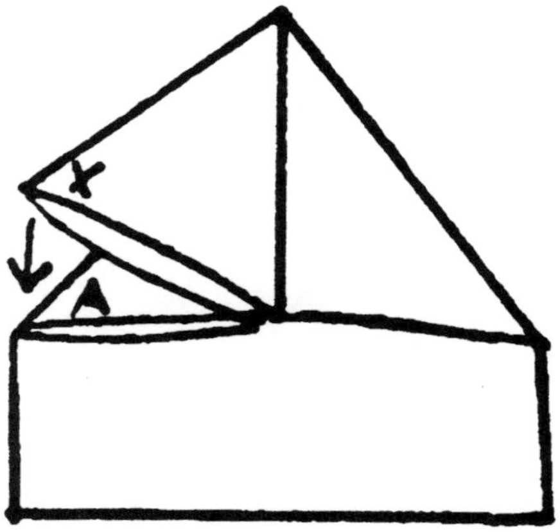


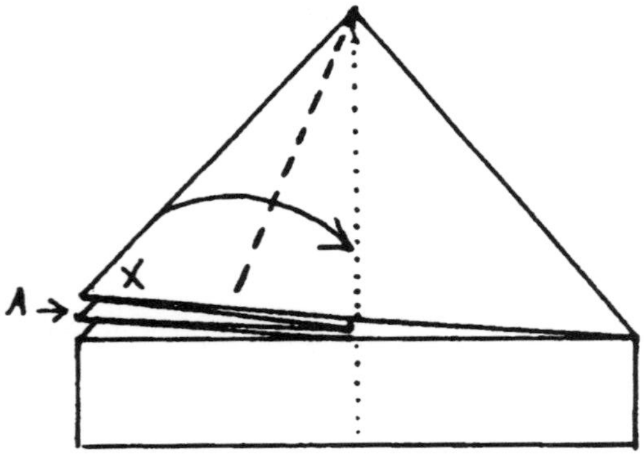


# 9

Now, fold Flap X on the dotted line toward the centerline.

# 10

This is how your fold should look.

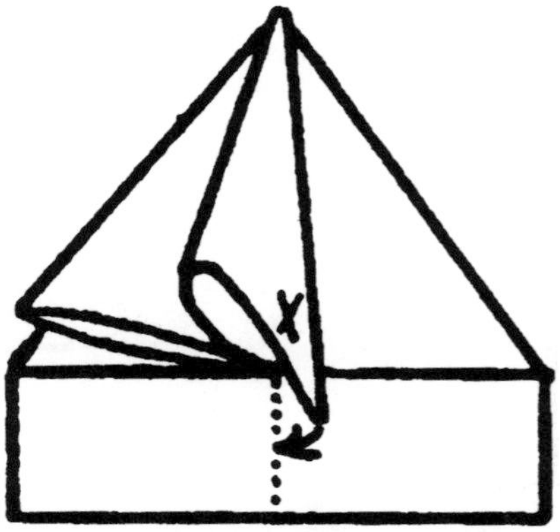

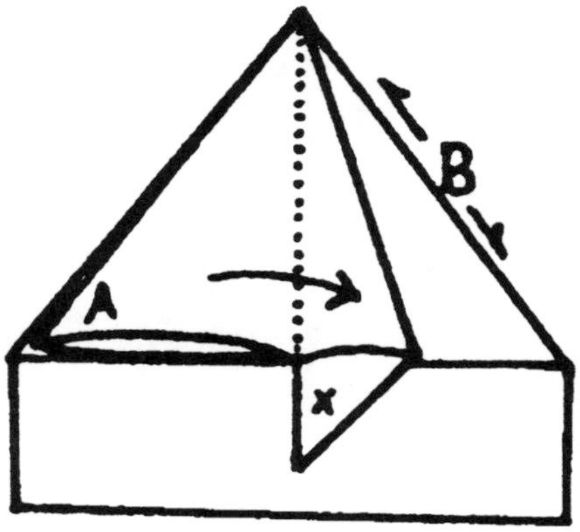


## 11

After you have folded Flap X toward the middle flap, flip it to the right side. Notice the B Edge.

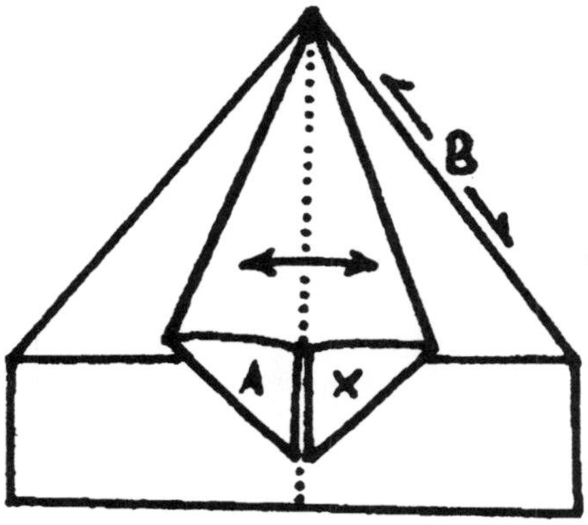


## 12

Now, repeat Steps 9–11 for the left side, and open the flaps to look like this.

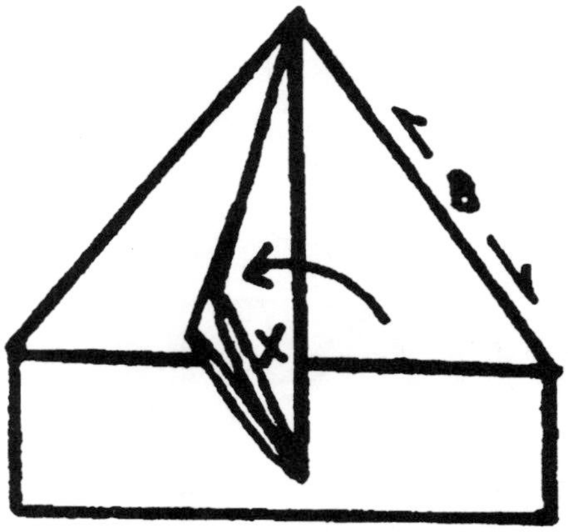


## 13

Now, flip Flap X to the left, over Flap A again.

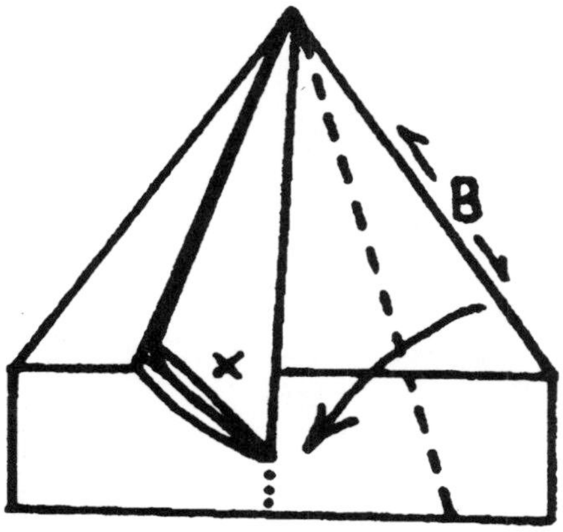


## 14

Then fold Side B on the dotted line to the centerline.

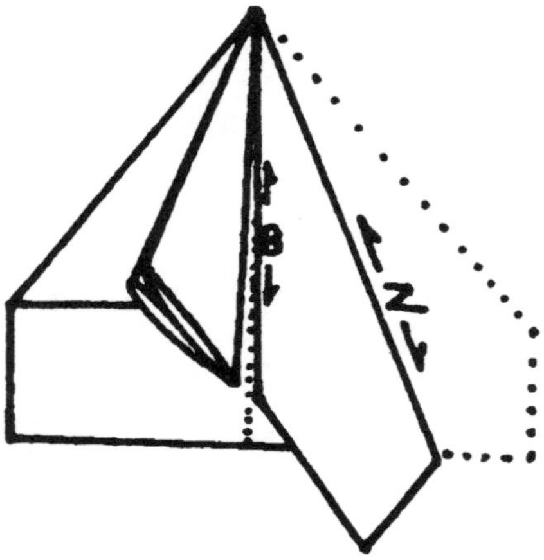


## 15

Now it should look like this.

## 16

Now, flip both Flaps A & X to the right side. Repeat Step 14 for the left side.

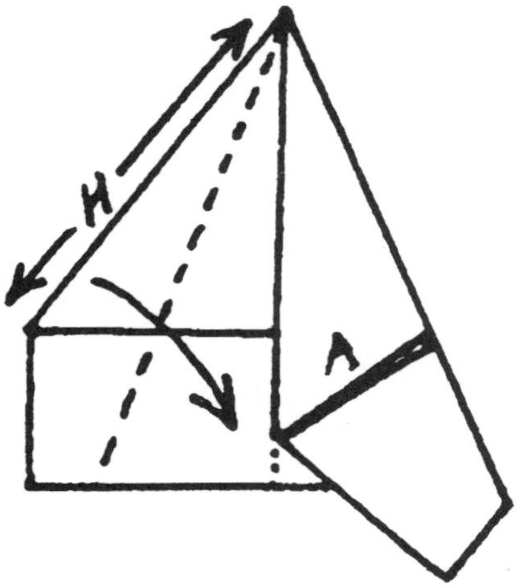

## 17

Spread Flaps A & X apart like this.

## 18

Now, flip Flap X to the left side. Then fold Edge B on the dotted line and match it evenly with Edge Z.

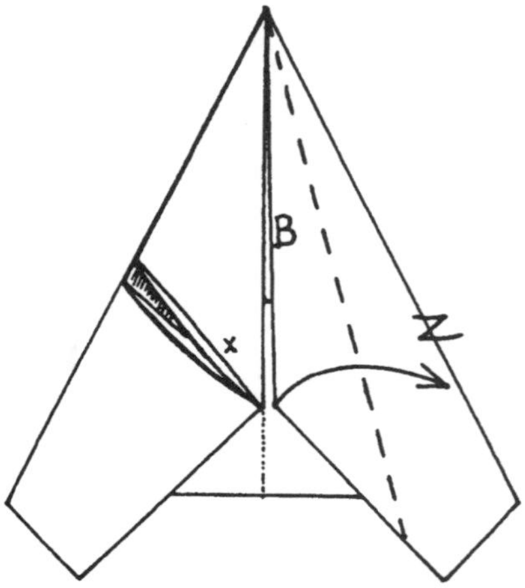

## 19

This is how the fold should look.

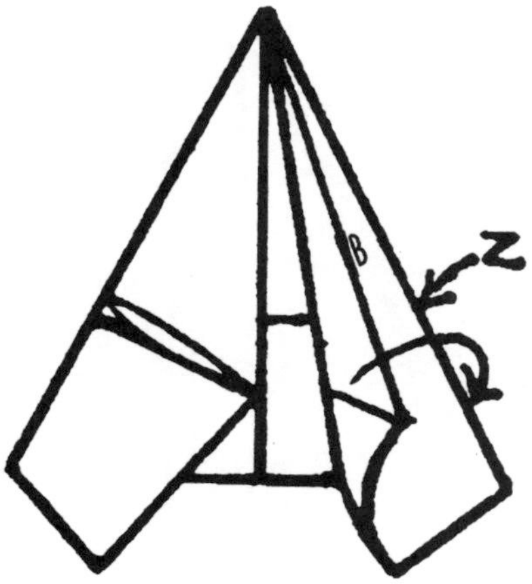


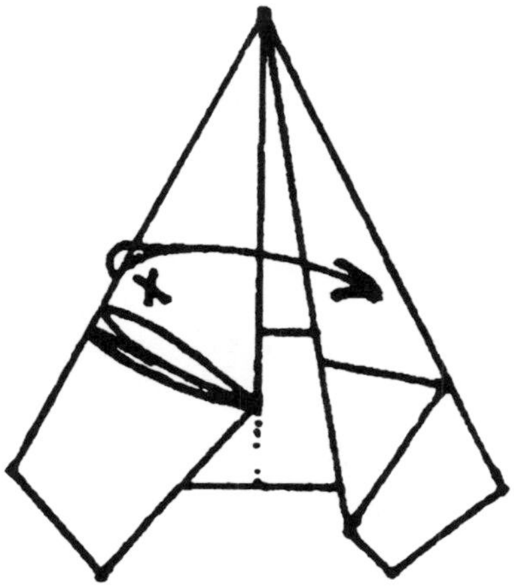


## 20

Now, flip Flaps A & X to the right.

## 21

Repeat Step 18 on the left side.

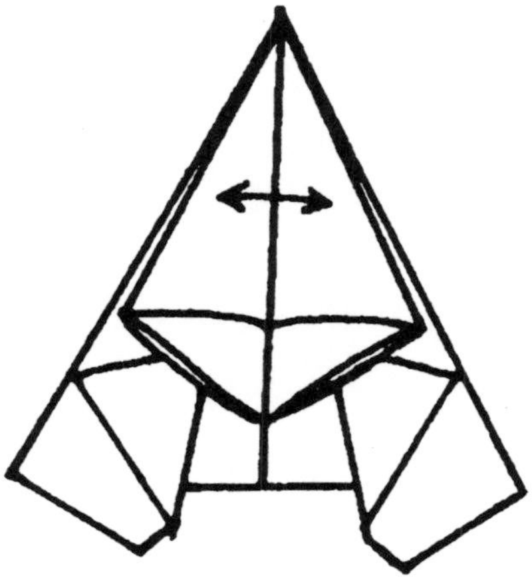

## 22

Then spread the flaps as shown here.

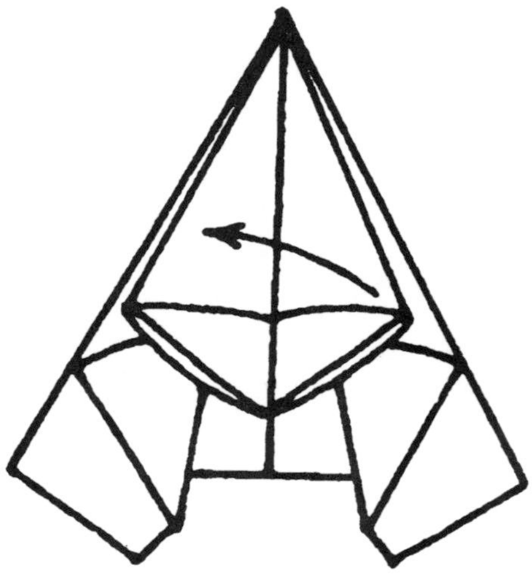

## 23

This is how your paper should look after completing Steps 1–22 In the Jet chapter. Now fold Flap X to the left as the arrow indicates.

## 24

Fold the right wing out to the right along the dotted line.

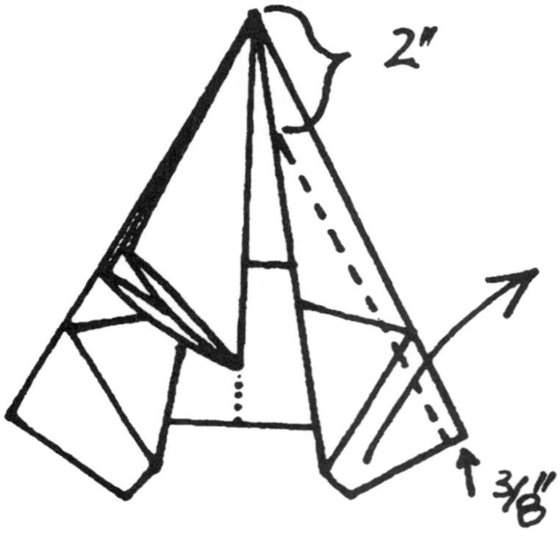


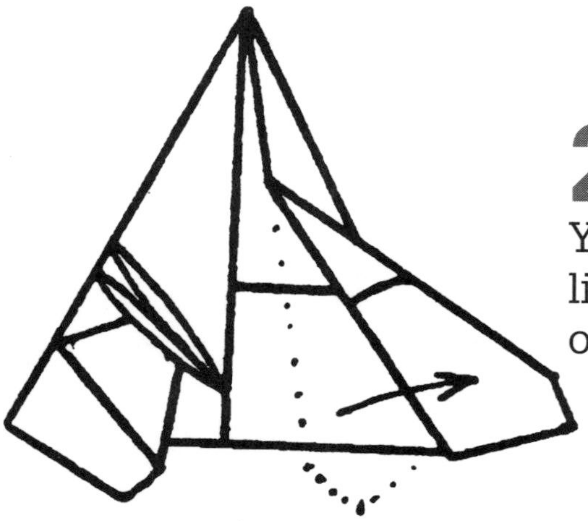

## 25

Your right wing fold should look like this. Now make the same fold on the left side.

## 26

Now, fully open Flap X to the left and fold along the dotted line so that Corner X is on Corner H.

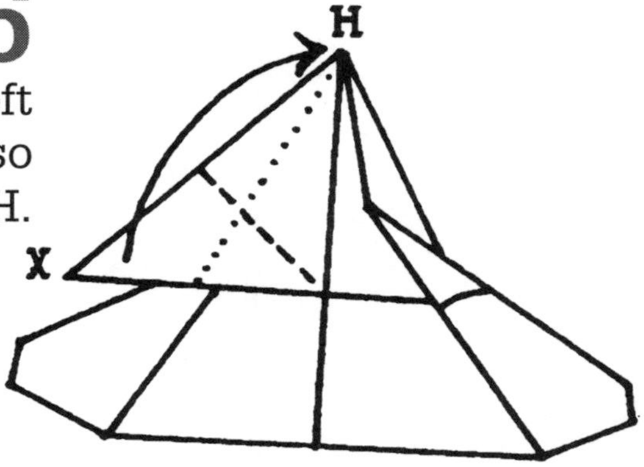


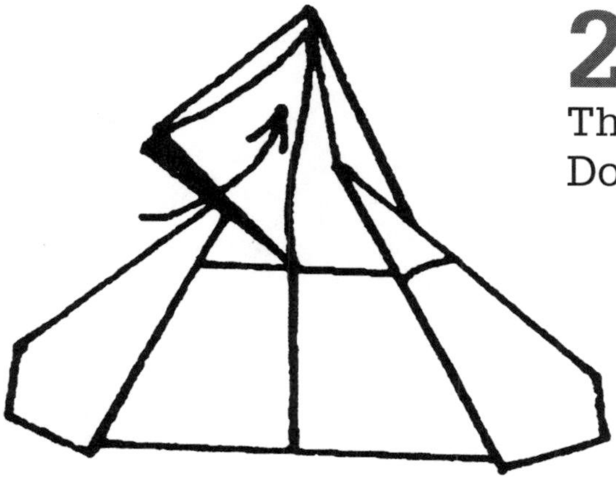

## 27

This is how your fold should look. Do the same on the other side.

## 28

Separate your newly folded flaps. This is the front stabilizer. Fold the nose along the dotted line.

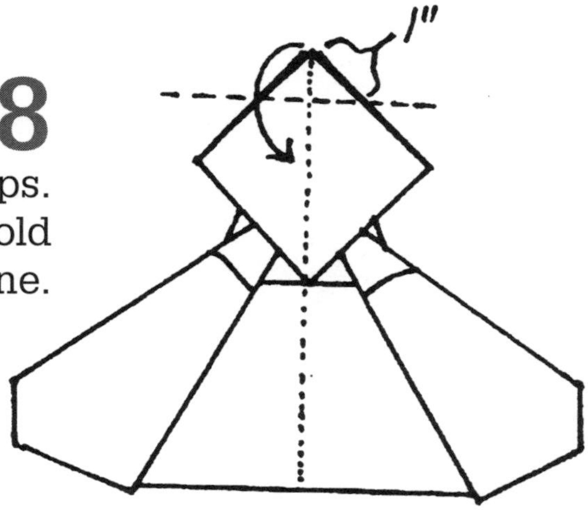

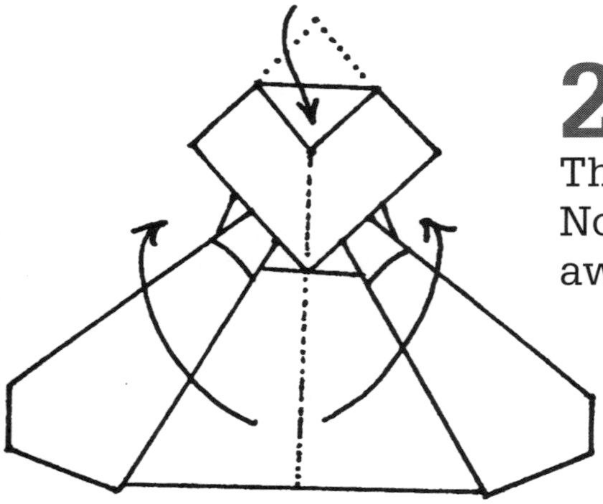

## 29

This is how the fold should look. Now fold both sides of the plane away from you.

## 30

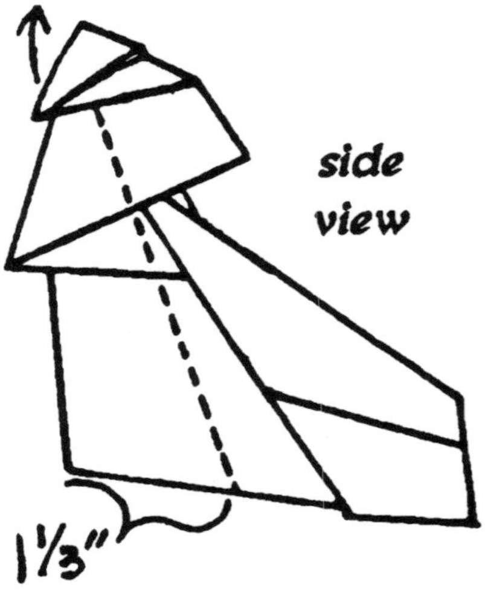


The plane should look like this. Next, turn the plane over and pinch the belly about 1⅓" into the fuselage (along the dotted line) while you press the back of the plane against your work surface.* Fold the belly from side to side a few times. As you did with the Jet, pull up the nose and pinch the fuselage together.

*NOTE: This will properly align the tail and the wings.

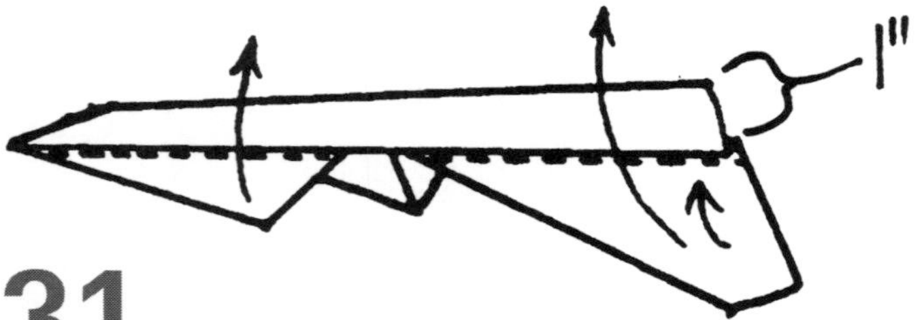


## 31

After you have pulled up the nose, line it up with the back. Then fold the wings up. You can now push the tail fin up.

## 32

With the tail pulled up, the plane should look like this.

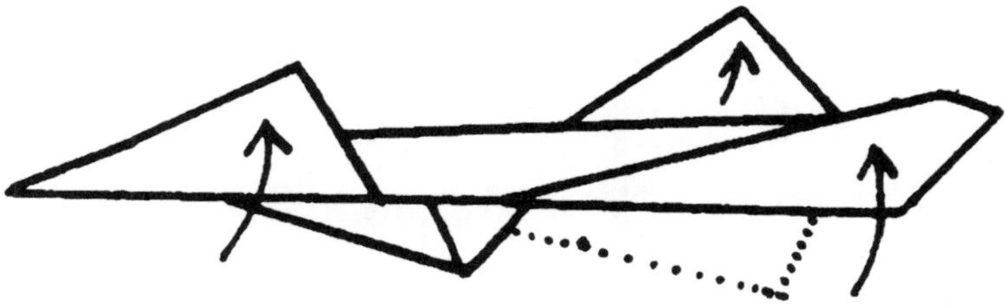

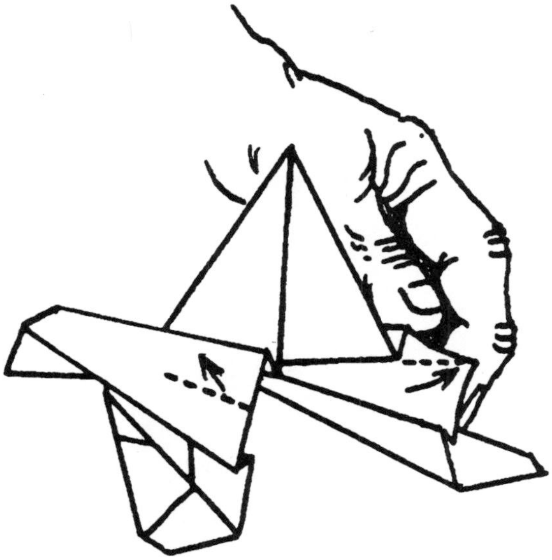

## 33

Make another fold as shown here for the engine.

## 34

The finished version of the Shuttle.

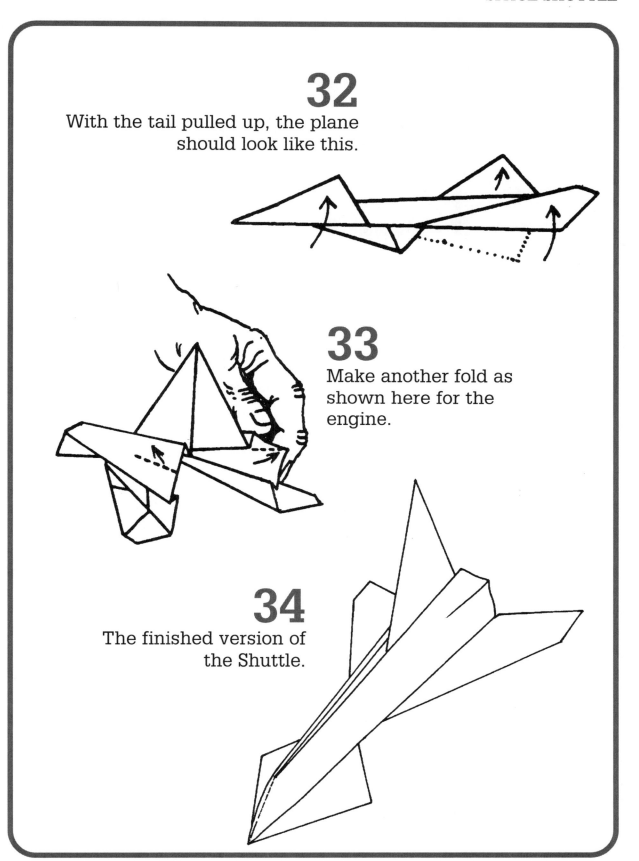

# SPACE SHUTTLE

# FUTURE FIGHTER

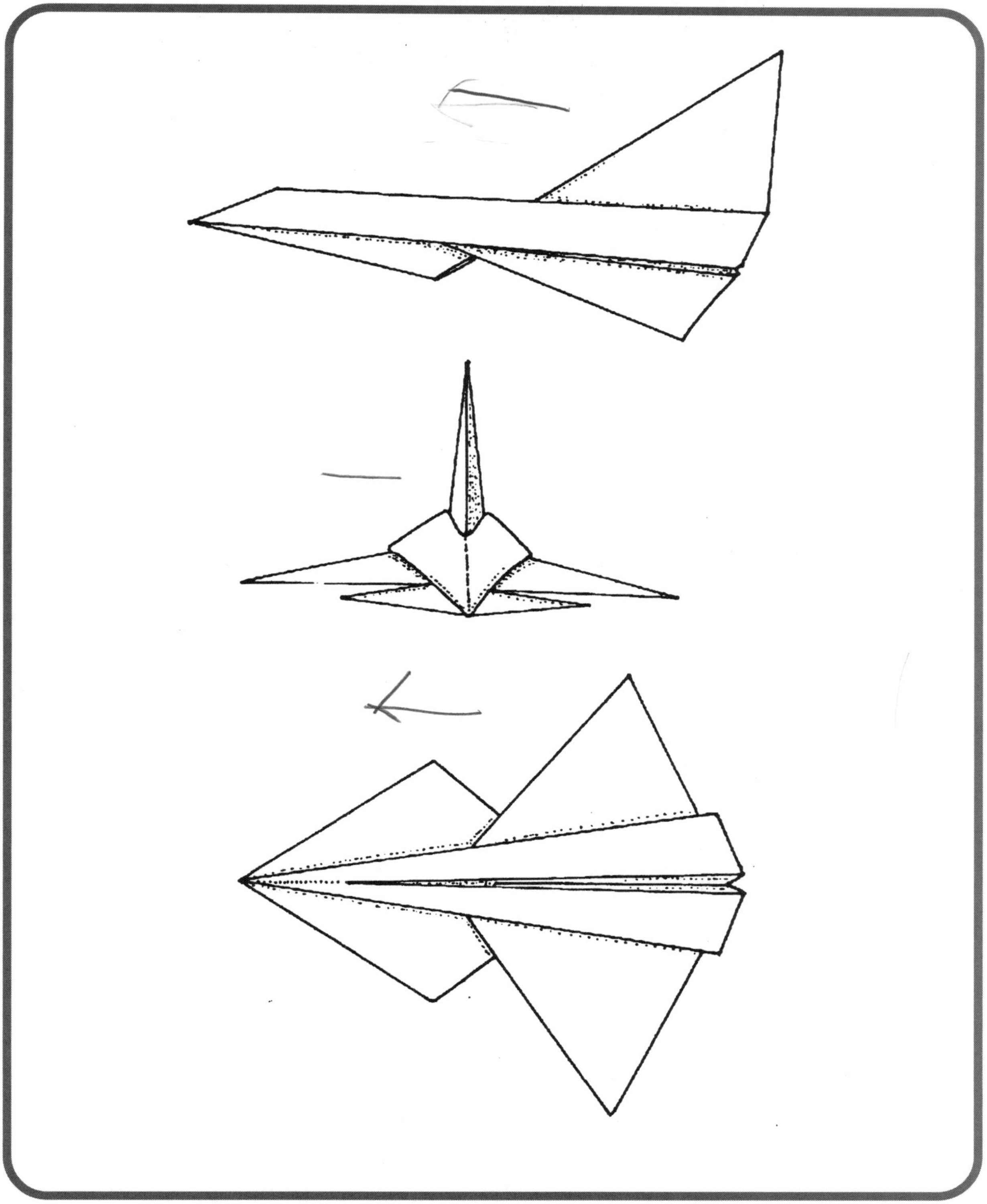

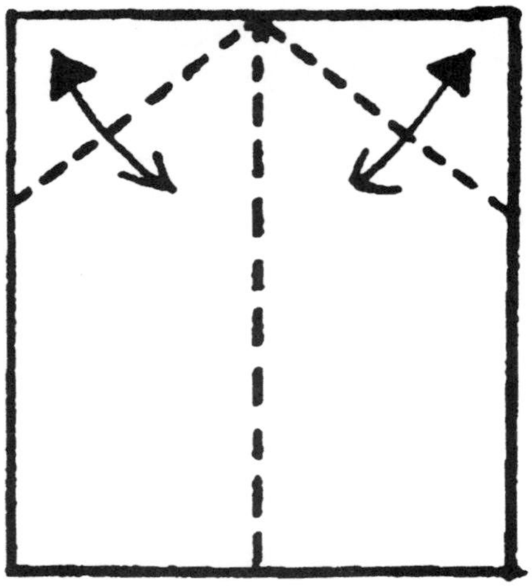

**1**

Fold the paper in half. Unfold it, then fold down the two corners.

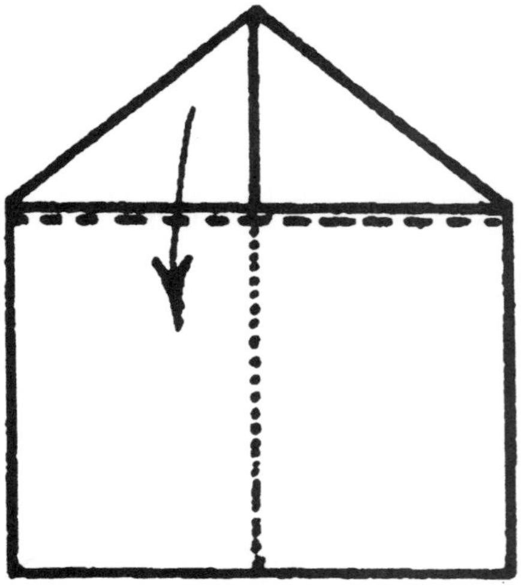

**2**

Fold down on the dotted line.

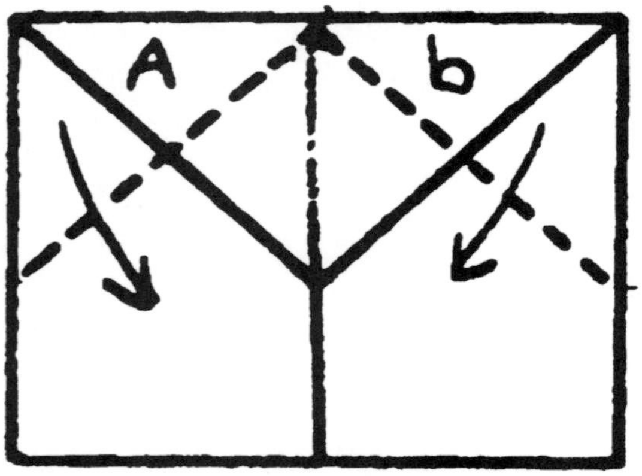


**3**

Fold the corners diagonally again.

# 4

Your fold should look like this.
Now, unfold the corners again.

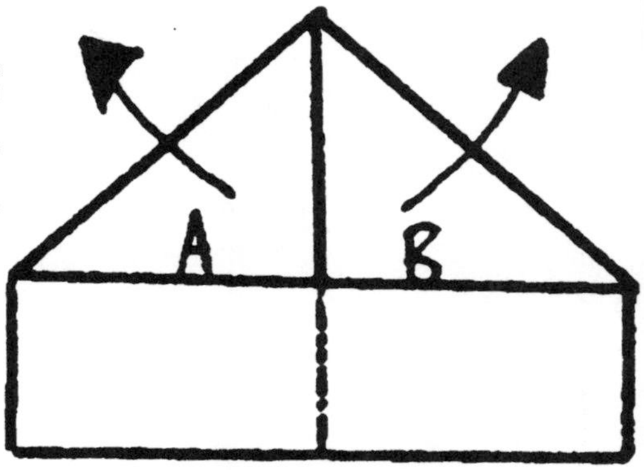


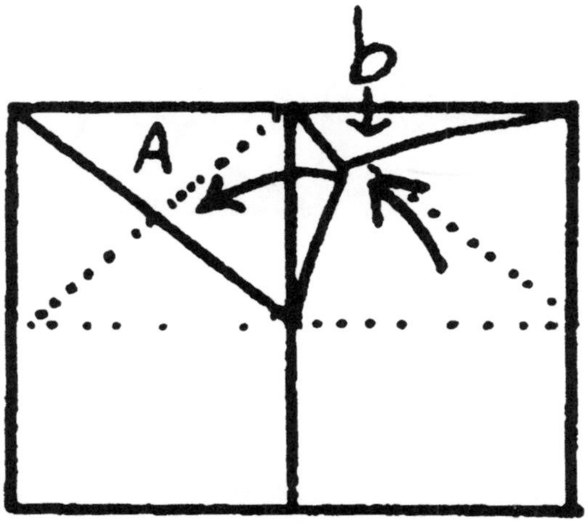


# 5

Put your hand under the Side B fold, then lift and reverse the fold to the left, as shown.

# 6

The fold should look like this.

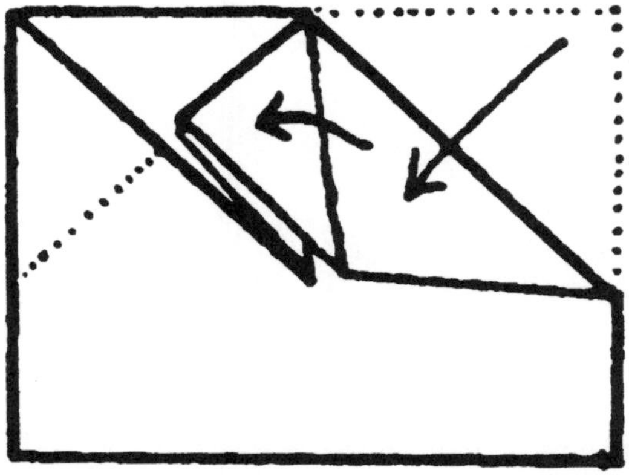

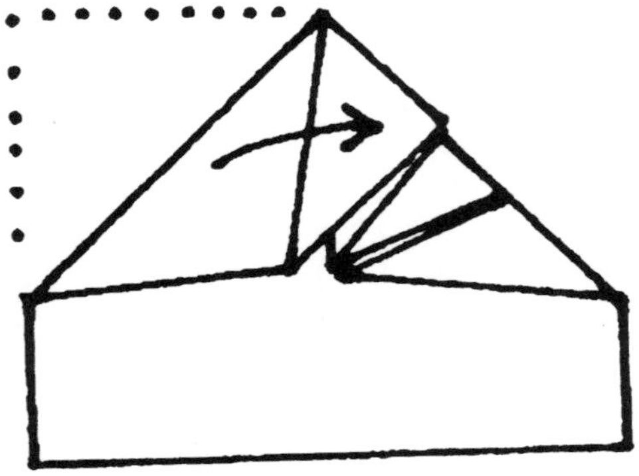

# 7

Now do the same to the other side. This is how it should look.

NOTE: These are the two front stabilizers.

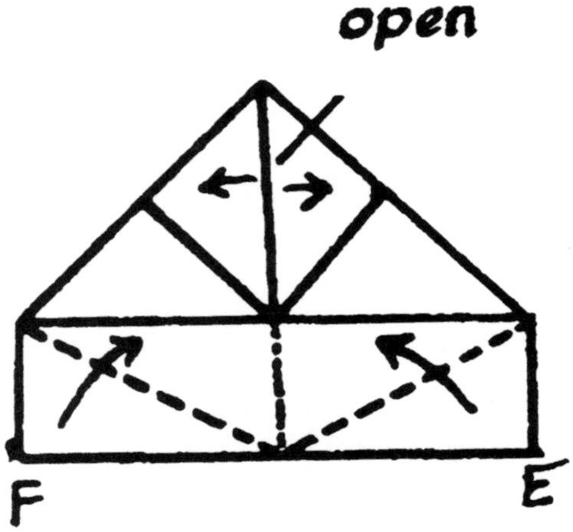


# 8

Now, open at the center as shown here. Fold Sides F & E diagonally up as indicated.

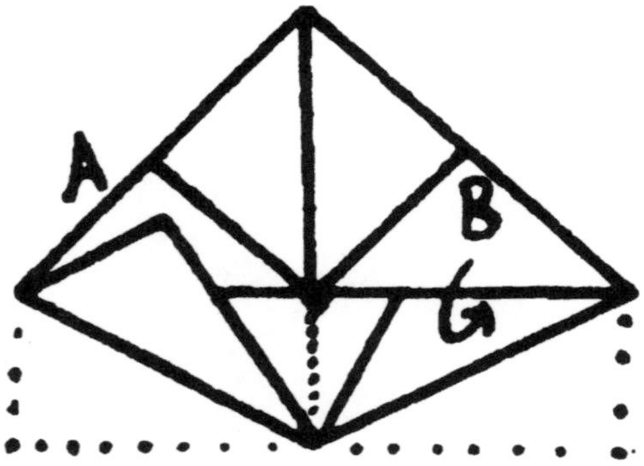


# 9

The folds of the lower corners should look like this. Tuck the corners under Sides A & B as shown here.

# 10

After you have tucked both corners under Sides A & B respectively, flip the stabilizers to the left side and make a fold on the dotted line toward the middle. Repeat on the left side.

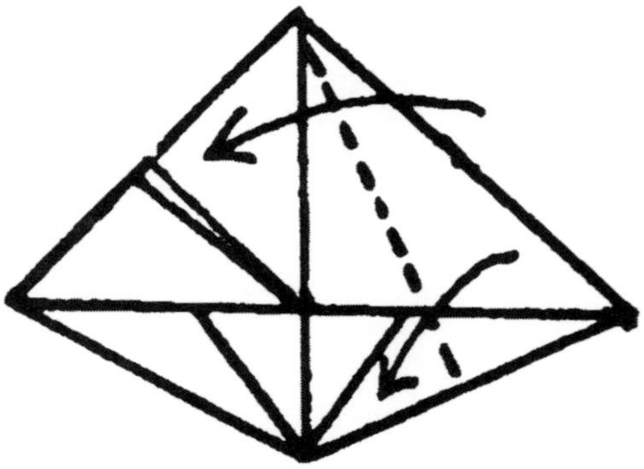

## 11

After you have folded both sides toward the middle and separated the two stabilizers, it should look like this.

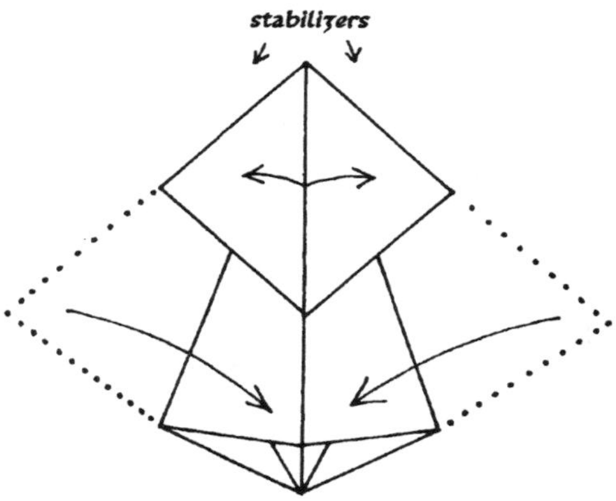


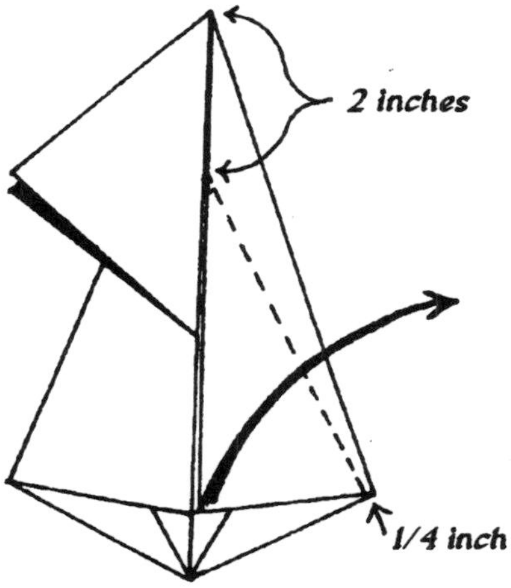


## 12

Fold the right wing out along the dotted line as indicated.

## 13

The folded right wing should look like this. Do the same thing on the left side before going on.

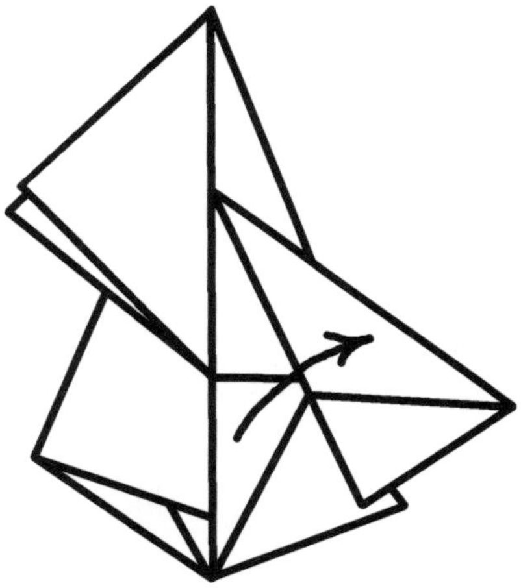

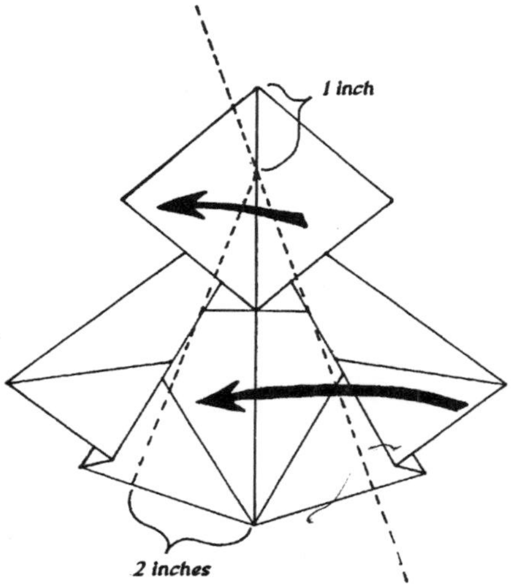


## 14

Fold the right side to the left along the dotted lines indicated by the arrows.

NOTE: Use the technique you learned with the Concord to complete the plane.

# 15

This is how the fold from Step 14 should look. Do the same on the left side.

NOTE: This new fold is great for compact planes when you don't fold the nose down first.

# 16

After you fold both sides, push the fuselage downward.

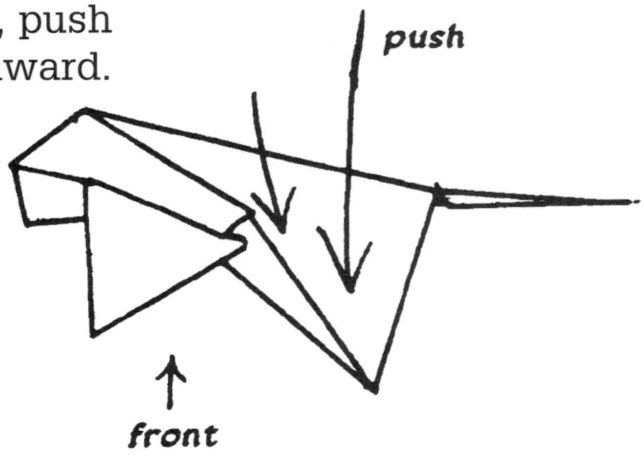


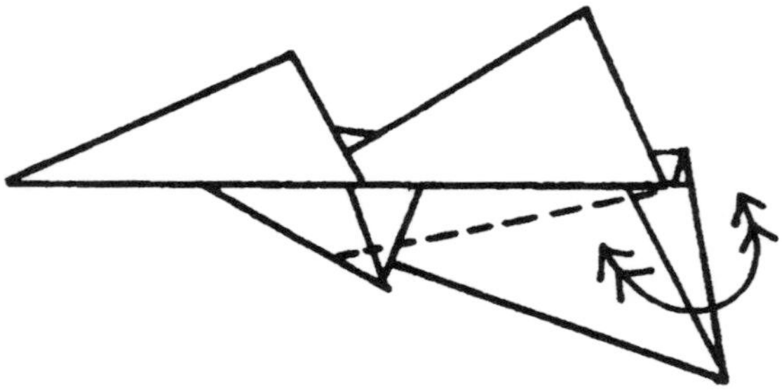

# 17

After you have pushed the tail down, press the two sides together. Fold the wings up, then fold the tail back and forth along the dotted lines. Now push inward and up.

## 18

This is how the plane looks with the tail up.

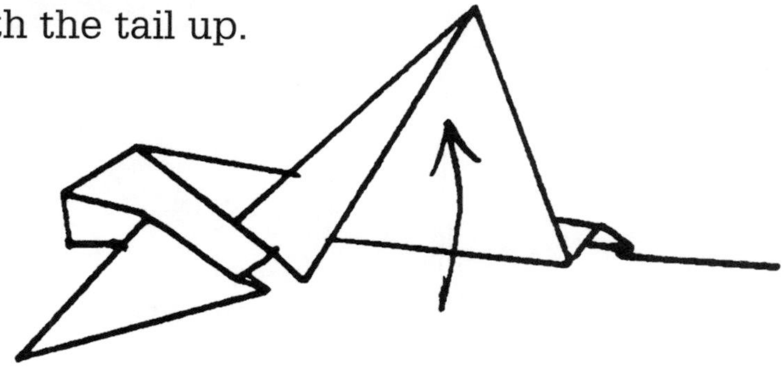

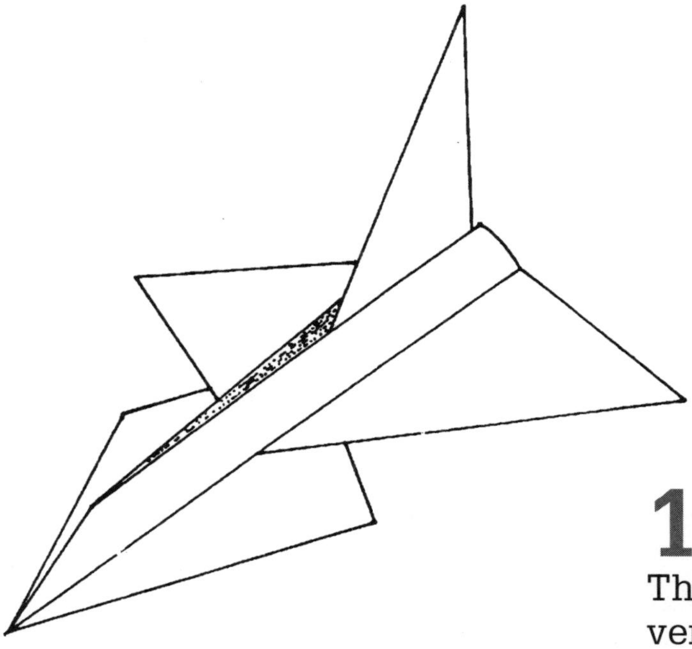

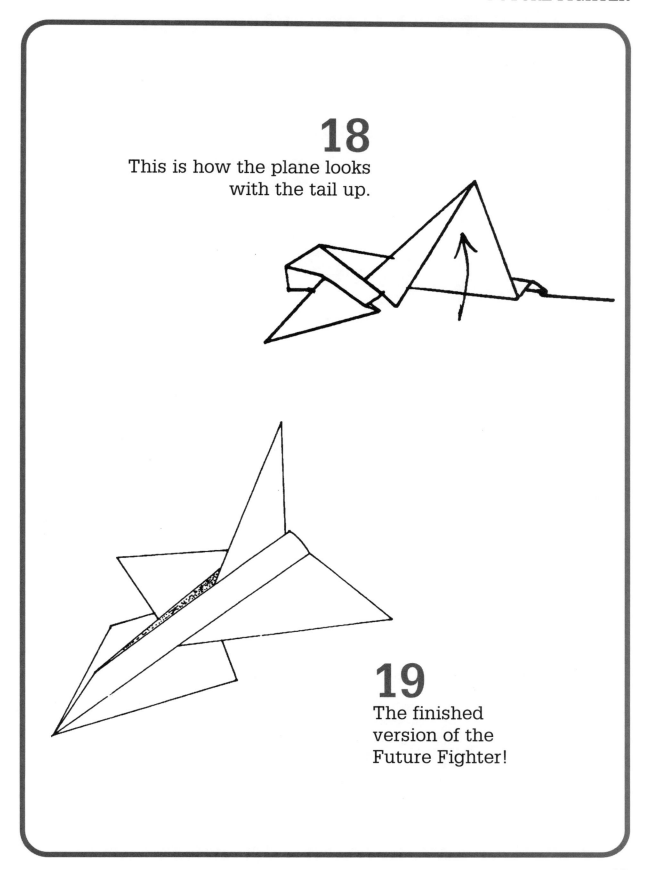

## 19

The finished version of the Future Fighter!

# FUTURE FIGHTER

# F-15 EAGLE

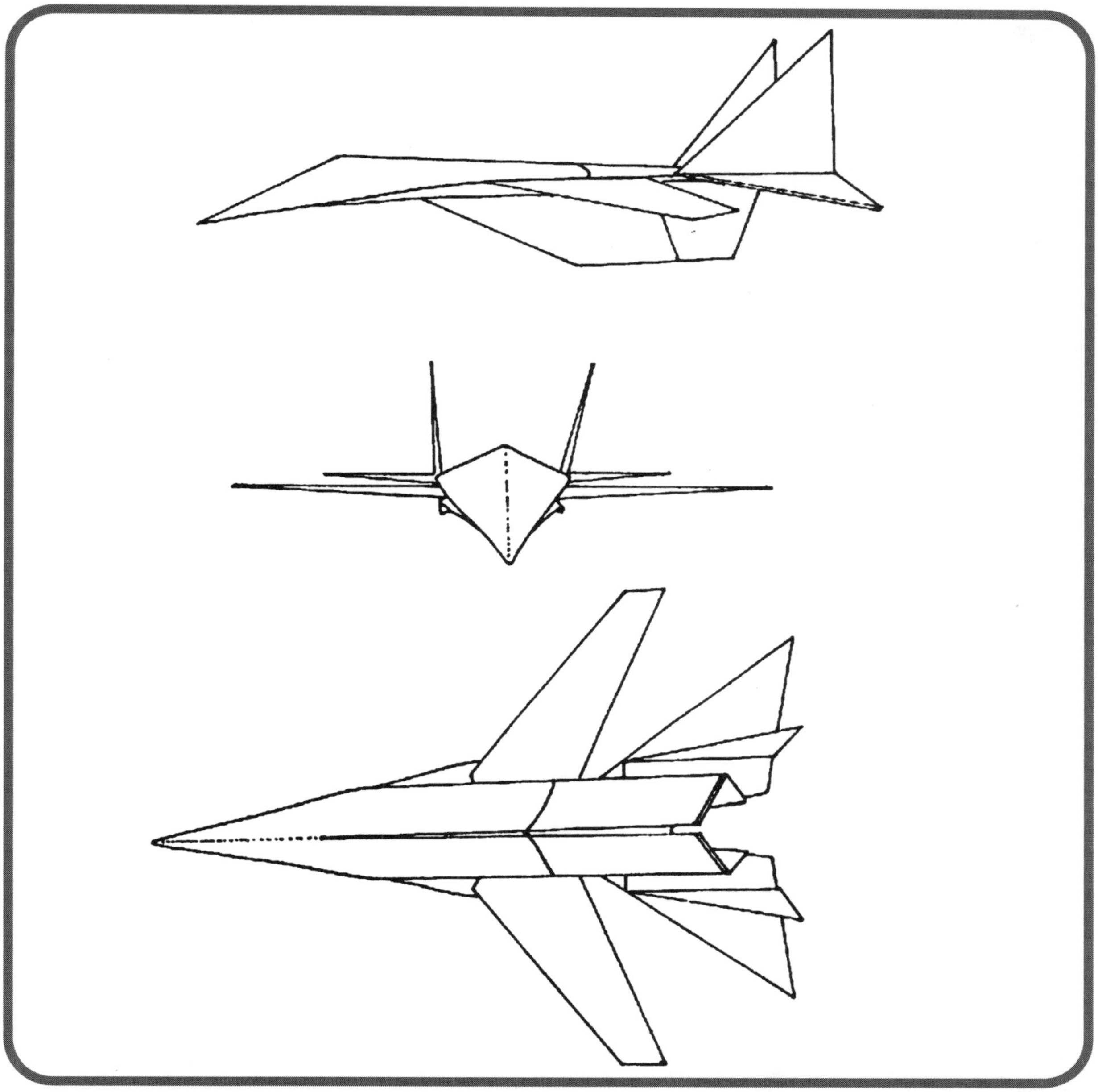

The F-15 will repeat some of the same steps and folds as the Jet, so many of these first steps should seem familiar.

(NOTE: Make sure you've mastered the F-15 Eagle before folding the F-14 Tomcat.)

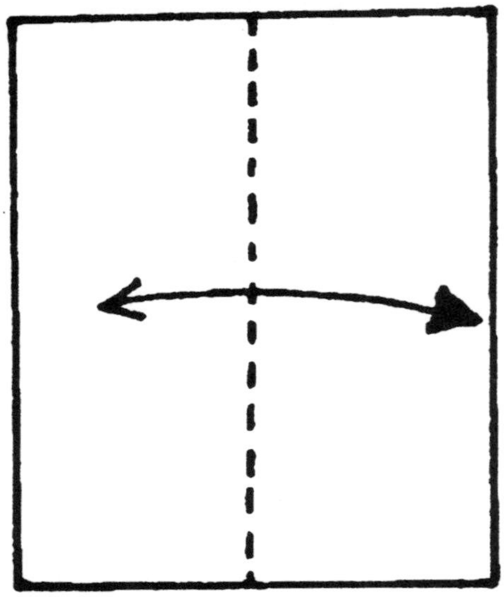

1

Fold paper in half, then unfold.

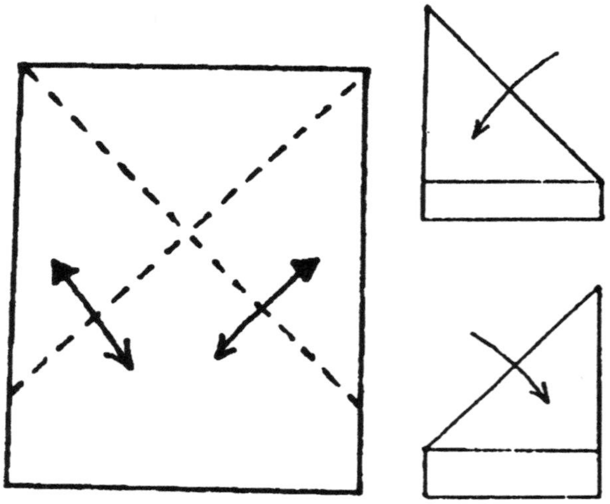

2

Fold diagonally at dotted lines, then unfold.

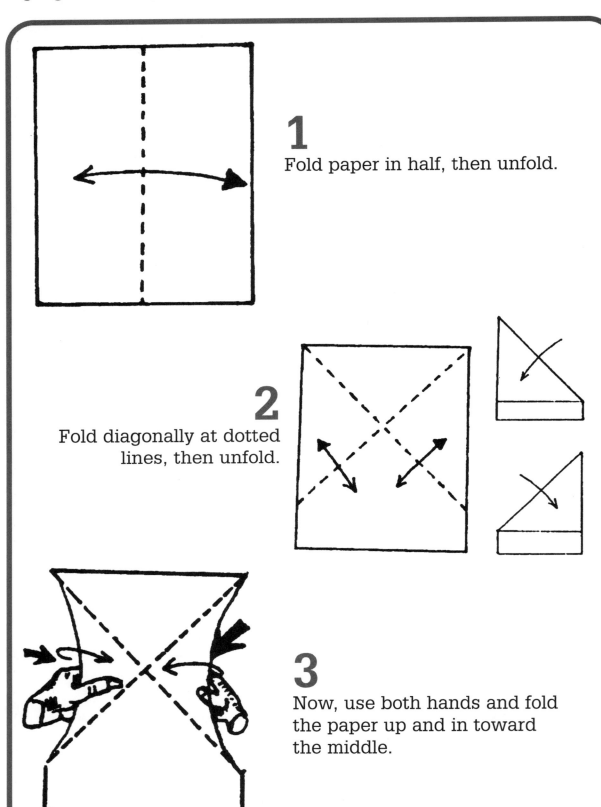

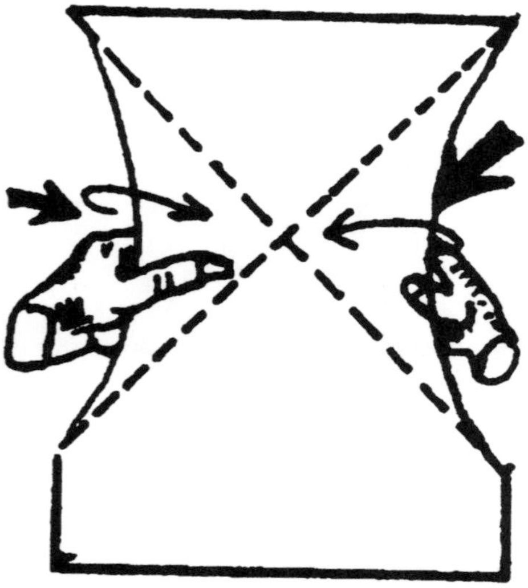

3

Now, use both hands and fold the paper up and in toward the middle.

# 4

This is how the paper should look. Gently press down from the top.

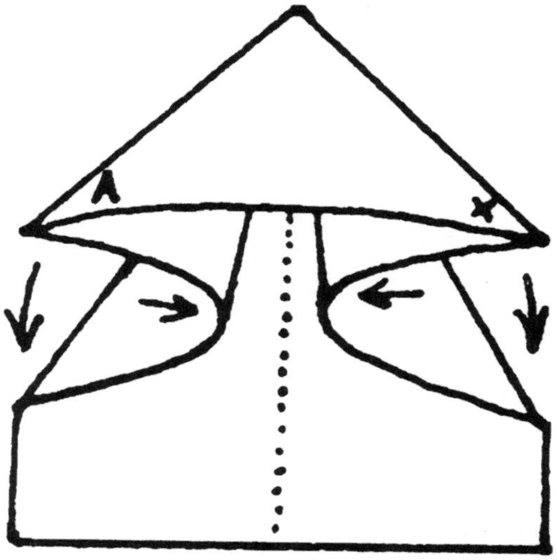


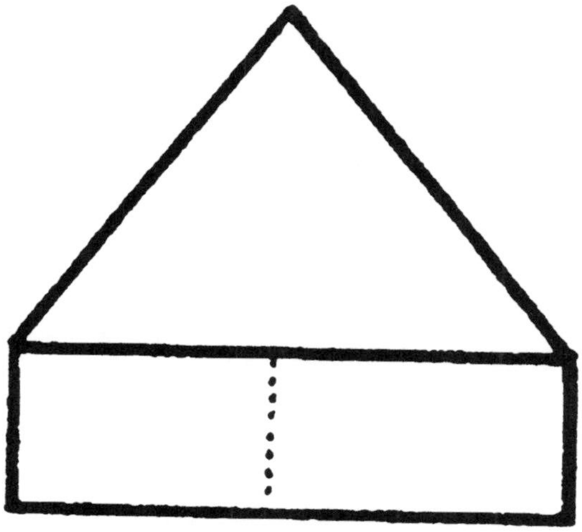

# 5

Now, it should look like this.

# 6

Slide your right hand under Flap X as shown here.

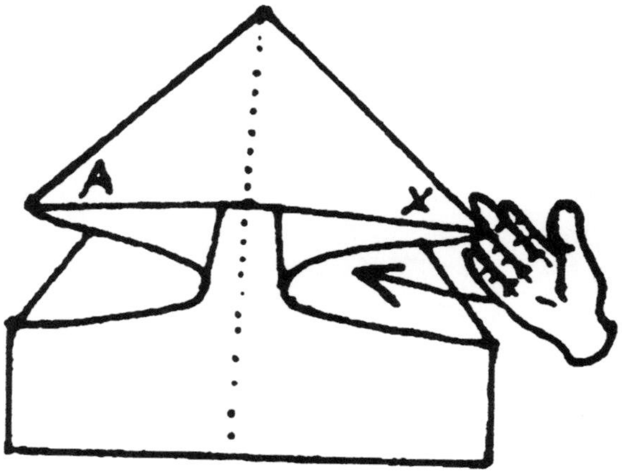

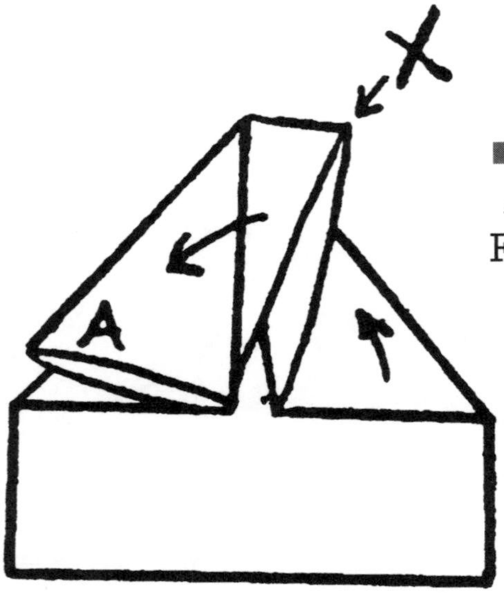


# 7

Flip Flap X over and onto Flap A.

# 8

Flap X should line up evenly with Flap A on the left side.

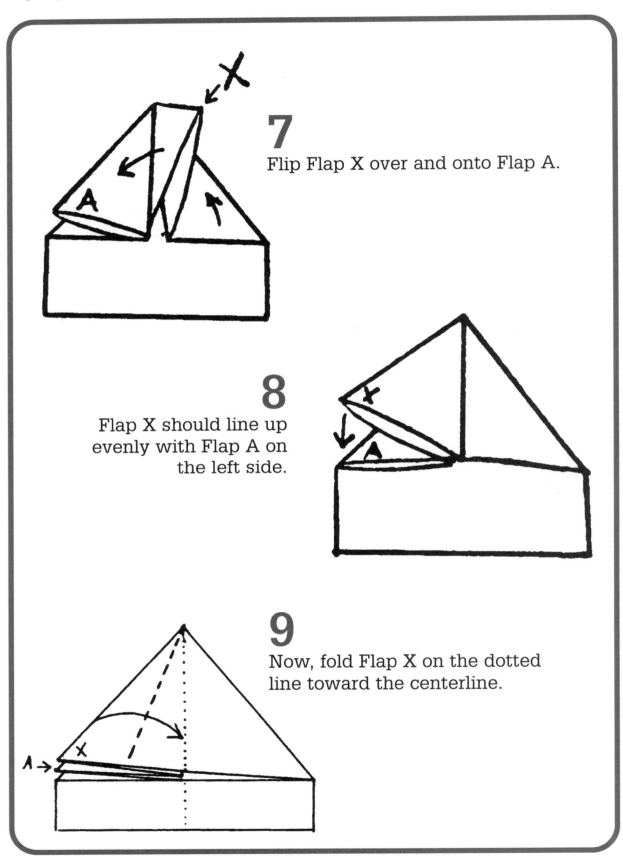

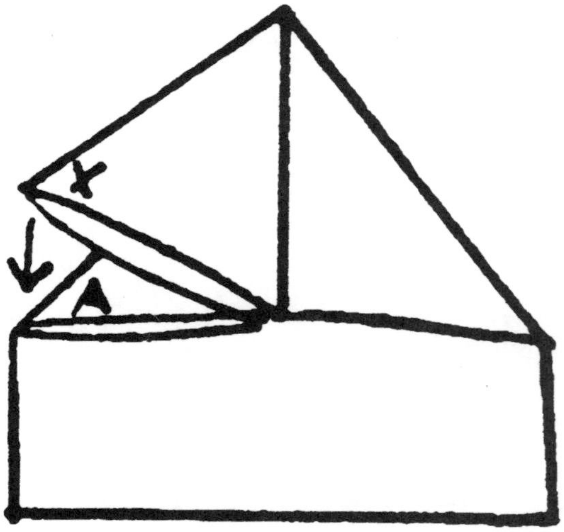


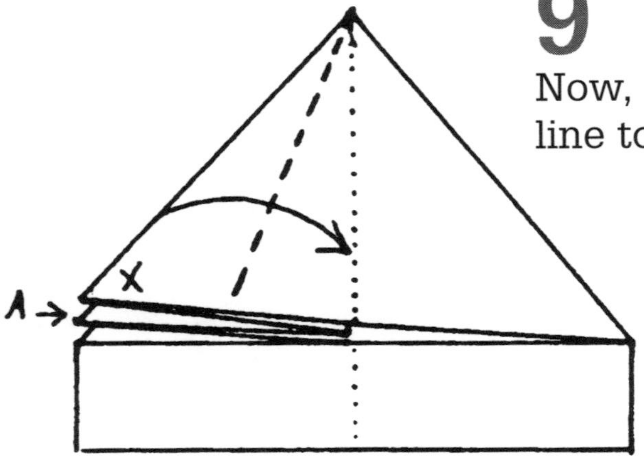


# 9

Now, fold Flap X on the dotted line toward the centerline.

## 10

This is how your fold should look.

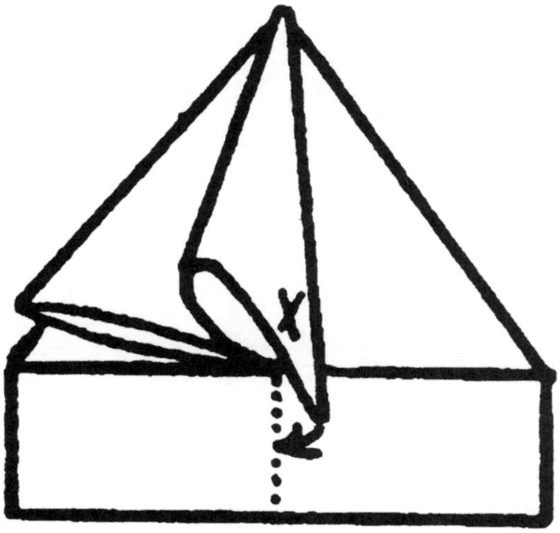


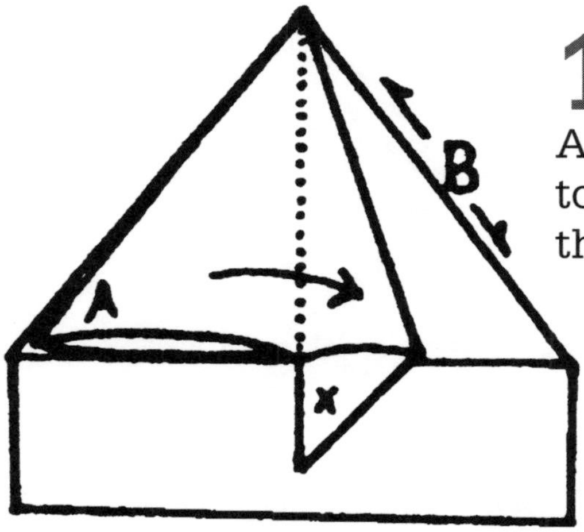


## 11

After you have folded Flap X toward the middle flap, flip it to the right side. Notice the B edge.

## 12

This is how your plane should look. Now, unfold & flip the right wing to the left side.

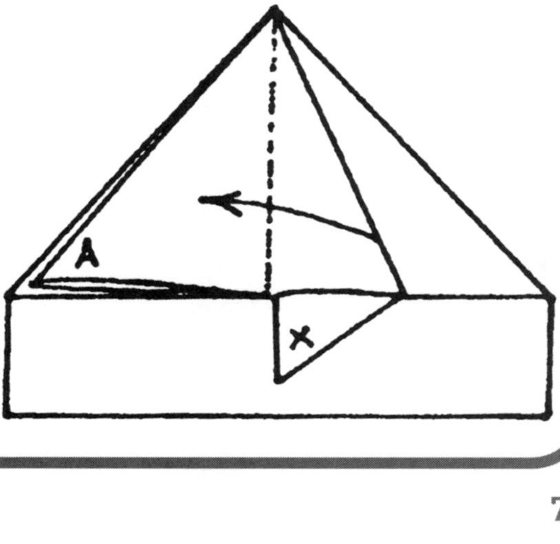

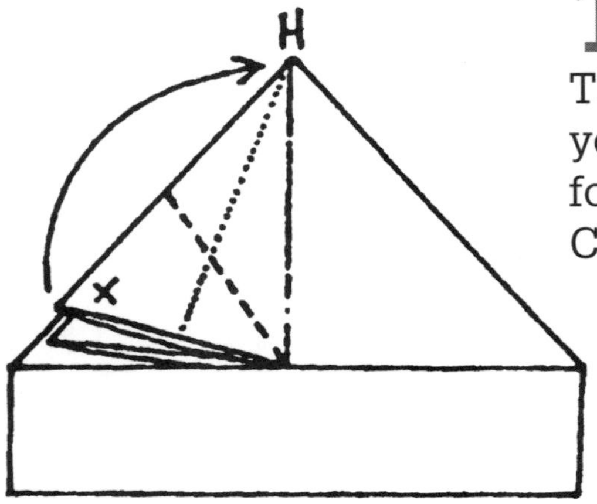


## 13

This is how it should look after you've flipped it to the left. Now fold on the dotted line so that Corner X meets Corner H.

## 14

This is how Step 13 should look. Repeat this fold on the left side.

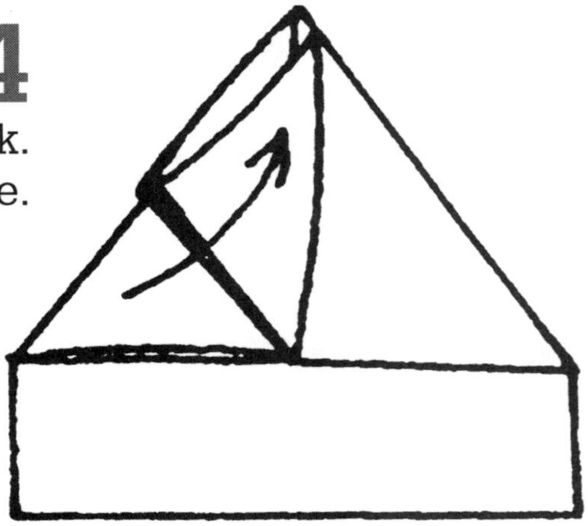

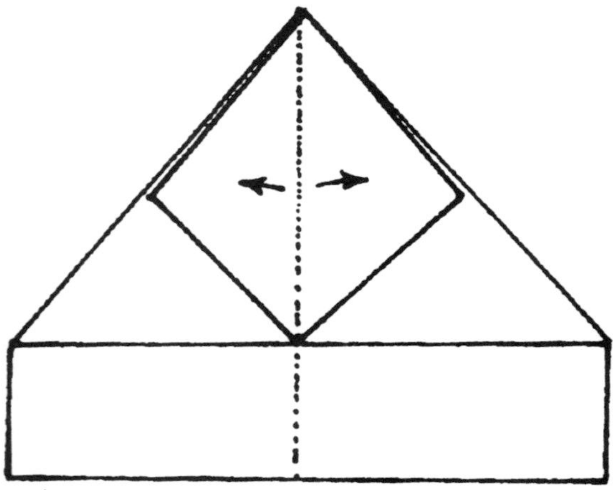

## 15

After you fold the left side, open both sides as indicated here.

# 16

Now open the wings further. The front wings now have two intersecting crease lines. Label them P and O.

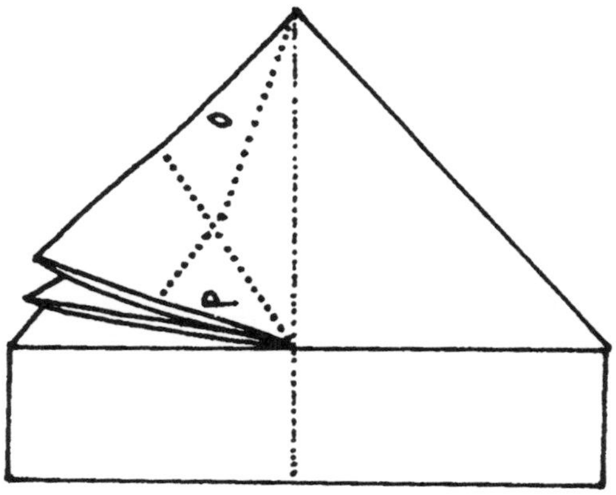


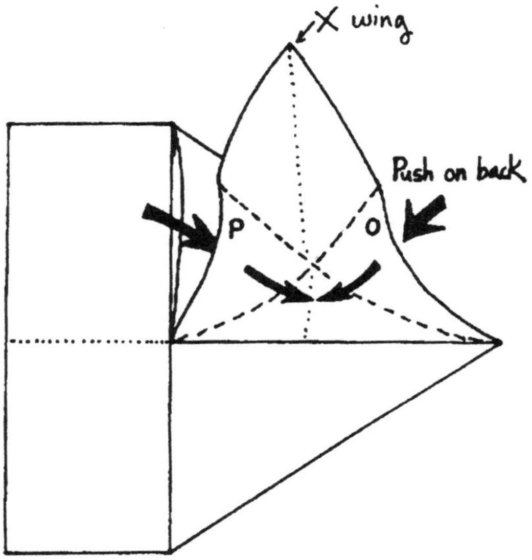


# 17

Rotate your paper ¼ turn to the right and fold P & O together and toward you on the crossing crease lines.

# 18

Your folds on P & O should look exactly as shown here. Put your hand behind the wing at M & N and press the two sides together.

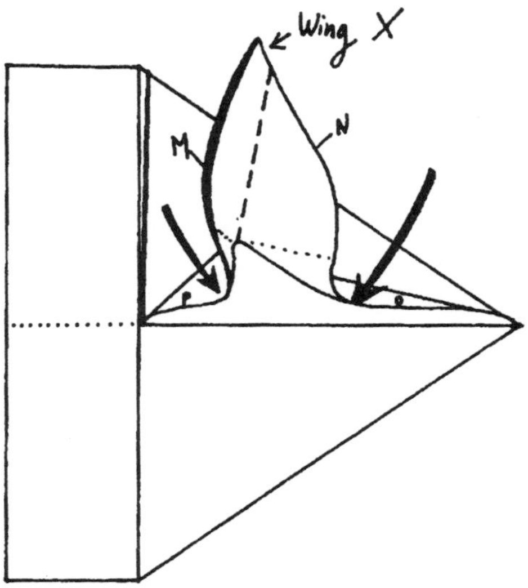

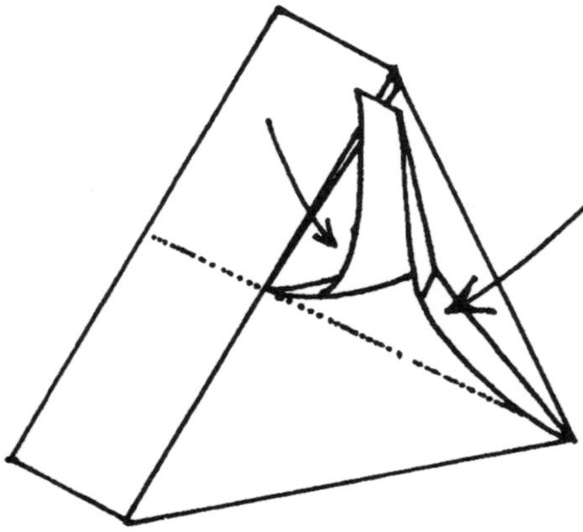

## 19

After pressing sides M & N together, this is how your plane should look. Do the same on the left side, beginning with Step 16, before going on.

## 20

Your finished folds of the wing should look like this. Fold the wing up toward the nose exactly as the arrow indicates.

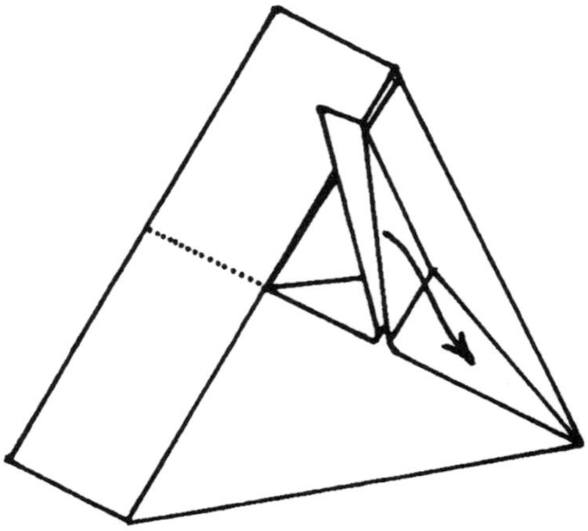

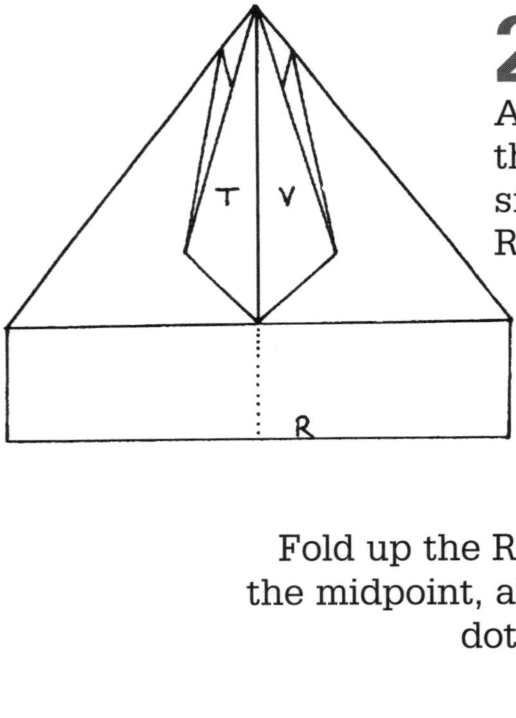


## 21

After you have finished with the other side, separate both sides as displayed. (Notice the R edge.)

## 22

Fold up the R edge at the midpoint, along the dotted line.

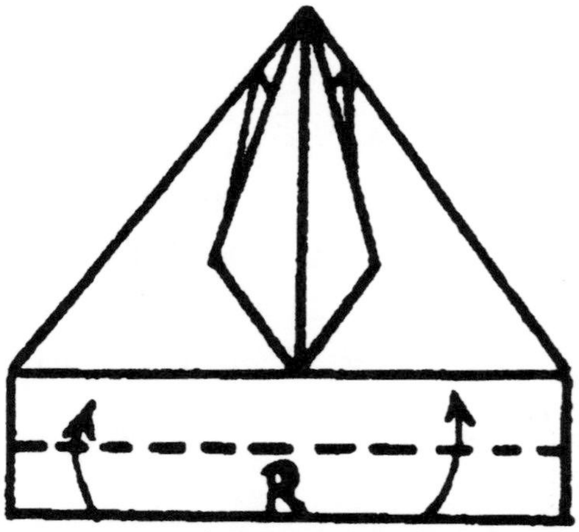

## 23

Now, fold back along the dotted line.

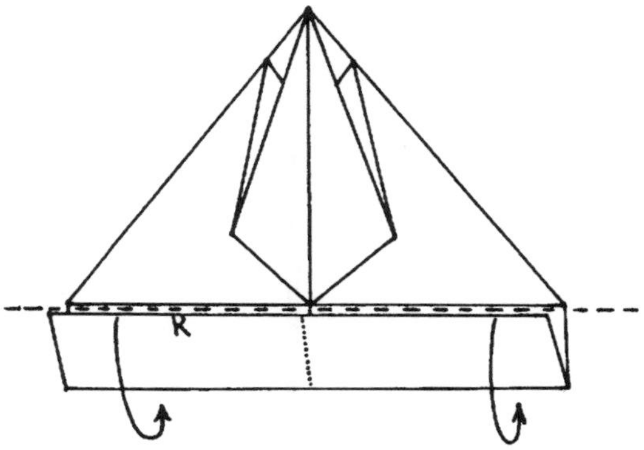


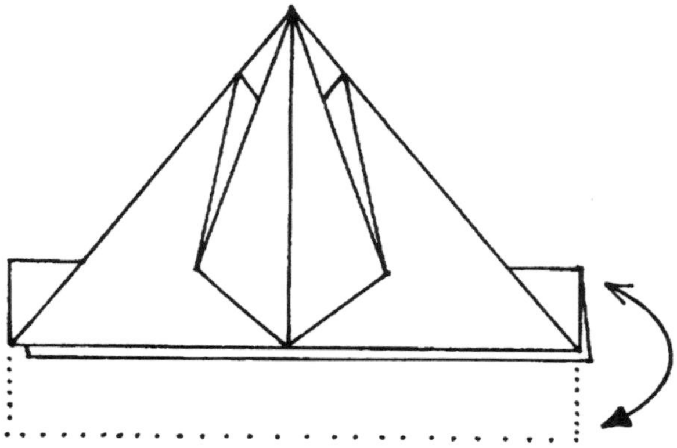

## 24

This is how your fold toward the back should look. Now unfold it as shown, so that it looks like the end of step 22.

## 25

Fold diagonally up, then back and forth at each corner, as shown here.

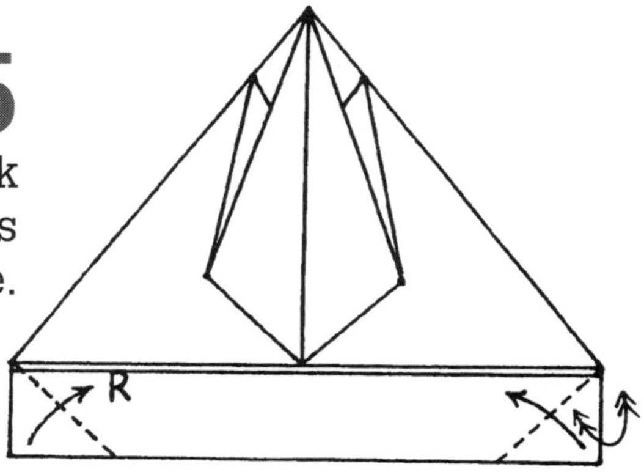


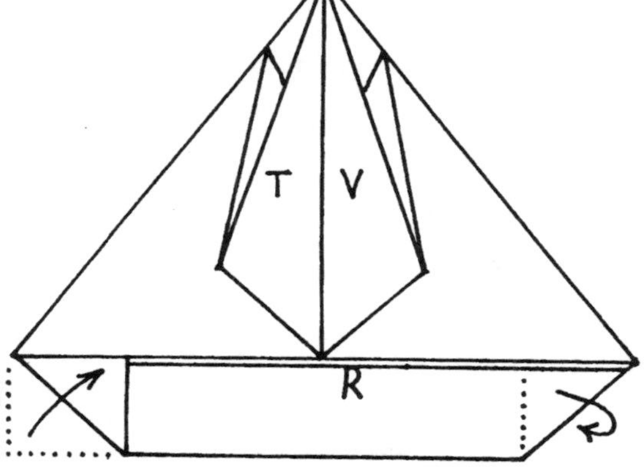


## 26

This is how the folds on step 25 should look. Fold back and forth five or six times.

# 27

After you've folded the corners, unfold the R edge fold as shown. You should have two triangular shapes.

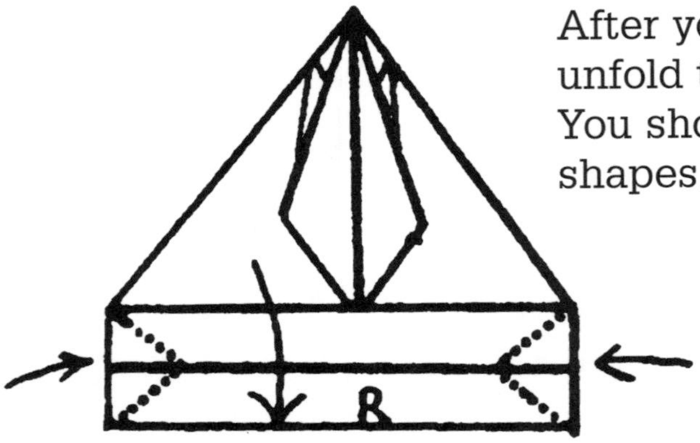


# 28

Push the two triangular sides inward as shown.

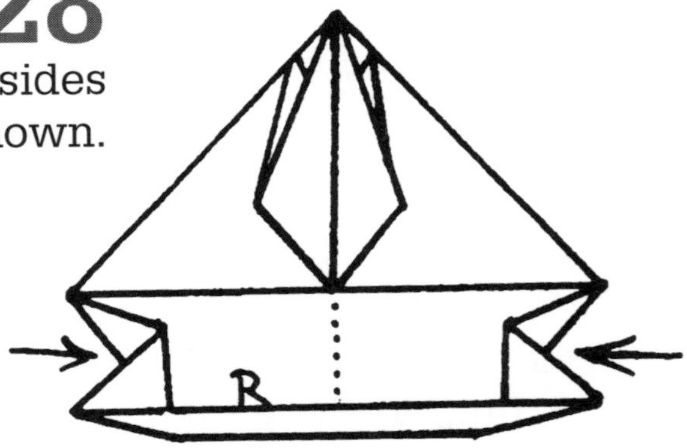


# 29

After you have pressed both triangular sides inward, it should look like this. Now, fold this part back on the dotted line. Next, flip the V wing to the T wing on the left side.

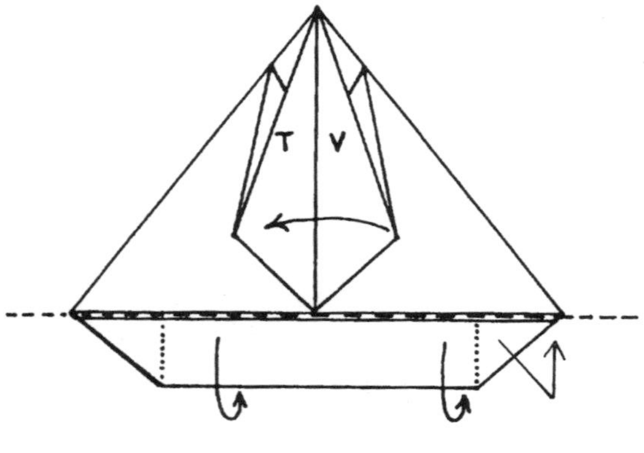

# 30

Now, fold Edge B to Centerline C on the dotted line. Do the same to the left side.

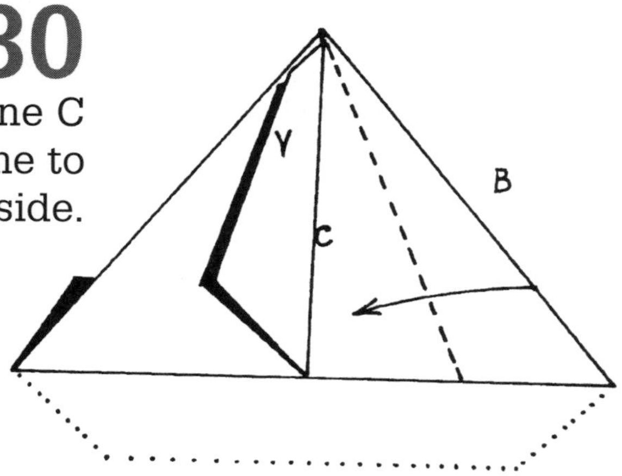


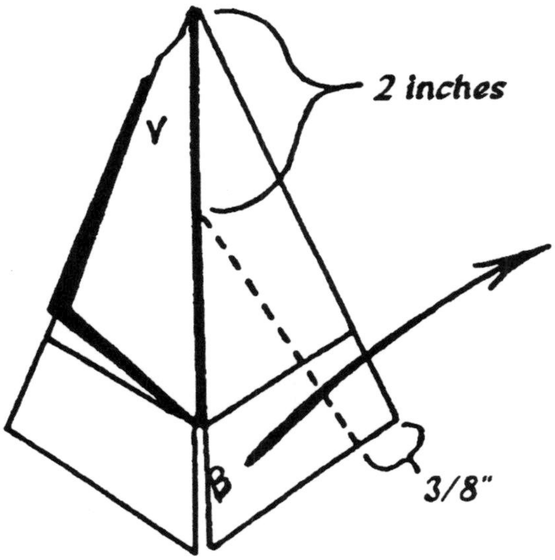


# 31

Fold Edge B to the right on the dotted line.

# 32

This is how your fold should look. Fold the left side the same way. Now fold the right side toward the center as shown.

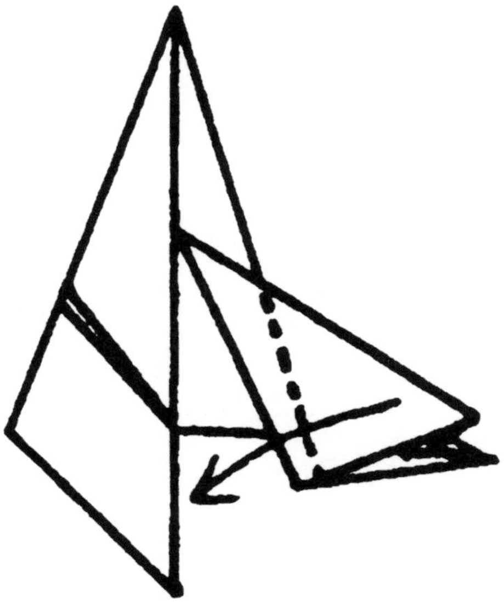

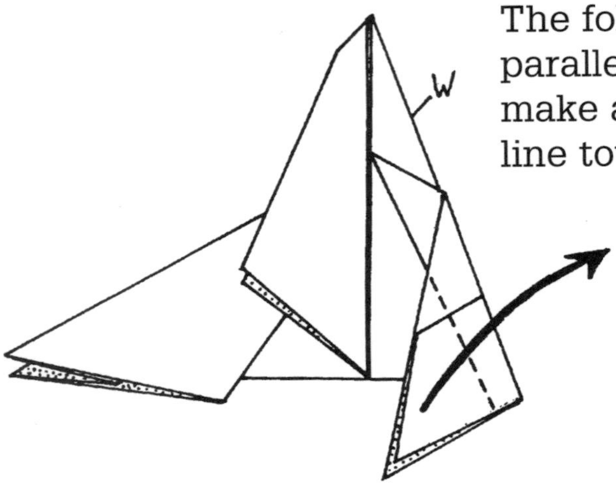

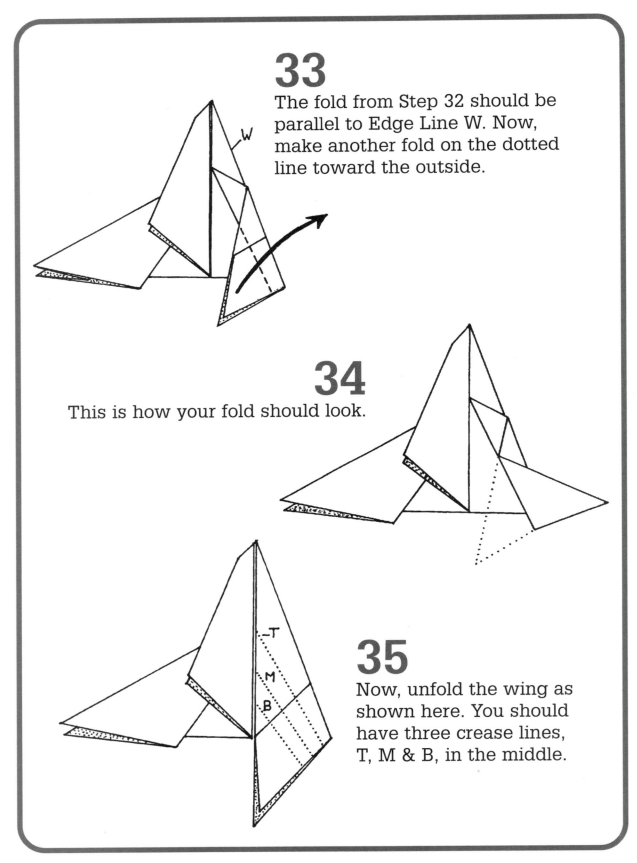

# 33

The fold from Step 32 should be parallel to Edge Line W. Now, make another fold on the dotted line toward the outside.

# 34

This is how your fold should look.

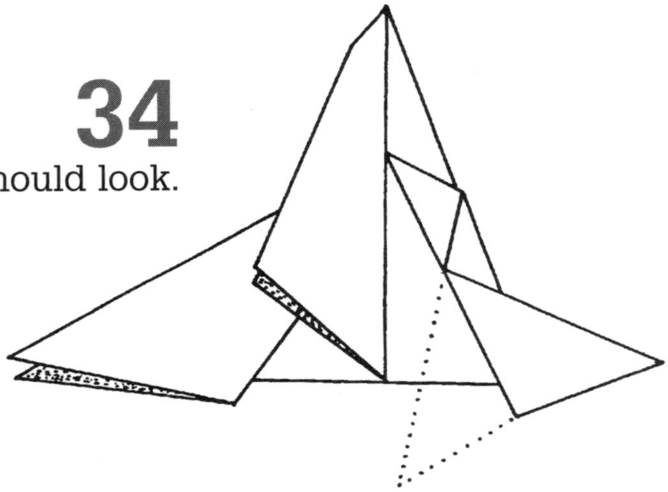

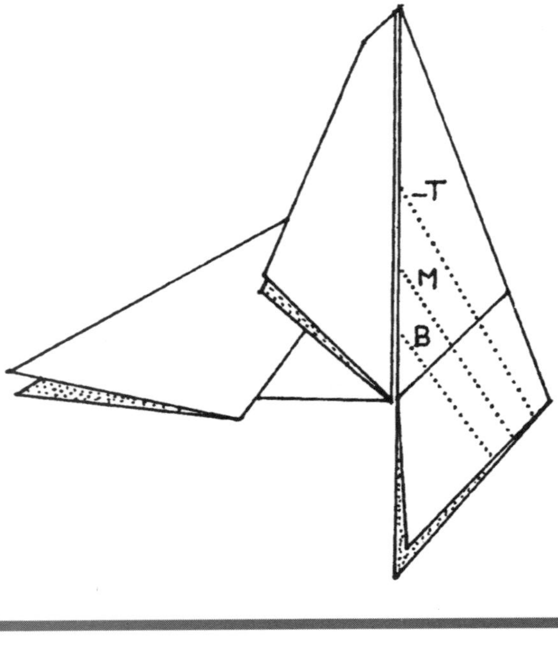


# 35

Now, unfold the wing as shown here. You should have three crease lines, T, M & B, in the middle.

# 36

Hold the paper straight; fold toward the outside along dotted crease Line M.

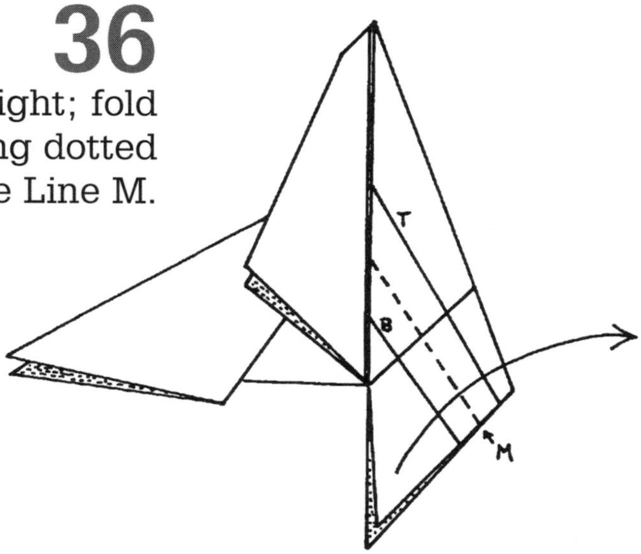


# 37

Your fold should look like this. Again, fold Edge M to Edge W.

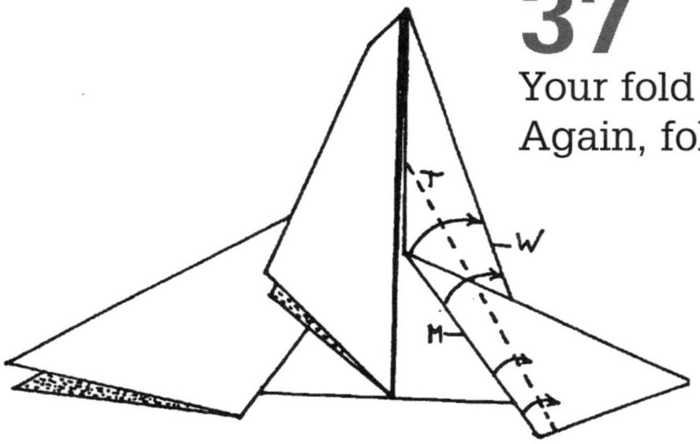


# 38

This is how the fold from Step 37 should look.

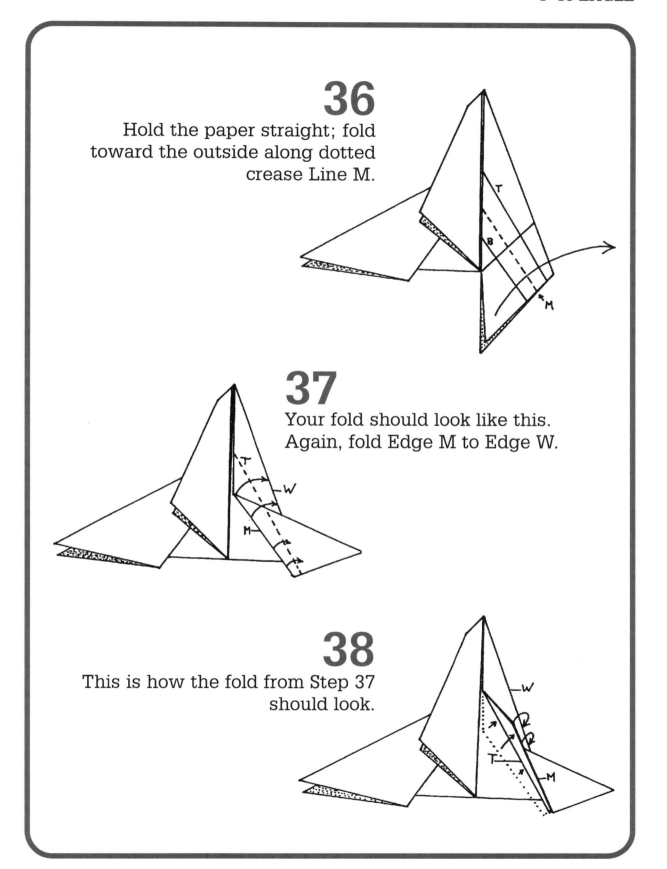

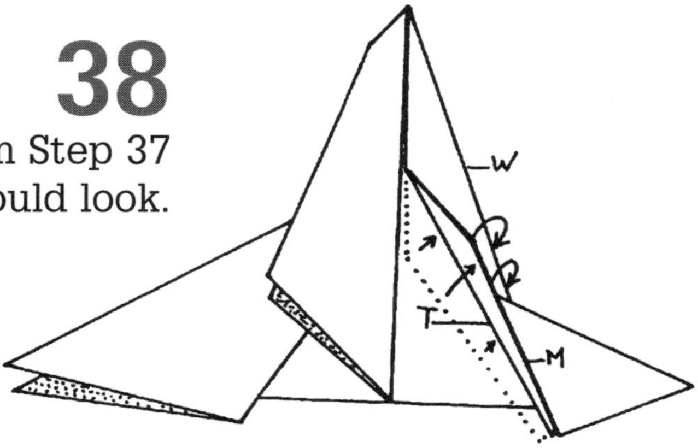

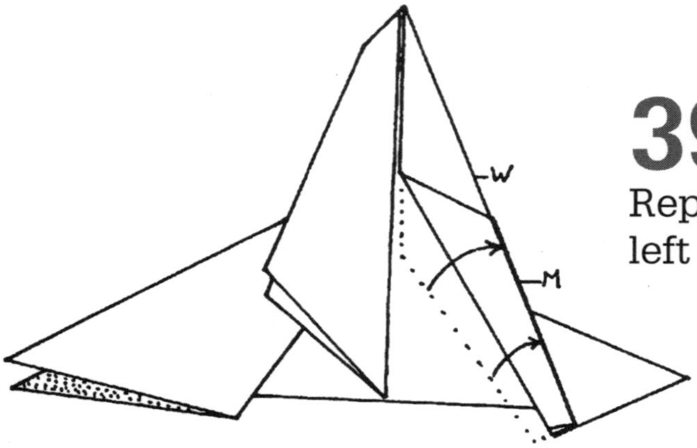

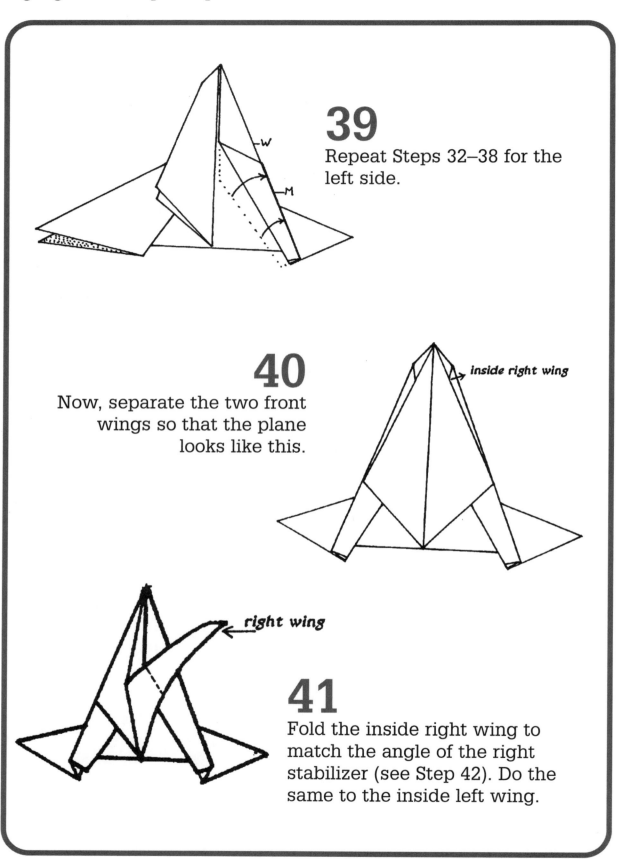

## 39

Repeat Steps 32–38 for the left side.

## 40

Now, separate the two front wings so that the plane looks like this.

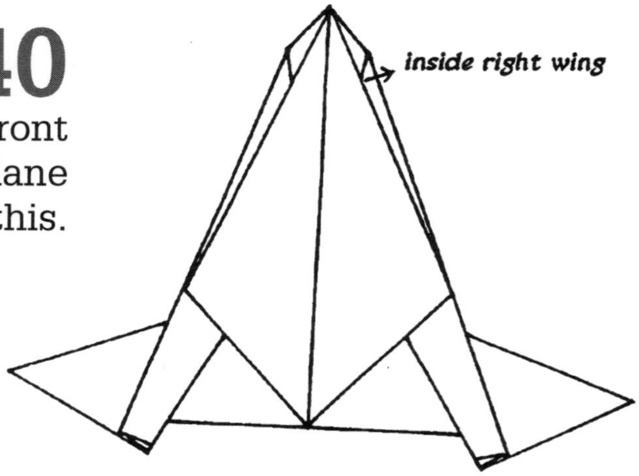


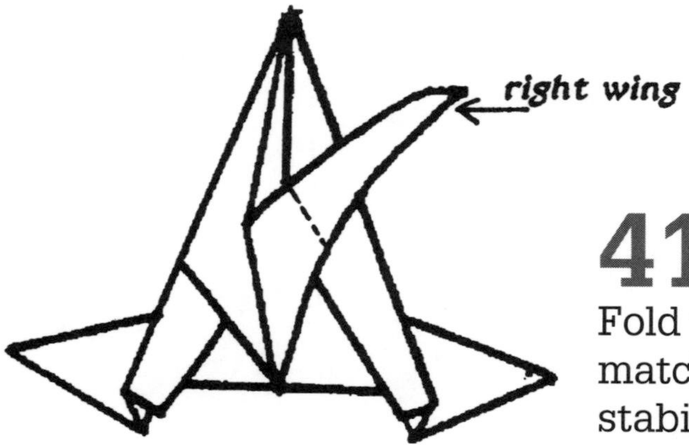


## 41

Fold the inside right wing to match the angle of the right stabilizer (see Step 42). Do the same to the inside left wing.

## 42

Match the angle of the front wing to the stabilizer. Do the same to the other side.

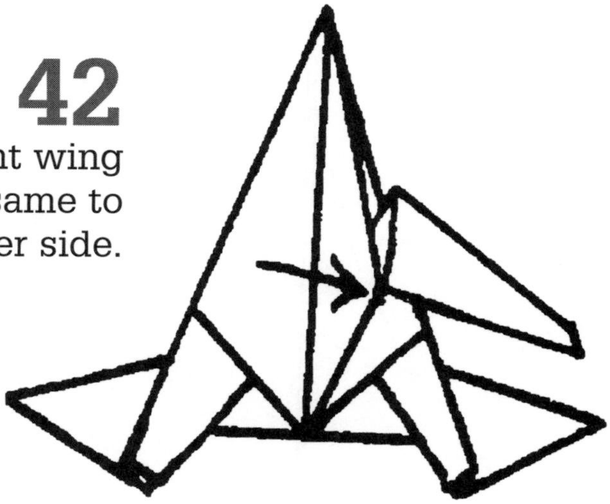

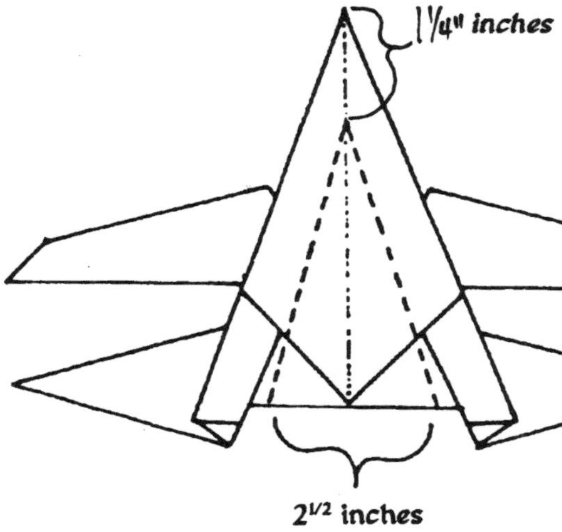


## 43

This is what your plane should look like.

## 44

Now, fold the right side to the left and fold the left side to the right.

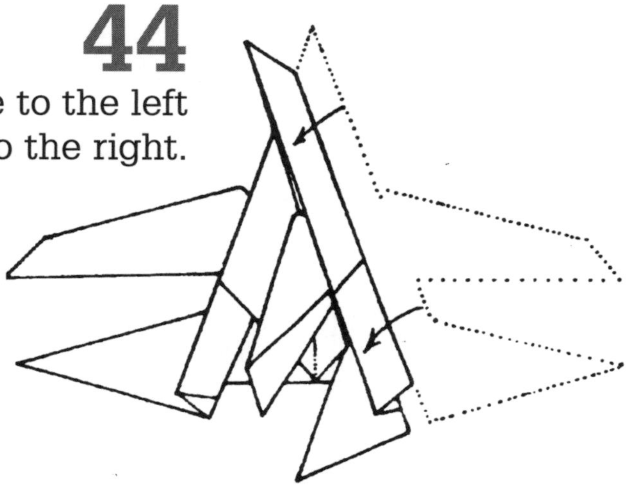

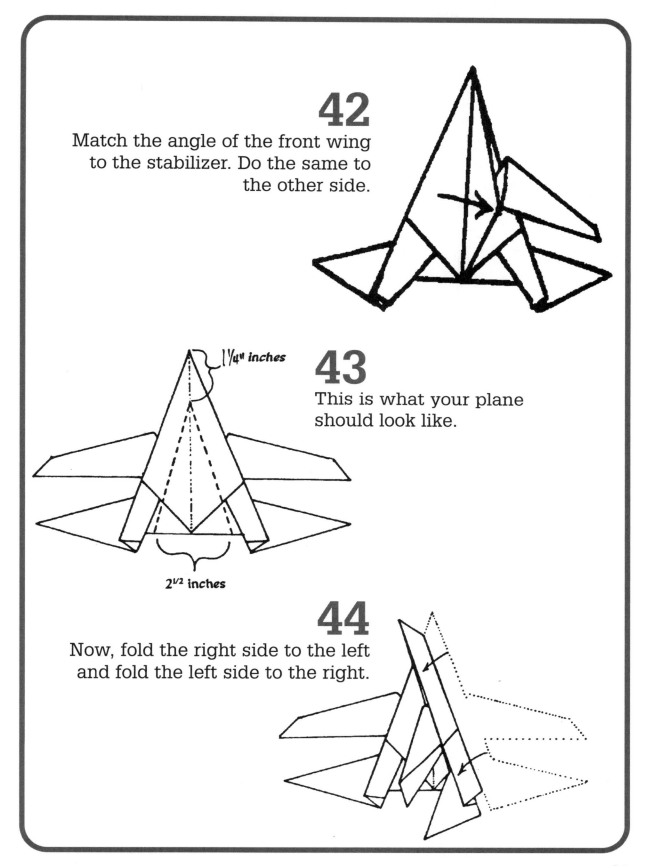

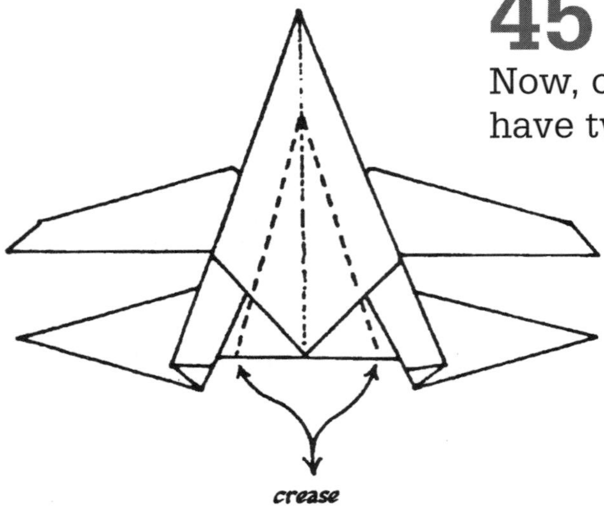


## 45

Now, open the folds; you should have two crease lines.

## 46

After you have folded the two sides, you should be able to push the belly downward without losing the sharp nose.

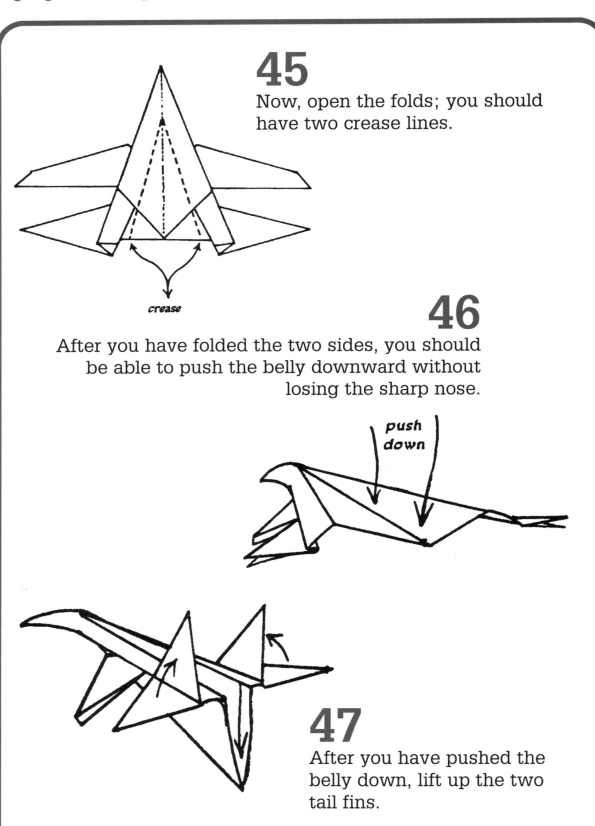

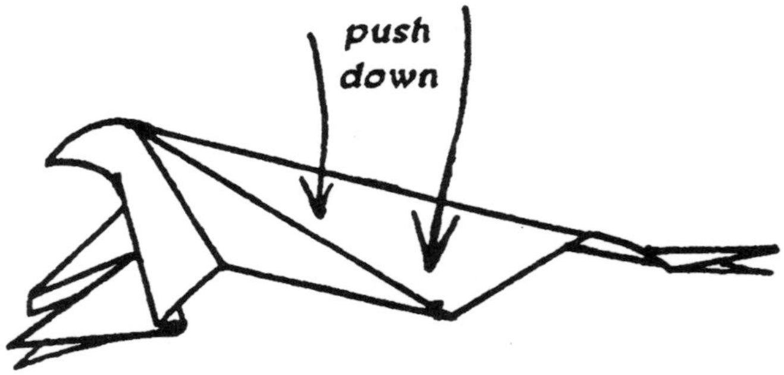


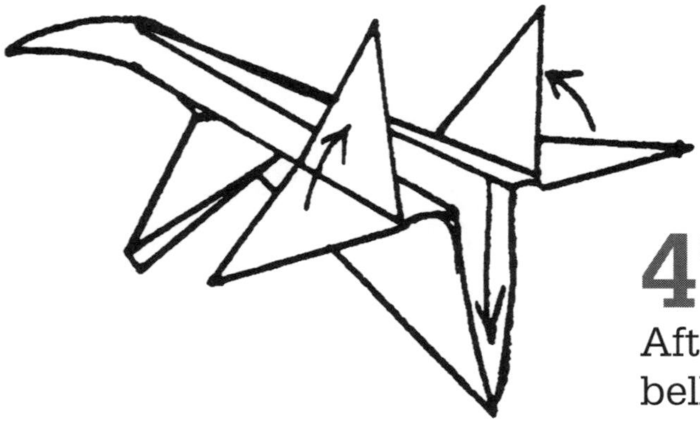

## 47

After you have pushed the belly down, lift up the two tail fins.

## 48

Make an inward-up fold of about ½ inch.

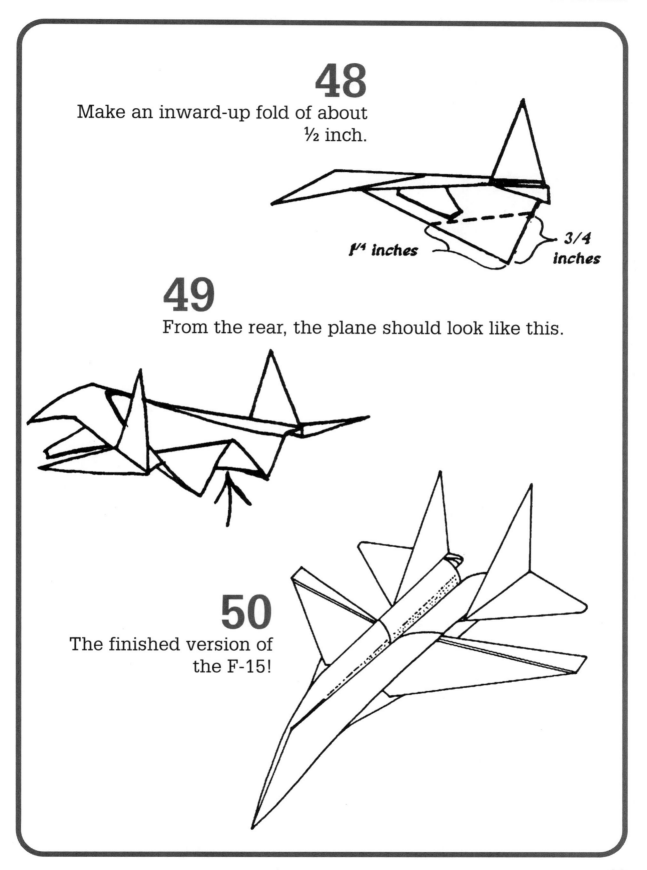

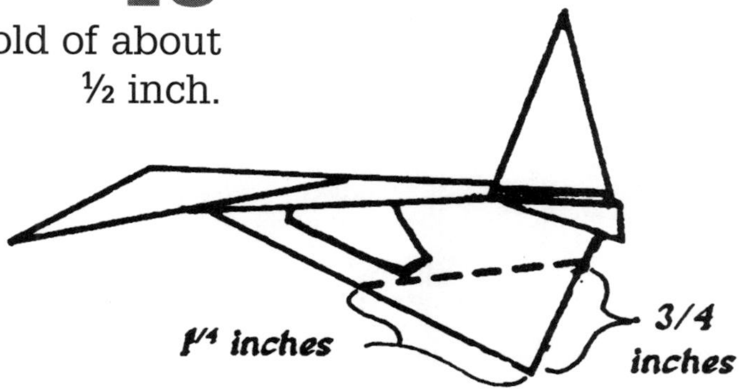


## 49

From the rear, the plane should look like this.

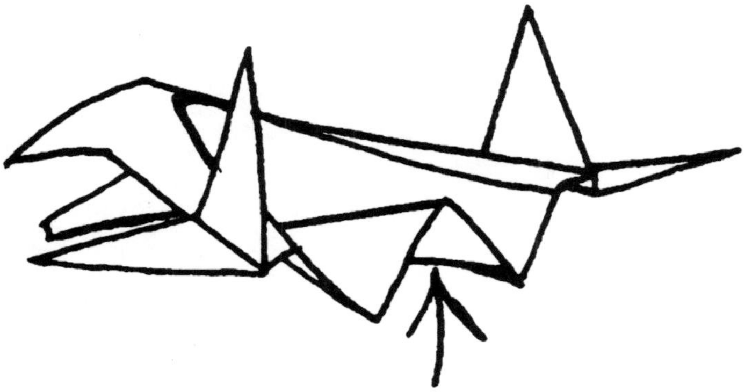

## 50

The finished version of the F-15!

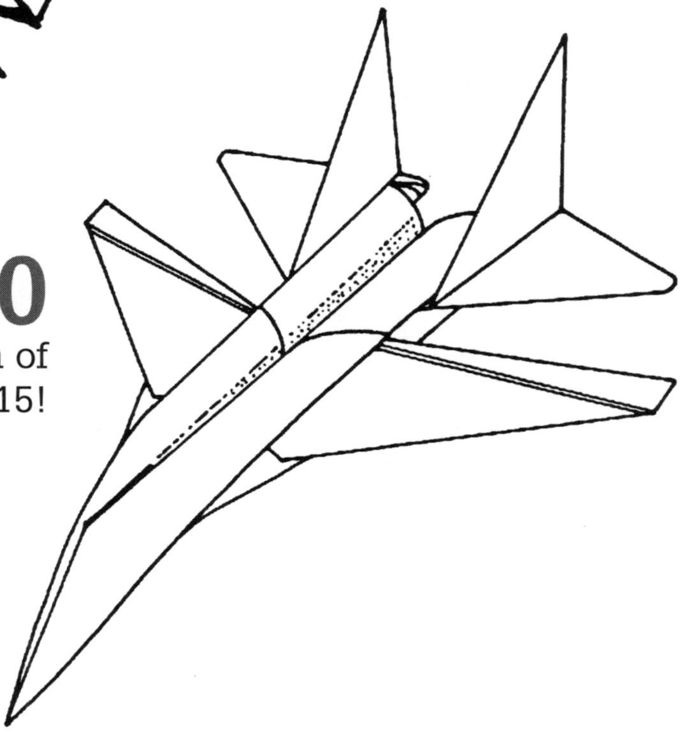

# F-15 EAGLE

# STEALTH-X

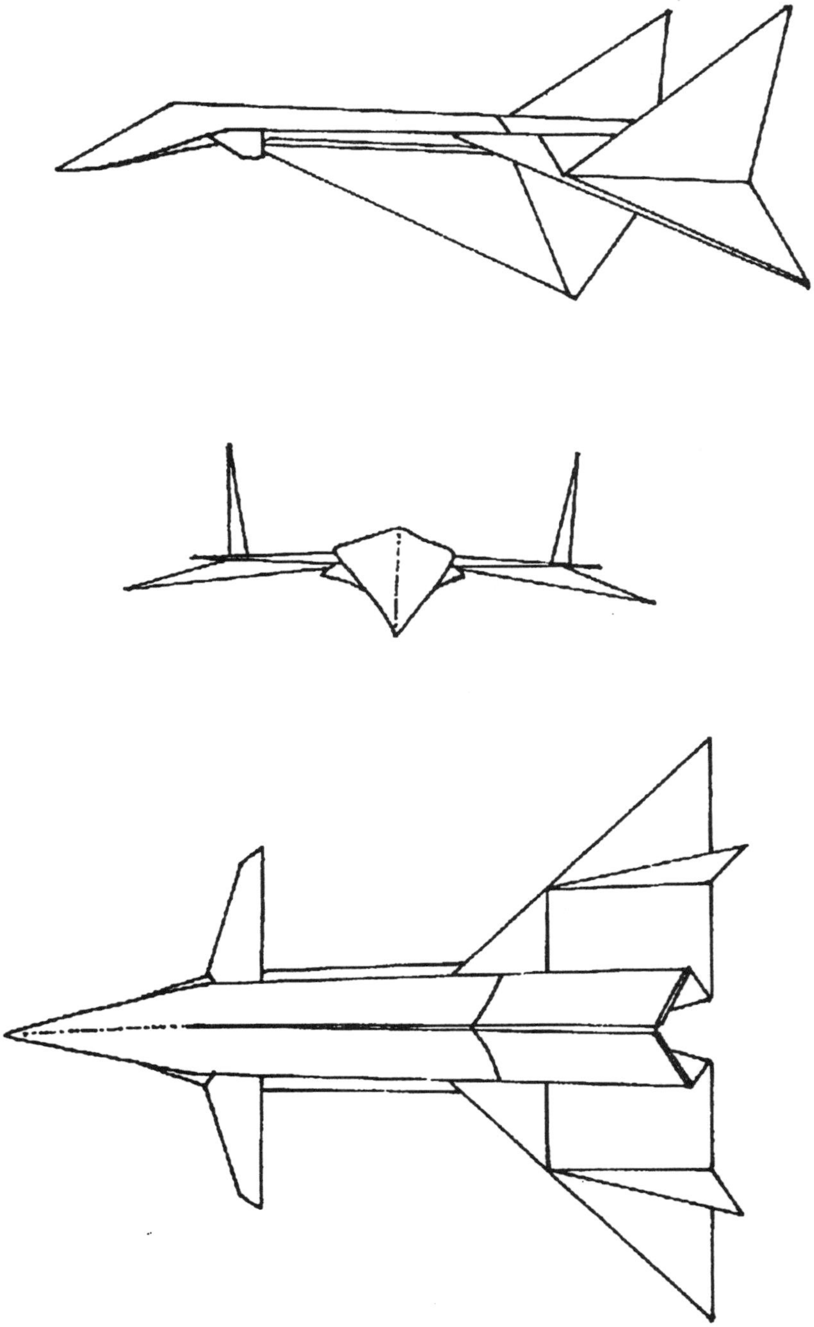

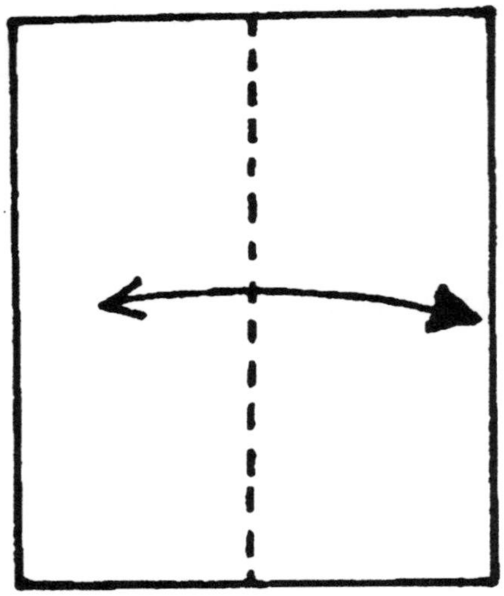

1

Fold paper in half, then unfold.

2

Fold diagonally at dotted lines, then unfold.

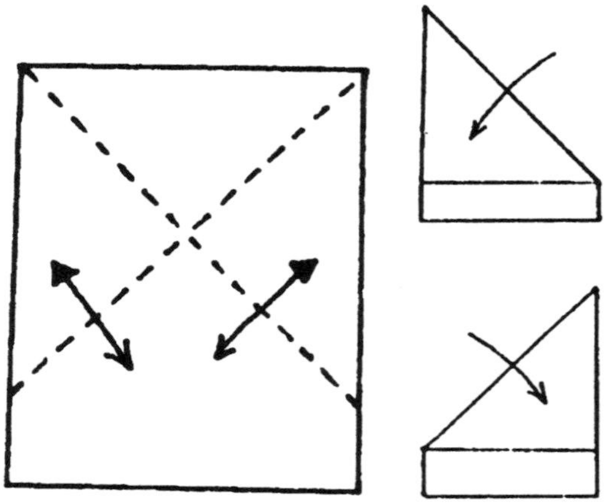

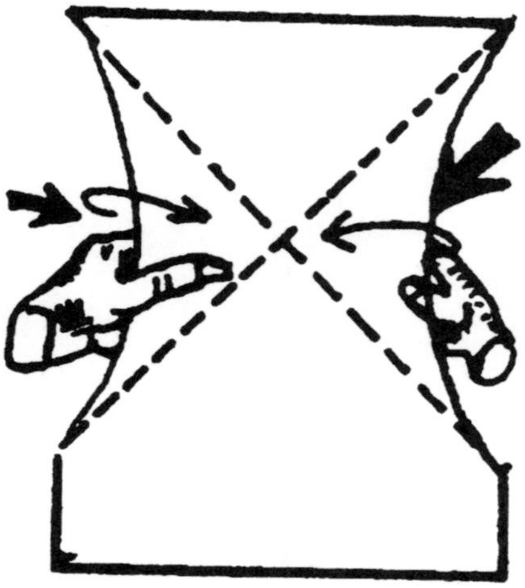

3

Now, use both hands and fold the paper up and in toward the middle.

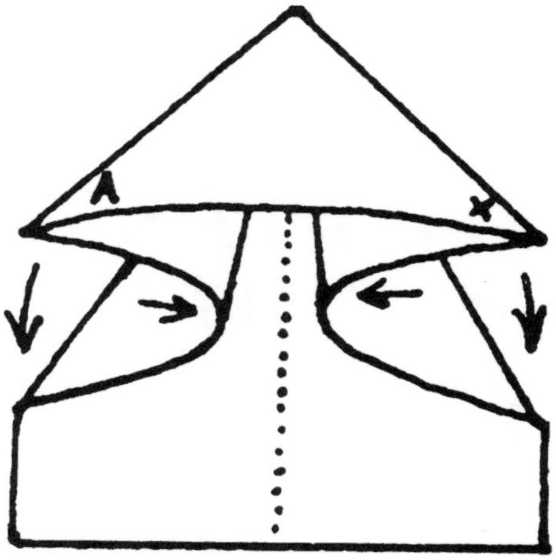


## 4

This is how the paper should look. Gently press down from the top.

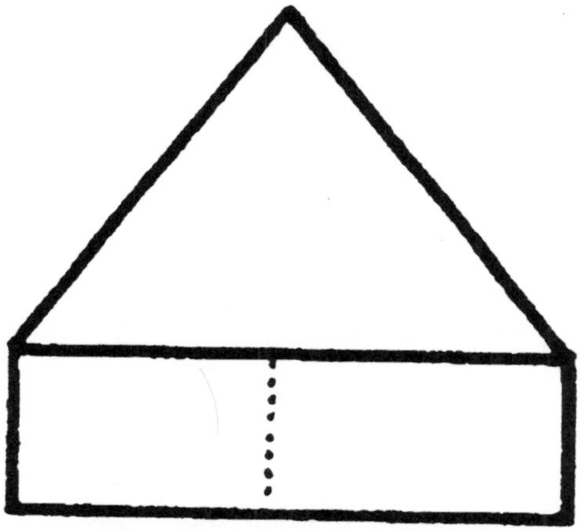

## 5

Now, it should look like this.

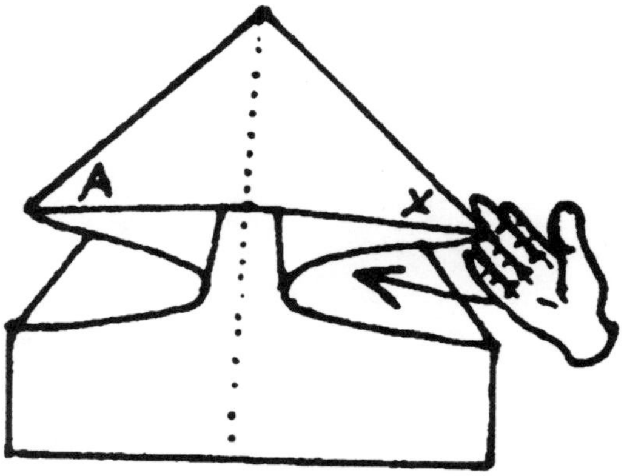


## 6

Slide your right hand under Flap X as shown here.

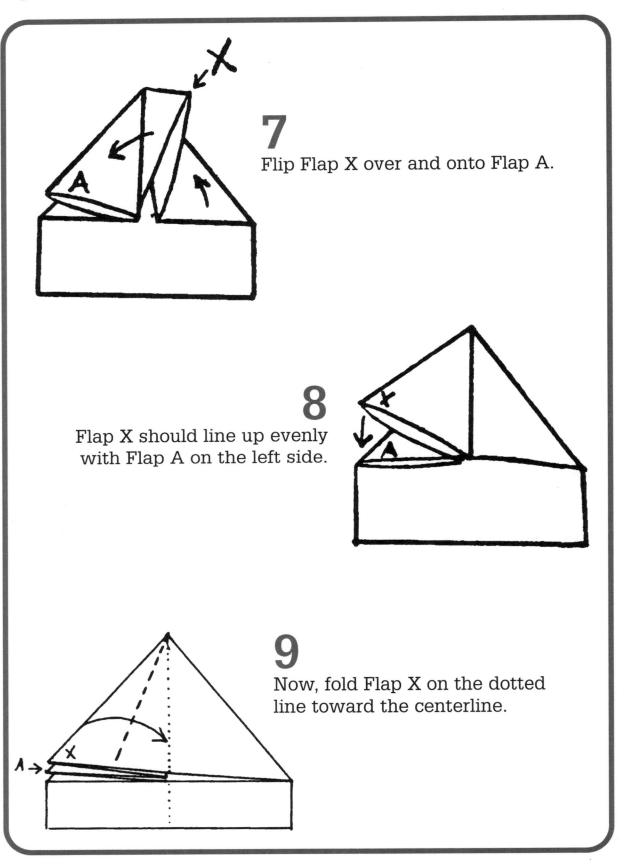

## 7

Flip Flap X over and onto Flap A.

## 8

Flap X should line up evenly with Flap A on the left side.

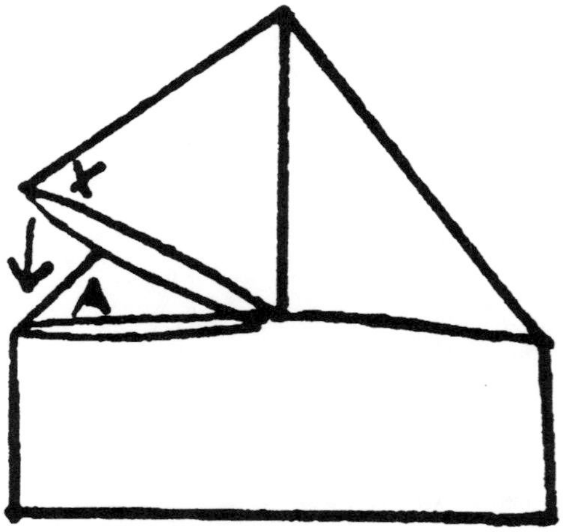


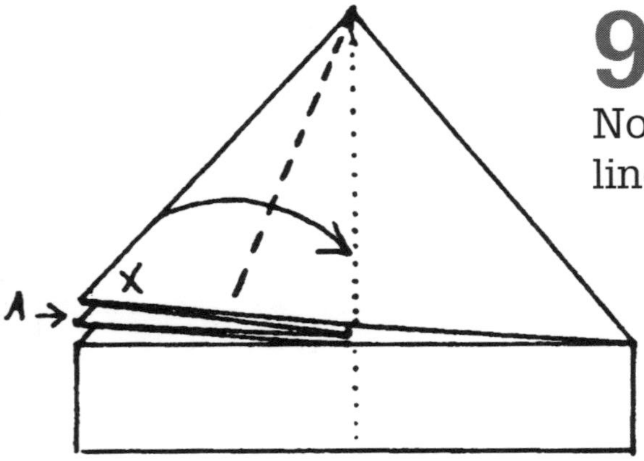


## 9

Now, fold Flap X on the dotted line toward the centerline.

## 10

This is how your fold should look.

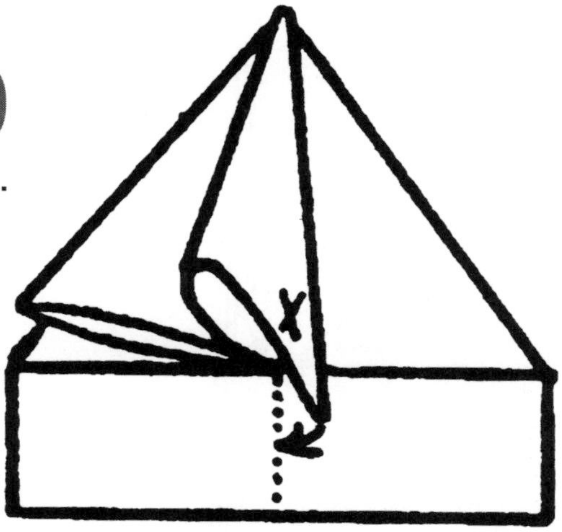


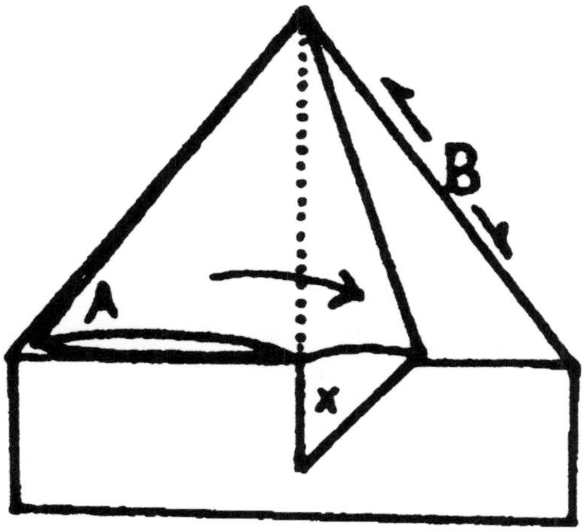


## 11

After you have folded Flap X toward the middle flap, flip it to the right side. Notice the B Edge.

## 12

This is how your plane should look. Now, unfold & flip the right wing to the left side.

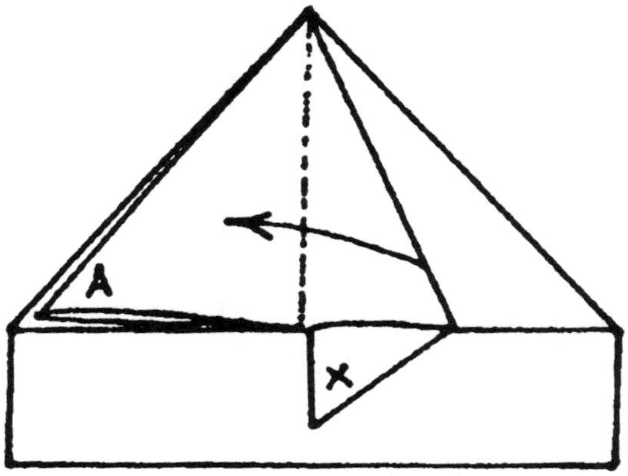

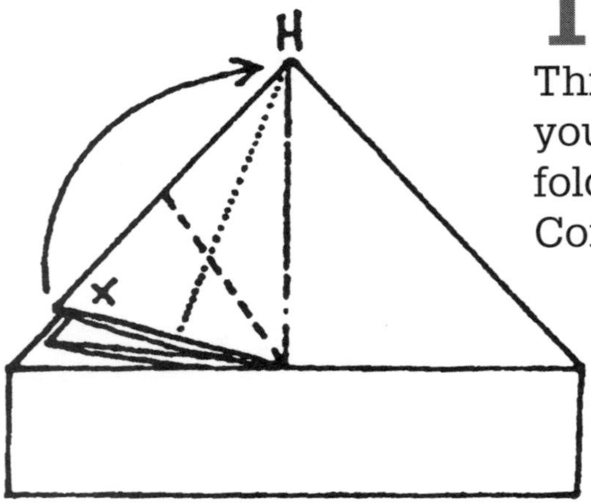


## 13

This is how it should look after you've flipped it to the left. Now fold on the dotted line so that Corner X meets Corner H.

## 14

This is how Step 13 should look. Repeat this fold on the left side.

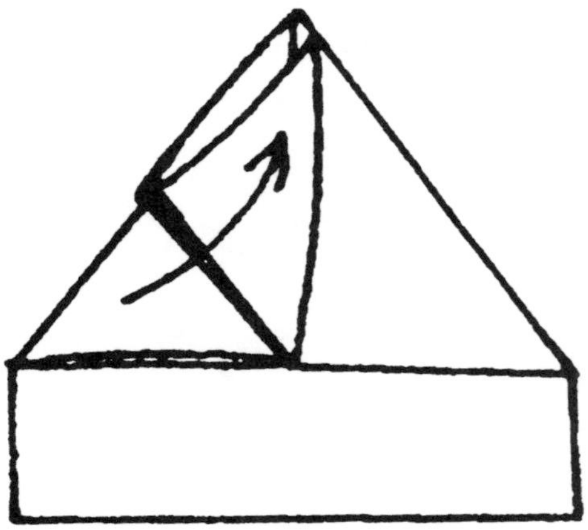

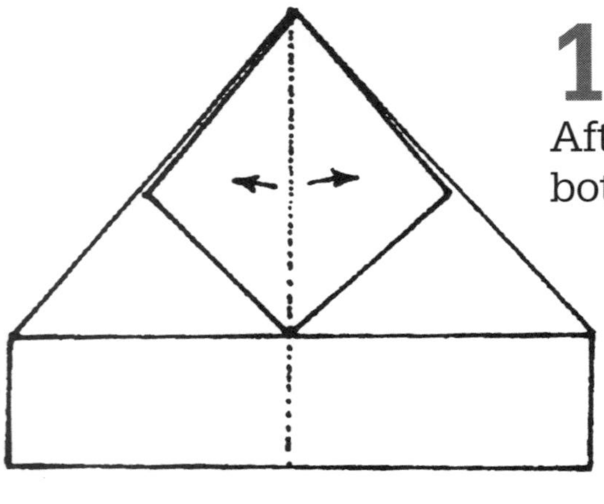

## 15

After you fold the left side, open both sides as indicated here.

# 16

Now open the wings further. The front wings now have two intersecting crease lines. Label them P and O.

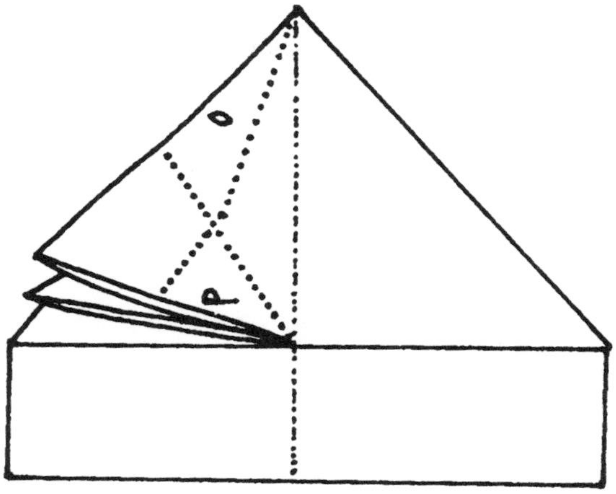


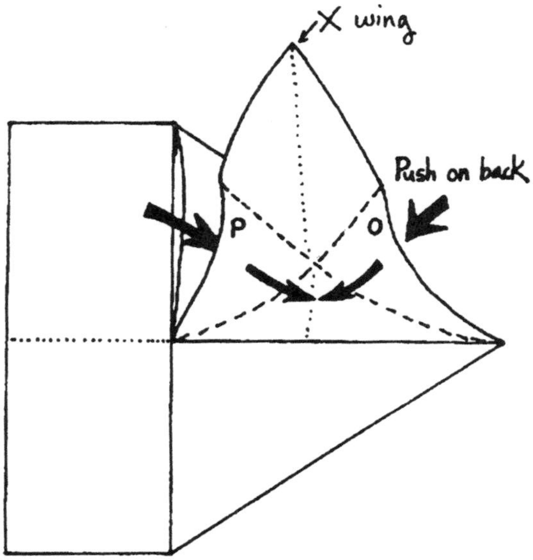


# 17

Rotate your paper ¼ turn to the right and fold P & O together and toward you on the crossing crease lines.

# 18

Your folds on P & O should look exactly as shown here. Put your hand behind the wing at M & N and press the two sides together.

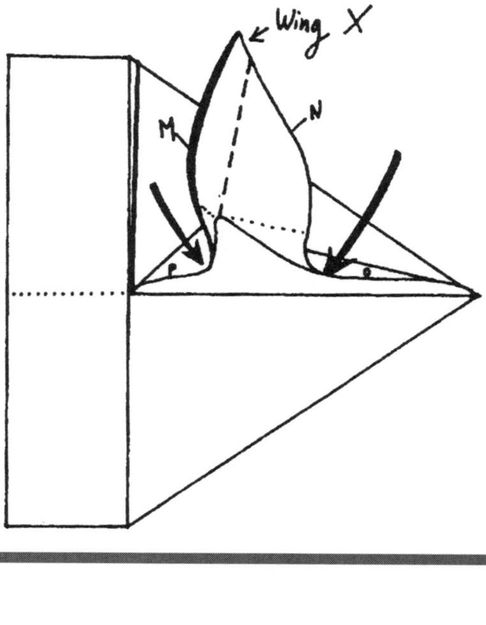

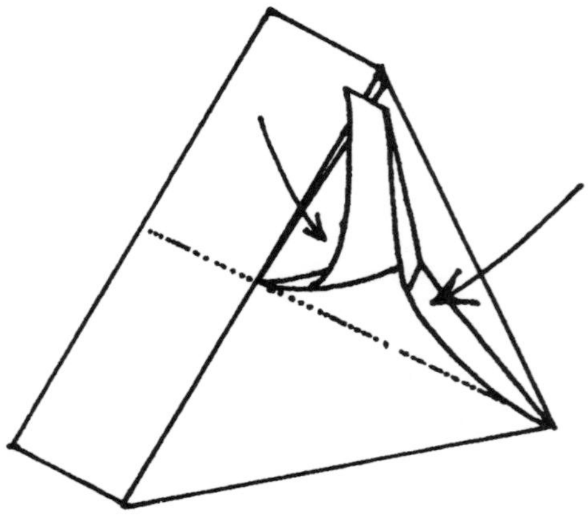

## 19

After pressing sides M & N together, this is how your plane should look. Do the same on the left side, beginning with Step 16, before going on.

## 20

Your finished folds of the wing should look like this. Fold the wing up toward the nose exactly as the arrow indicates.

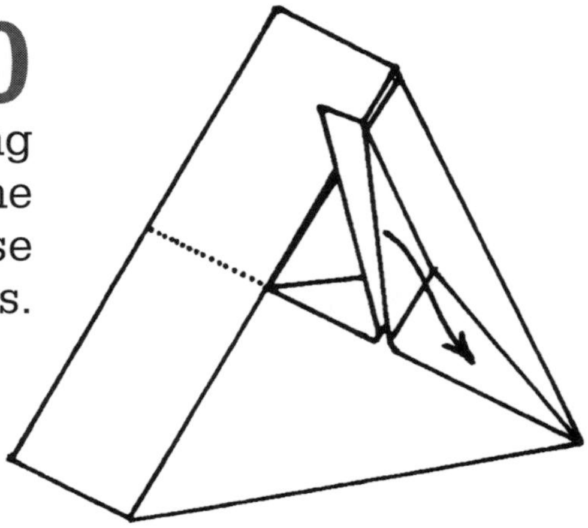

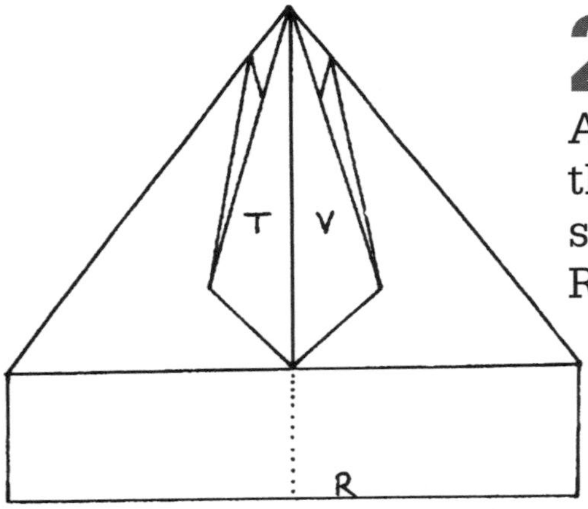


## 21

After you have finished with the other side, separate both sides as displayed. (Notice the R edge.)

## 22

Fold up the R edge at the mid-point, along the dotted line.

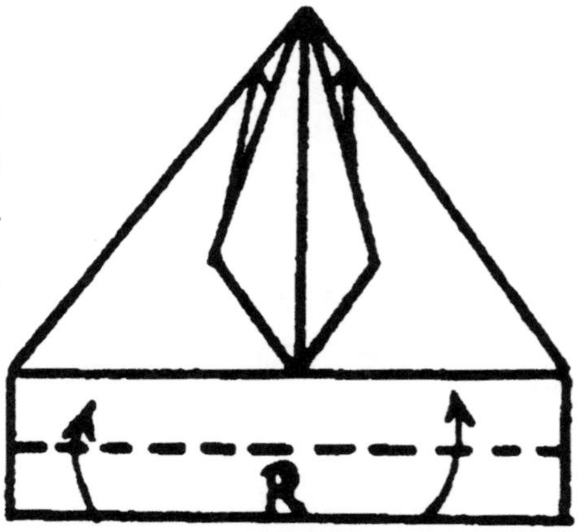

# 23

Now, fold back along the dotted line.

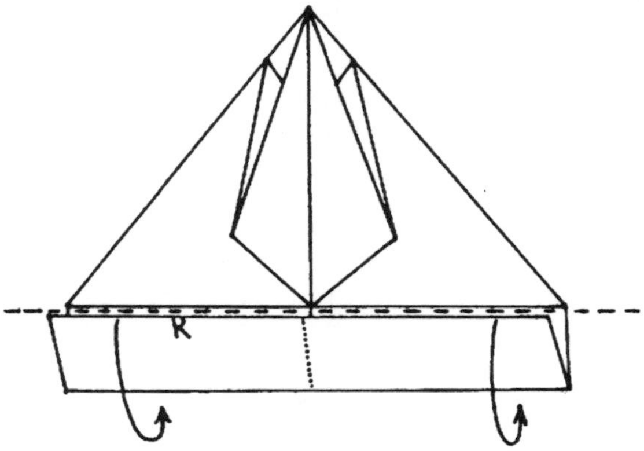


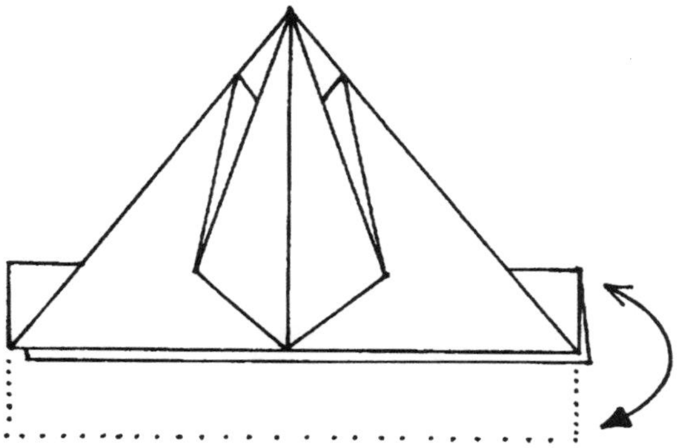

# 24

This is how your fold toward the back should look. Now unfold it as shown, so that it looks like the end of step 22.

# 25

Fold diagonally up, then back and forth at each corner, as shown here.

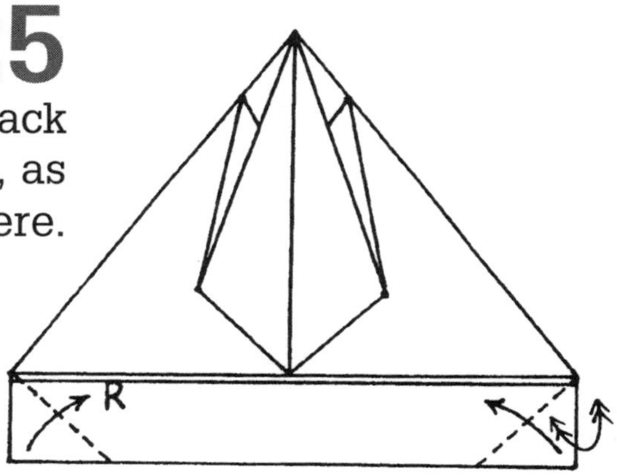


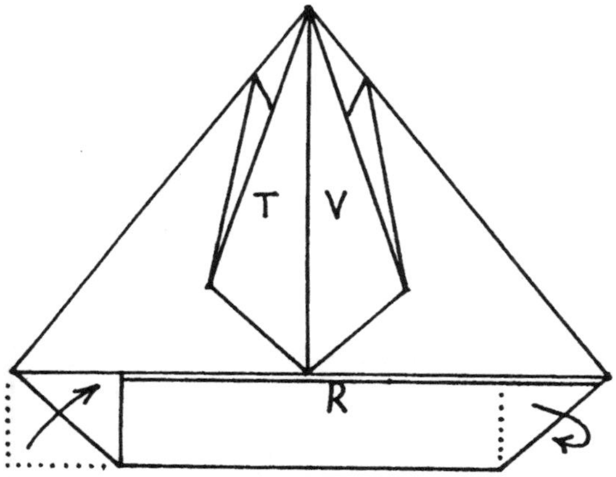


# 26

This is how the folds on step 25 should look. Fold back and forth five or six times.

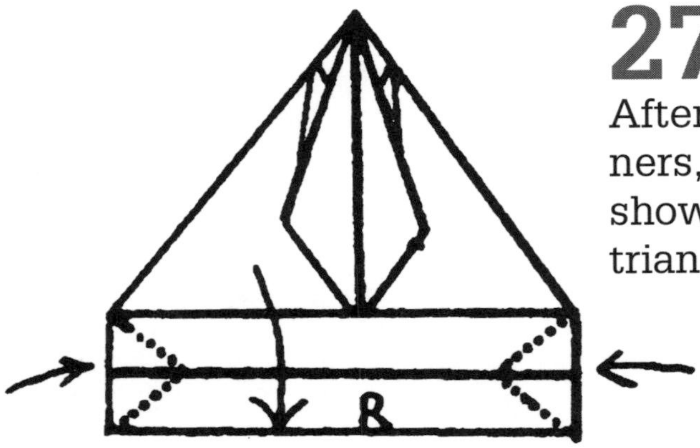


## 27

After you've folded the corners, unfold the R edge fold as shown. You should have two triangular shapes.

## 28

Push the two triangular sides inward as shown.

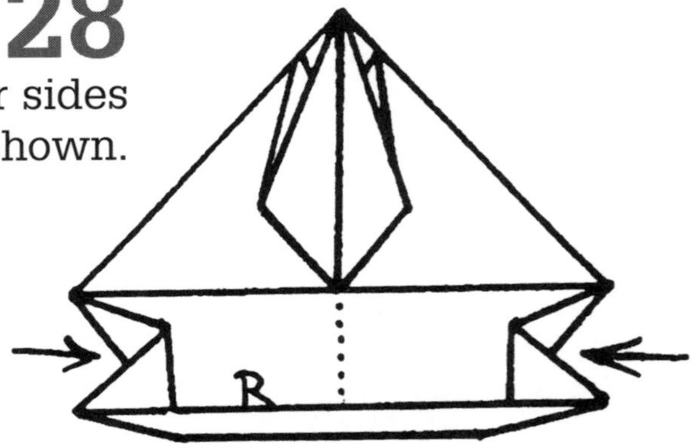


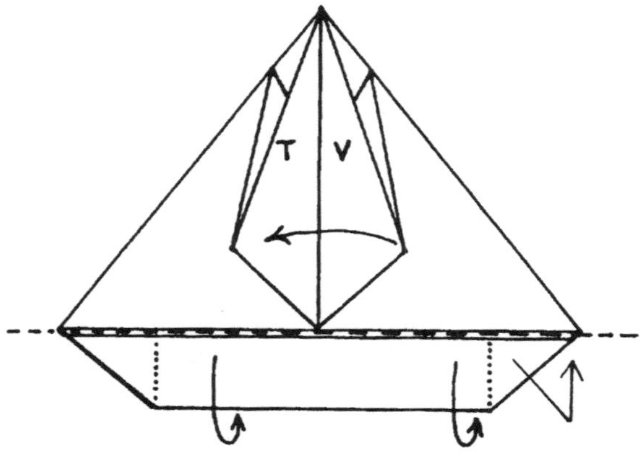


## 29

After you have pressed both triangular sides inward, it should look like this. Now, fold this part back on the dotted line. Next, flip the V wing to the T wing on the left side.

## 30

Now, fold Edge B to Centerline C on the dotted line. Do the same to the left side.

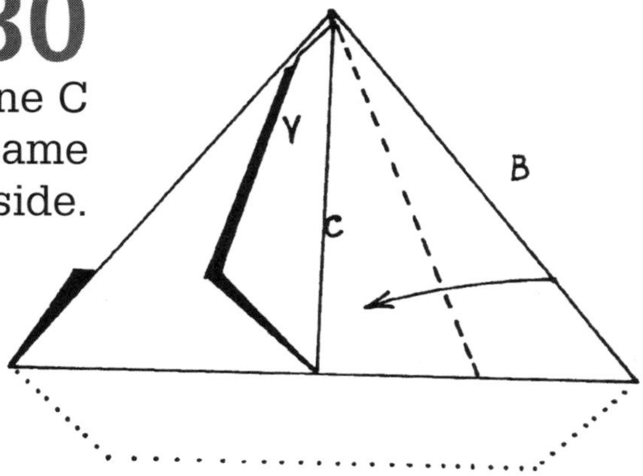


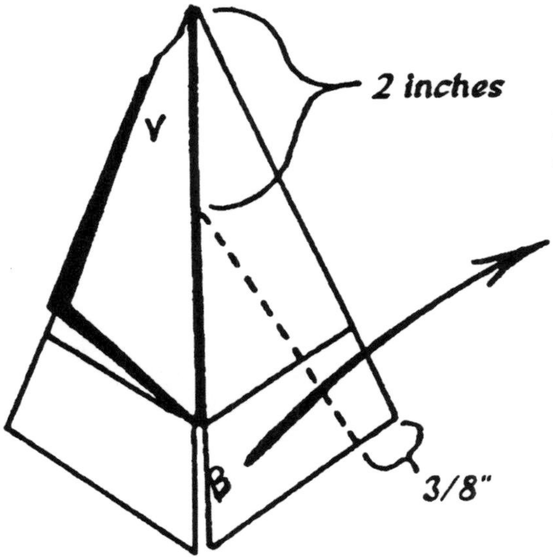


## 31

Fold Edge B to the right on the dotted line.

## 32

Your plane should look like this. Fold the front stabilizer straight to the left side as shown by the top arrow.

NOTE: The left side has not been folded toward the middle in this drawing.

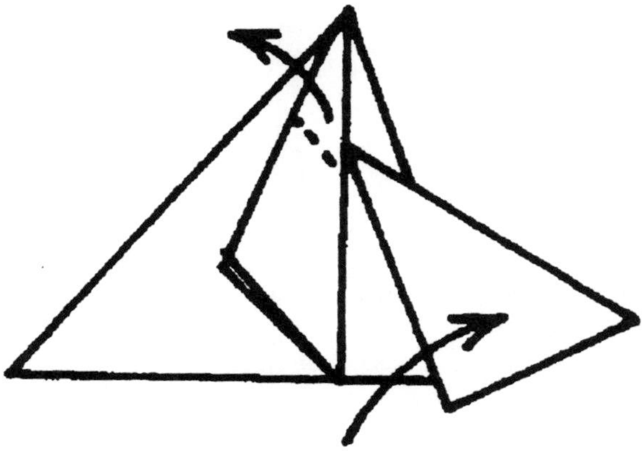

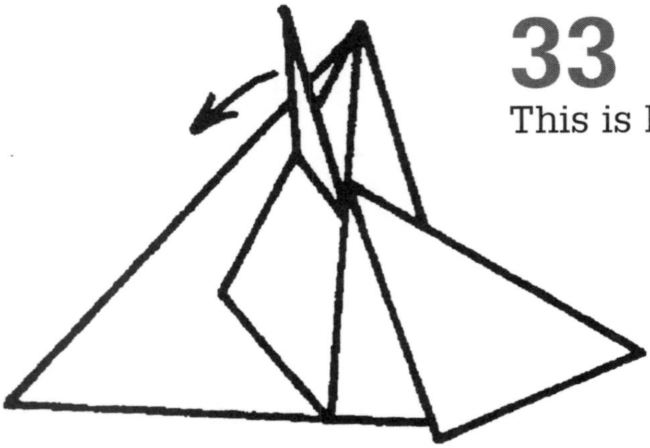

## 33

This is how the fold should look.

## 34

This is how your fully folded stabilizer should look. Flip the right stabilizer to the right and do the same on the other side.

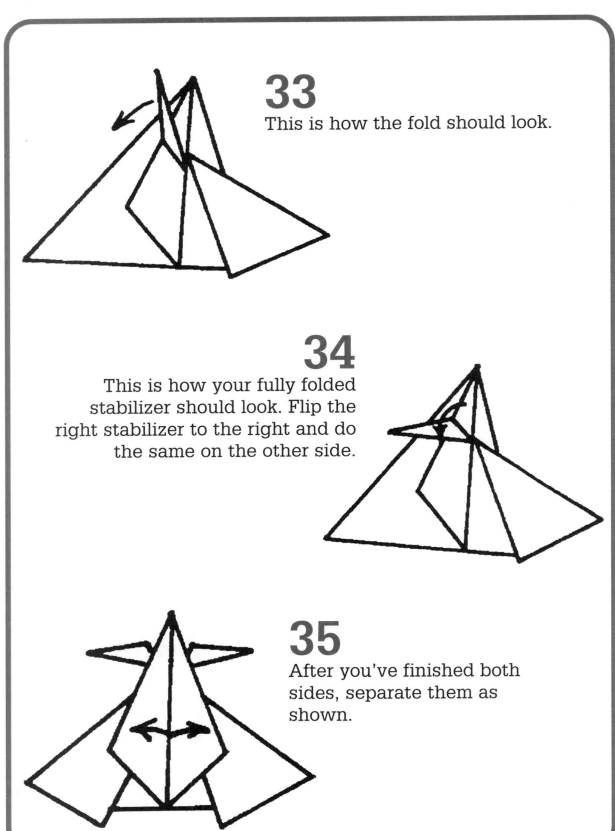

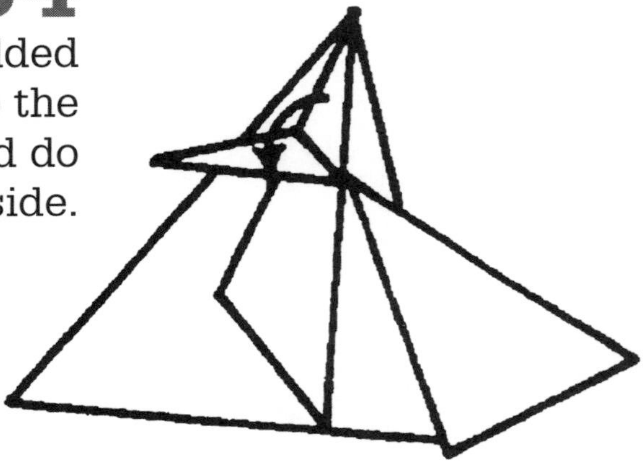

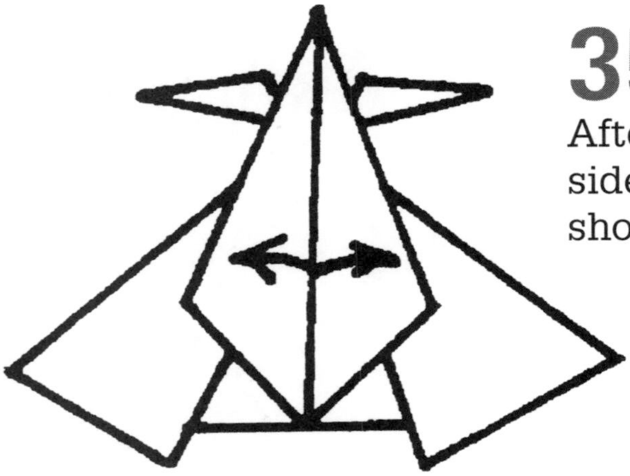

## 35

After you've finished both sides, separate them as shown.

## 36

Fold on the dotted lines, as indicated. Fold the right side to the left and the left side to the right exactly as on the F-15.

NOTE: Work on a flat surface.

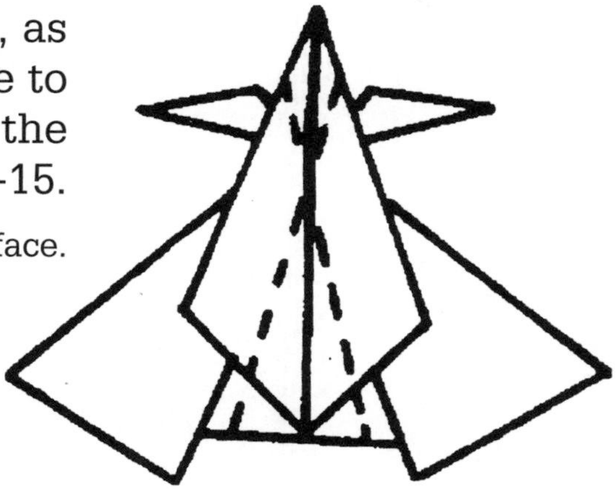

## 37

This is how your fold to the left side should look. Press hard on the fold, then unfold it and do the same on the left side.

## 38

After you've folded the two sides of the plane, open it up. You should see two crease lines (as shown by the dotted lines.)

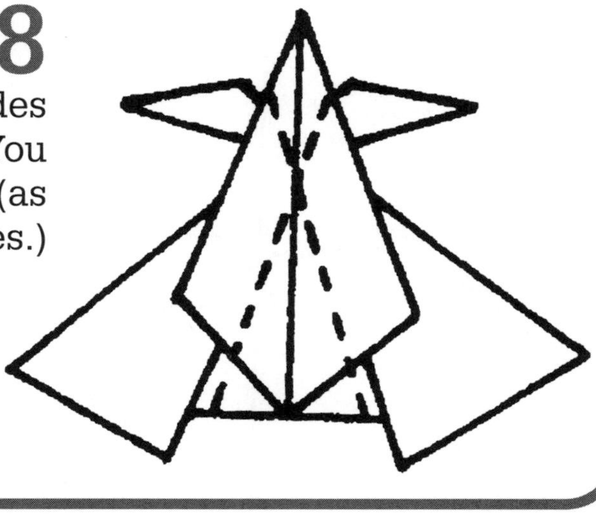

## 39

Now, turn your plane over, with the belly down. Press the centerline down as indicated by the arrows until the two sides come close together. With your thumb and fingers, press the plane's fuselage tightly together.

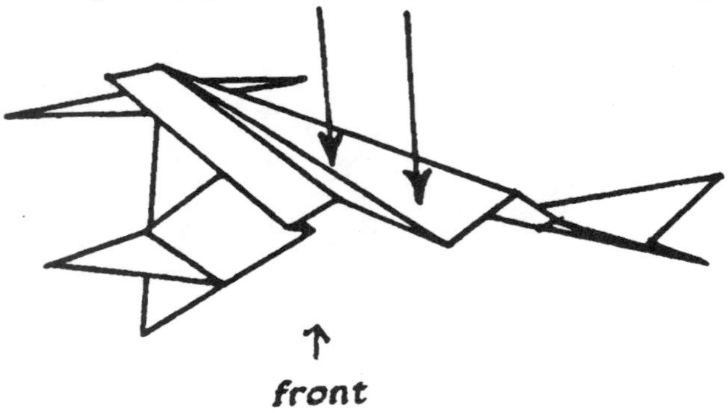


## 40

This is how your plane should look from the side.

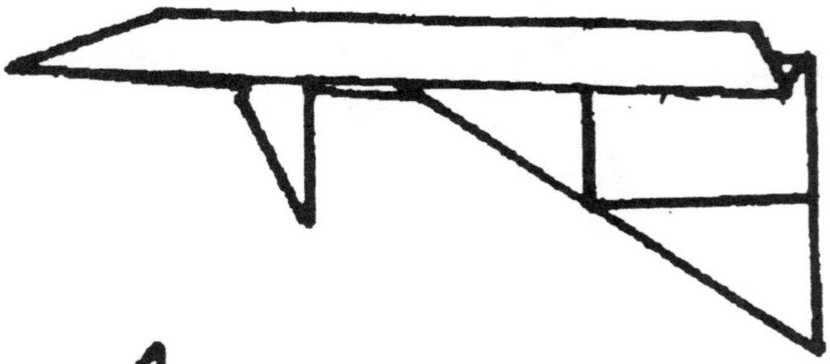

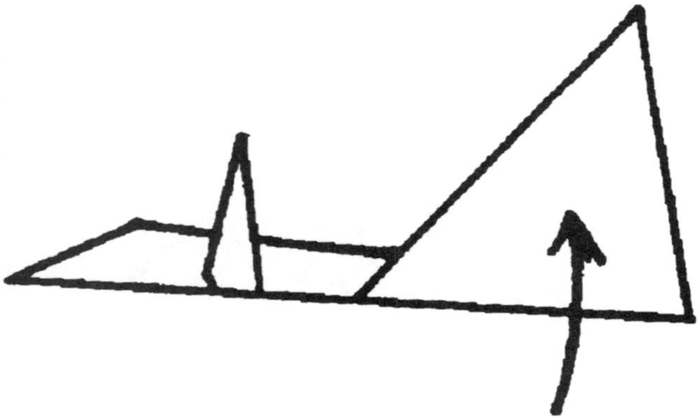

## 41

Now fold the wings up.

## 42

Fold up the two tail wings as shown.

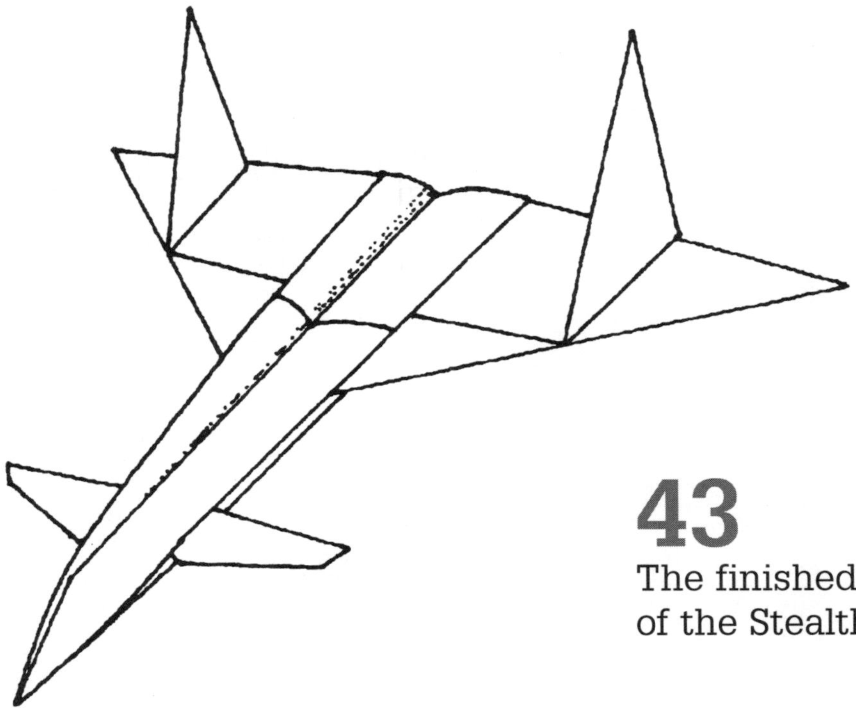

## 43

The finished version of the Stealth-X!

# STEALTH-X

# BOMBER

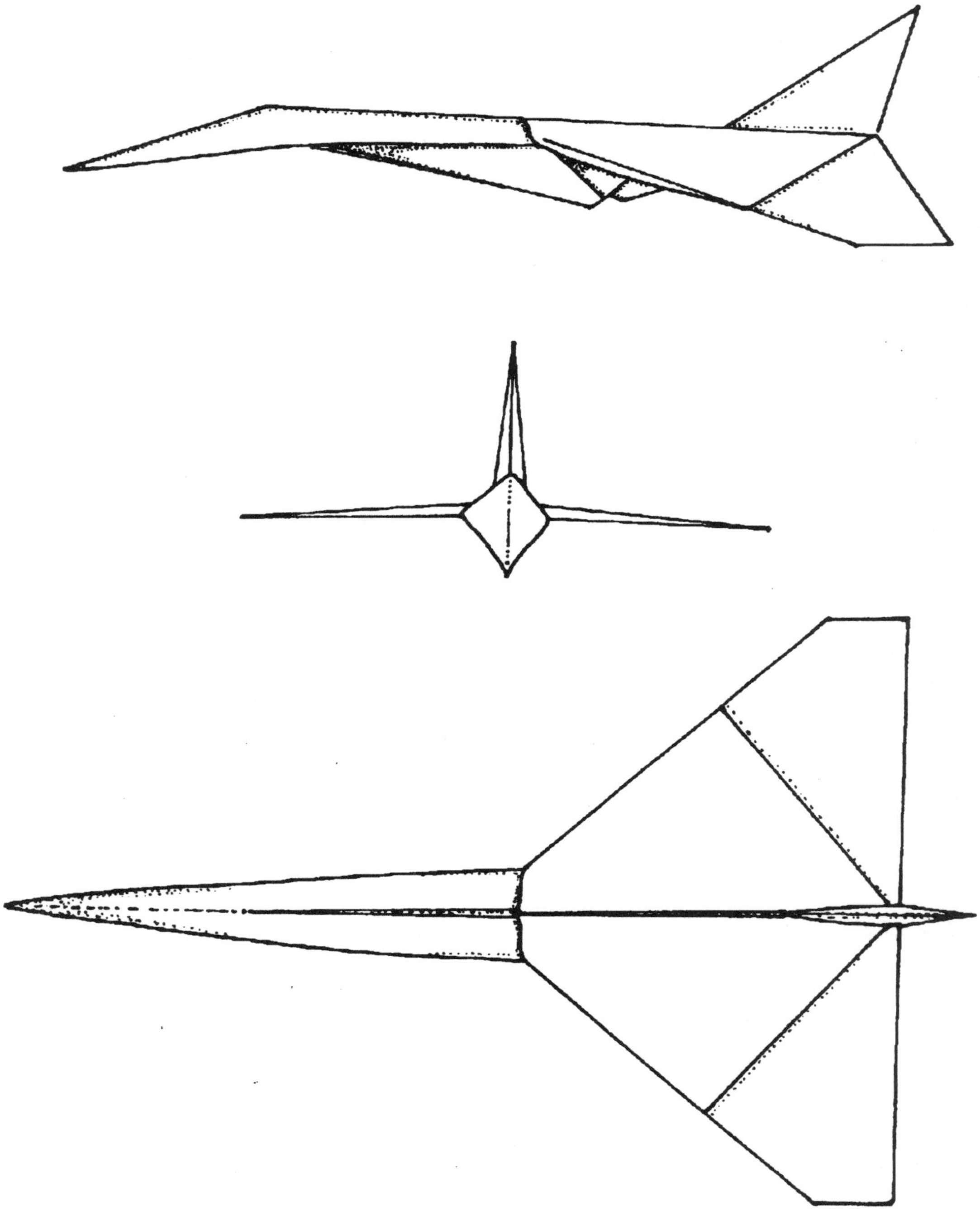

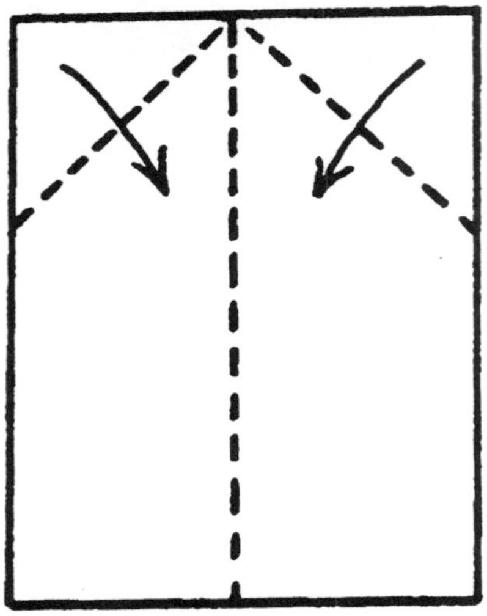

1

Fold the paper in half. Then open it and fold the two top corners toward the centerline.

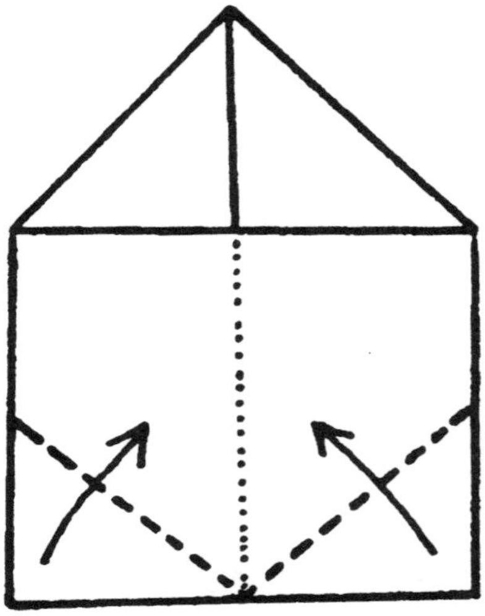

2

This is how your folds should look. Now make the bottom folds at the corners, as indicated.

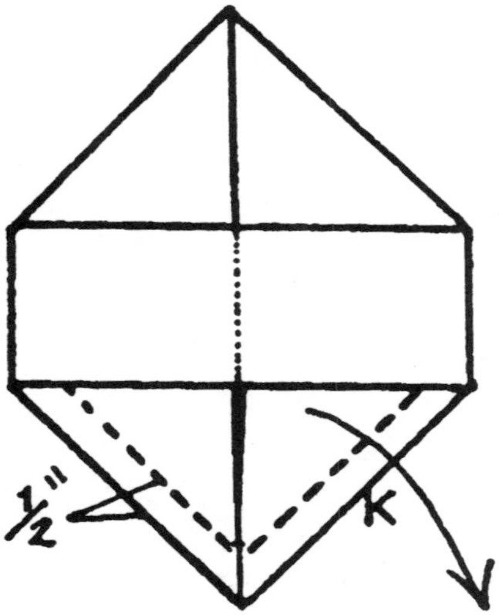


3

This is how the folds on the four corners should look. Make a downward-out fold as indicated, leaving about ½ inch.

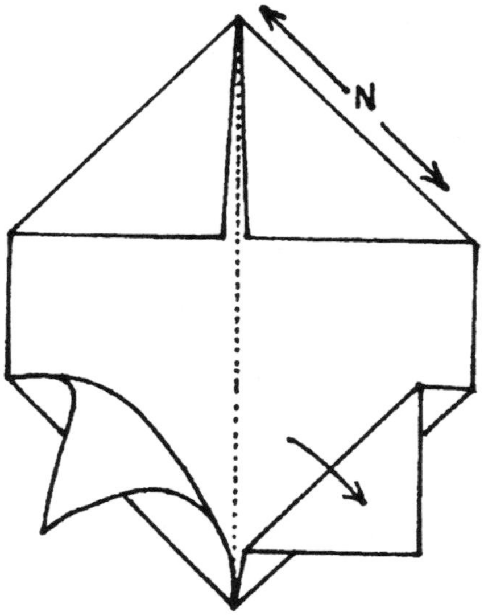


4

This is how your downward-out fold should look.

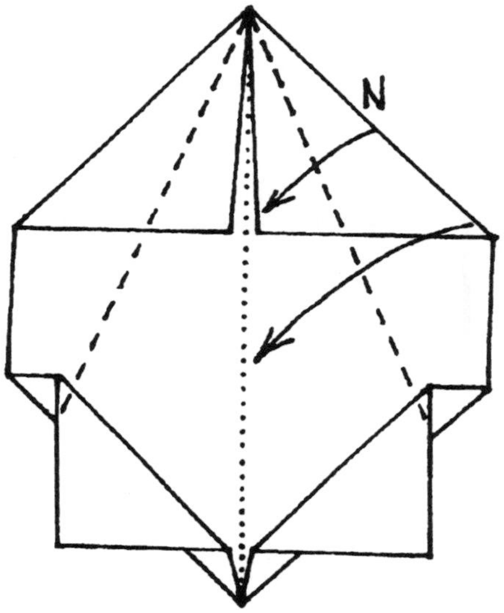


5

Now, fold Edge N on the dotted line to the centerline.

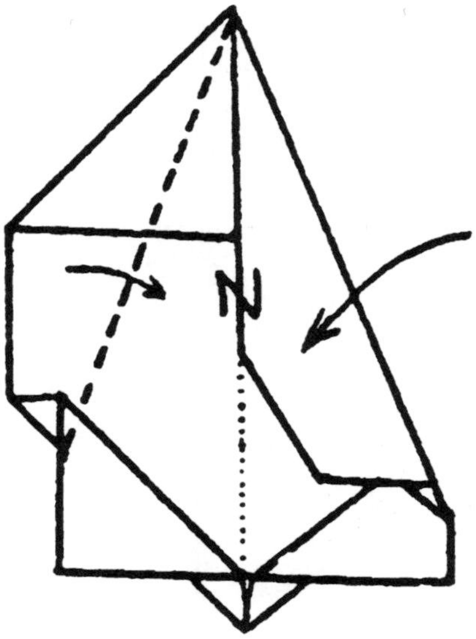


6

This is how your N Line fold toward the centerline should look. Do the same to the other side.

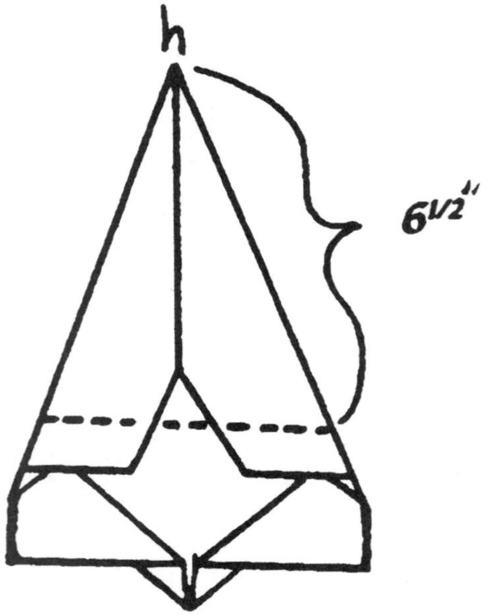


# 7

The plane should now look like this. Next, measure 6½ inches from H and fold down along the dotted line.

# 8

This is how the fold should look. Now, fold up on the dotted line, which should be about 1 inch from Line D.

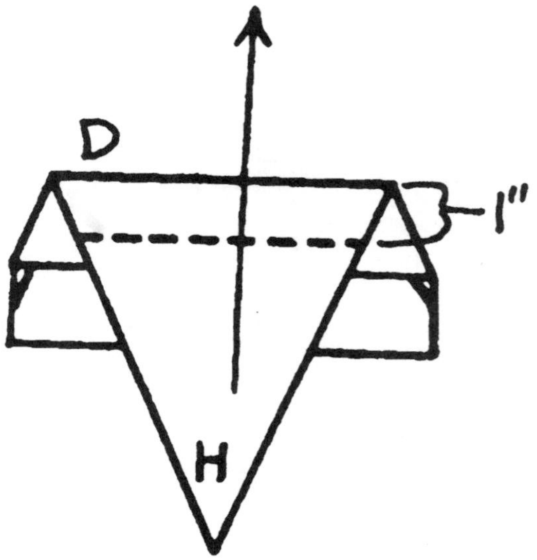


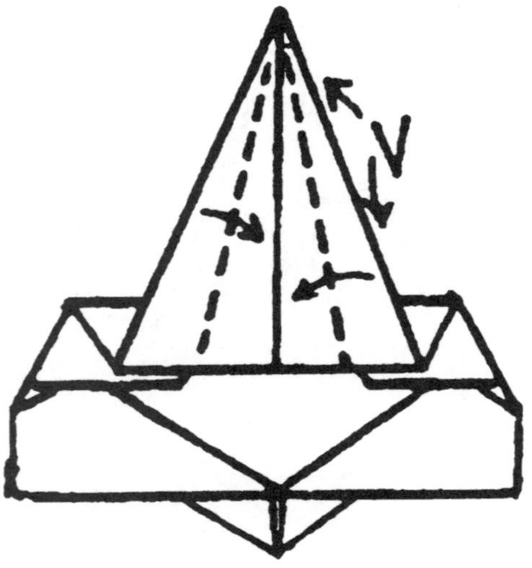


# 9

Now the plane should look like this. Fold Edge V to the centerline.

## 10

This is how your fold toward the centerline should look. Open it back up and do the same on the other side.

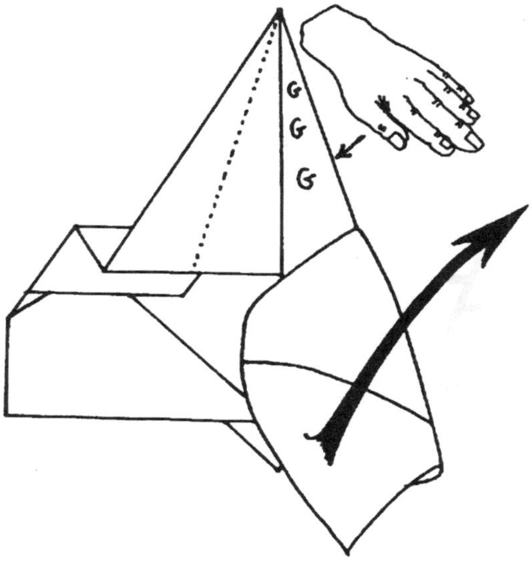


## 11

After you open it up again, close it and put your left hand over the G spots and open the lower part of the wing with your right hand.

## 12

You should be able to spot a pocket where you see the A. Stick your finger in as shown and place your left thumb above the pocket where the C is shown.

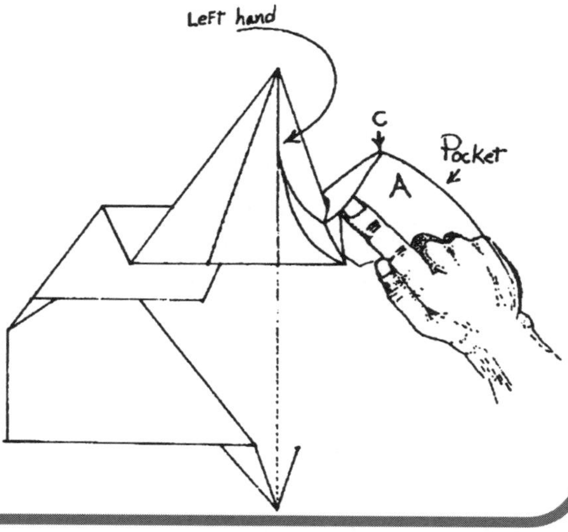

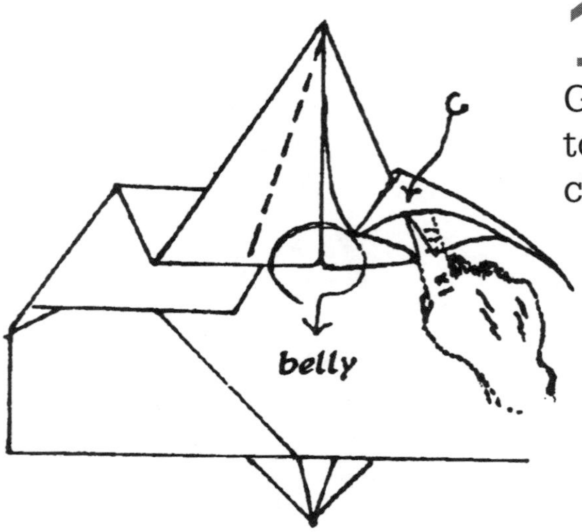


## 13

Gently, press down from the top of the pocket; it should close easily.

## 14

After pressing down both pockets, the plane should look like this. (Notice the ¾" wing edge.) Fold the indicated edges under the wings and belly as shown by the arrows.

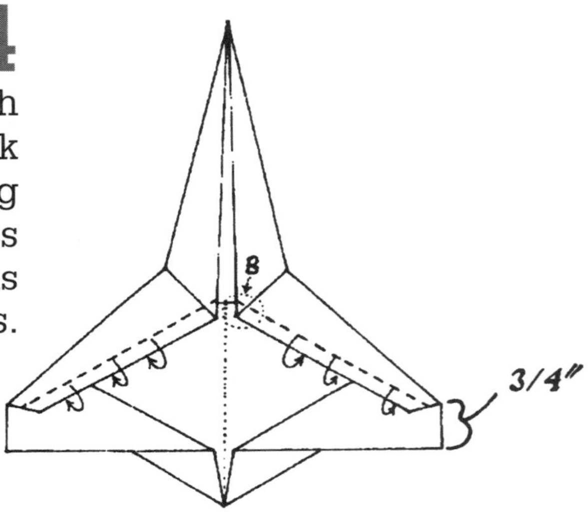


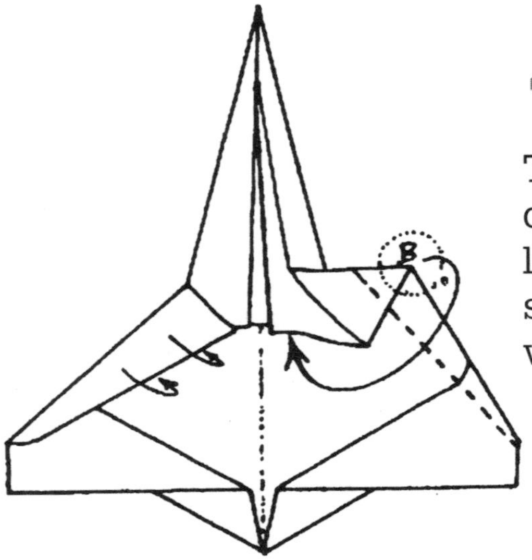


## 15

The B corner should be folded directly under the belly. It should look exactly like the left finished side on the diagram. This is a very important step.

## 16

After you have folded the two parts under the belly, your plane should look exactly as shown. Now, 2½ inches down from H, fold along the dotted line.

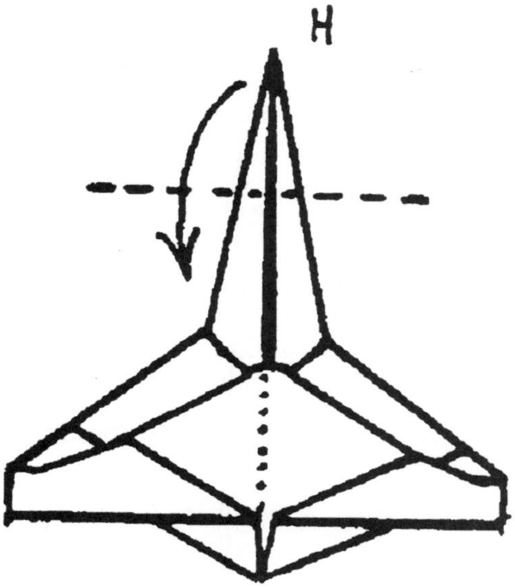


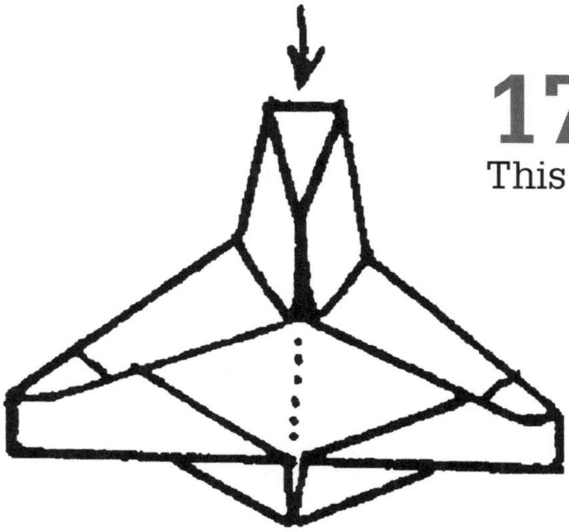

## 17

This is how your fold should look.

## 18

After you have folded the nose down, fold the two sides of the plane toward the back so that it looks like this from the side view. Then, lift up the nose.

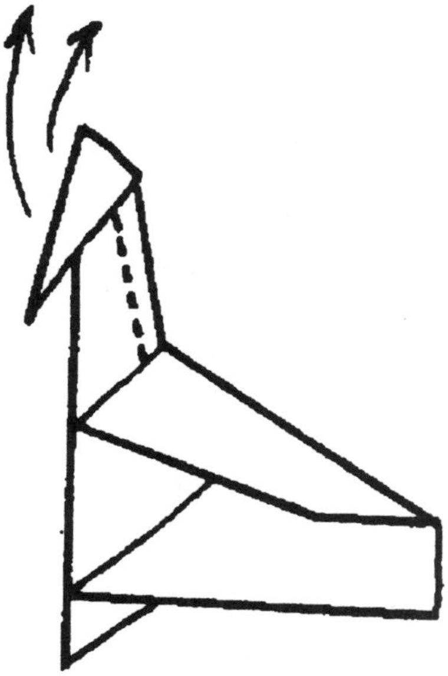

# 19

Hold your right hand under the plane as shown and, with your left hand, pull up the nose of the plane.

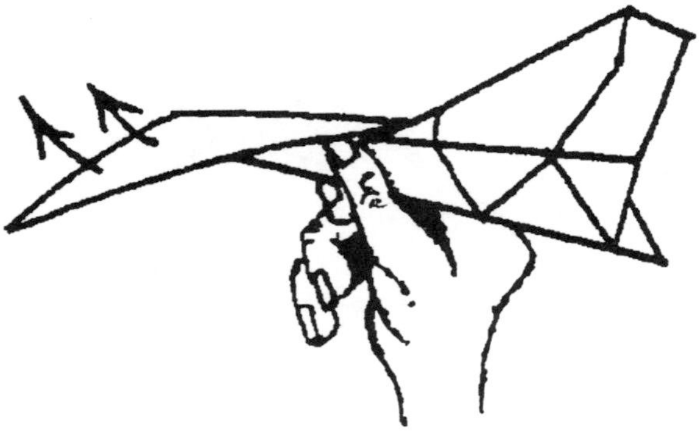

# 20

After you have pulled up the nose, carefully line up the plane's back so that it looks exactly as shown here.

# 21

Now, lift up the plane's wings so that they are flat and even. Then lift the tail fin as indicated. Fold the wings back down and press hard on them from both sides of the fuselage. Finally, lift the wings up again and you're done.

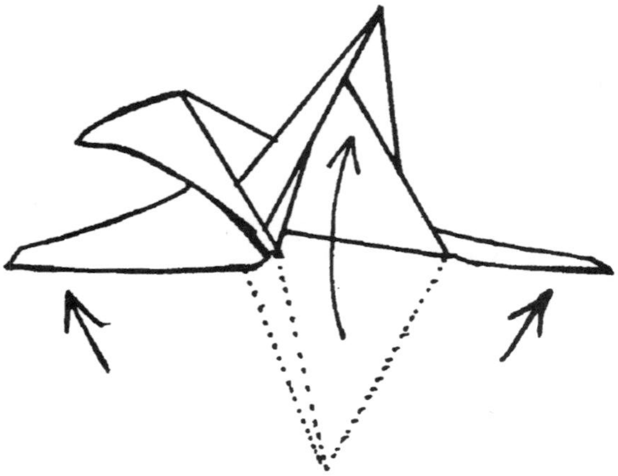

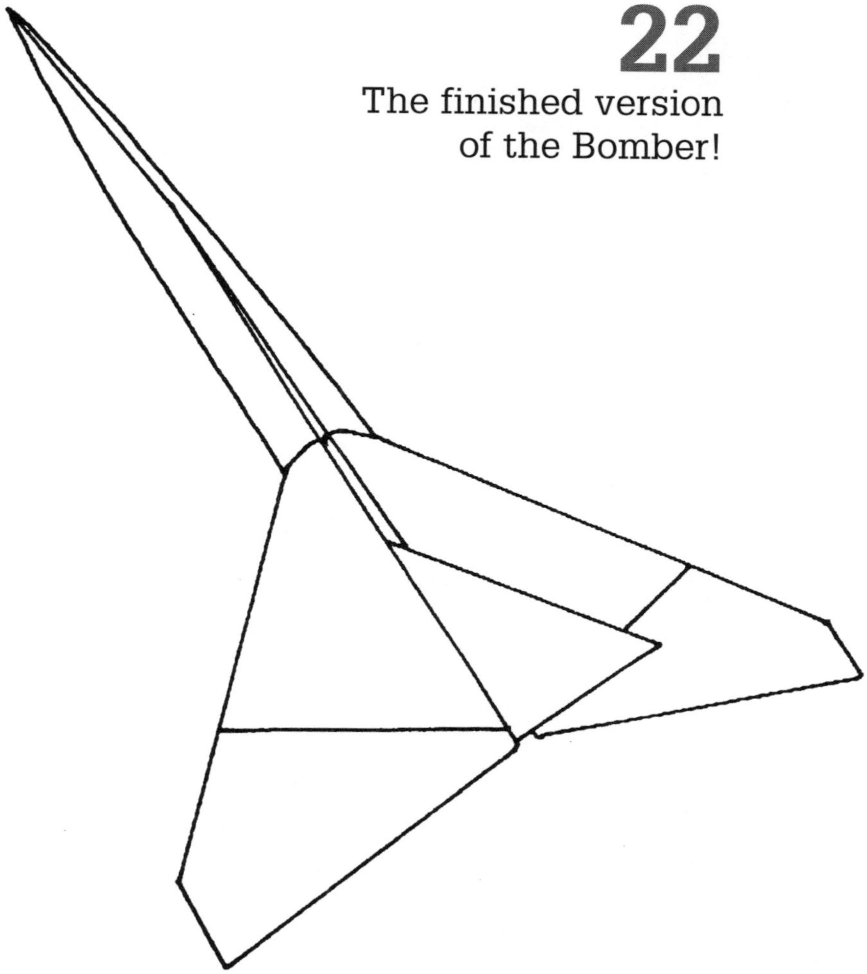

**22**
The finished version
of the Bomber!

# BOMBER

# STAR FIGHTER

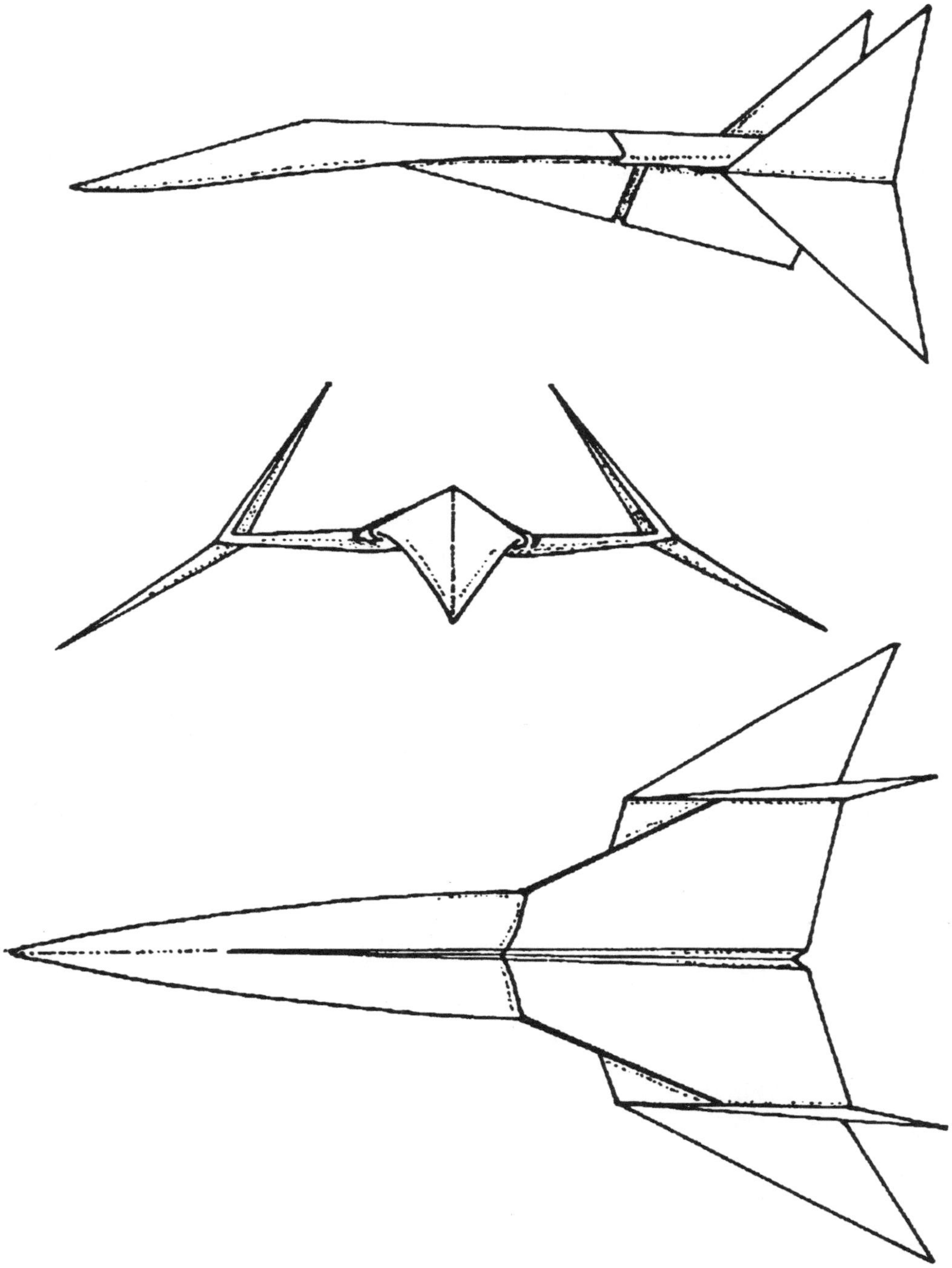

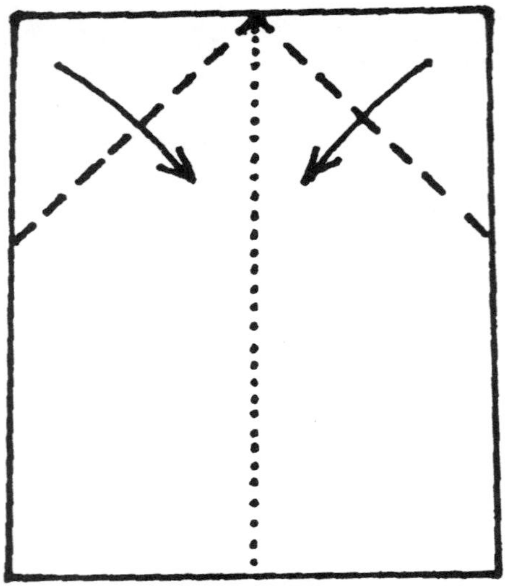

# 1

Fold the paper in half and open it back up. Fold the top two corners toward the middle line.

# 2

Your folds should look like this.

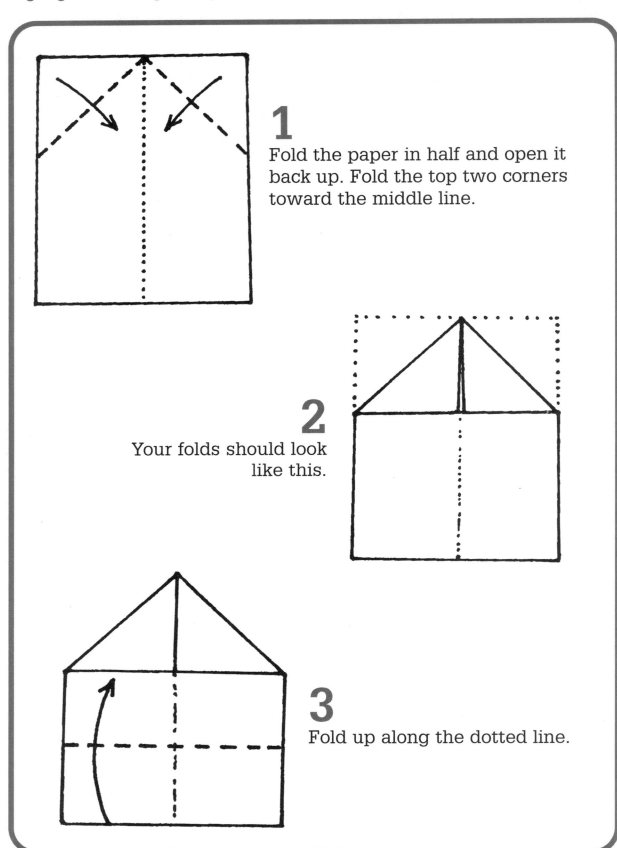

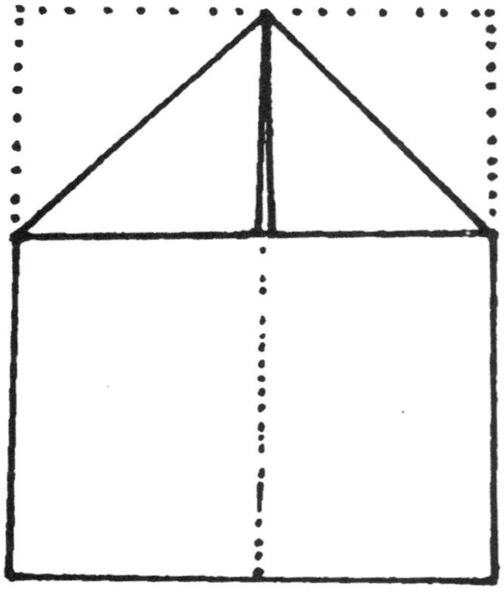

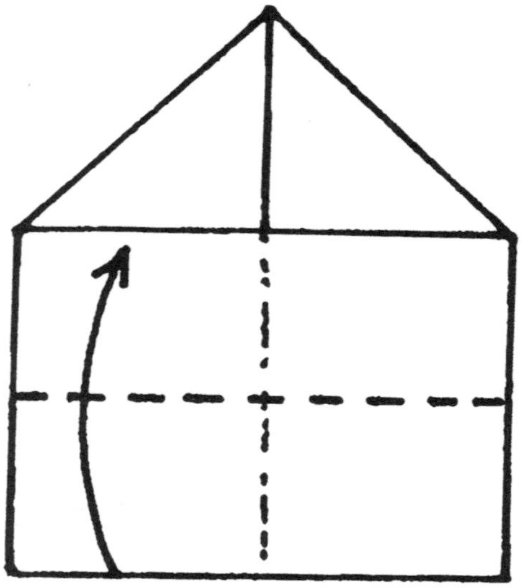

# 3

Fold up along the dotted line.

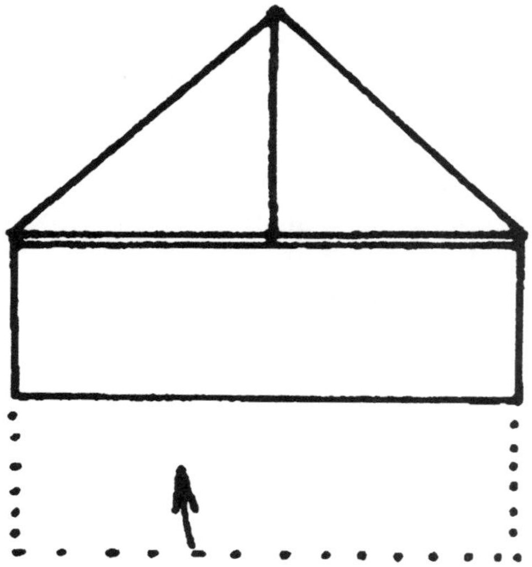

# 4

Your fold should look like this.

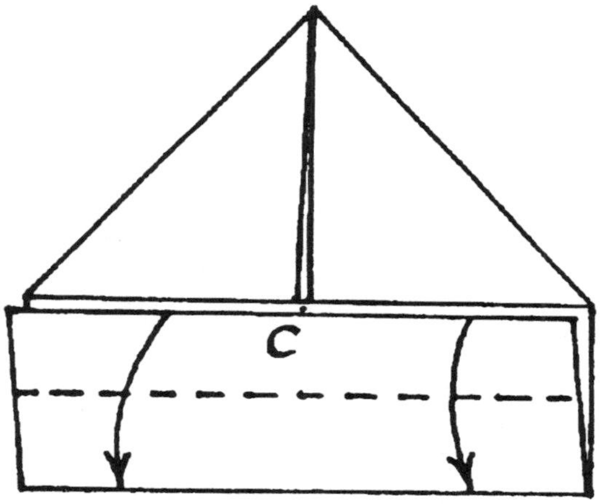


# 5

Fold down Edge C at the midpoint.

# 6

Your fold should look like this.

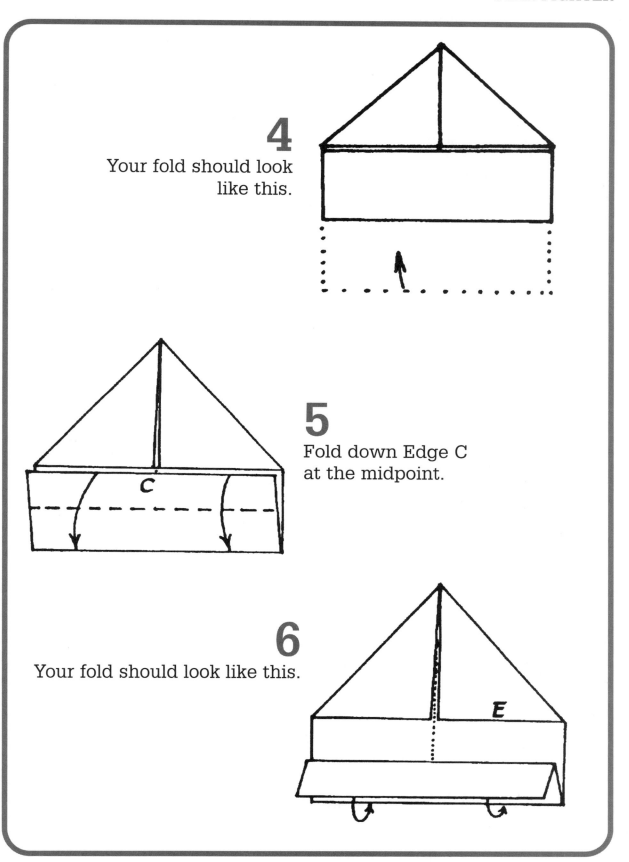

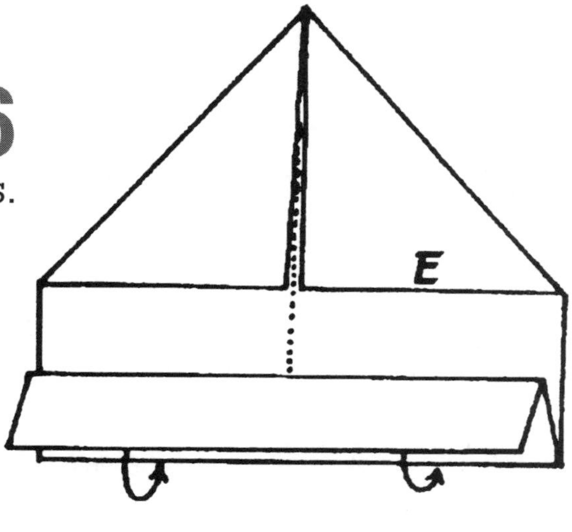

## 7

Unfold Edge E.

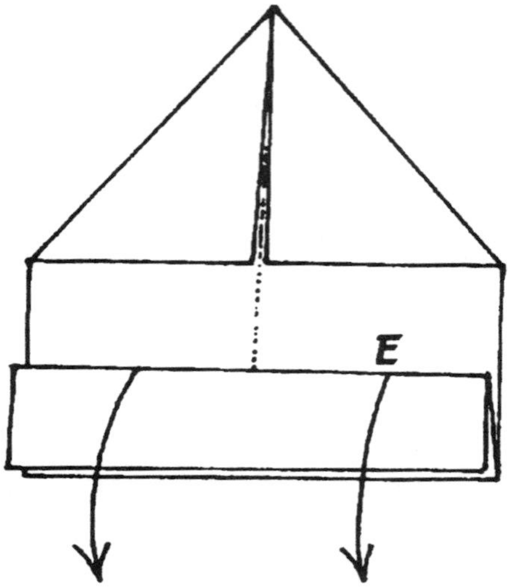


## 8

Make two upward folds from the two bottom corners as shown, along the diagonal dotted lines.

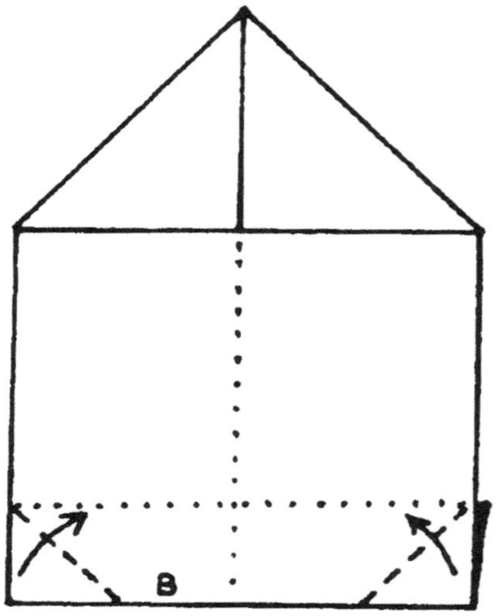


## 9

This is how your bottom corner folds should look. Fold back and forth four to five times at each corner.

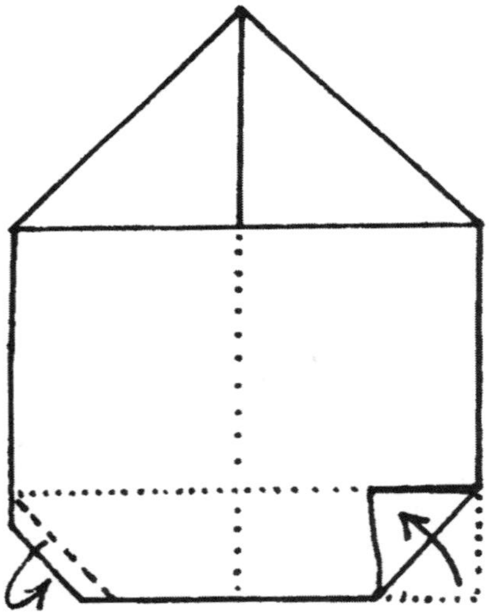

## 10

Open the corners as shown. Then fold the bottom edge line B upward, along the dotted line.

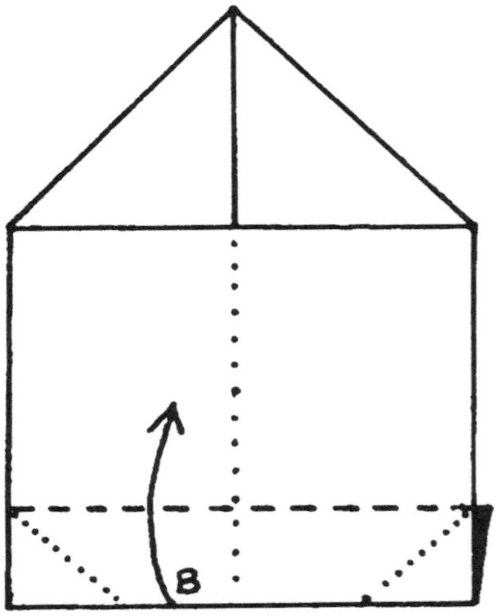

## 11

Your fold should look like this.

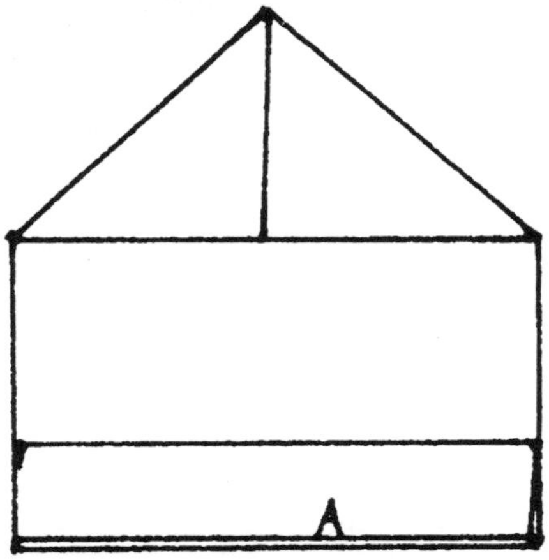


## 12

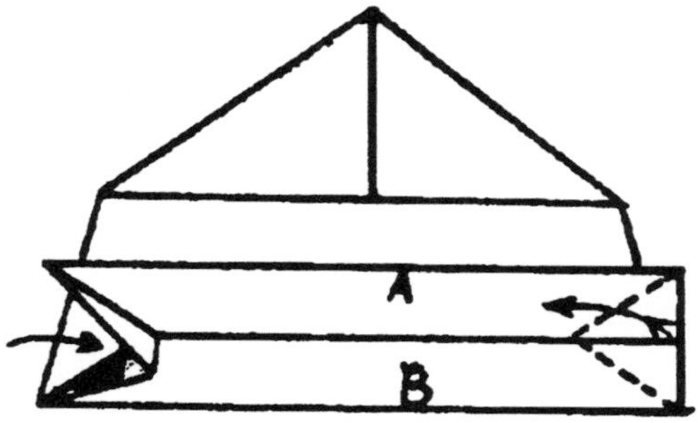


Lift Edge A halfway up, as shown. Now you should have a triangular shape on each side. Push both triangular shapes inward and toward each other.

## 13

This is how it should look. Now fold the right fin as indicated to the left side on the dotted line. Do the same on the left side.

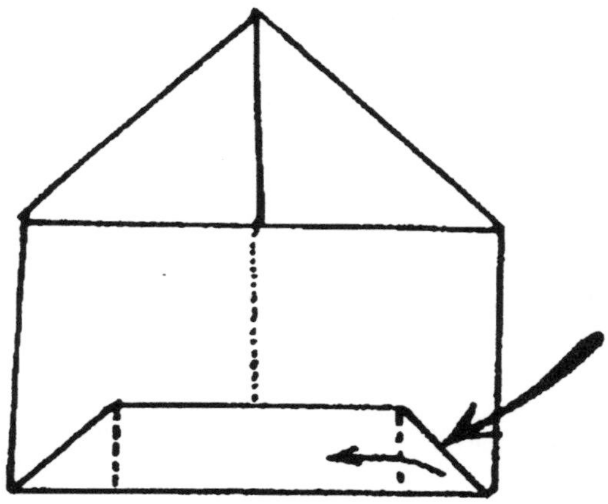

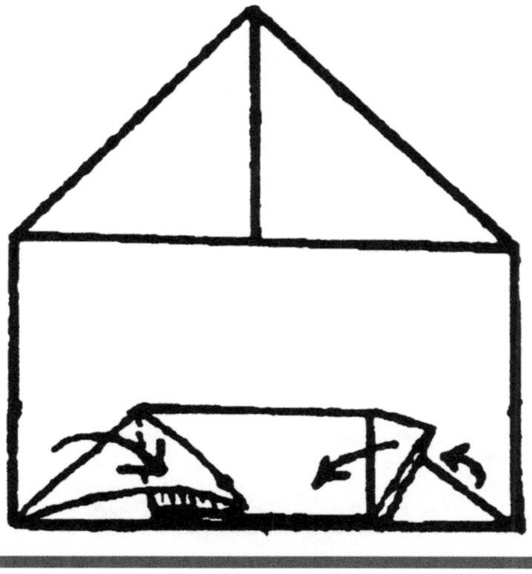

## 14

Your fold to the center should look like this.

## 15

Now, unfold to the outside as indicated.

## 16

After you have completed the folds toward the outside, you should have this.

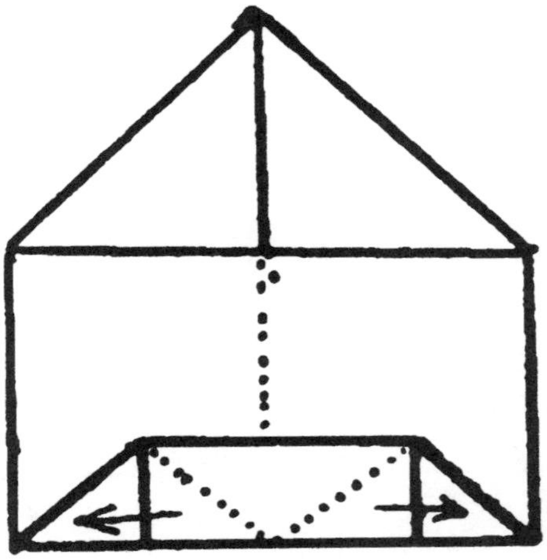

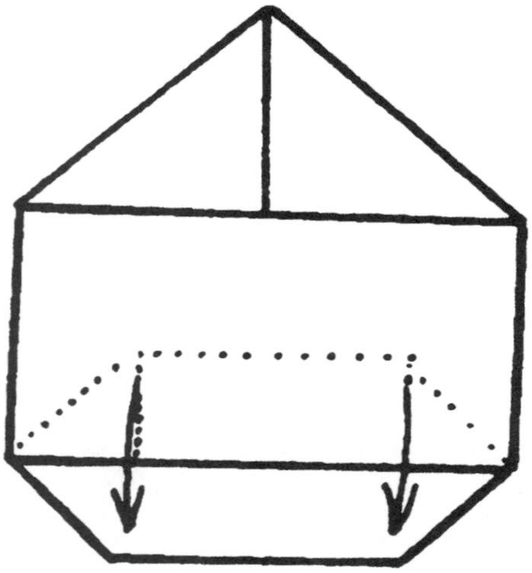

## 17

Unfold down as shown.

## 18

Fold the two P corners as shown along the dotted lines toward the centerline.

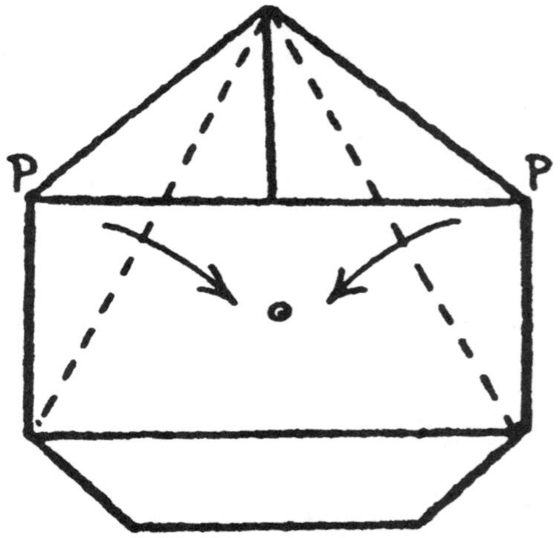

## 19

After you fold the two sides inward, your plane should look like this.

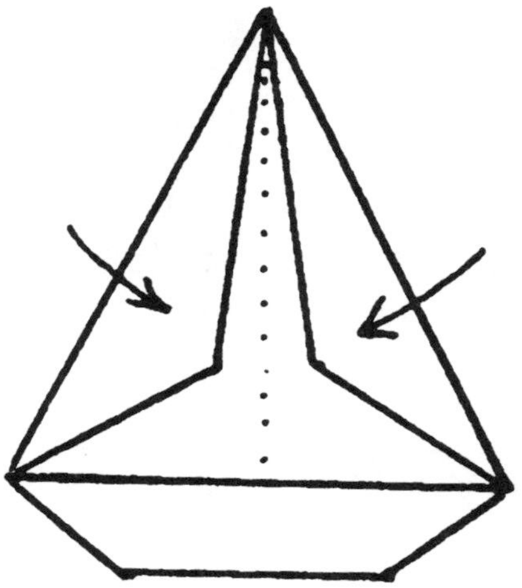

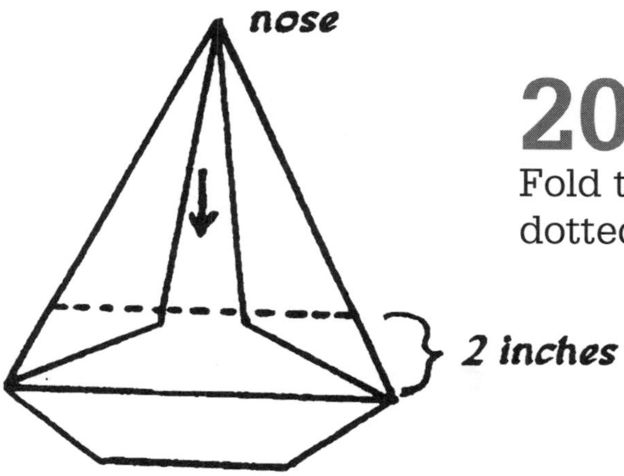


## 20

Fold the nose down along the dotted line.

## 21

Now fold up along the dotted line, as shown.

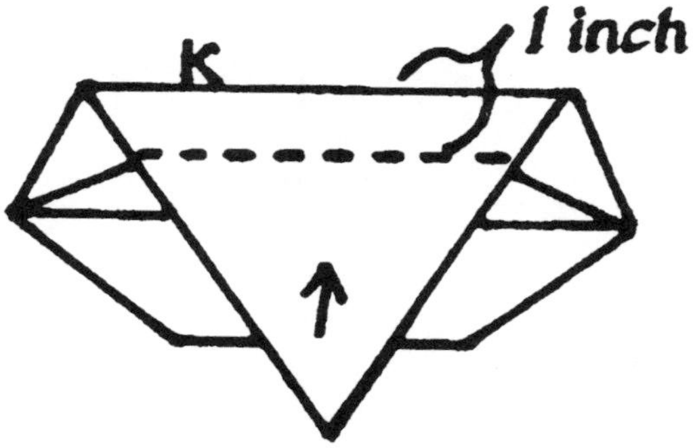


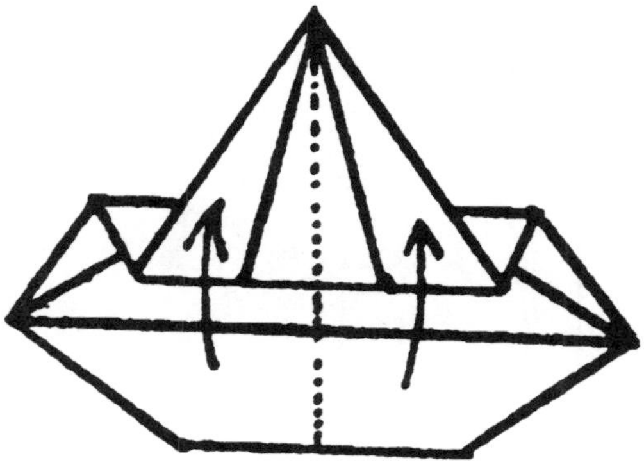

## 22

Your fold should look like this.

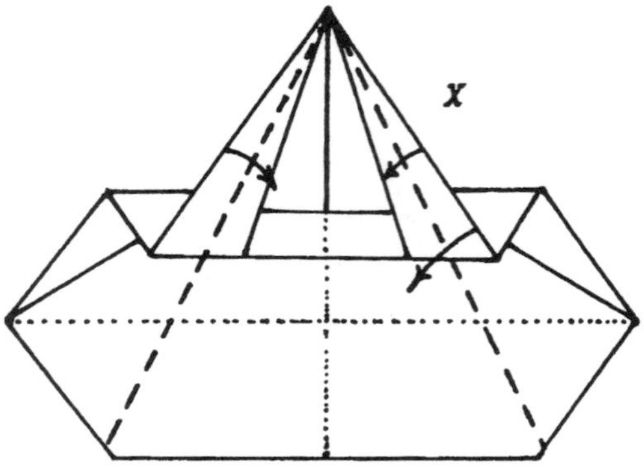


## 23

Now fold Edge X toward the centerline.

NOTE: The intent of this fold is to get two triangular shapes in Step 27.

## 24

This is how your fold should look. Now unfold it and repeat on the other side.

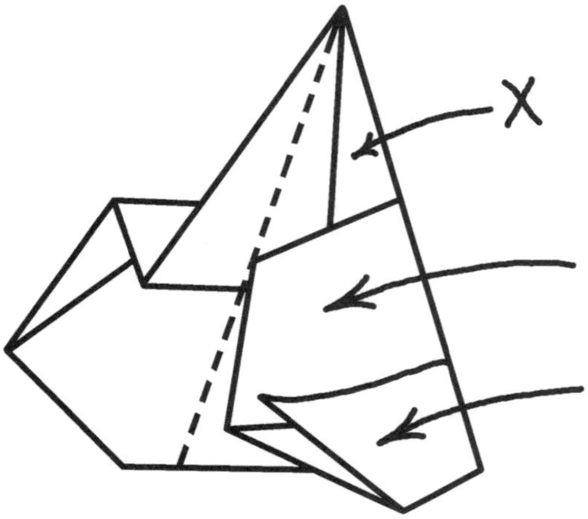


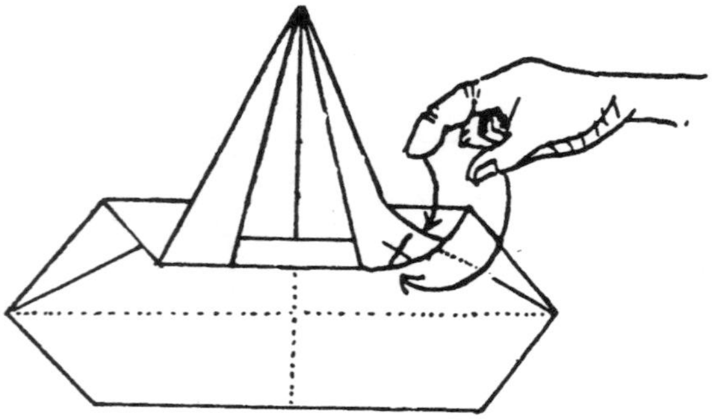

## 25

After you have unfolded the sides, you should have a little pocket behind the X. Put your index finger inside and your thumb on the X, as indicated by the arrows.

## 26

Simply place your left hand over the A's while your right finger and thumb press the pocket downward to look like Step 27.

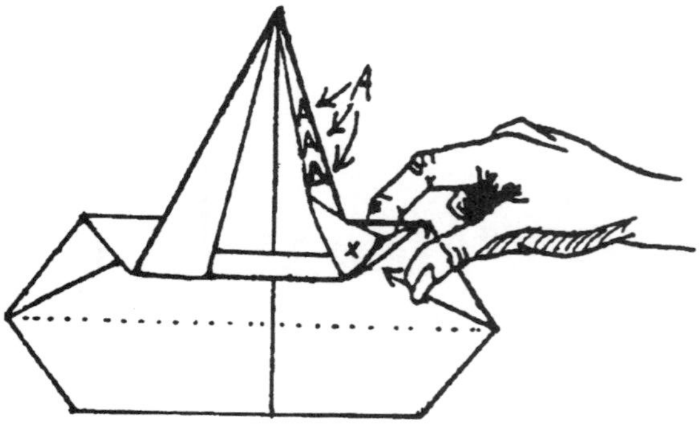

## 27

You should now have two upside-down triangular shapes. Yours may look a bit different, but carry on.

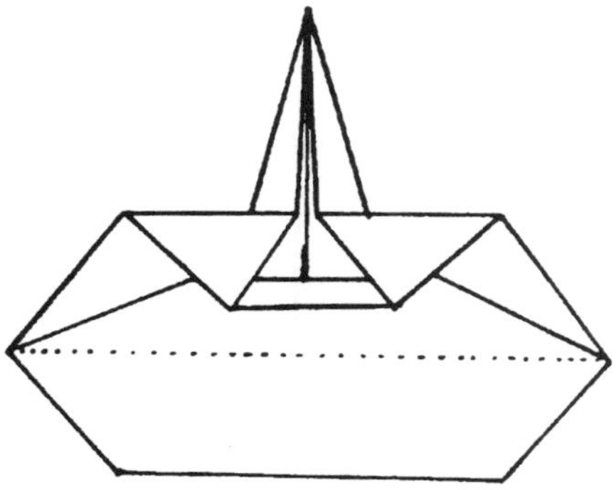

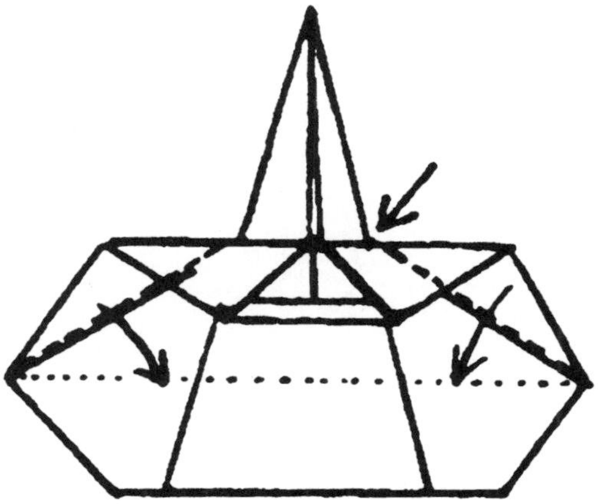

## 28

Now, fold both sides diagonally down as shown, along the dotted lines.

## 29

This is how the folds should look.

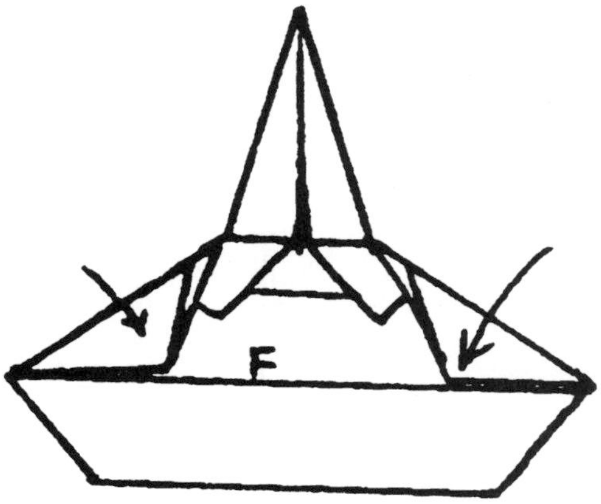


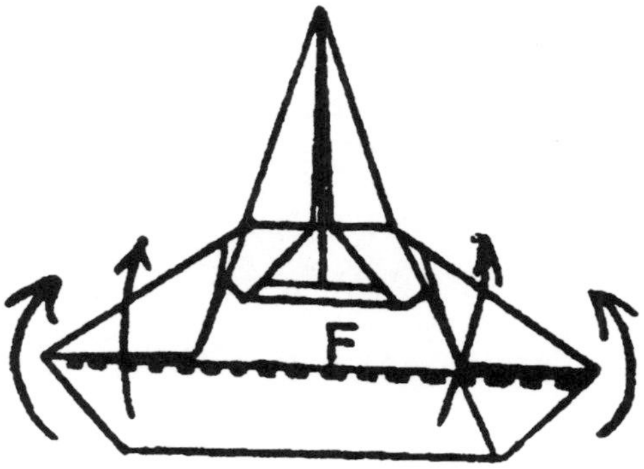


## 30

Fold up the lower part along dotted Line F.

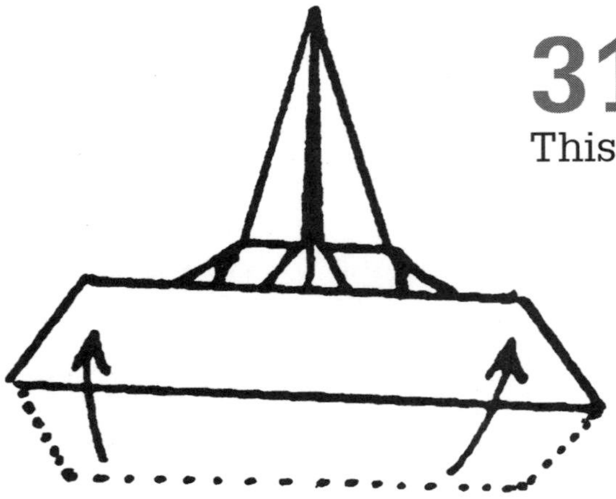

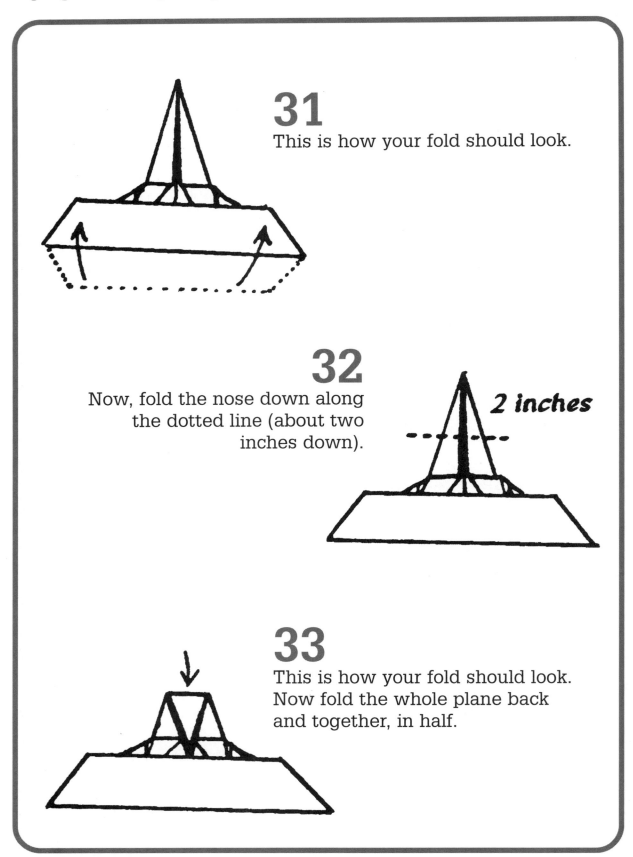

## 31

This is how your fold should look.

## 32

Now, fold the nose down along the dotted line (about two inches down).

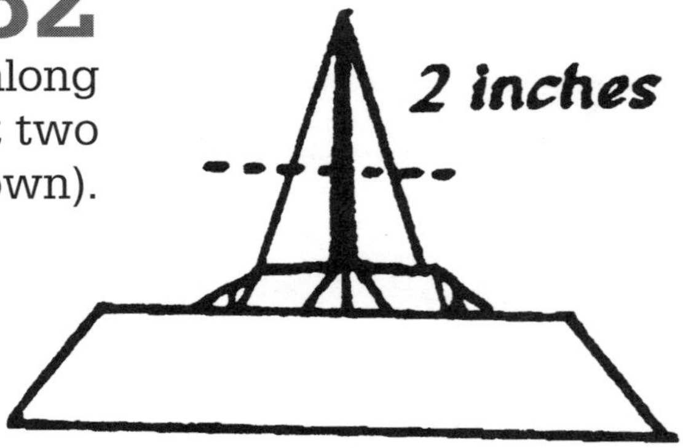


## 33

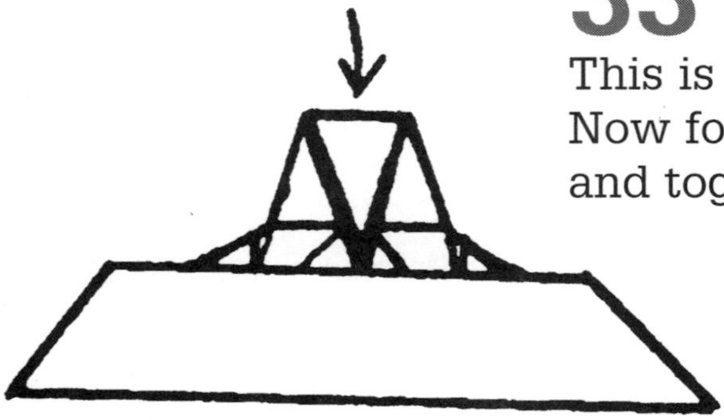

This is how your fold should look. Now fold the whole plane back and together, in half.

## 34

This is how the fold toward the back should look from the side. Next, lift up the nose and pinch along the belly about one inch up.

NOTE: For the best results, always place the plane's back against a flat surface.

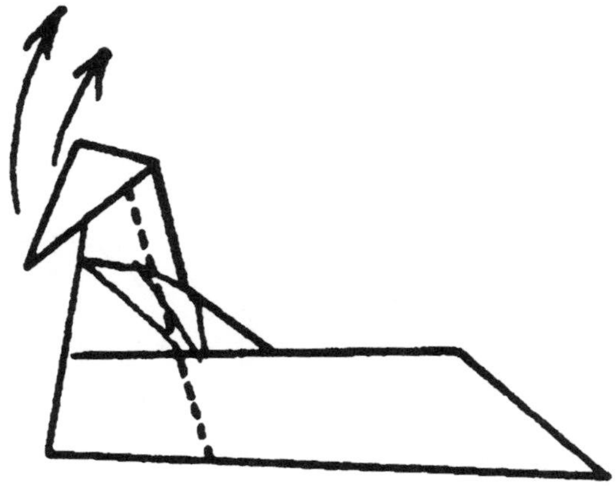

## 35

This is how the plane should look after you've lifted the nose and aligned the fuselage. The tiny Line M should be about ¼ inch long.

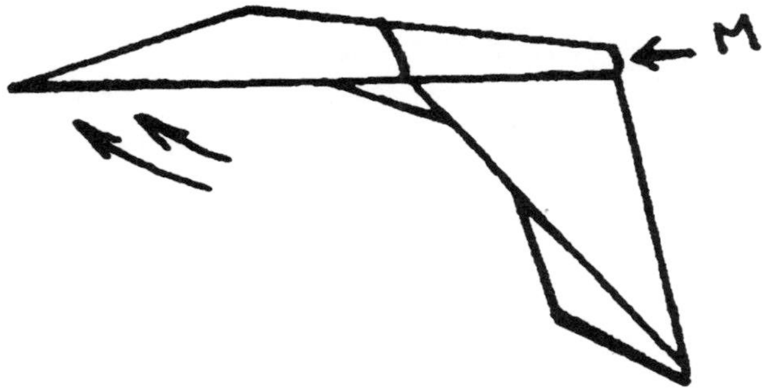


## 36

Now, lift up the wings as shown.

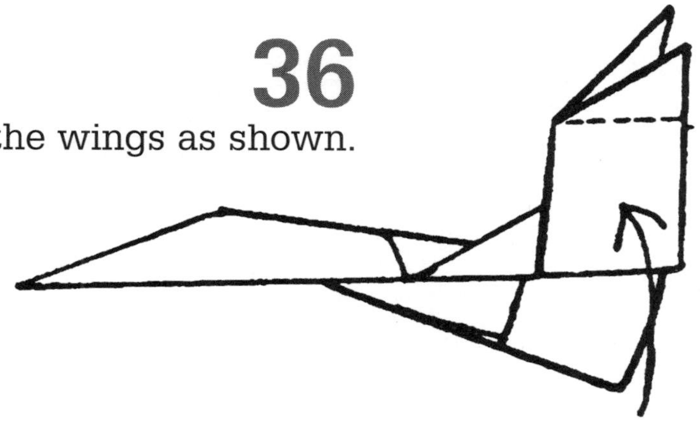

# 37

Separate the edges of each wing into two sides and fold them back and forth.

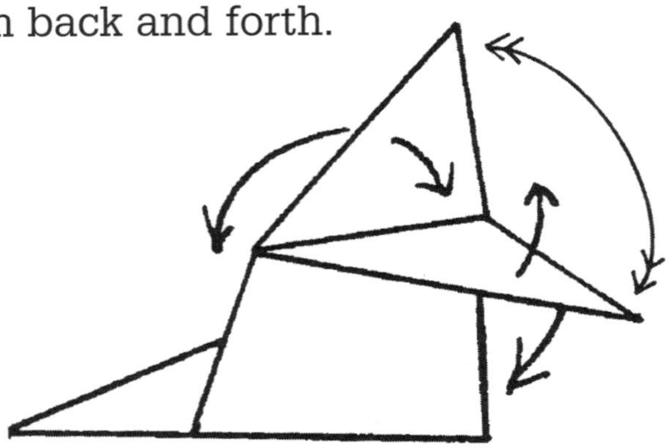

# 38

This is how your plane should look.

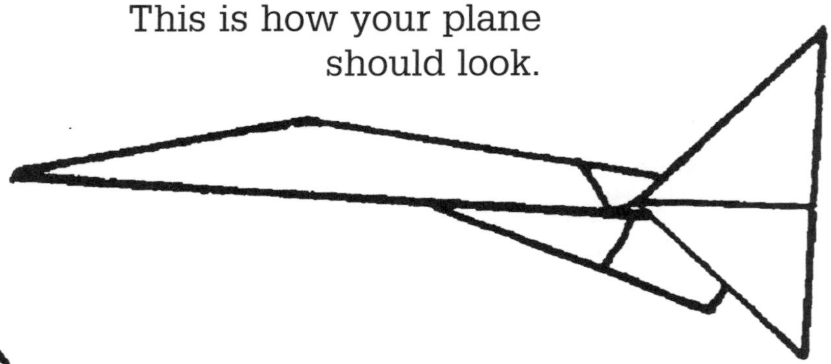

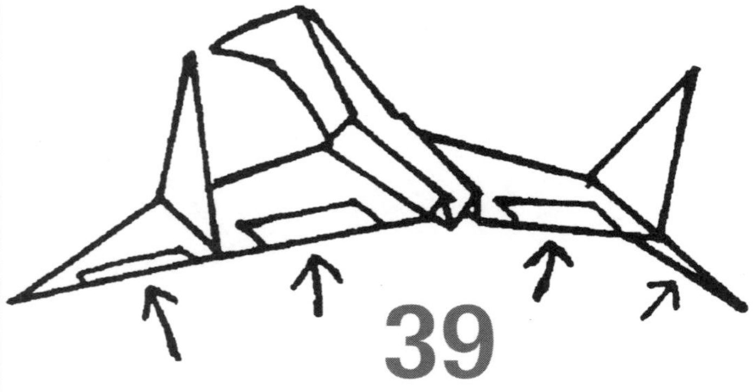

# 39

Trim up at the arrows for good lift.

OPTION: Make cuts for flaps for easier flying.

## 40

The finished version of the Star Fighter!

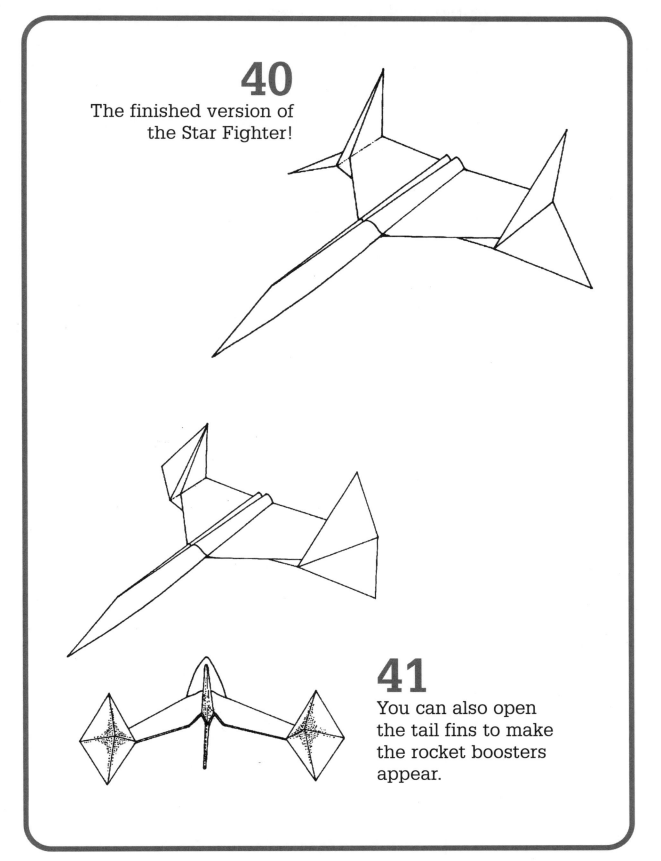

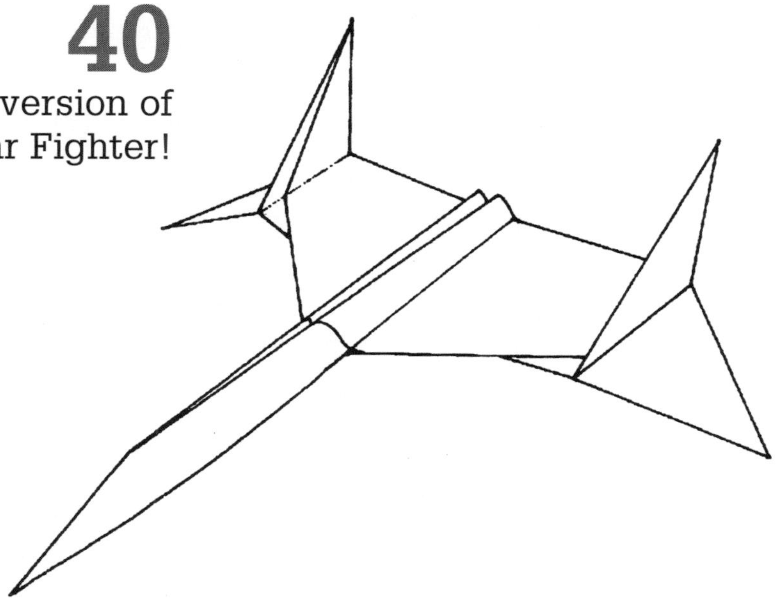

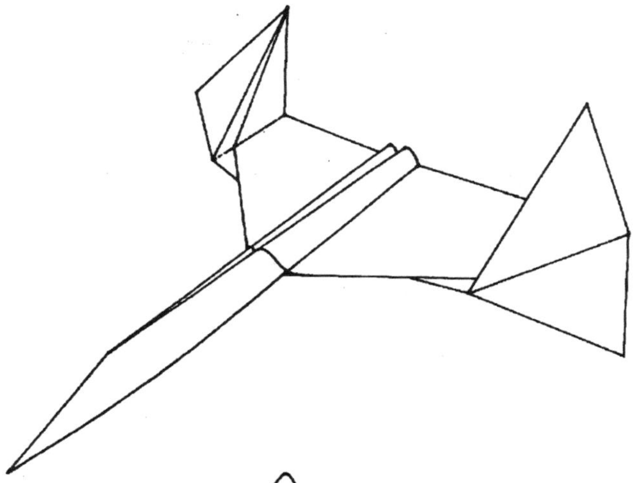

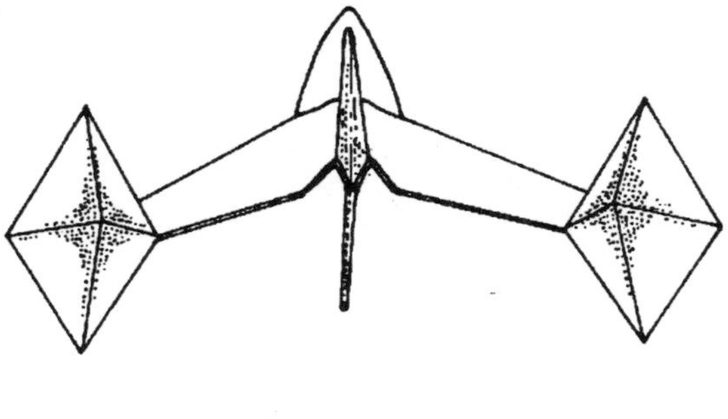

## 41

You can also open the tail fins to make the rocket boosters appear.

# STAR FIGHTER

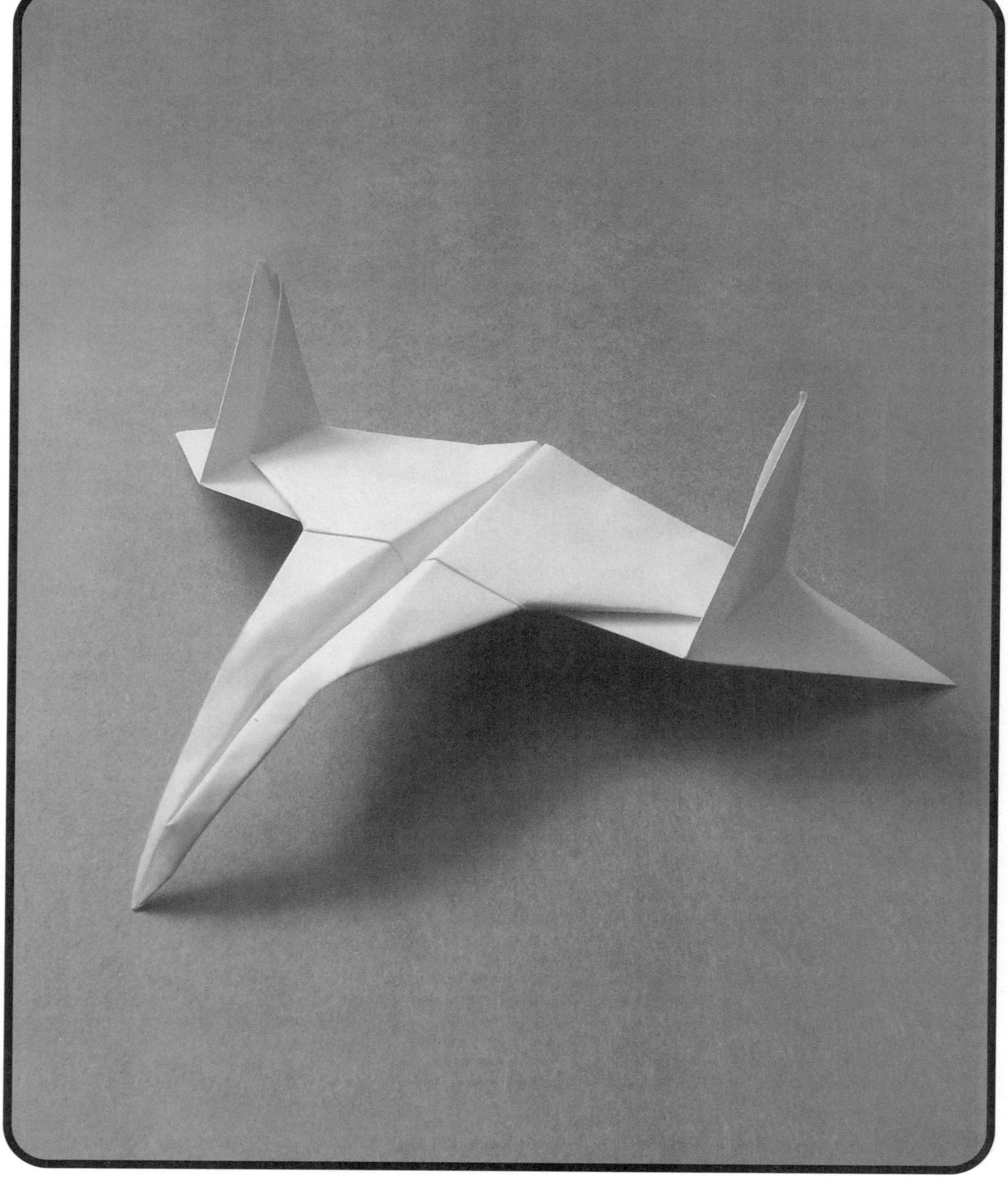

# F-117 NIGHTHAWK

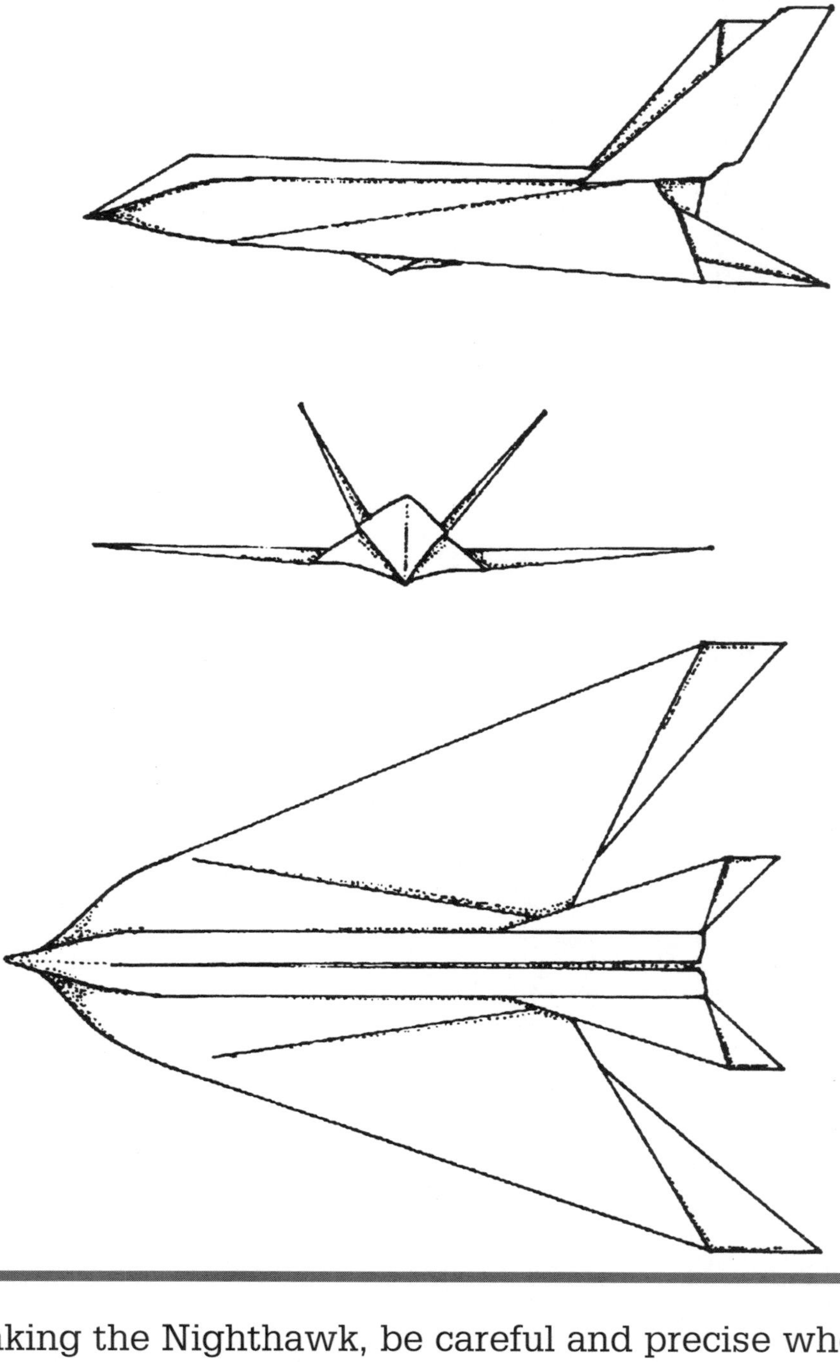

In making the Nighthawk, be careful and precise when you tear and tuck the wing inward.

NOTE: This technique will also be necessary for the MIG-27.

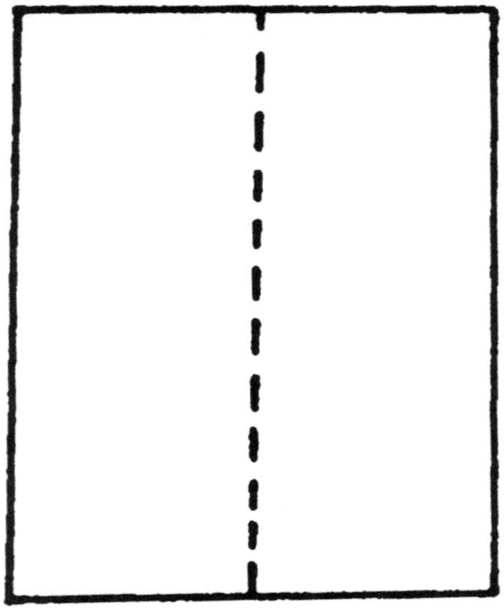

1

Fold the paper in half, then open it back up.

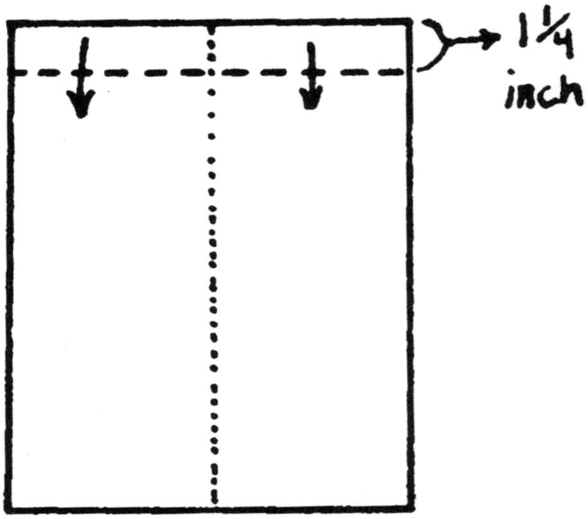


2

Fold it down about 1¼" from the top.

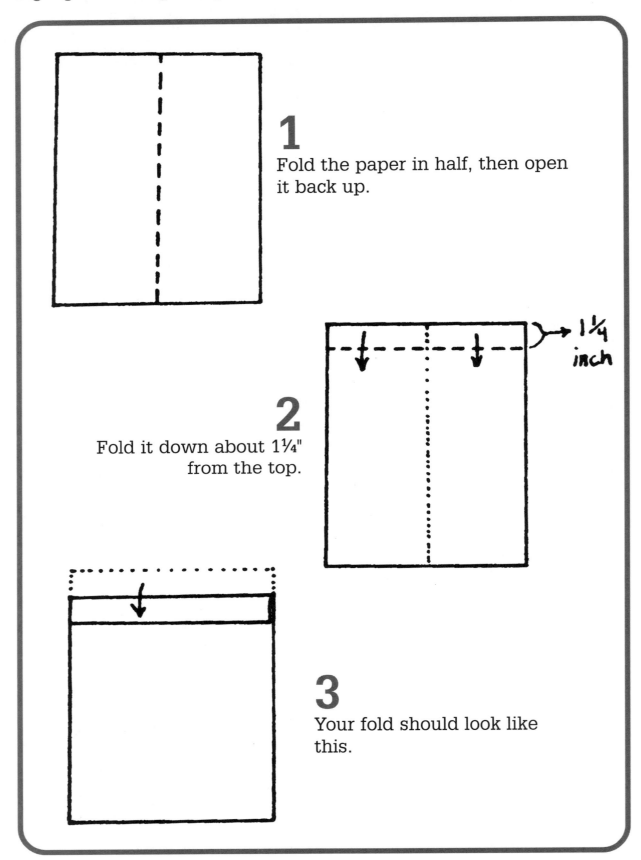

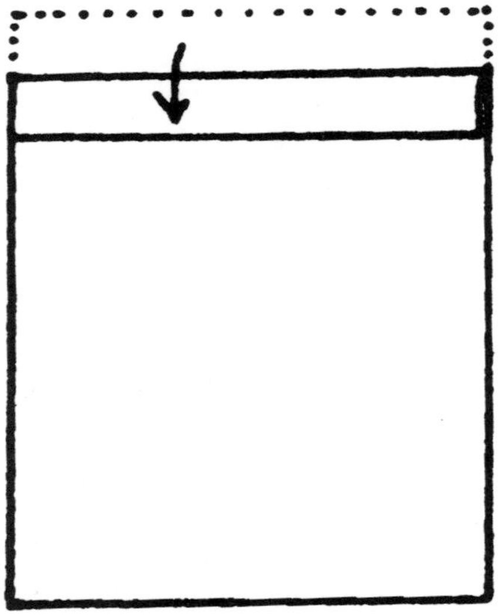

3

Your fold should look like this.

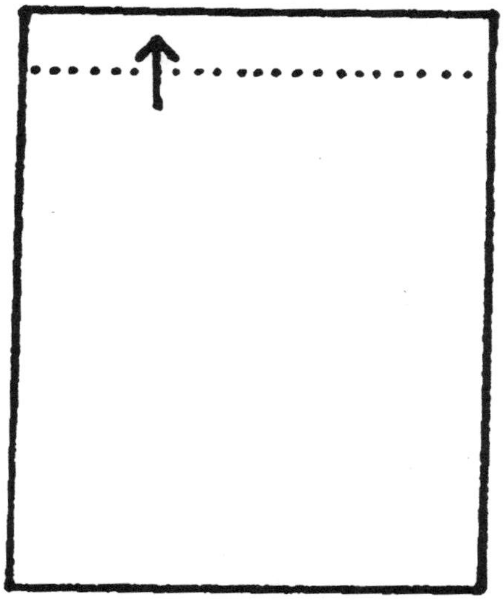

**4**

Open it back up.

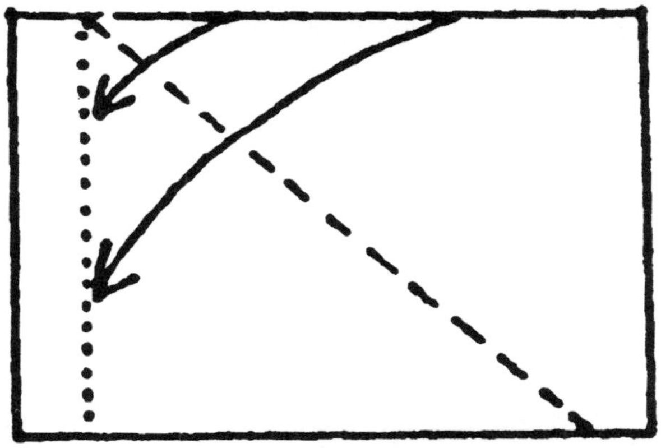

**5**

Turn your paper sideways. Fold the top right corner diagonally down to the left crease line as indicated.

**6**

Fold from the top right corner.

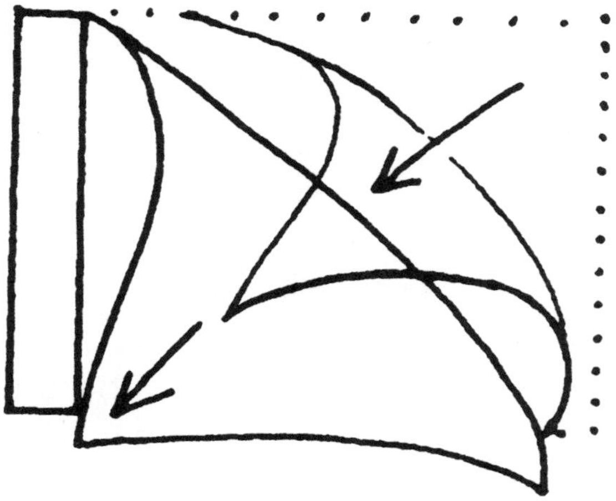

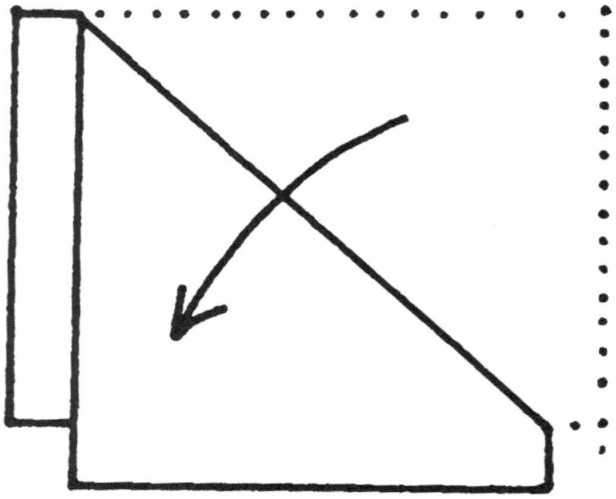

## 7

It should look like this.

## 8

Now, open it back up.

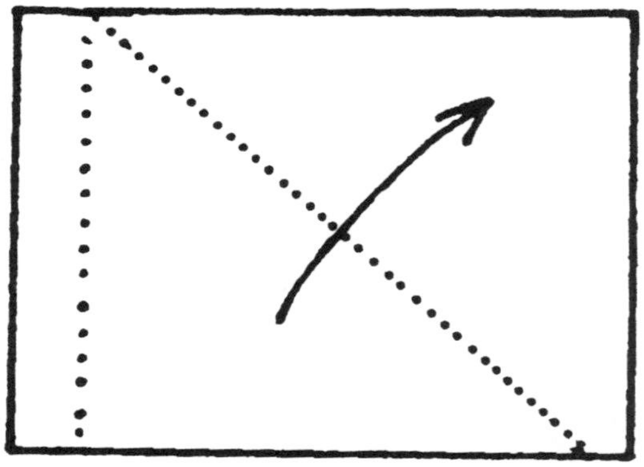

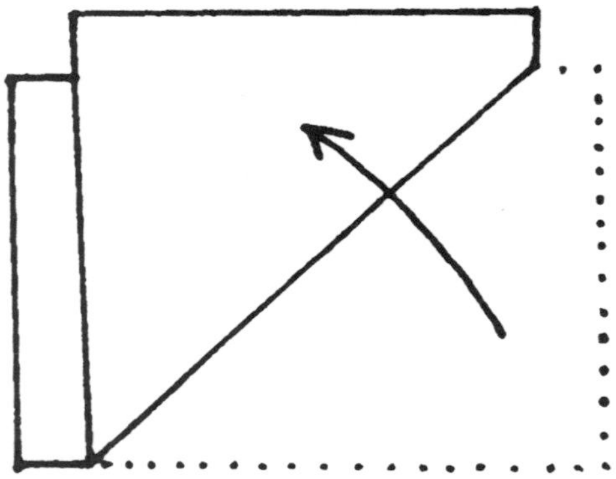

## 9

Make a fold from the lower right-hand corner diagonally up and left as shown.

## 10

Open it back up, rotate your paper a quarter turn and you should have the crossing lines you see here.

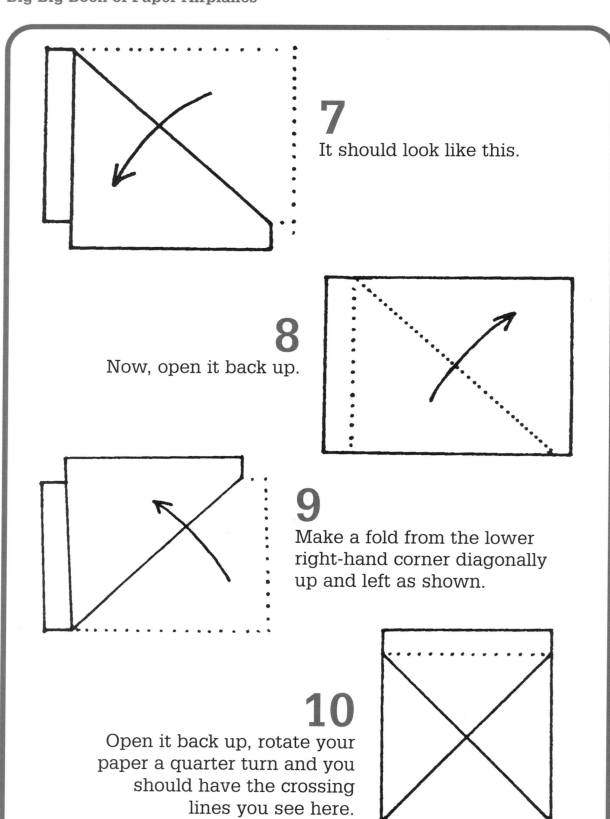

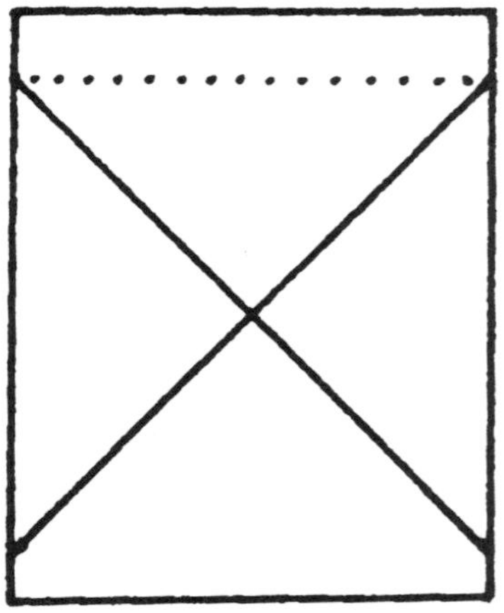

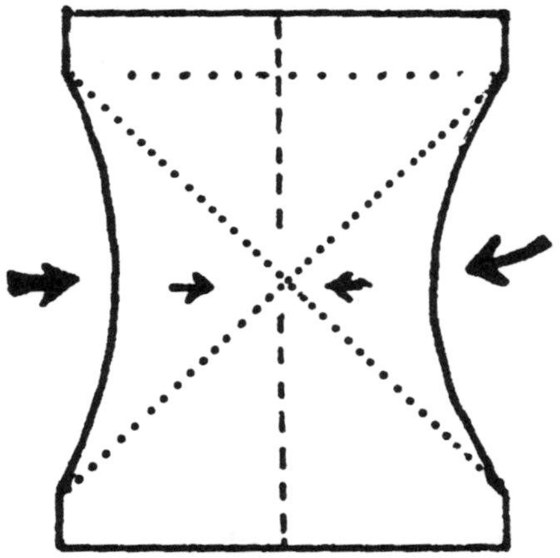

# 11

Fold the sides inward.

# 12

Your inward fold should look like this.

# 13

Press down and it should look like this. The base might not be even, but don't worry about it.

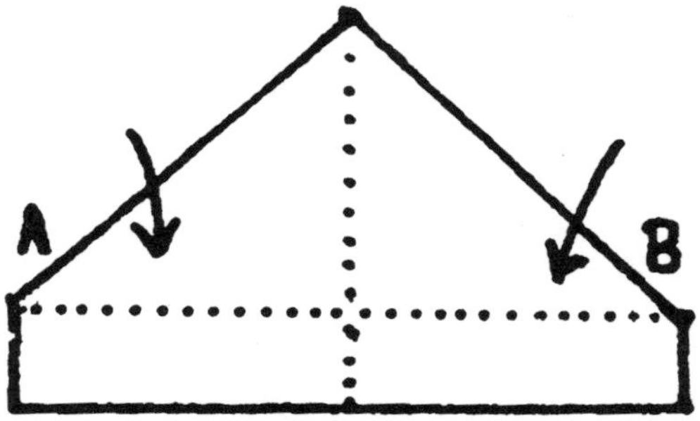


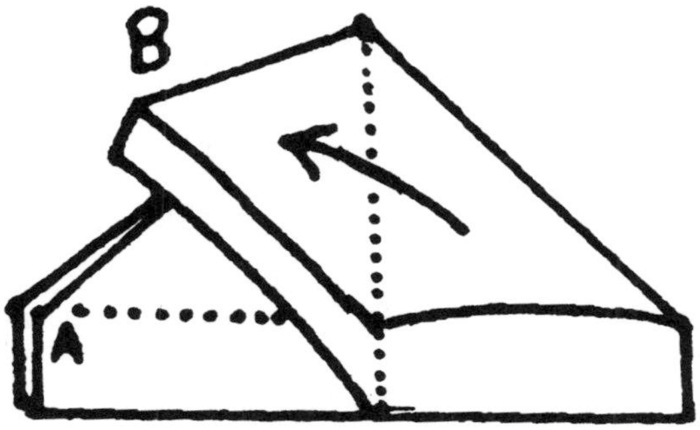


# 14

Flip Fin B to the left side.

## 15

Make a fold toward the middle line as shown by the arrows.

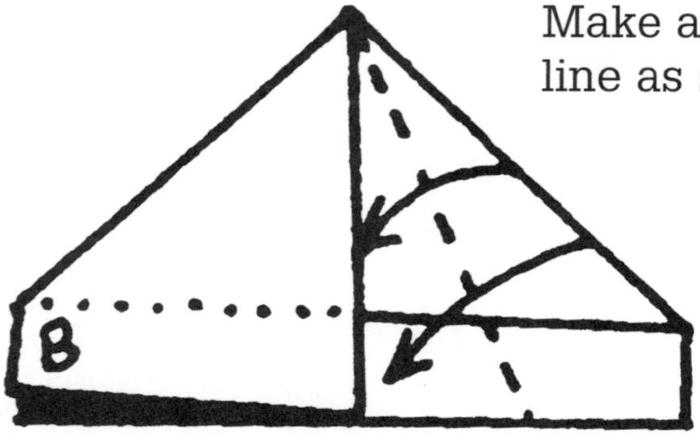


## 16

Your fold should look like this.

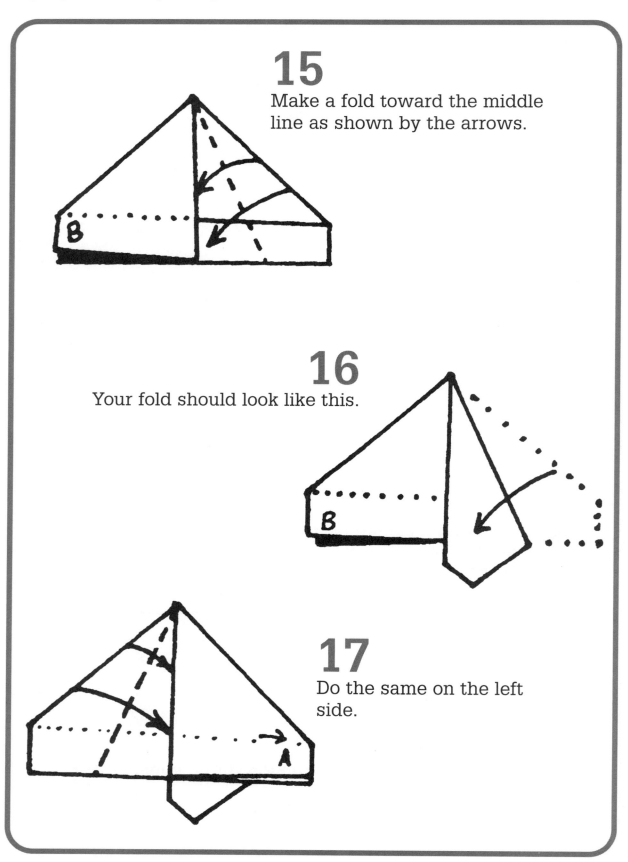

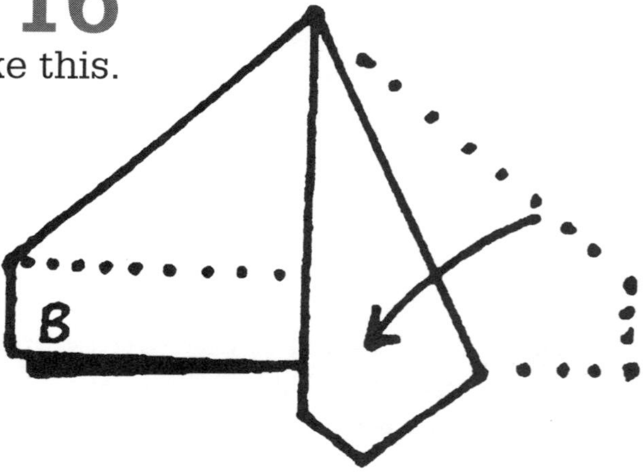


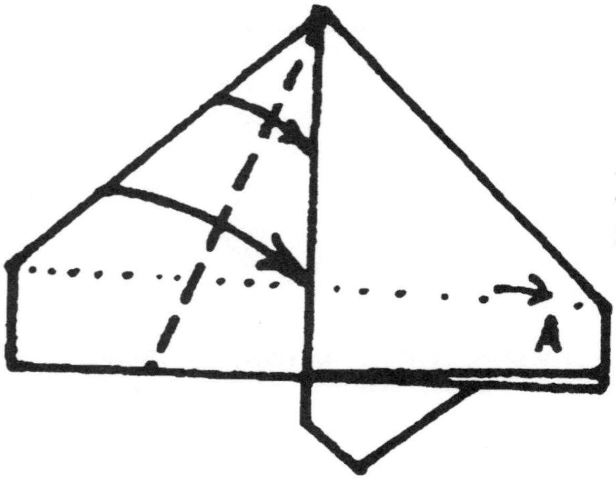


## 17

Do the same on the left side.

## 18

Flip Flaps A & B to the left. Fold outward along the dotted line.

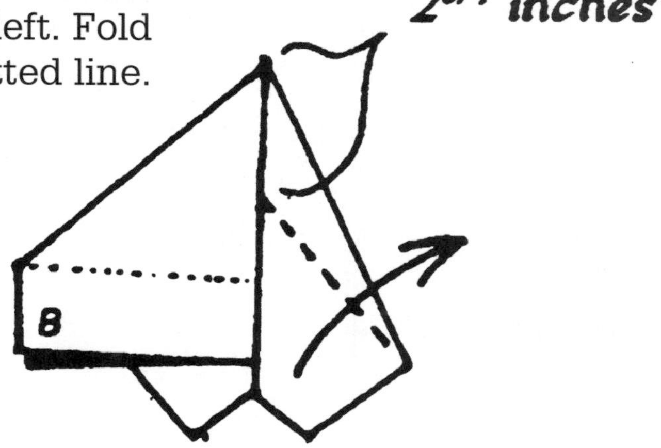


## 19

Your fold should look like this.

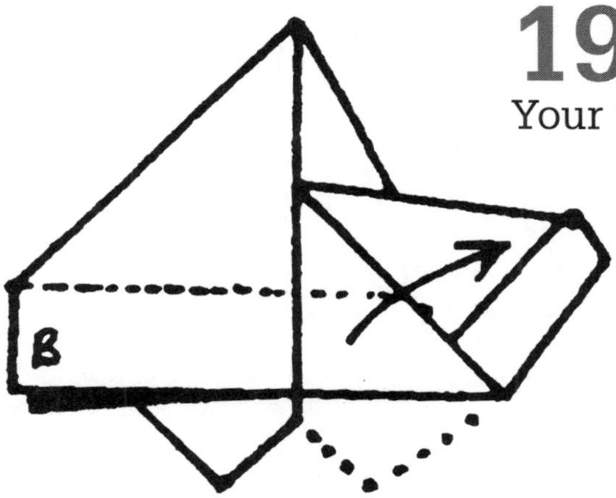


## 20

Fold Edge C to Edge D.

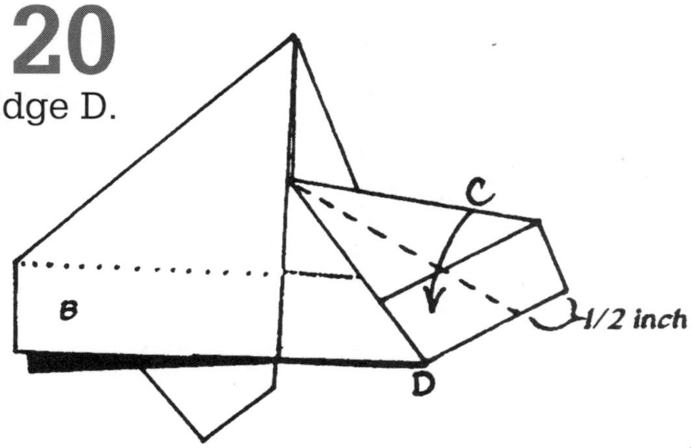

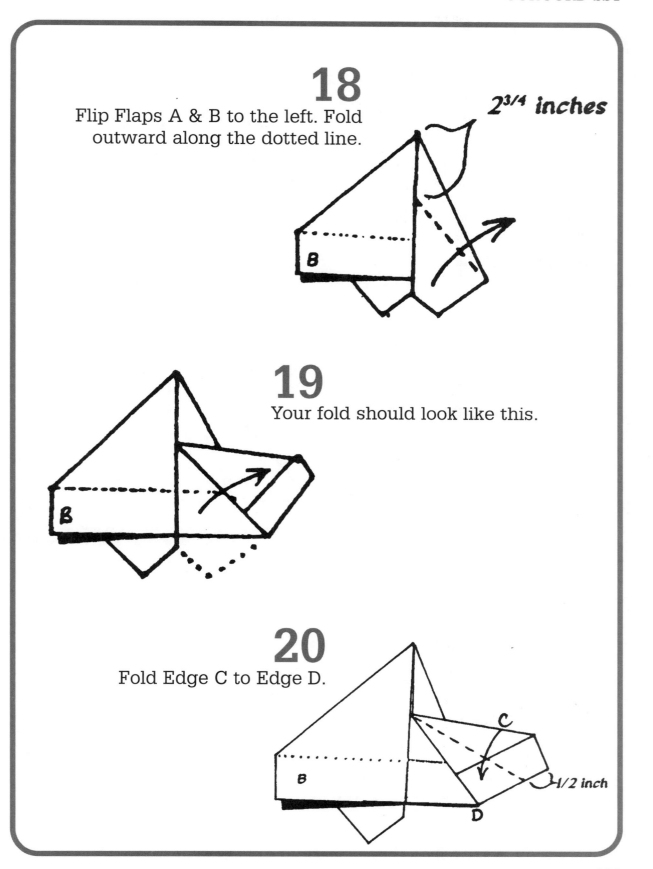

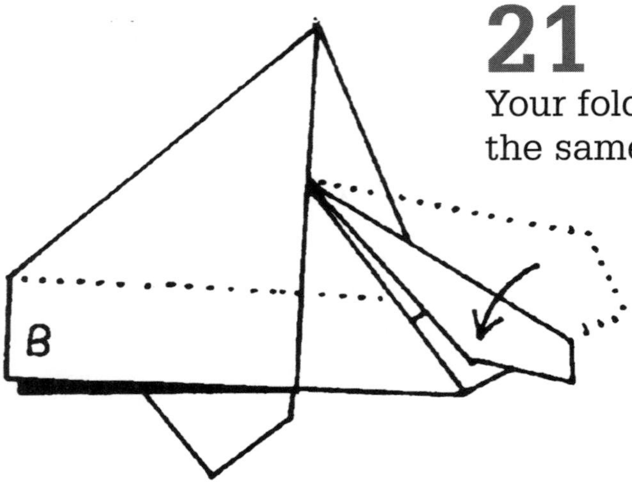

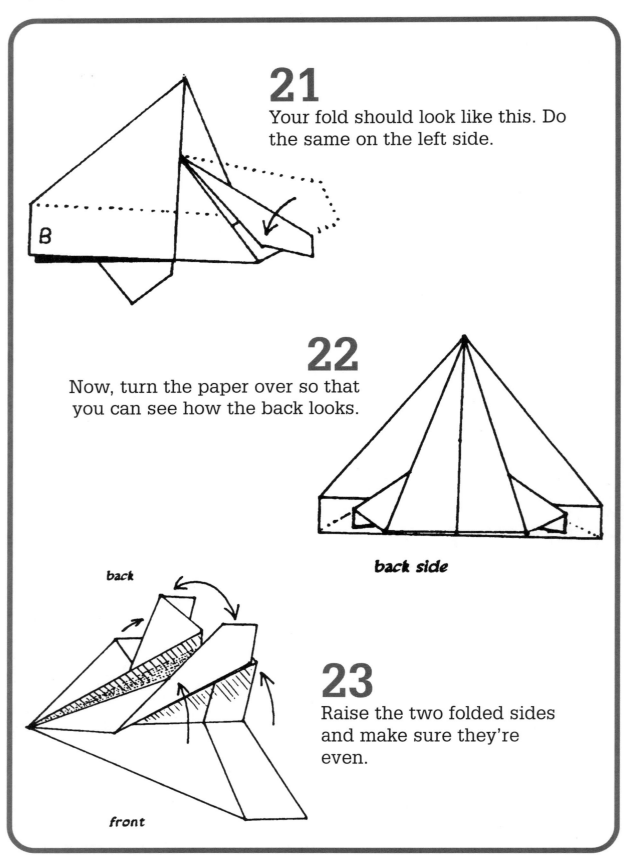

## 21

Your fold should look like this. Do the same on the left side.

## 22

Now, turn the paper over so that you can see how the back looks.

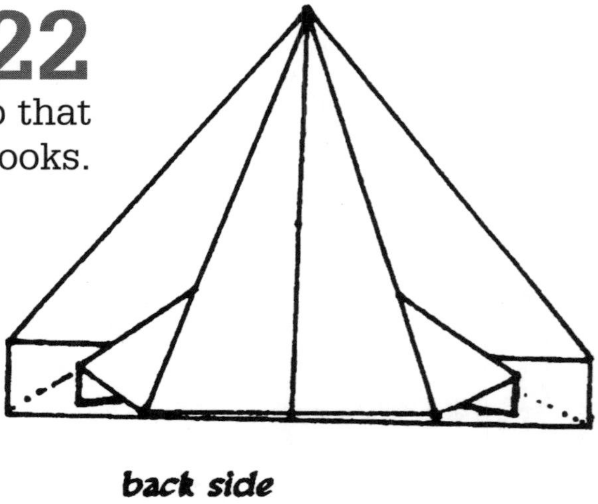


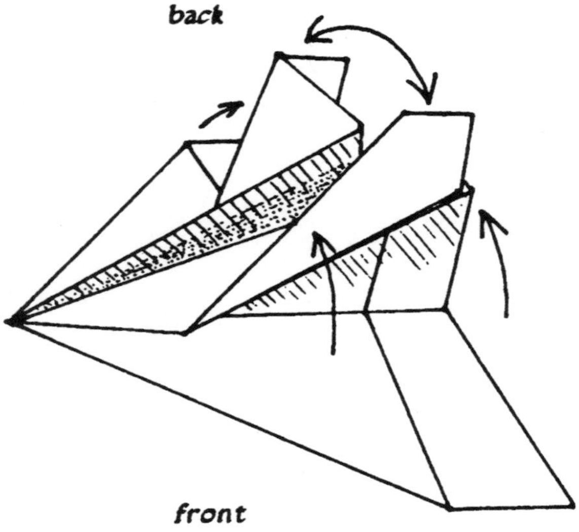


## 23

Raise the two folded sides and make sure they're even.

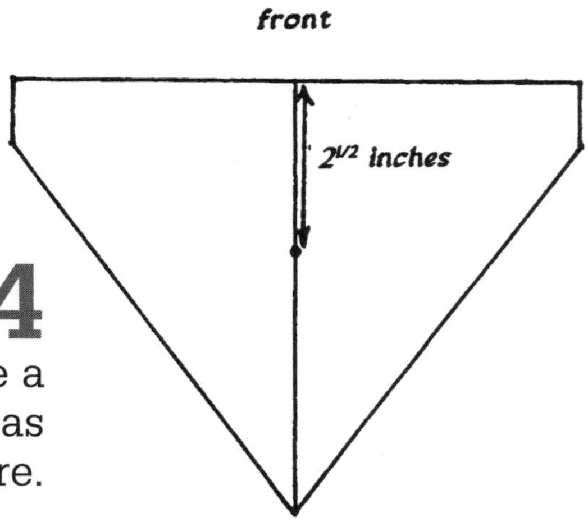


# 24

Turn the plane over and make a tear about 2½ inches long as indicated here.

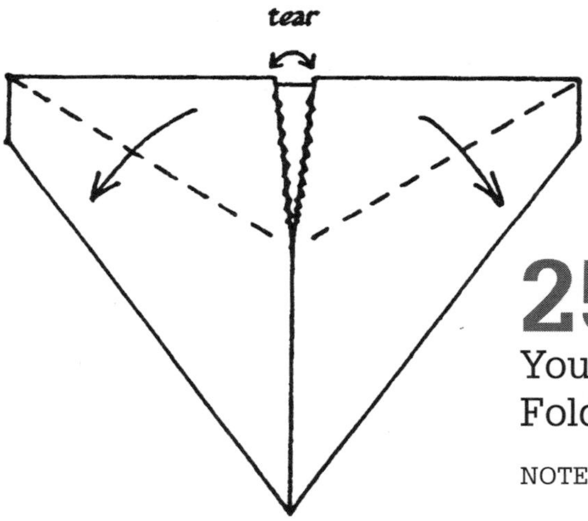


# 25

Your tear should look like this. Fold the two sides as indicated.

NOTE: Cutting is optional.

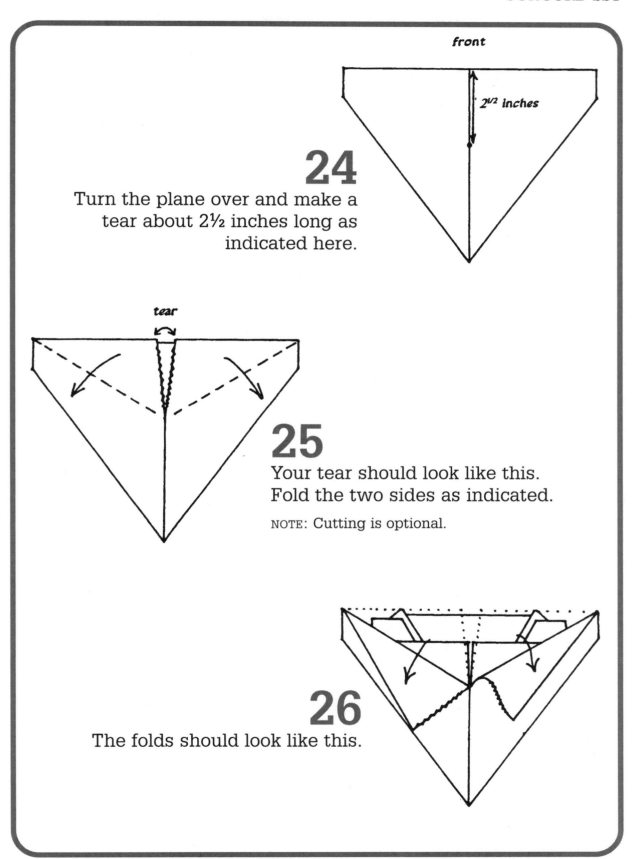

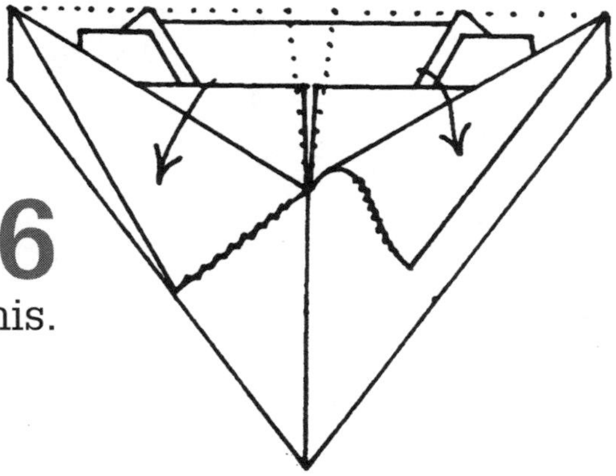

# 26

The folds should look like this.

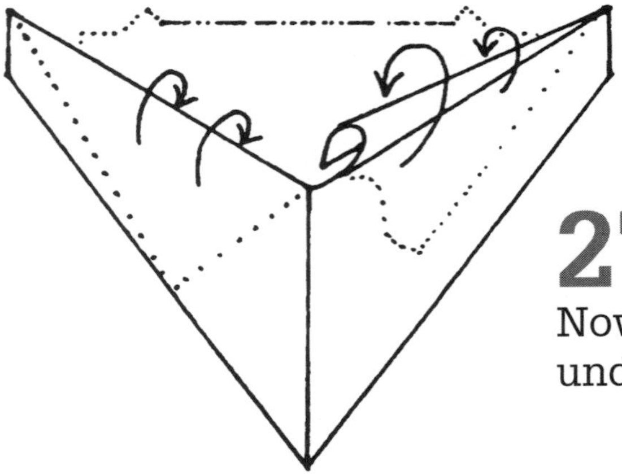

# 27

Now, fold the two flaps inward under the wings.

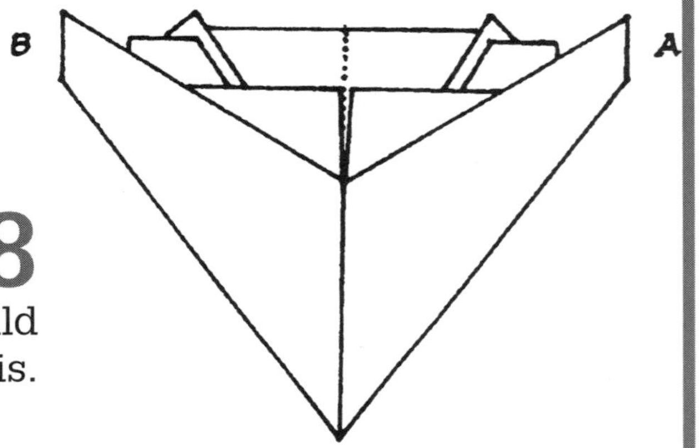


# 28

Now the plane should look like this.

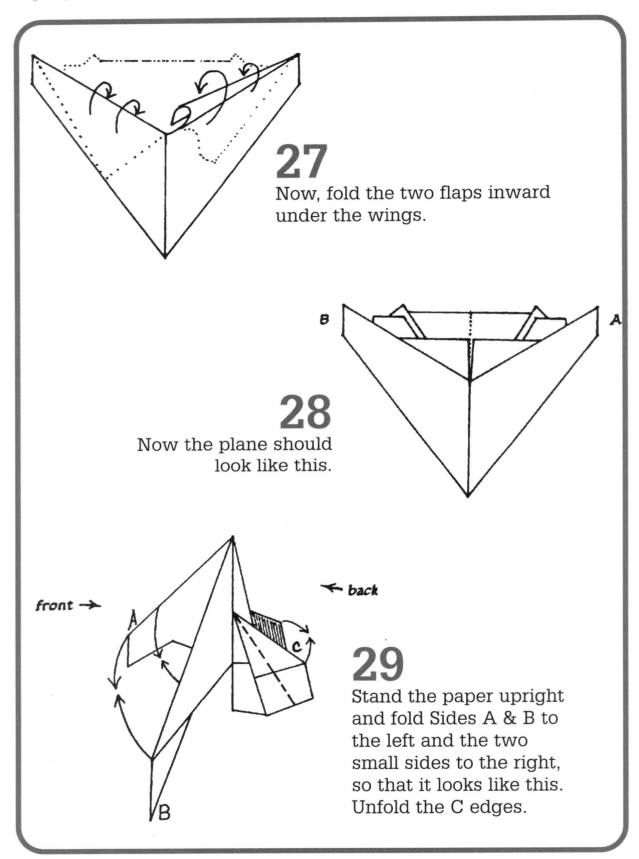

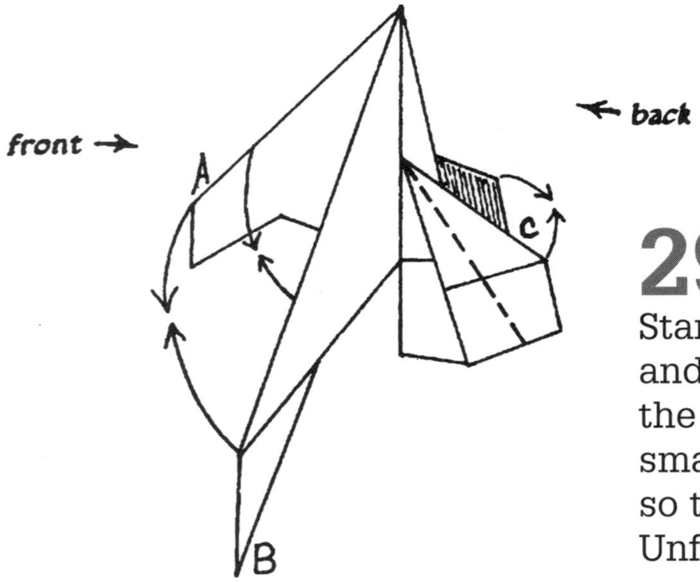


# 29

Stand the paper upright and fold Sides A & B to the left and the two small sides to the right, so that it looks like this. Unfold the C edges.

## 30

Your plane should look like this. Make a small fold up on the bottom as indicated, on the top flap only. Do the same on the other side.

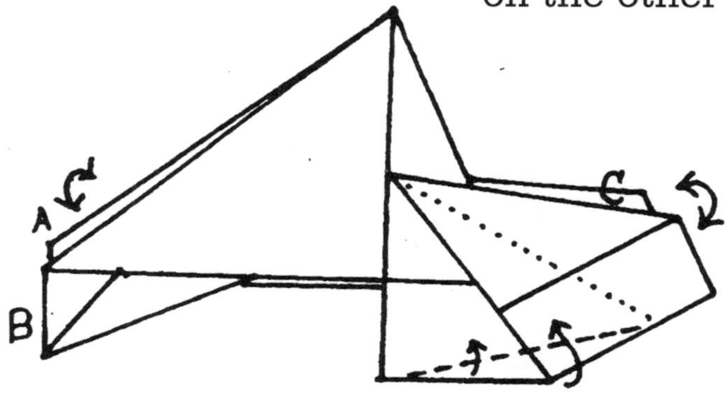


## 31

Now, fold the upper portion of the tail fin down. Do the same on the other side.

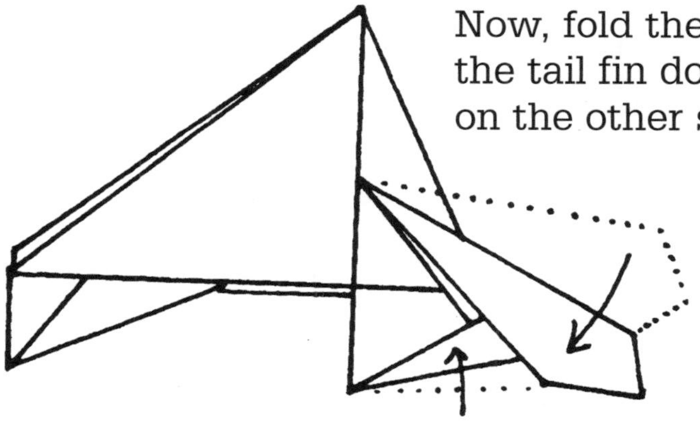

## 32

Now spread the plane open. It should look like this.

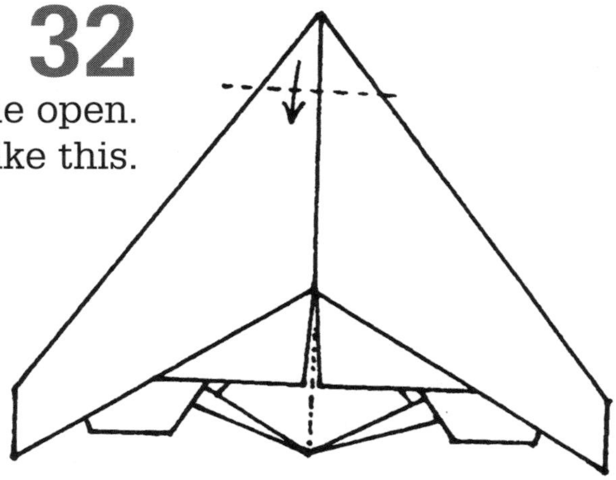

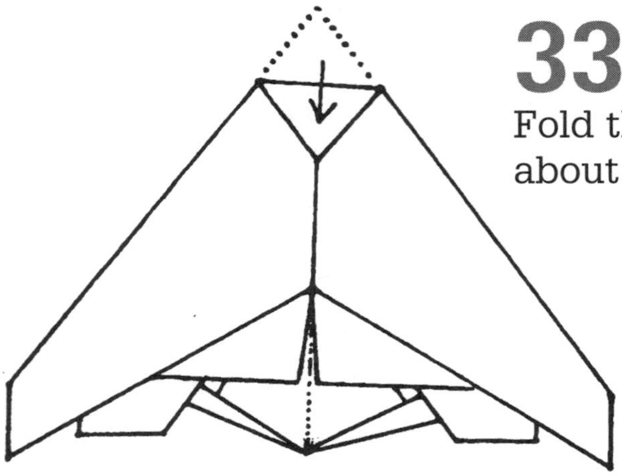

## 33

Fold the nose down toward you about one inch from the top.

## 34

With your hand in the position shown, turn the plane sideways.

NOTE: Remember this procedure from previous airplanes.

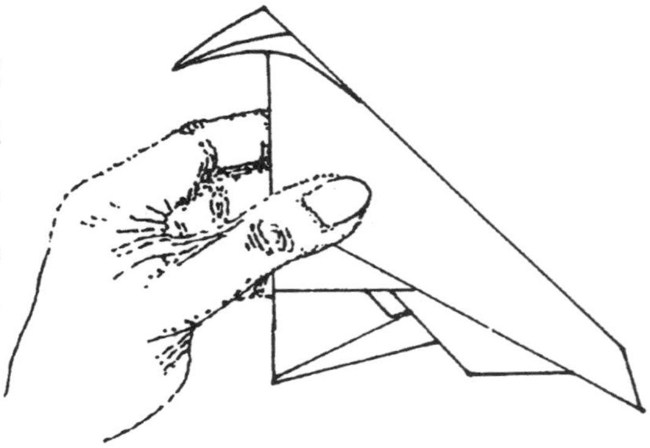

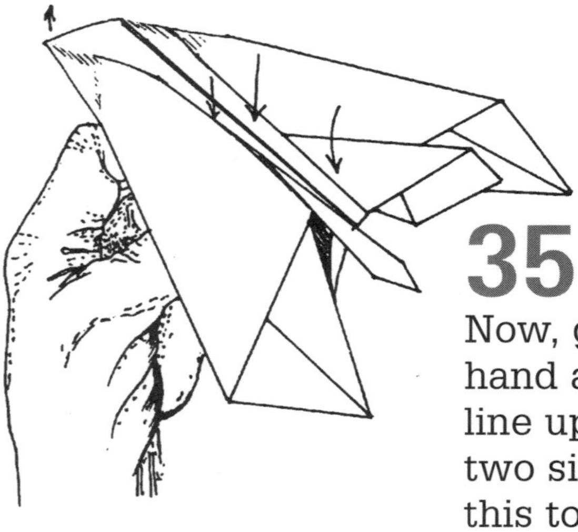

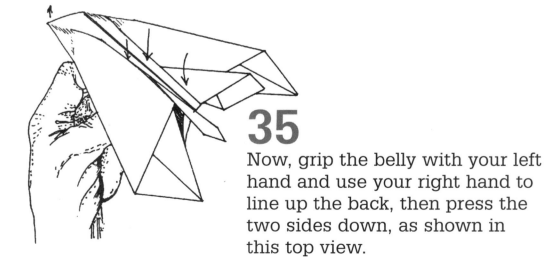

## 35

Now, grip the belly with your left hand and use your right hand to line up the back, then press the two sides down, as shown in this top view.

## 36

This is how your plane should look after you have folded the two sides down.

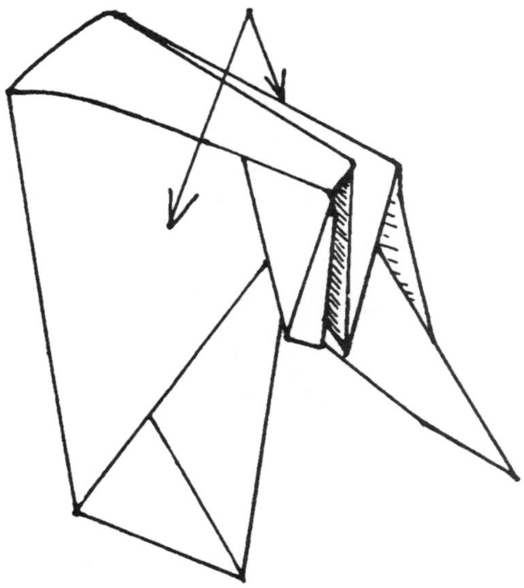

## 38

Fold along the dotted line for a more authentic looking plane.

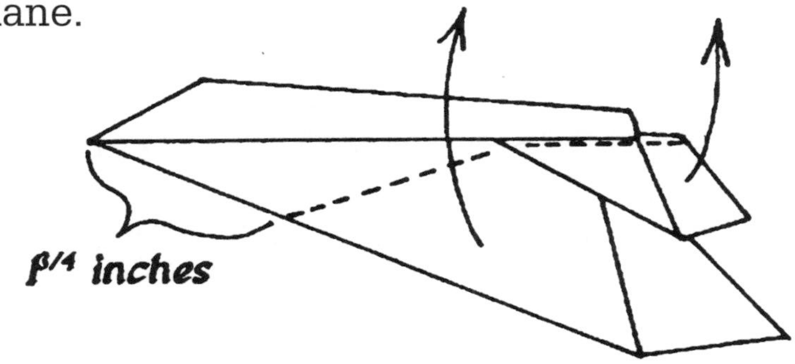


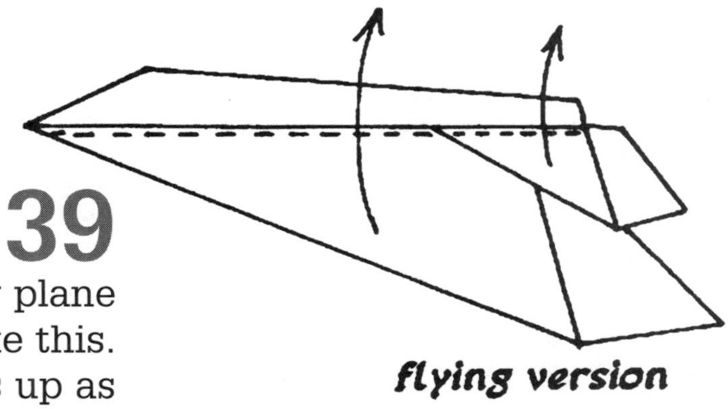


## 39

From the side, your plane should now look like this. Fold the wings up as indicated & do the same on the other side.

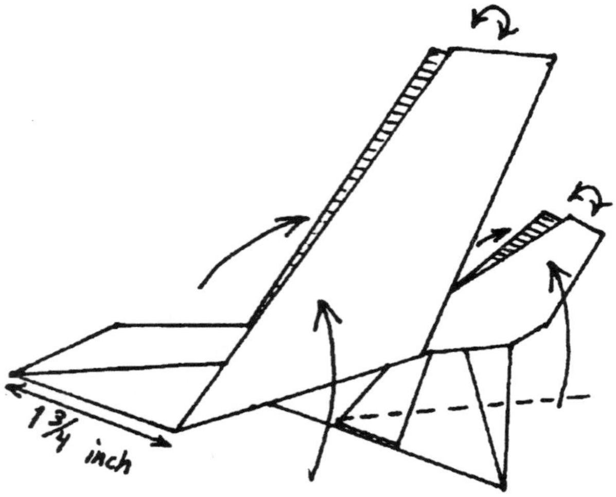


## 39

This is how the plane should look after you have folded the four wings up. Make sure they're even.

## 40

Make an inward-up fold as indicated, similar to the ones you have made on earlier planes in this book.

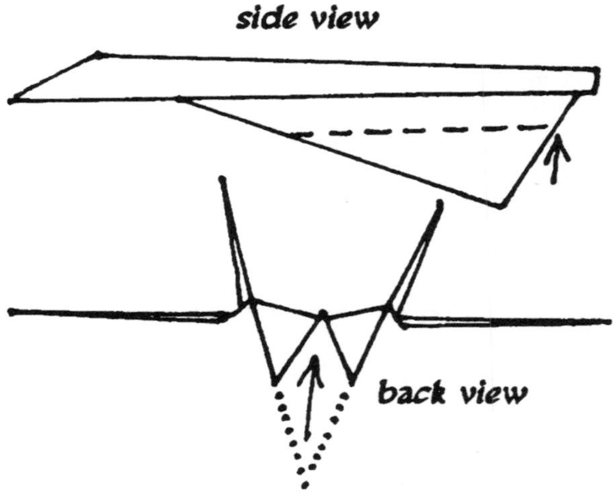


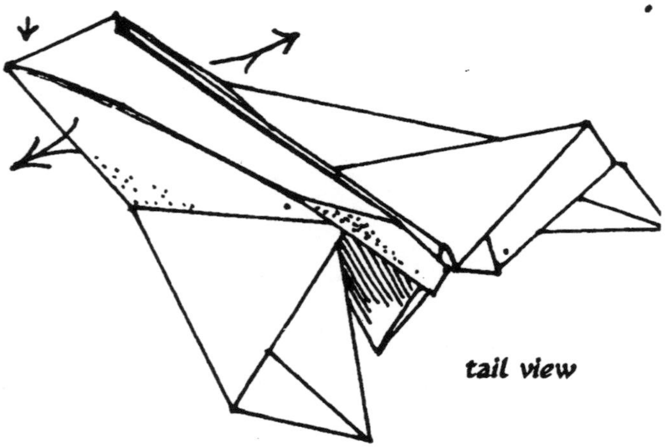


## 41

Lift up and widen the two sides as indicated by the arrows.

**42**

The finished version of the Nighthawk!

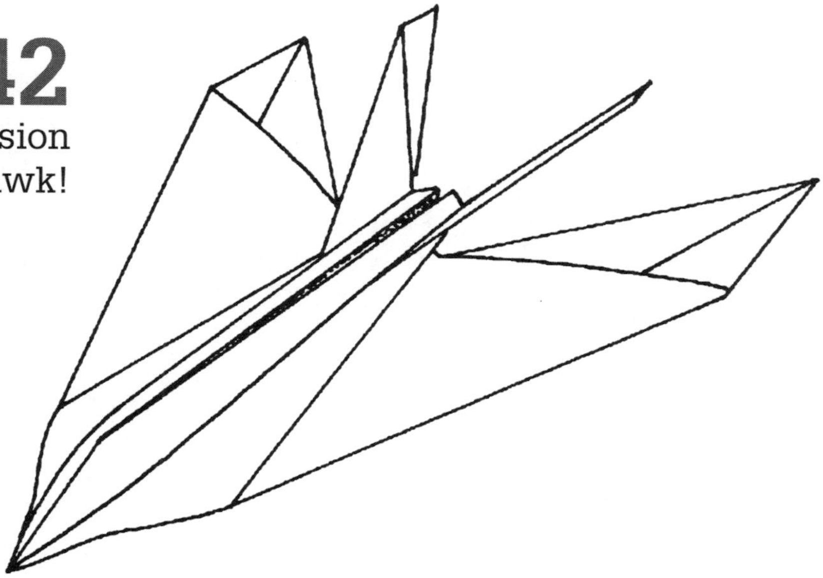

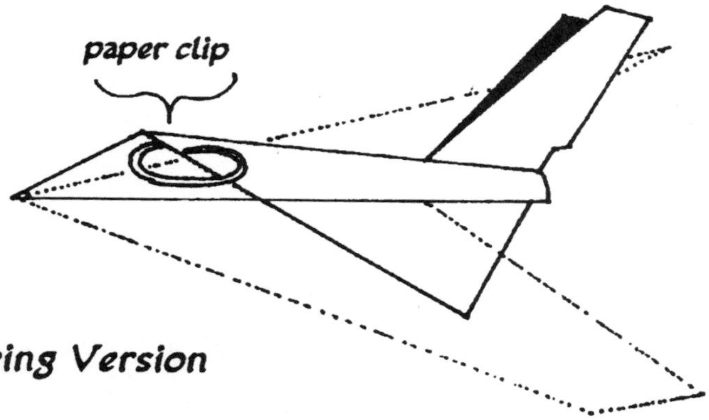


**43** *Flying Version*

To fly this plane, place a paper clip as shown, and tightly press the nose to make it pointed. Slide the paper clip back & forth for balance. Throw the plane straight out from your body and it should fly and glide smoothly.

# F-117 NIGHTHAWK

# MIG-27 FLOGGER

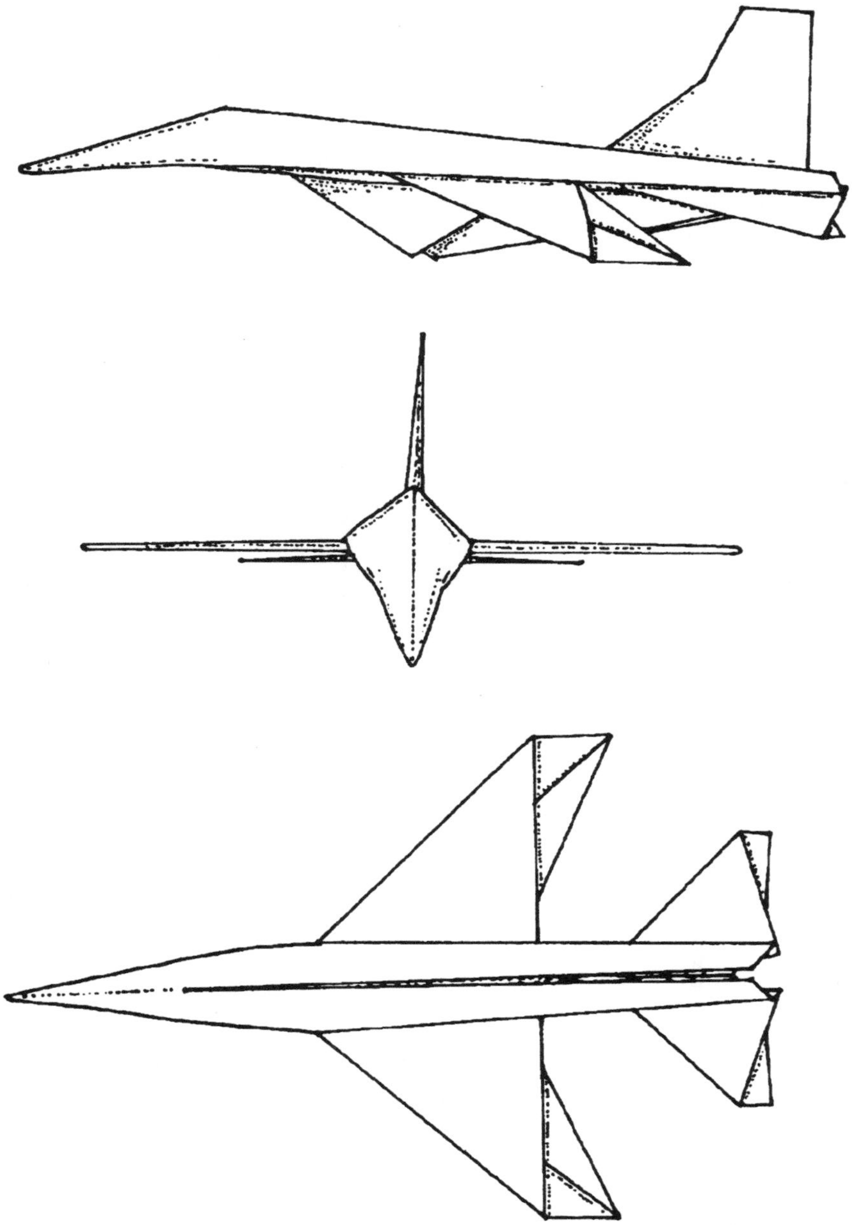

You will not be able to make this plane until you have mastered both the Nighthawk and the Jet. In making the MIG-27, after a few initial folds, you'll find yourself repeating some steps that you learned making the F-117 Nighthawk and a few steps from the Jet.

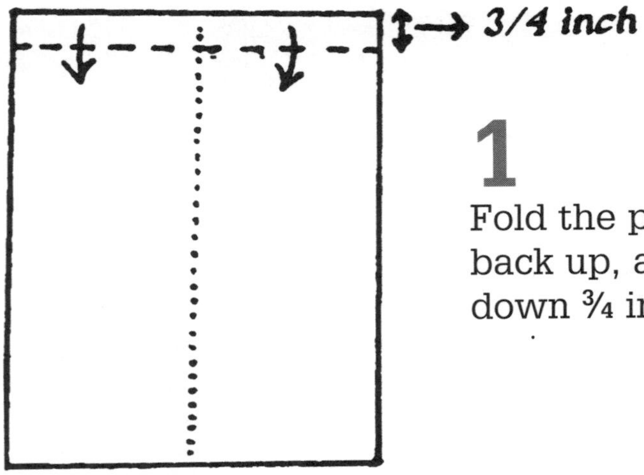


**1**

Fold the paper in half, open it back up, and fold the top part down ¾ inch.

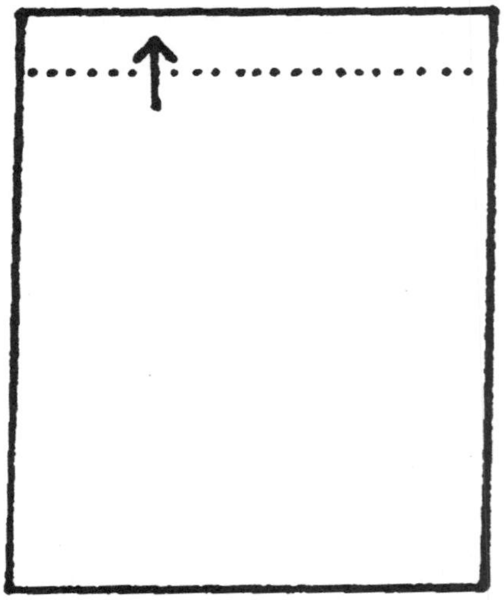

**2**

Open it back up.

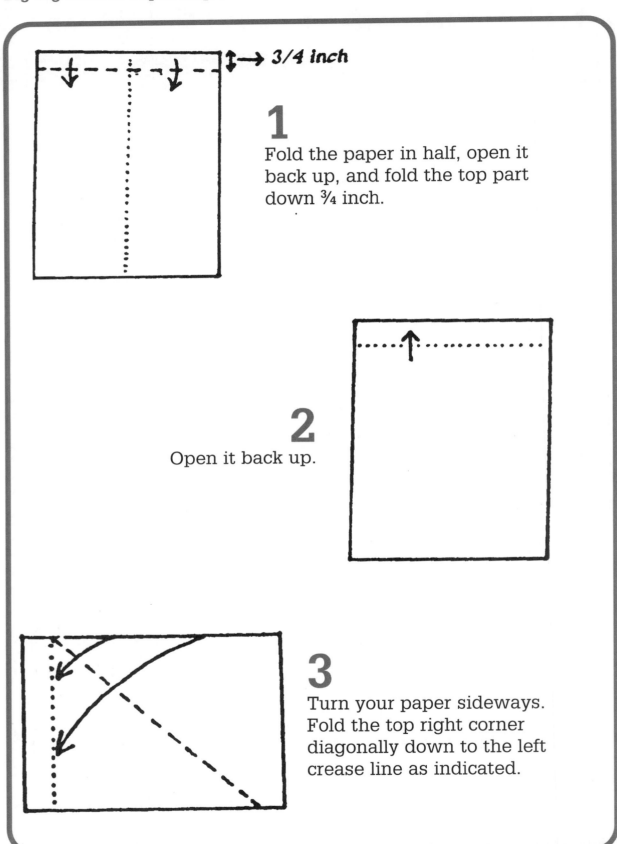

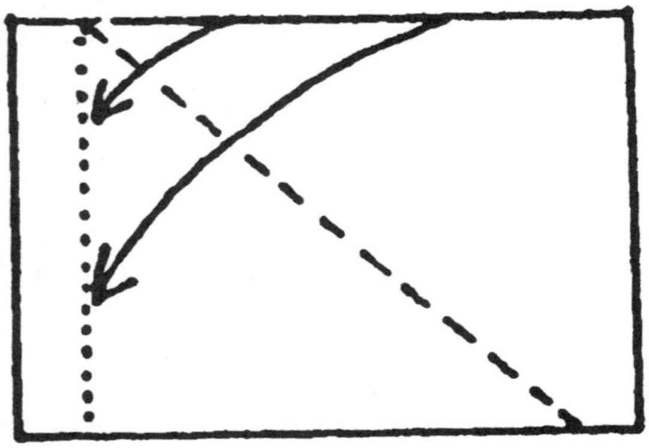

**3**

Turn your paper sideways. Fold the top right corner diagonally down to the left crease line as indicated.

# 4
Fold from the top right corner.

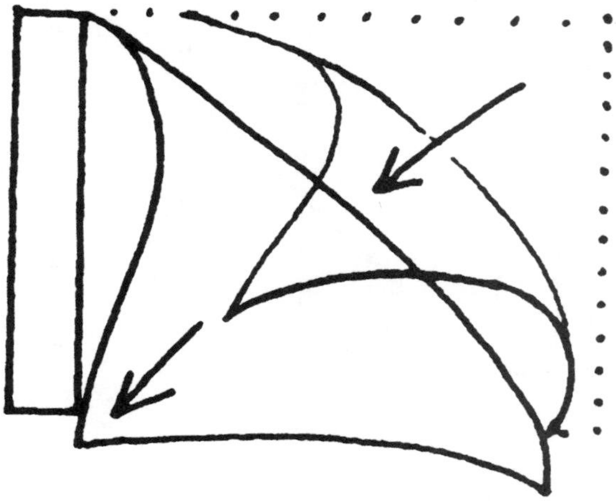

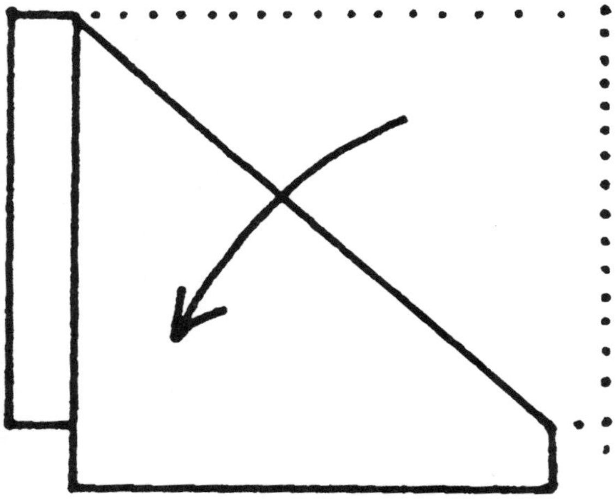

# 5
It should look like this.

# 6
Now, open it back up.

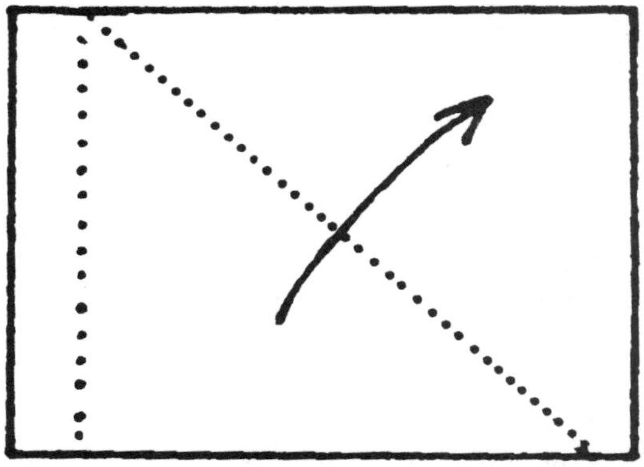

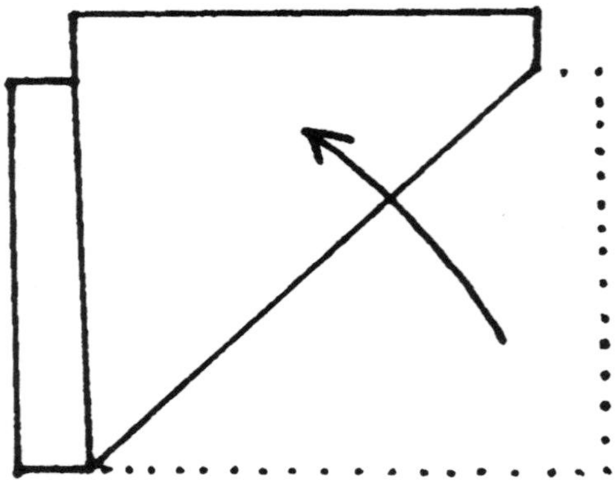

# 7

Make a fold from the lower right-hand corner diagonally up and left as shown.

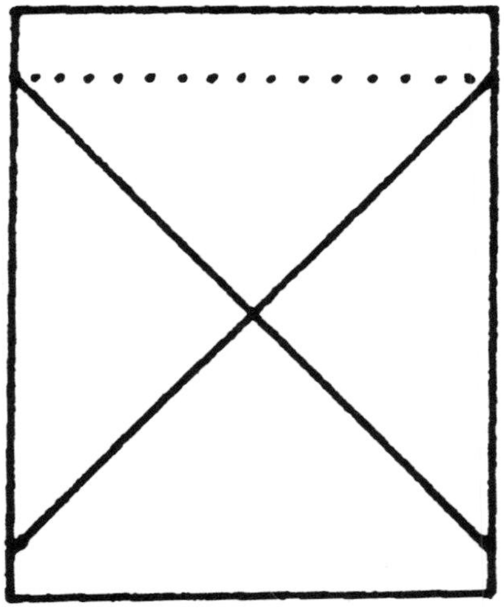

# 8

Open it back up, rotate your paper a quarter turn and you should have the crossing lines you see here.

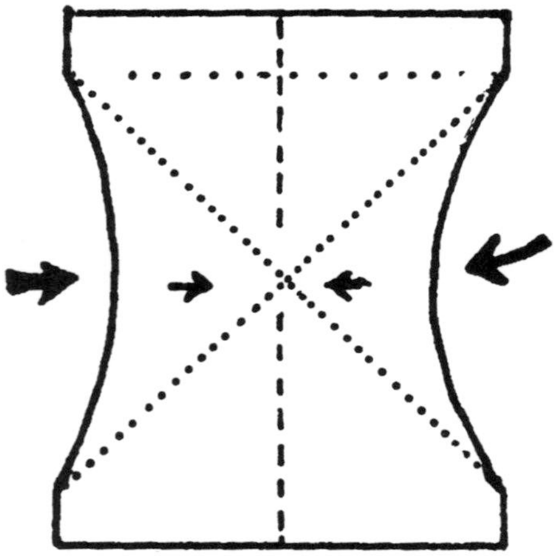

# 9

Fold the sides inward.

# 10

Your inward fold should look like this.

## 11

Press down and it should look like this. The base might not be even, but don't worry about it.

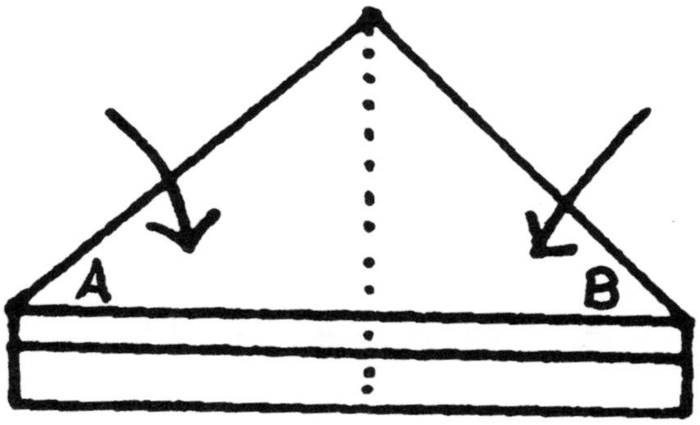


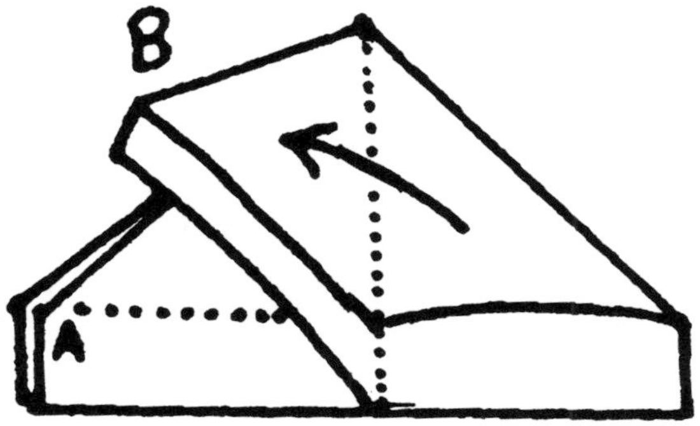


## 13

Flip Fin B to the left side.

## 14

Make a fold toward the middle line as shown by the arrows.

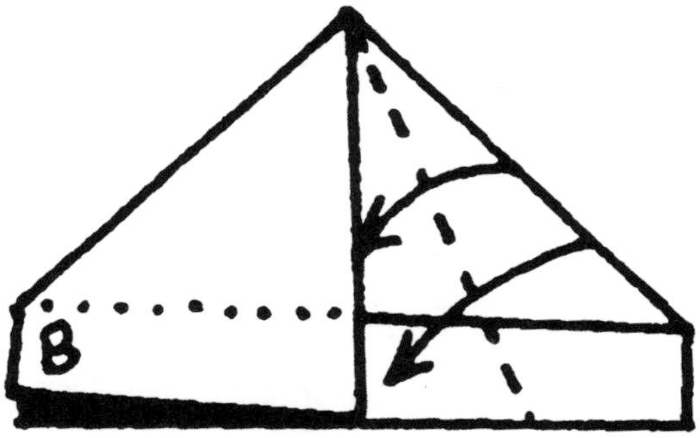


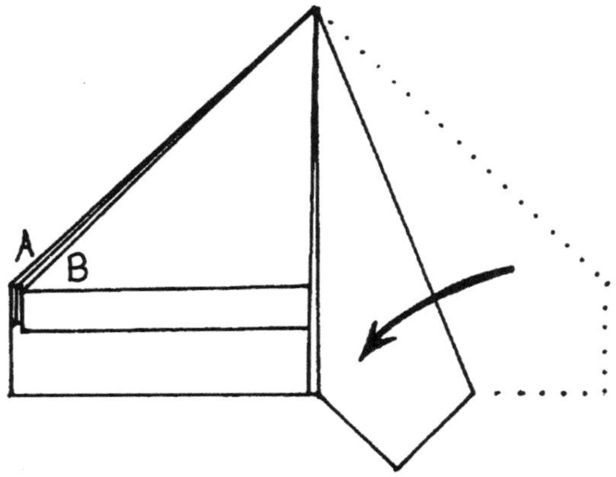


## 15

Your fold should look like this.

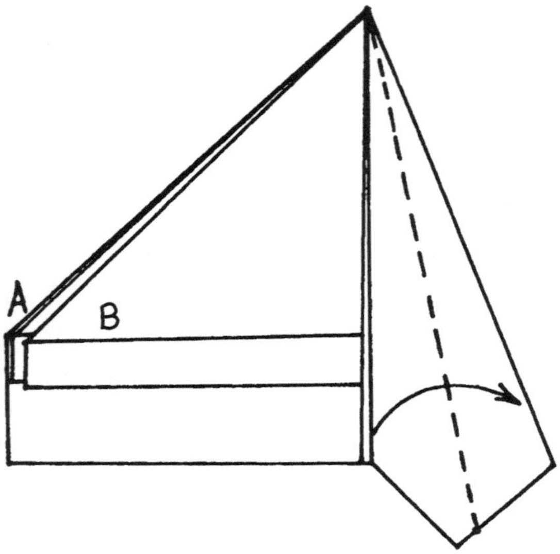

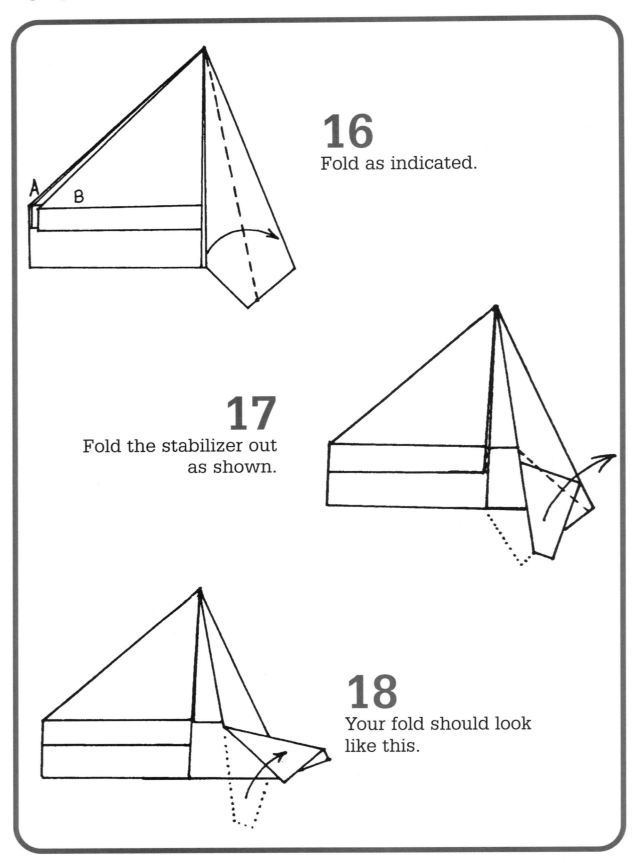

**16**

Fold as indicated.

**17**

Fold the stabilizer out as shown.

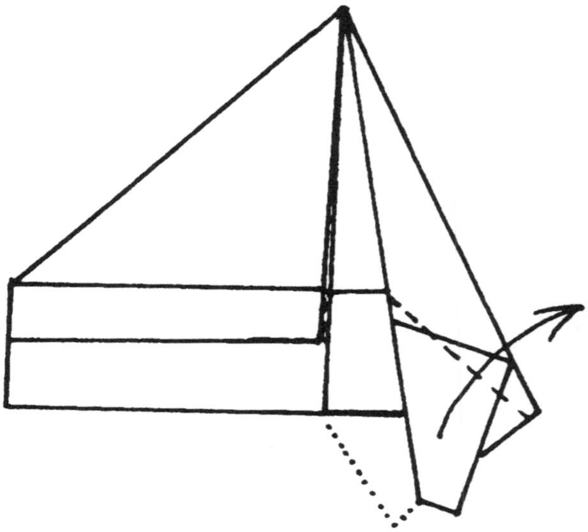

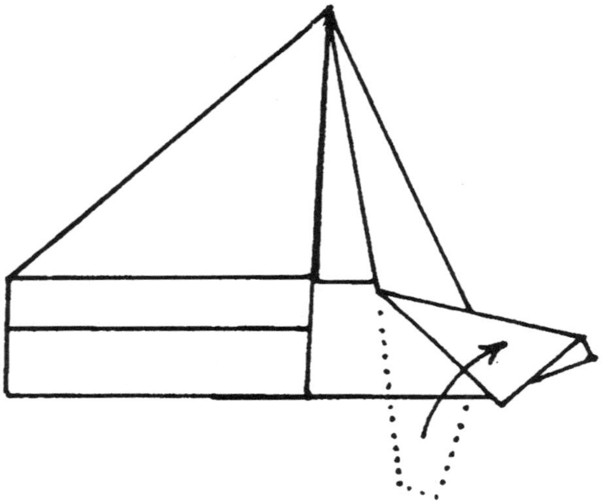

**18**

Your fold should look like this.

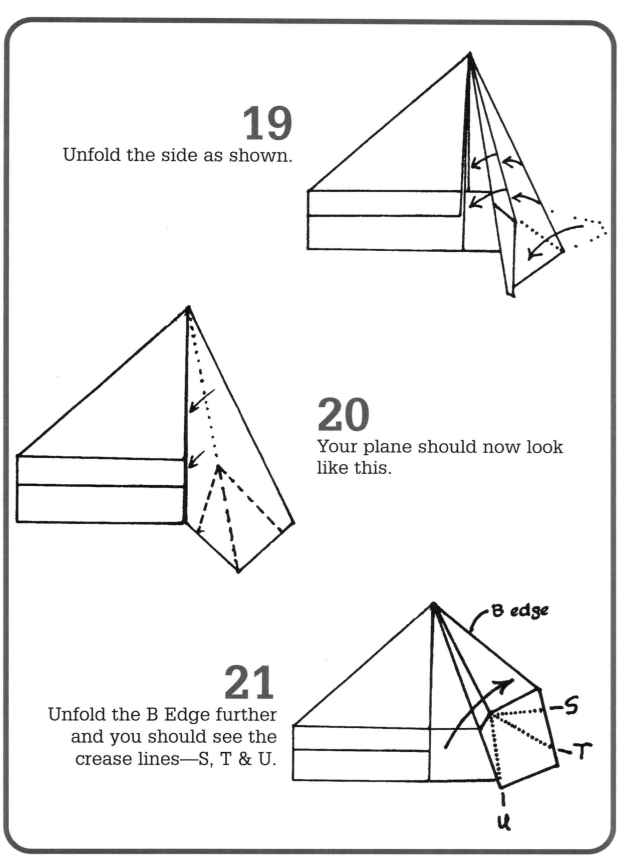

## 19

Unfold the side as shown.

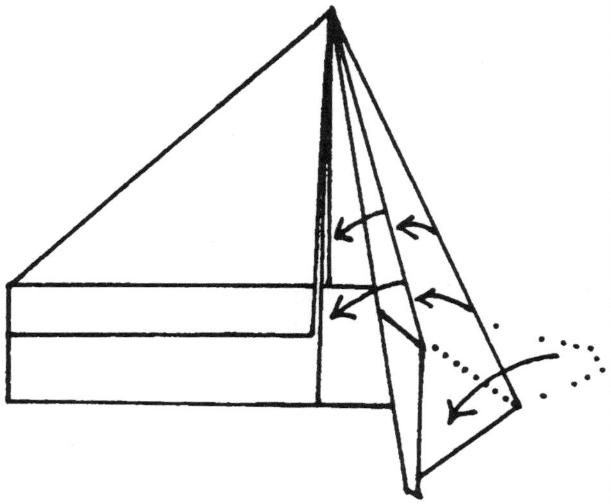

## 20

Your plane should now look like this.

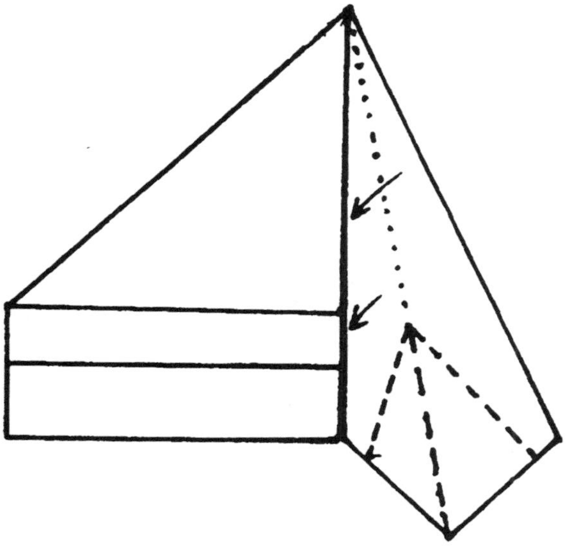

## 21

Unfold the B Edge further and you should see the crease lines—S, T & U.

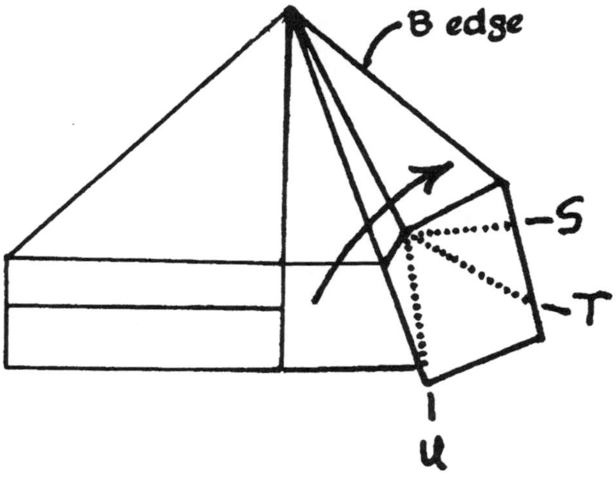

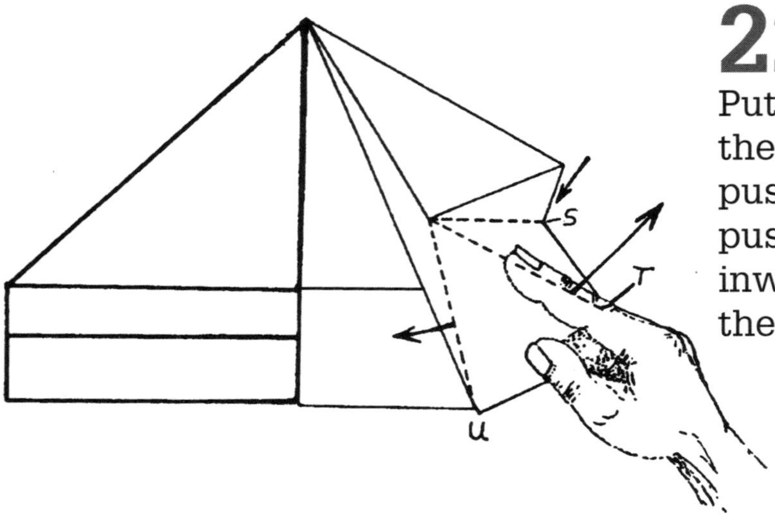

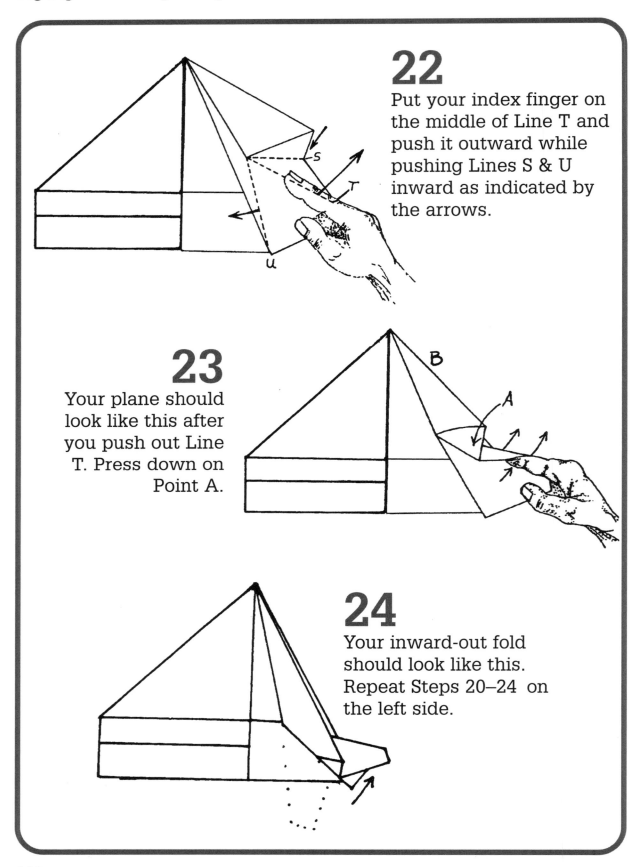

## 22

Put your index finger on the middle of Line T and push it outward while pushing Lines S & U inward as indicated by the arrows.

## 23

Your plane should look like this after you push out Line T. Press down on Point A.

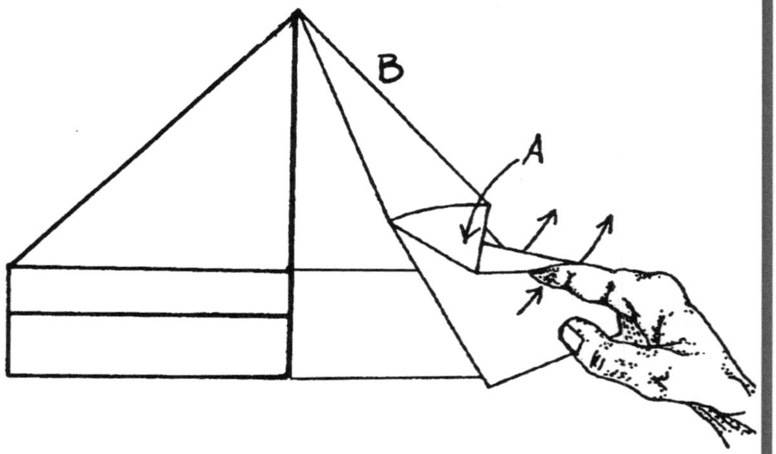


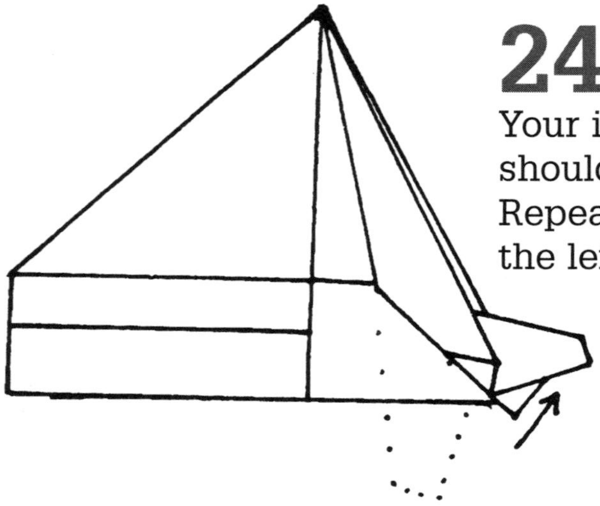

## 24

Your inward-out fold should look like this. Repeat Steps 20–24 on the left side.

## 25

Open up the plane so it looks like this.

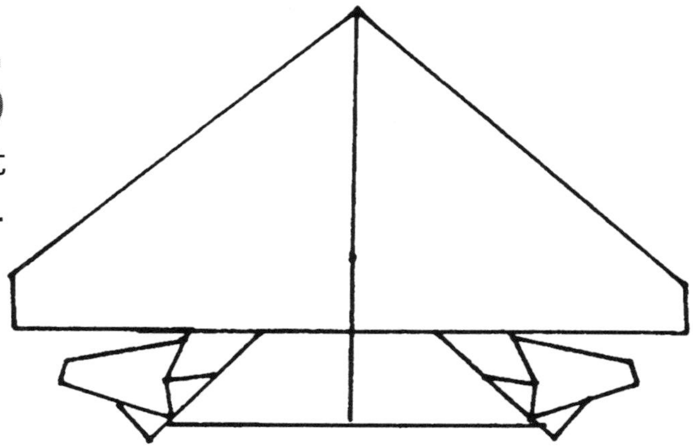

## 26

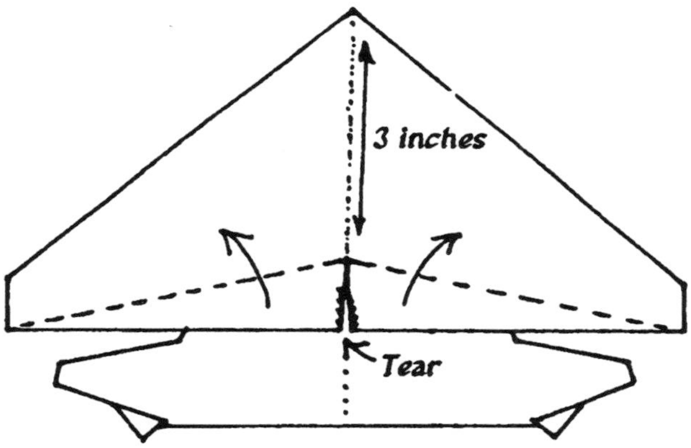


Make a tear as you did with the Nighthawk, and like the Nighthawk, fold toward the inside.

## 27

Your inside fold should look like this. (Notice the L left wing & R right wing.)

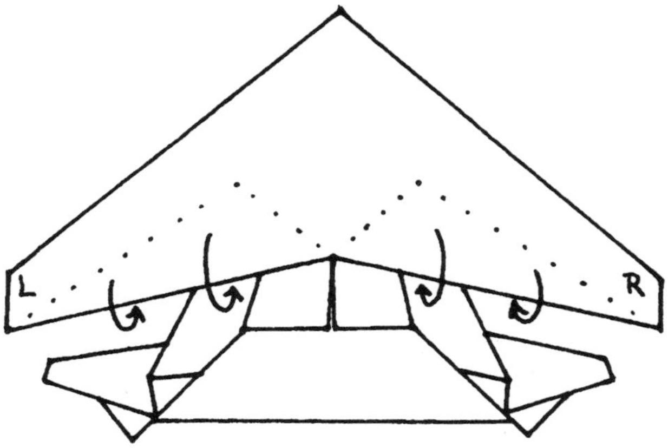

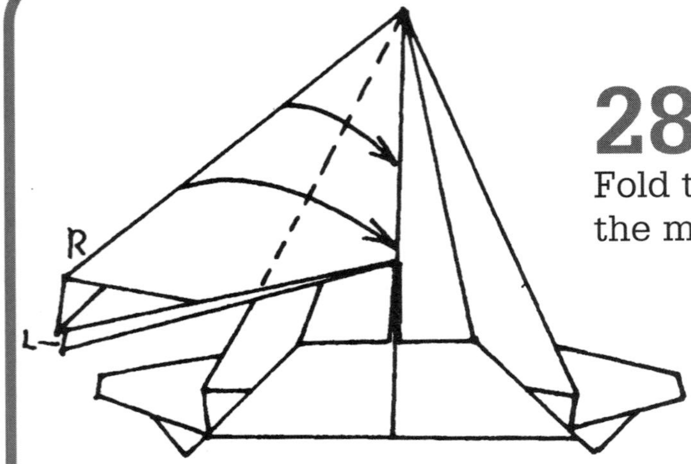

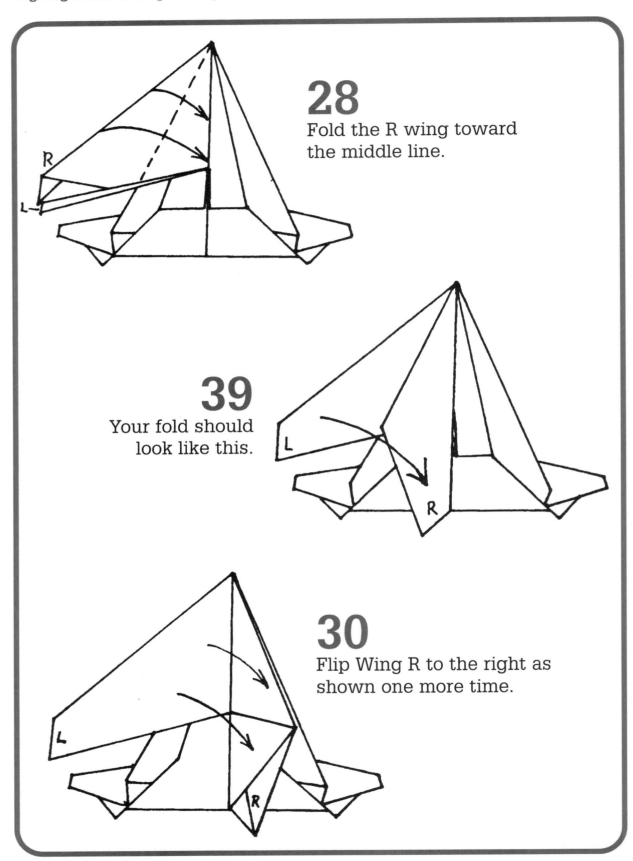

## 28

Fold the R wing toward the middle line.

## 39

Your fold should look like this.

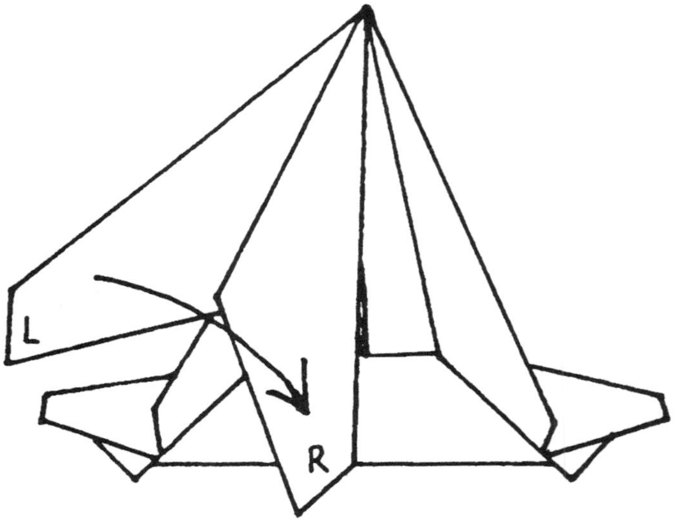


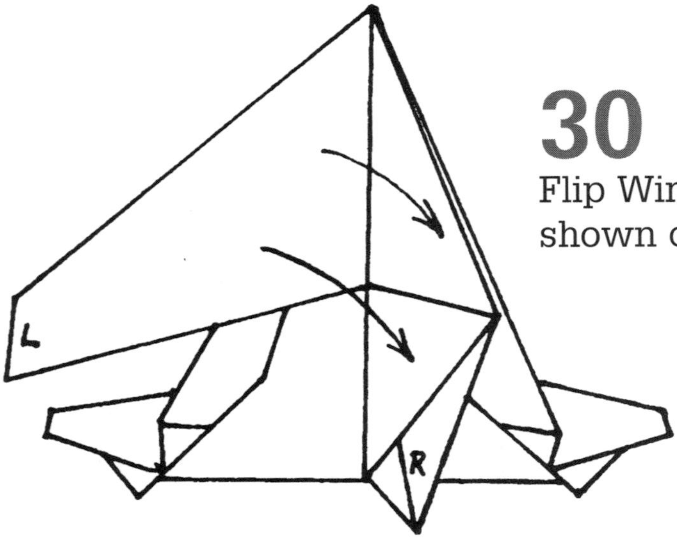


## 30

Flip Wing R to the right as shown one more time.

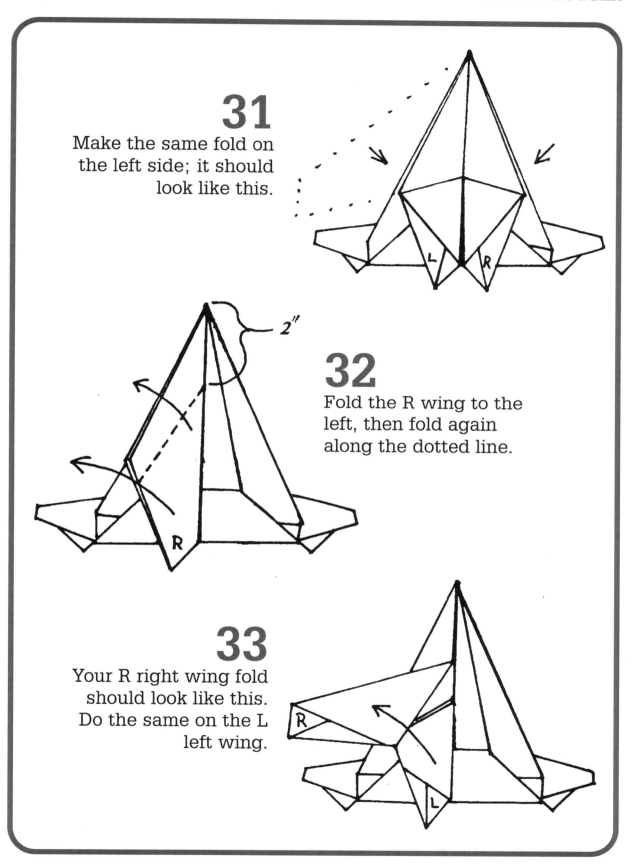

# 31

Make the same fold on the left side; it should look like this.

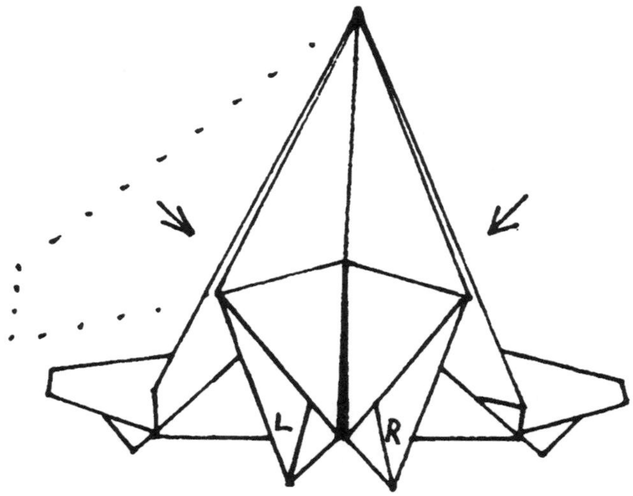


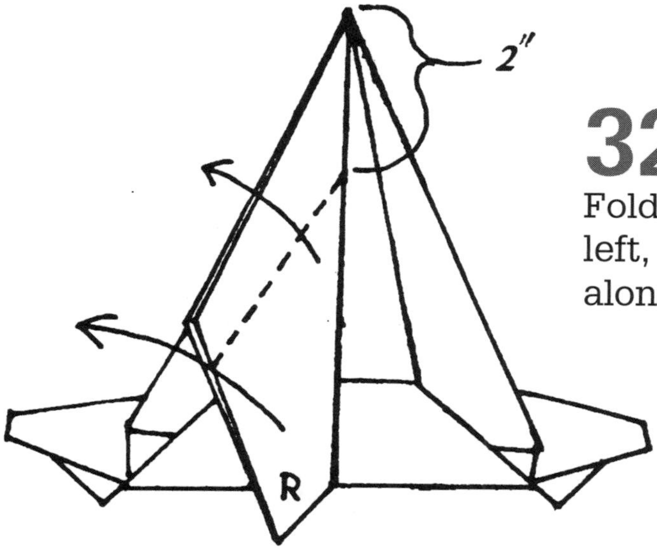


# 32

Fold the R wing to the left, then fold again along the dotted line.

# 33

Your R right wing fold should look like this. Do the same on the L left wing.

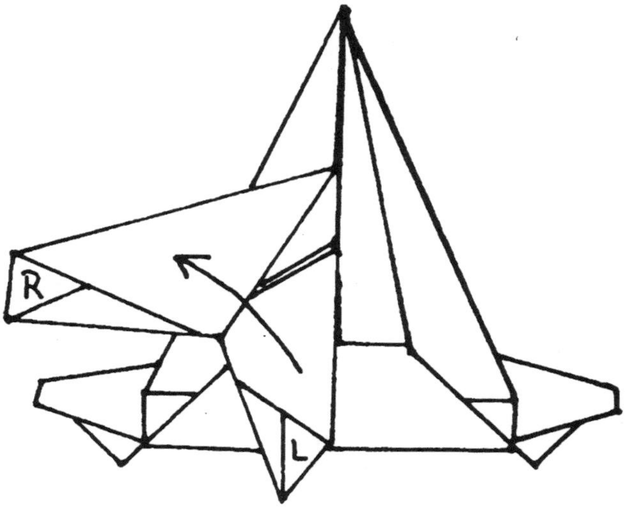

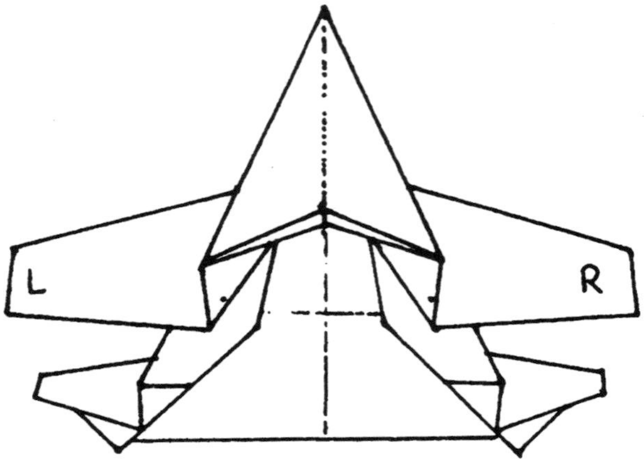


## 34

Open the R wing to the right side, L to the left and you should have this. Now, fold the nose down and finish the plane. If you have trouble, go on to the next step.

## 35

Measure about 1¼ inches from the end of the nose. Fold down the nose along the dotted line.

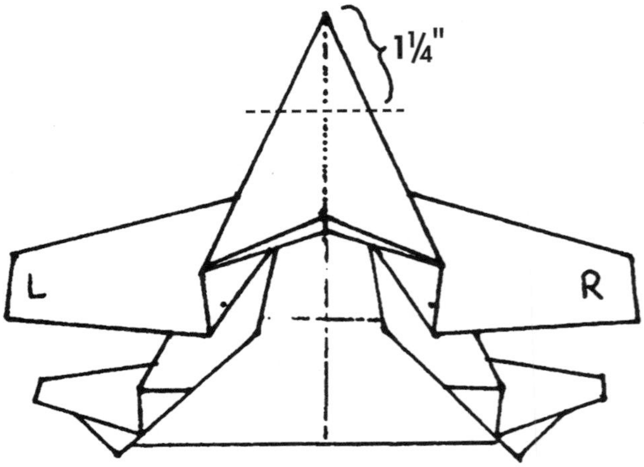


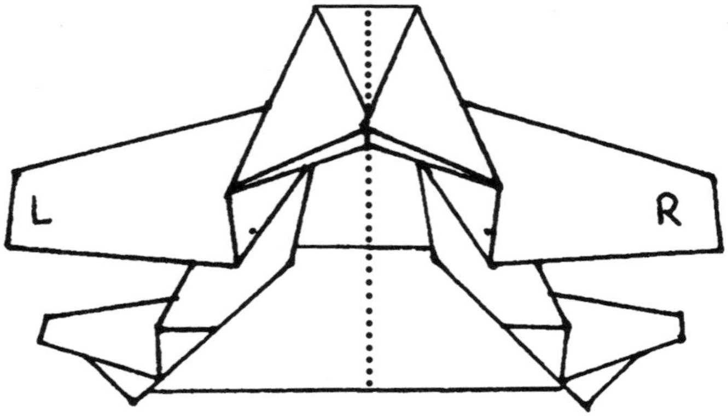


## 36

Your fold should look like this.

# 37

After folding down the nose, fold both sides of the plane's body toward the back as shown.

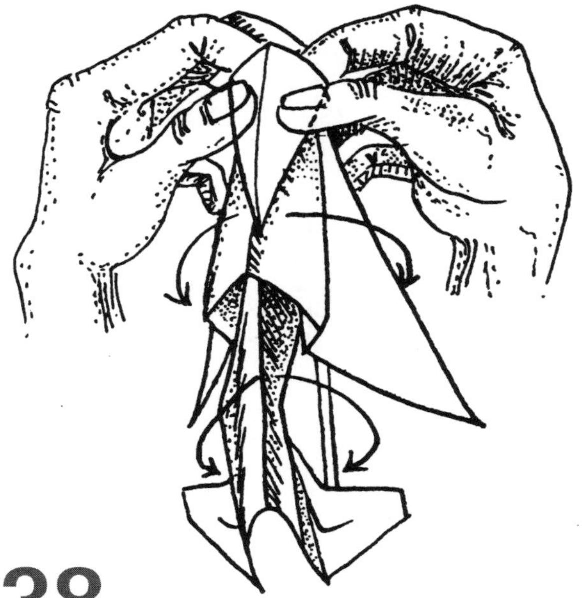

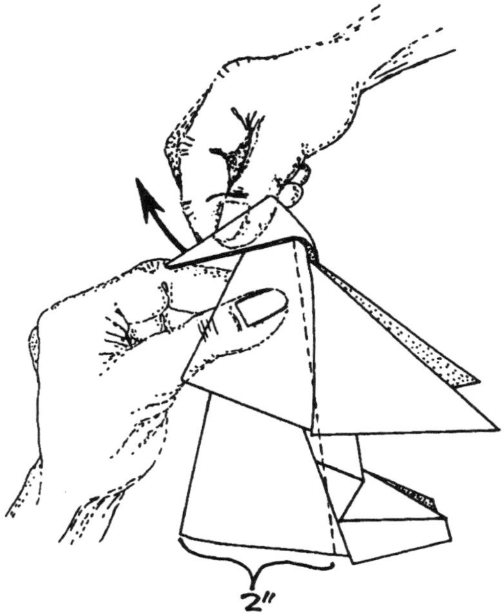


# 38

From the side, your plane should look like this. Now, hold the body with your left hand, and, with the other, pull up the nose. Then, as you did on the Concord (Steps 17–20), lay the plane, upside down, on a flat surface and fold the under fuselage back and forth. Notice the 2-inch depth.

# 39

Continue to grip the plane firmly in your left hand while using the thumb and index finger of your right hand to press hard along the plane's body, as shown here.

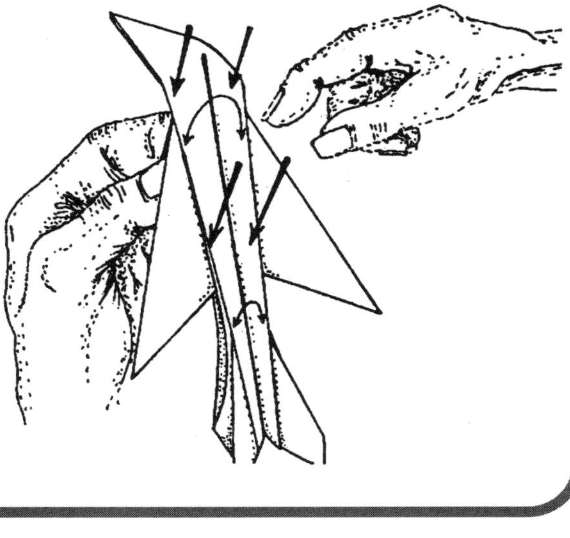

# 40

Move your right hand under the wings.

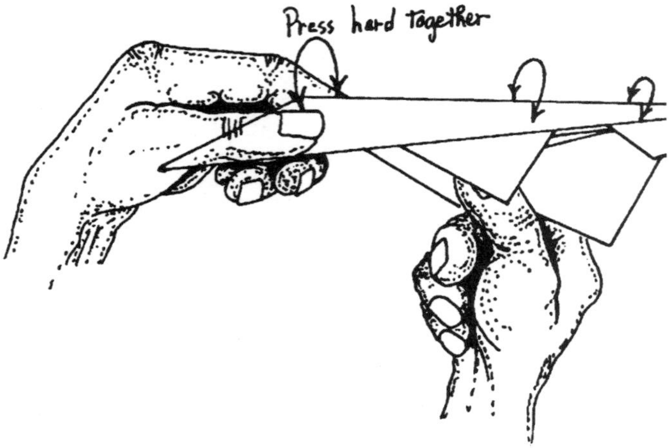


# 41

Carefully apply pressure while sliding your left hand along the back of the plane.

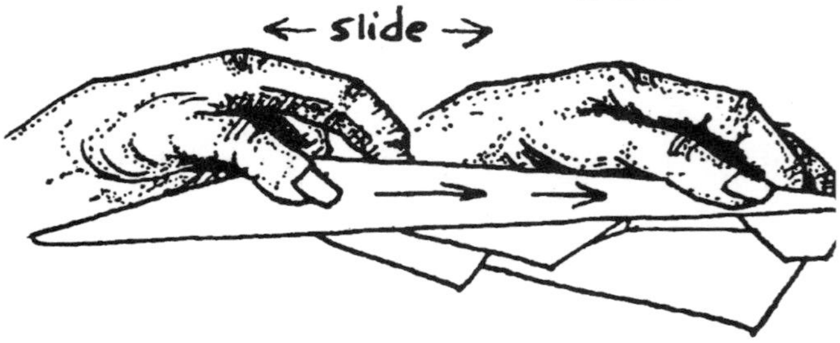


# 42

After you have completed the back, fold up the wings in the front and back as shown.

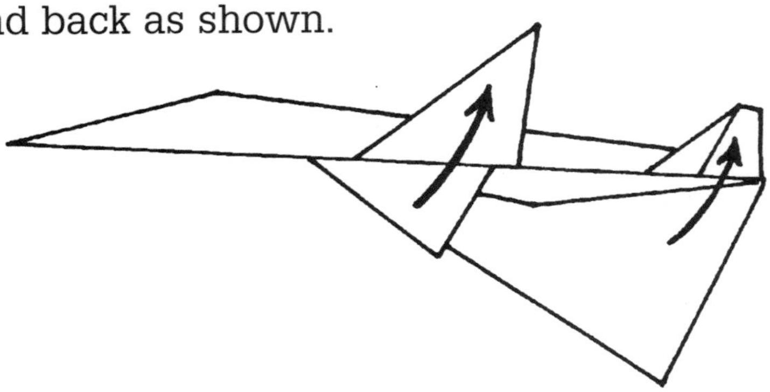

# 43

Fold along the dotted line four times from side to side.

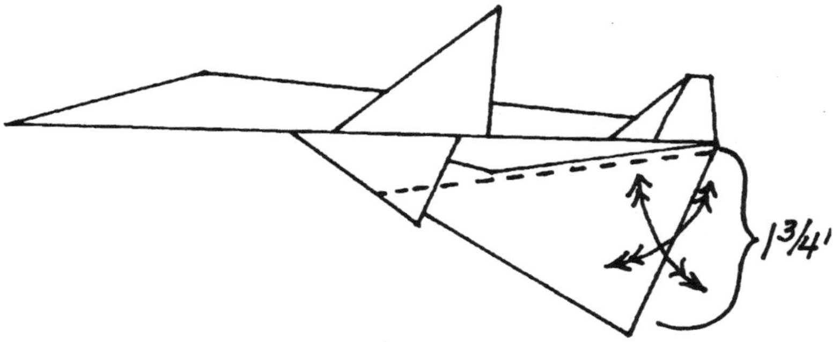


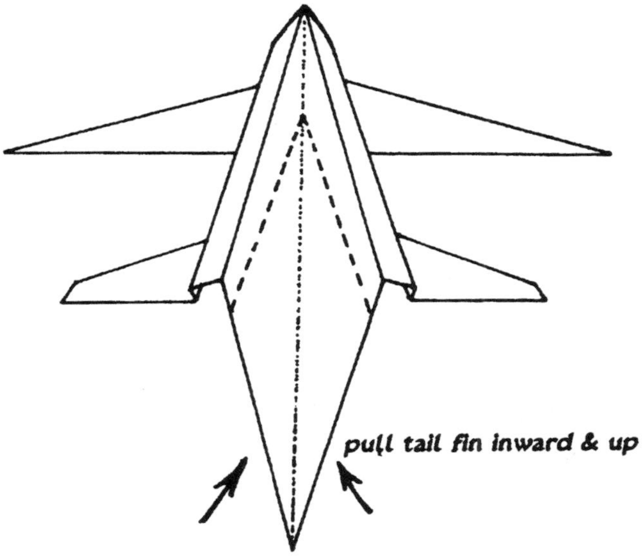


# 44

This is the rear view of the plane. Lift the tail inward & up as indicated by the arrows.

# 45

Your tail fin should come up like this.

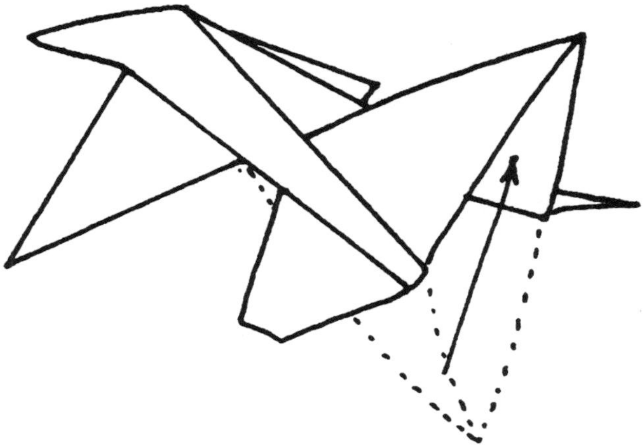

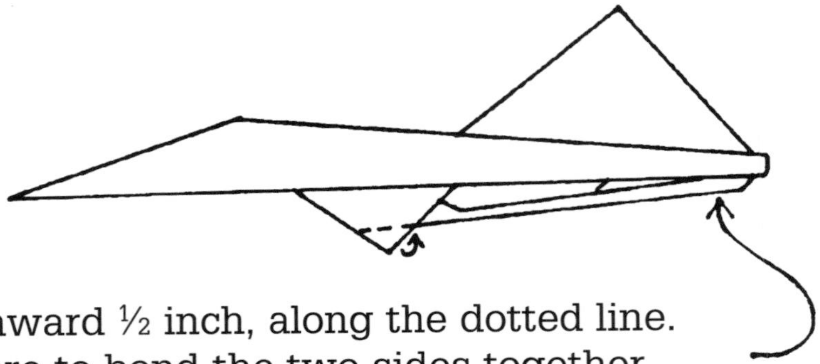

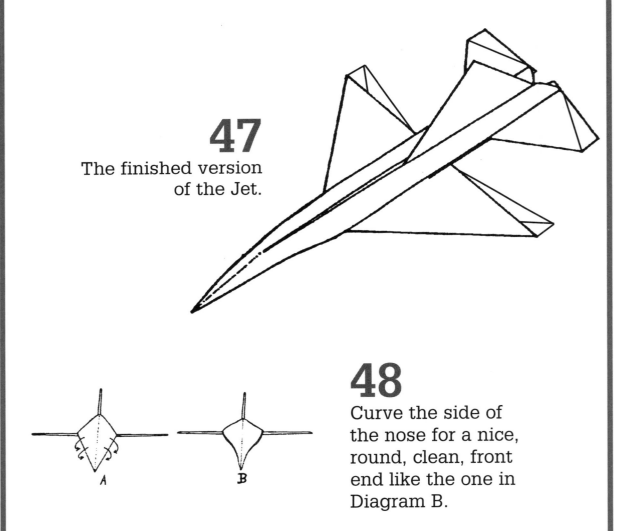

## 46

Fold the belly inward ½ inch, along the dotted line. You can tape here to bond the two sides together. Taping improves flight performance. You can tape all other planes, except the Hornet, in the same place.

## 47

The finished version of the Jet.

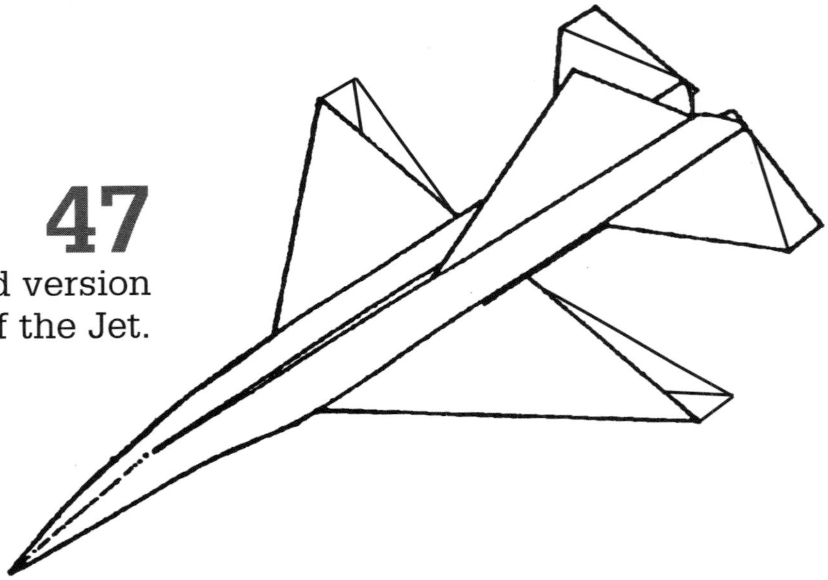

## 48

Curve the side of the nose for a nice, round, clean, front end like the one in Diagram B.

## 49

You are now finished with the MIG. If you want the tail to look more realistic, pull it down the way it was before you raised it, then cut along the dotted lines and push it back up. Make sure that it's even with the body.

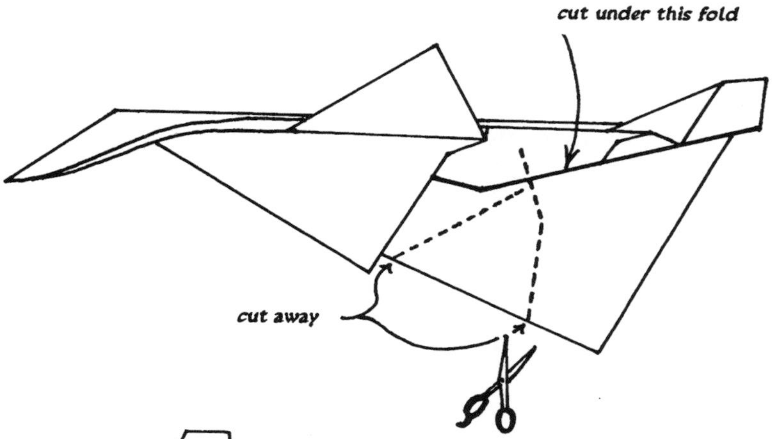


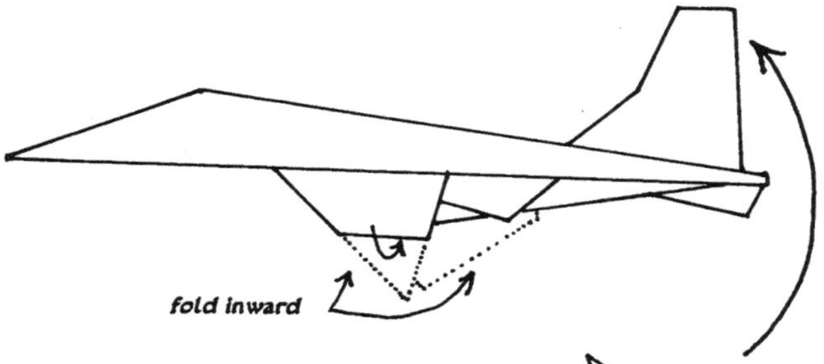

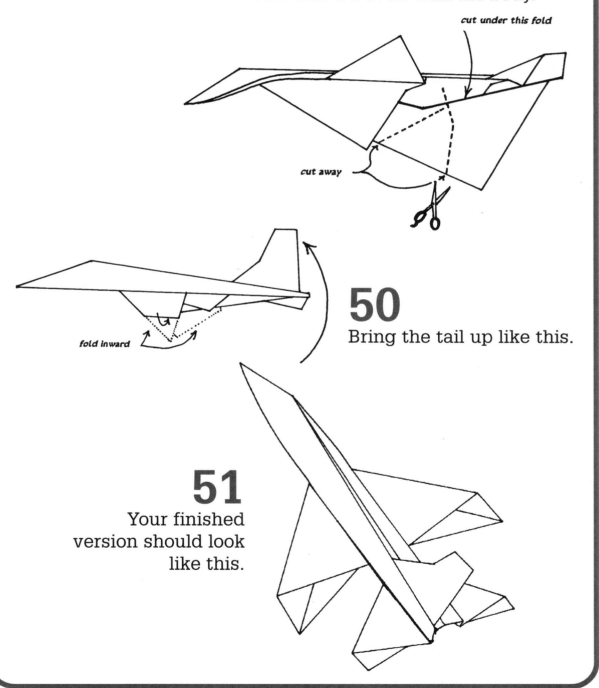

## 50

Bring the tail up like this.

## 51

Your finished version should look like this.

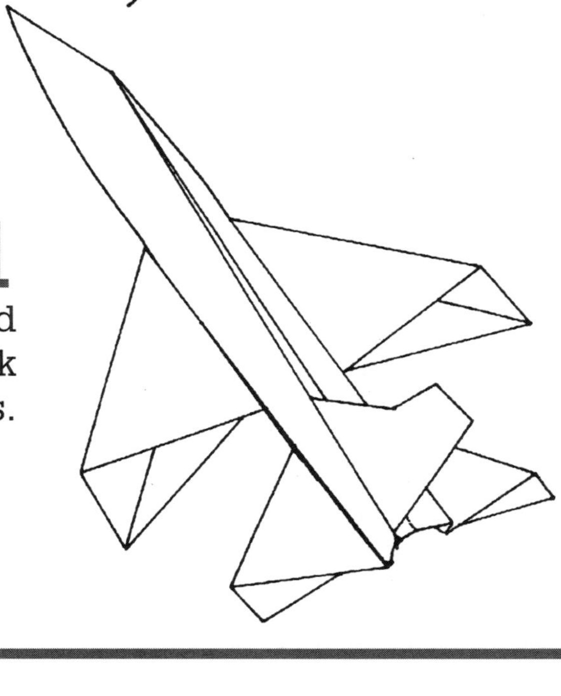

# MIG-27 FLOGGER

# SAAB 37 VIGGE

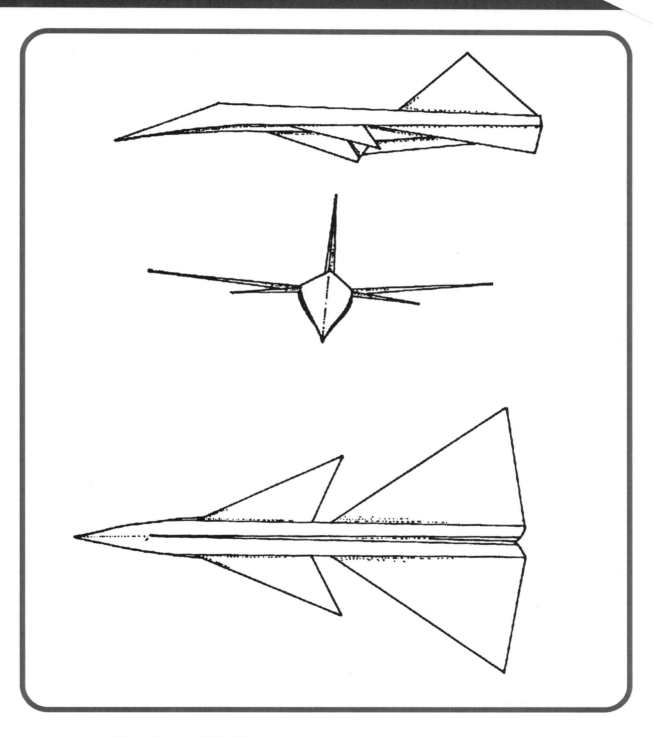

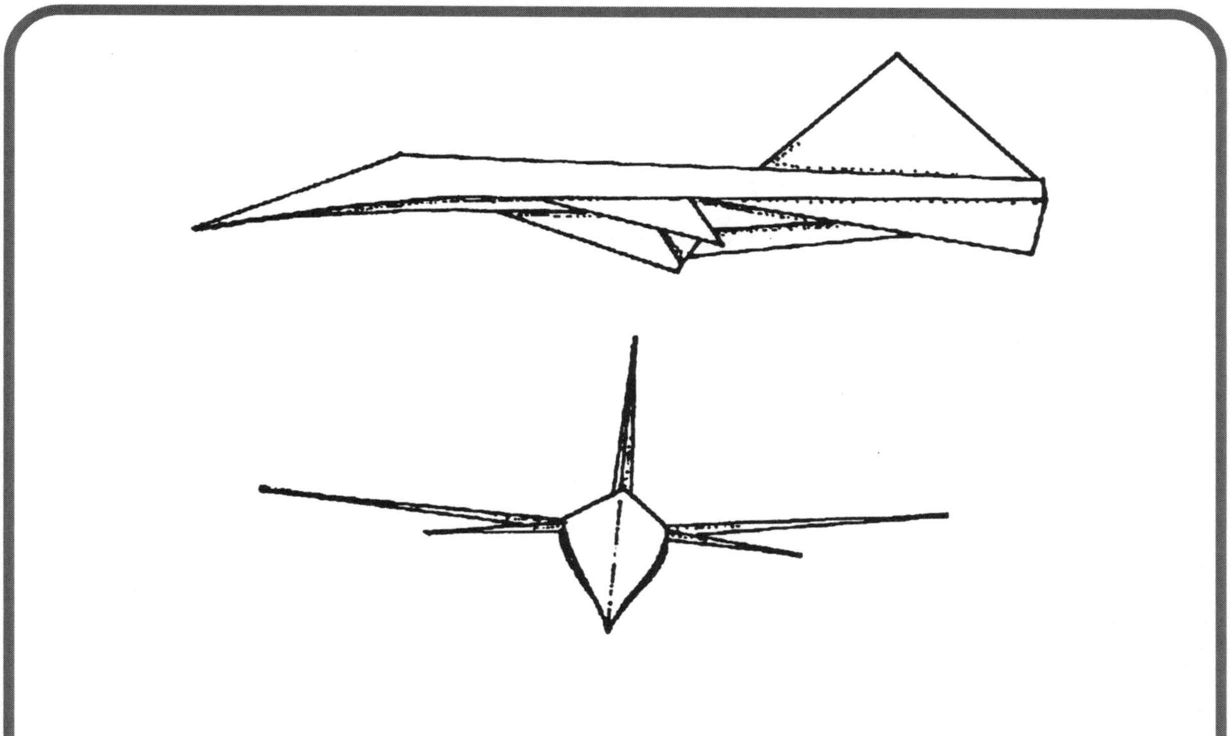

The Saab 37 Viggen also uses many of the folds
that you learned making the Jet.

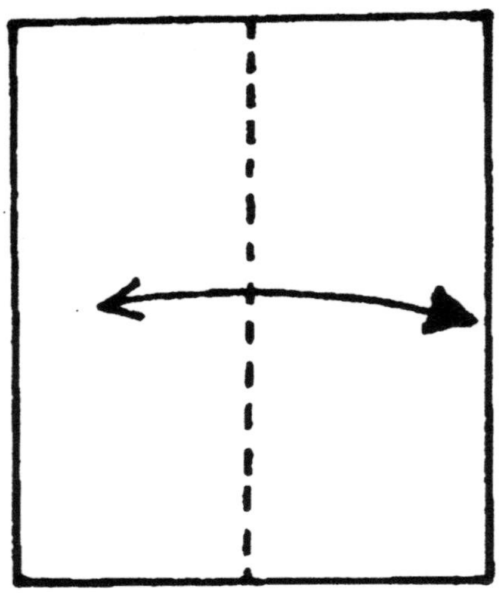

**1**

Fold paper in half, then unfold.

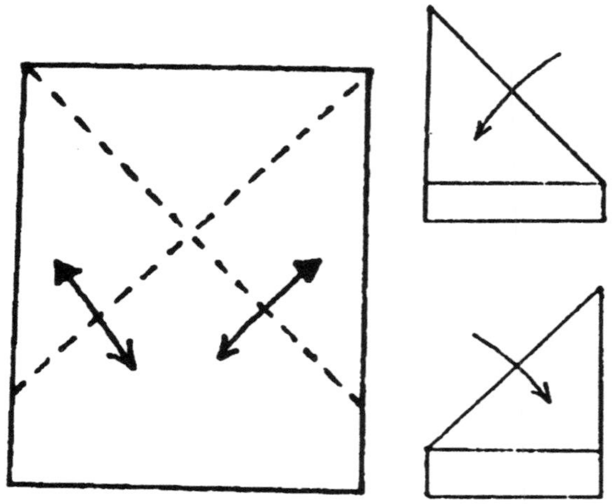

**2**

Fold diagonally at dotted lines, then unfold.

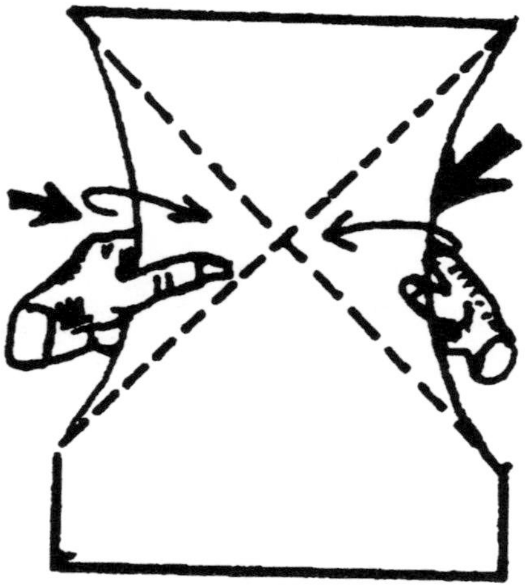

**3**

Now, use both hands and fold the paper up and in toward the middle.

**4**

This is how the paper should look. Gently press down from the top.

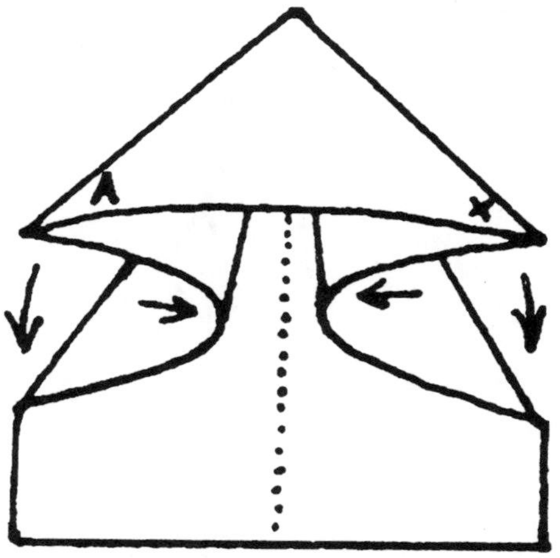


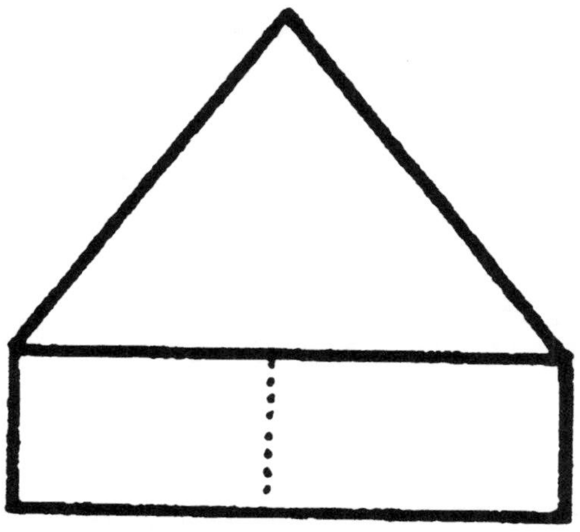

**5**

Now, it should look like this.

**6**

Slide your right hand under Flap X as shown here.

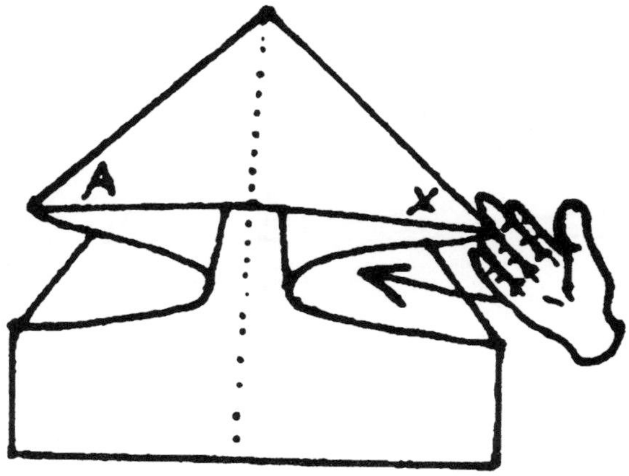

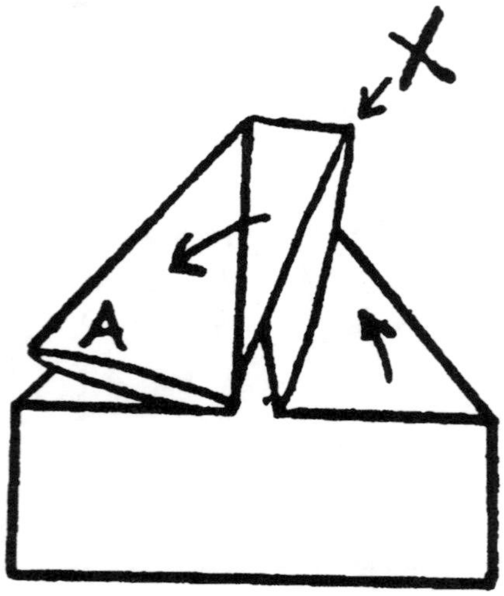


# 7

Flip Flap X over and onto Flap A.

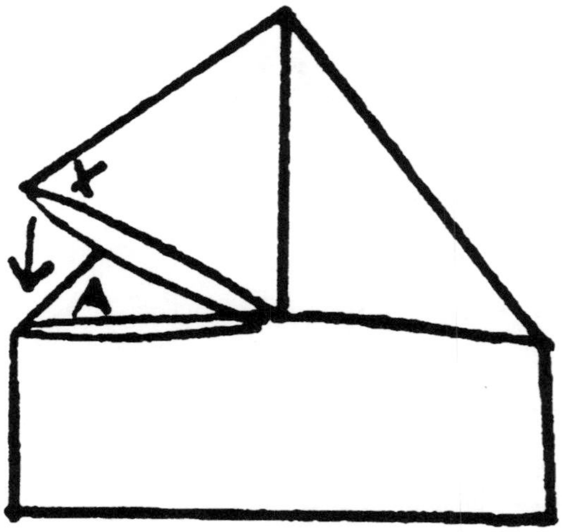


# 8

Flap X should line up evenly with Flap A on the left side.

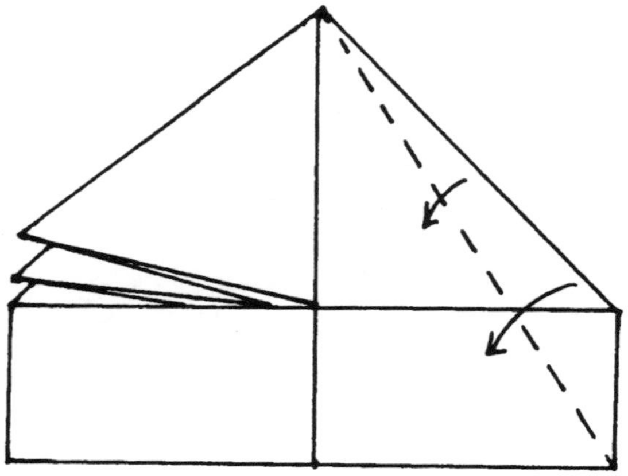

# 9

Your plane should look like this. Make a fold on the dotted line.

## 10

Your fold should look like this.

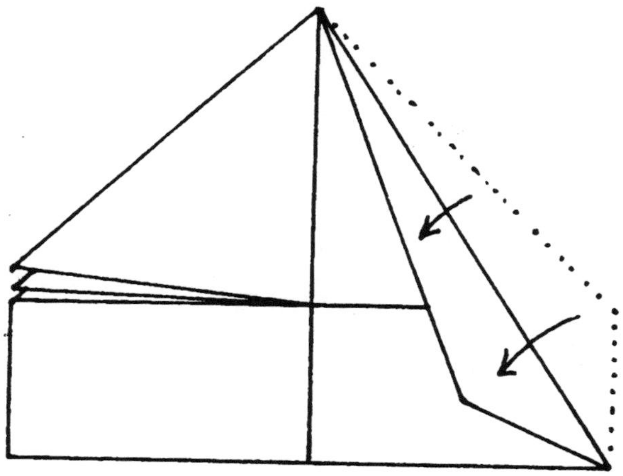

## 11

Make a fold to the center along the dotted line.

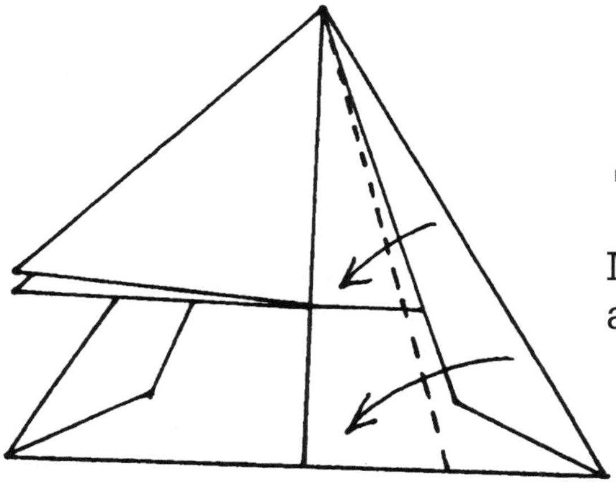

## 12

Make another fold along the dotted line.

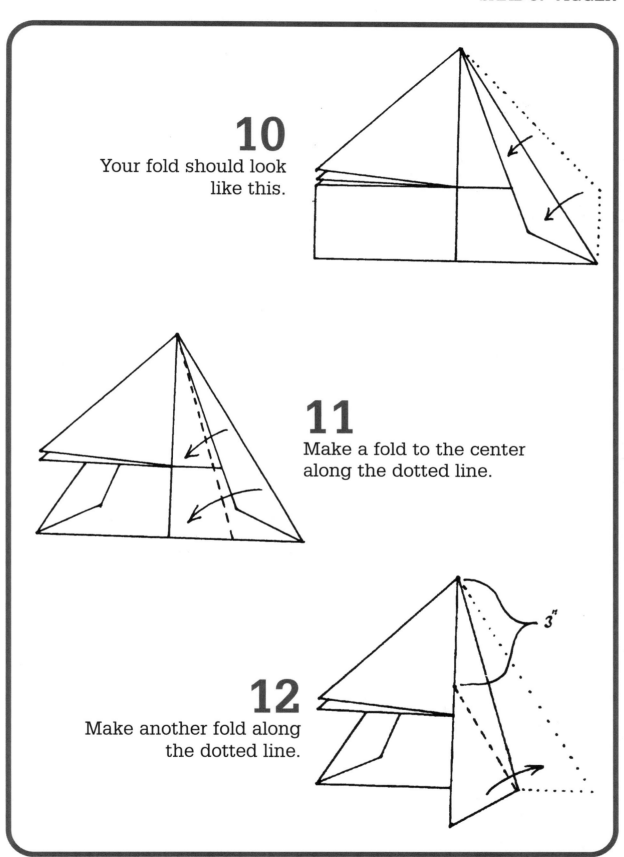

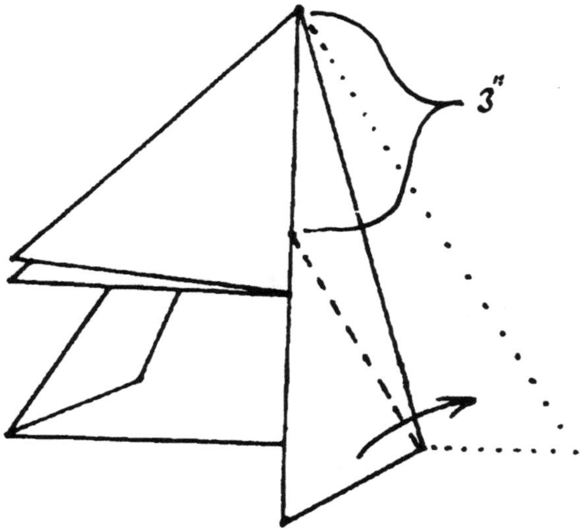

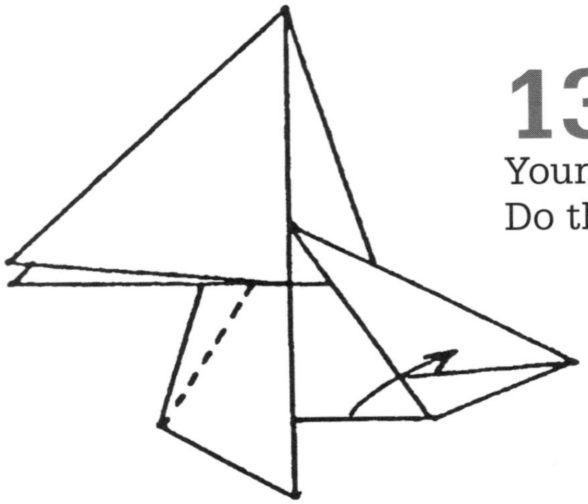

## 13

Your fold out should look like this. Do the same on the left side.

## 14

Fold up along the dotted line to the tip.

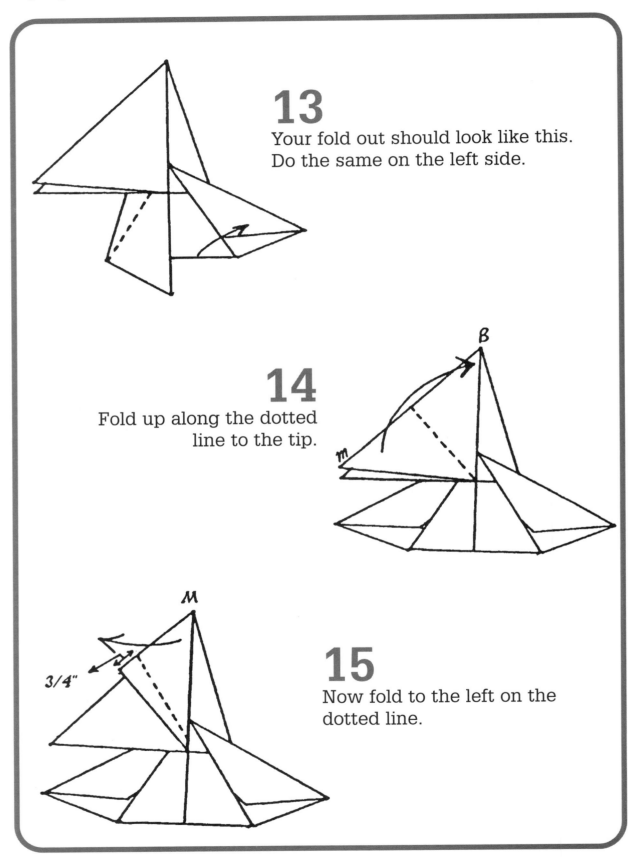

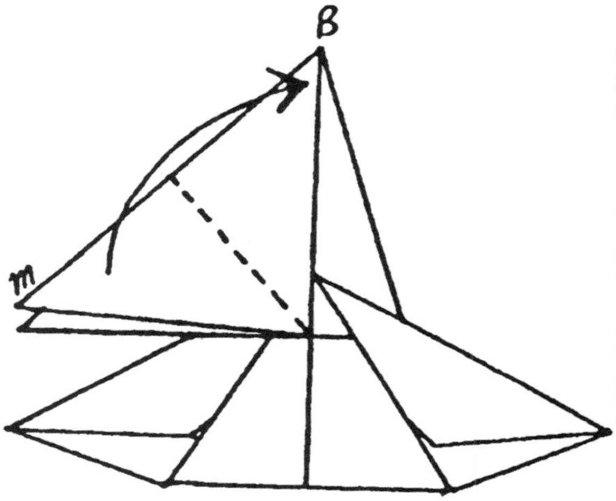


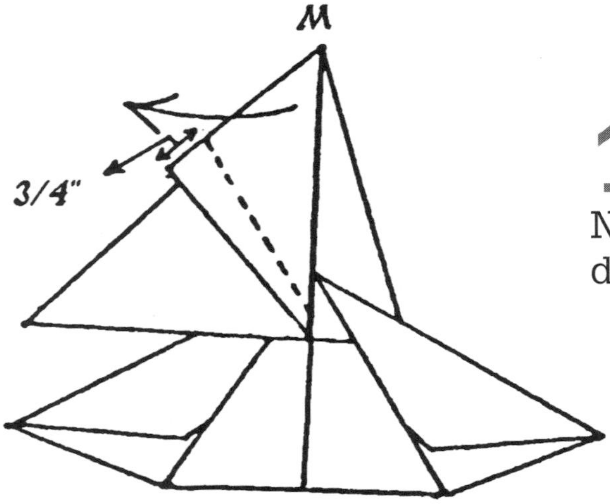


## 15

Now fold to the left on the dotted line.

## 16

Your fold to the left side should look like this. Repeat Steps 14 & 15 to the left side, (Fold Edge A to the right, even with Edge B.)

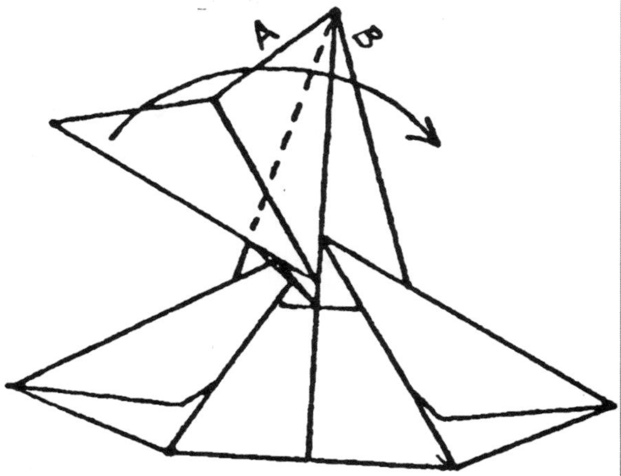


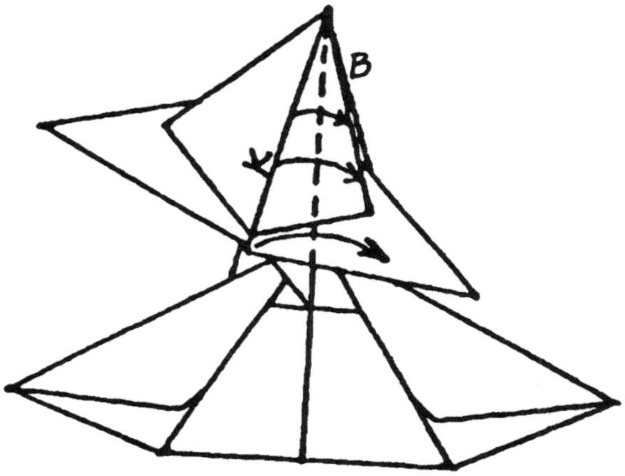


## 17

Your fold to the right should look like this. Now fold Edge K to the right so it's even with Edge B.

## 18

Your completed fold of Edge K should turn out like this.

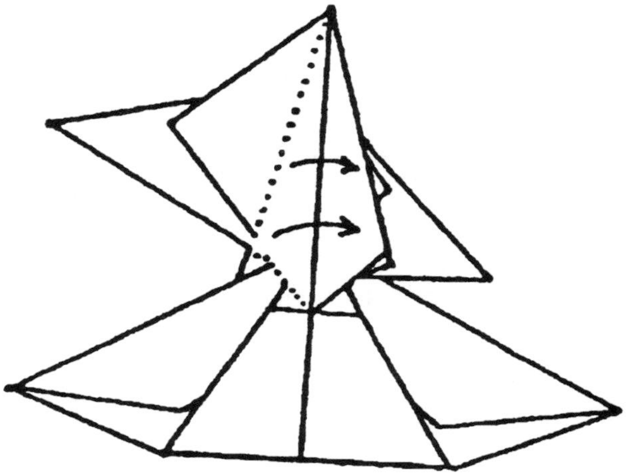

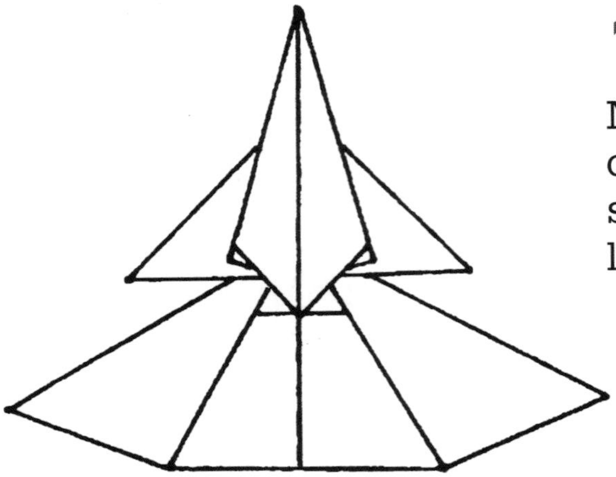

## 19

Now, repeat Steps 16–18 on the left side, and then separate the sides. It should look like this.

## 20

Measure about 1¼ inches from the end of the nose. Fold down the nose along the dotted line.

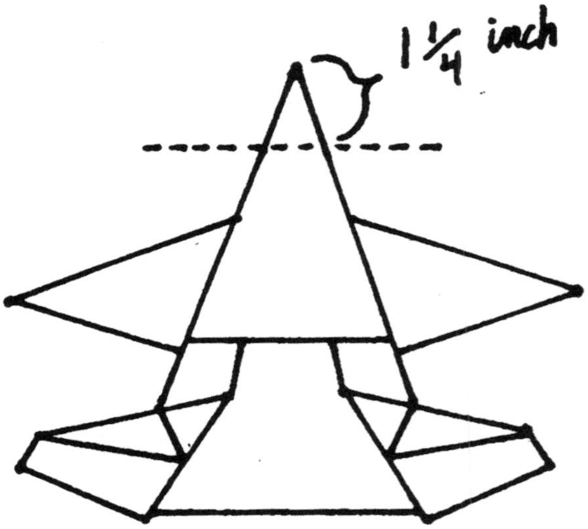


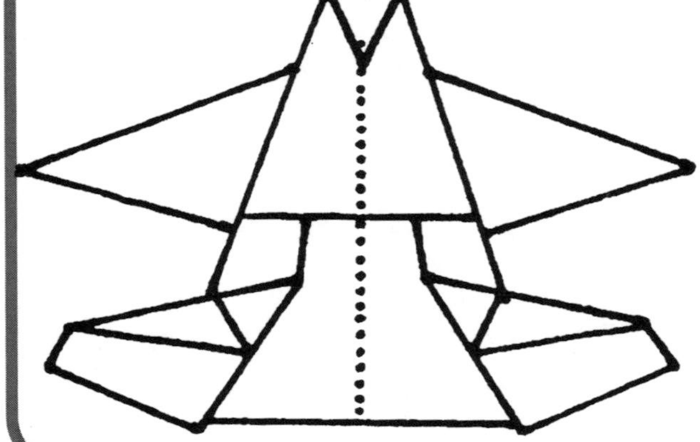

## 21

Your fold should look like this.

## 22

After folding down the nose, fold both sides of the plane's body toward the back as shown.

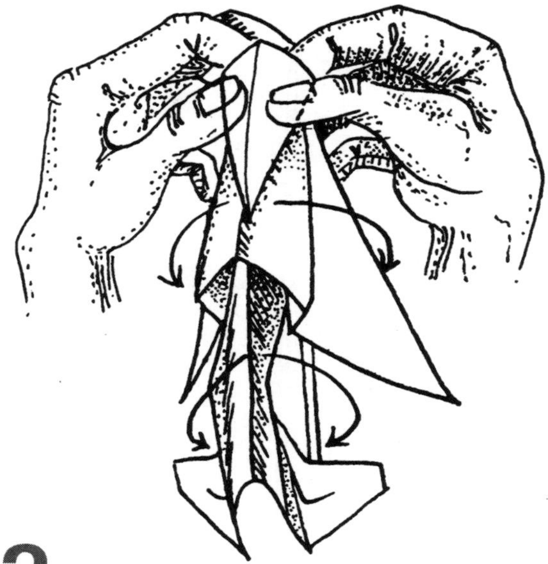

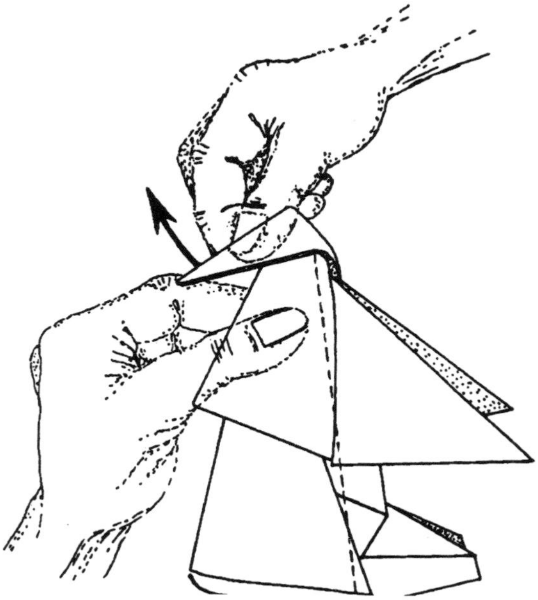

## 23

From the side, your plane should look like this. Now, hold the body with your left hand, and, with the other, pull up the nose. Then, as you did on the Concord (Steps 17–20), lay the plane, upside down, on a flat surface and fold the under fuselage back and forth. Notice the 2-inch depth.

## 24

Continue to grip the plane firmly in your left hand while using the thumb and index finger of your right hand to press hard along the plane's body, as shown here.

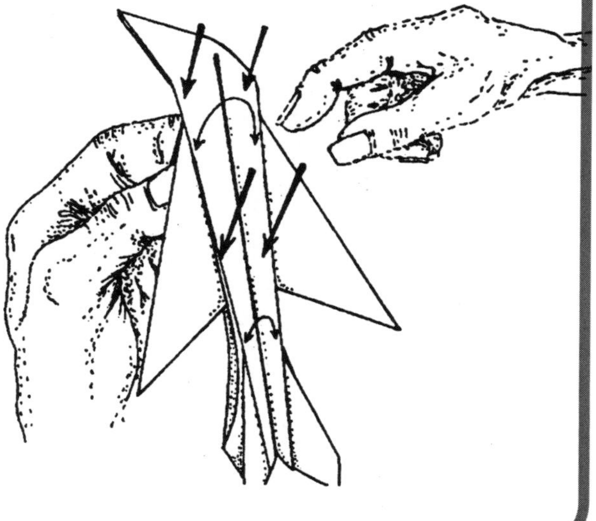

# 25

Move your right hand under the wings.

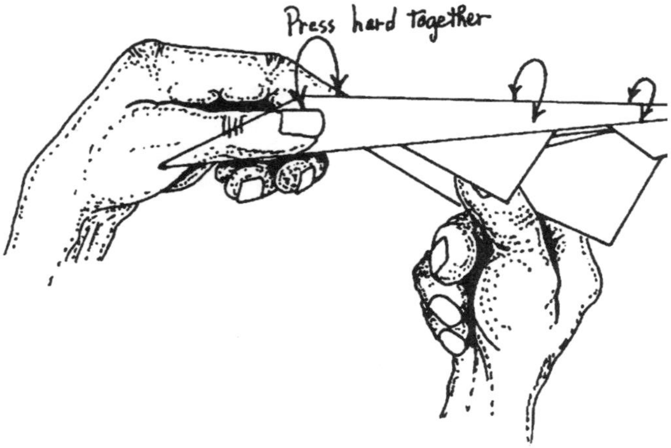


# 26

Carefully apply pressure while sliding your left hand along the back of the plane.

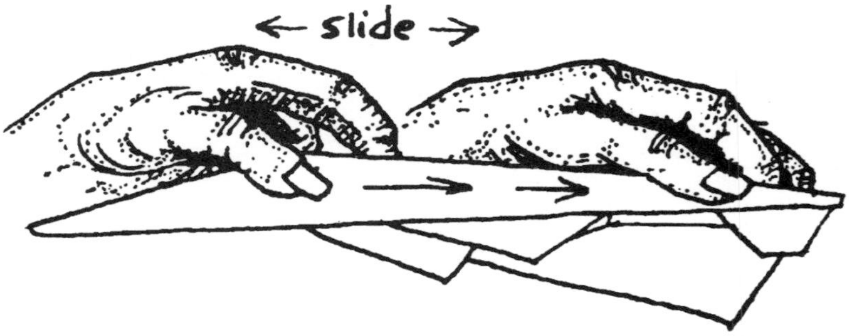


# 27

After you have completed the back, fold up the wings in the front and back as shown.

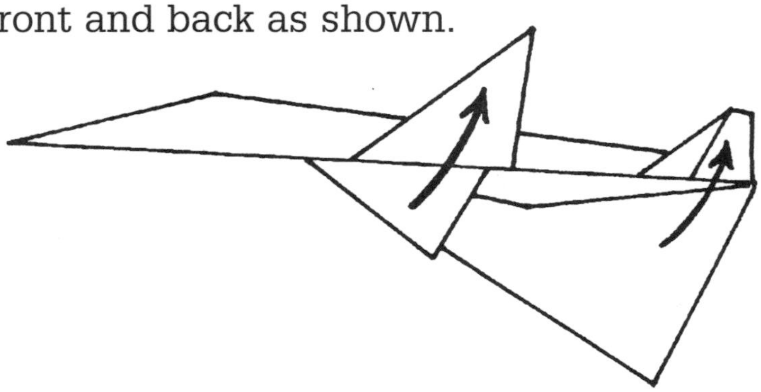

## 28

Fold along the dotted line four times from side to side.

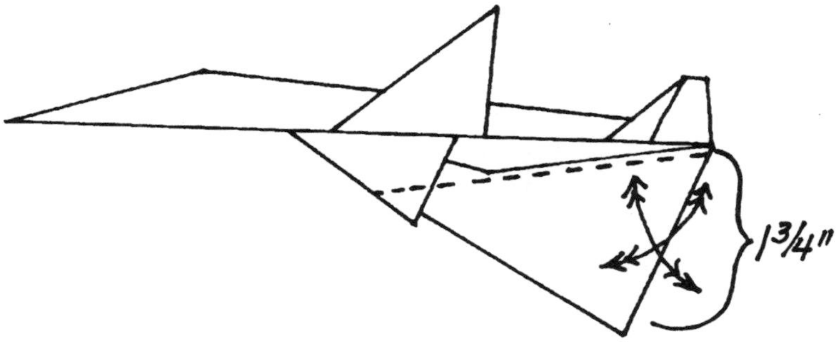


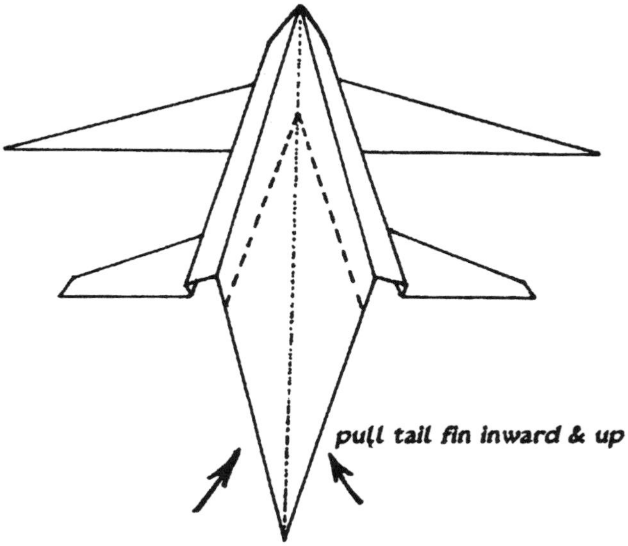


## 29

This is the rear view of the plane. Lift the tail inward & up as indicated by the arrows.

## 30

Your tail fin should come up like this.

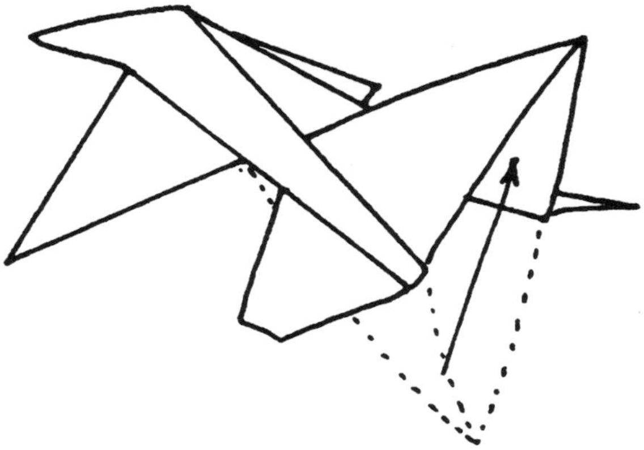

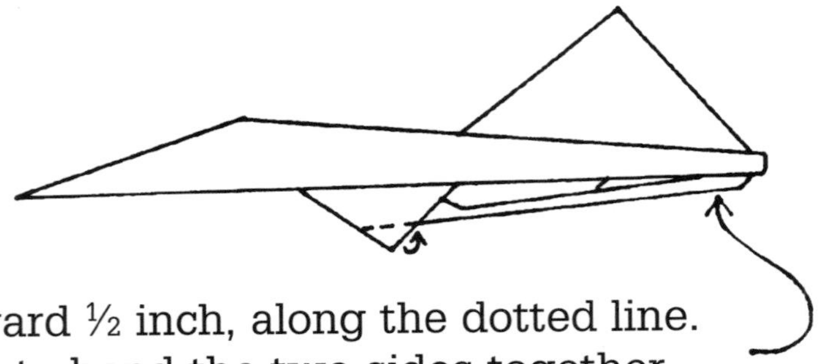

**31**

Fold the belly inward ½ inch, along the dotted line. You can tape here to bond the two sides together. Taping improves flight performance. You can tape all other planes, except the Hornet, in the same place.

**32**

The Viggen should now look like this.

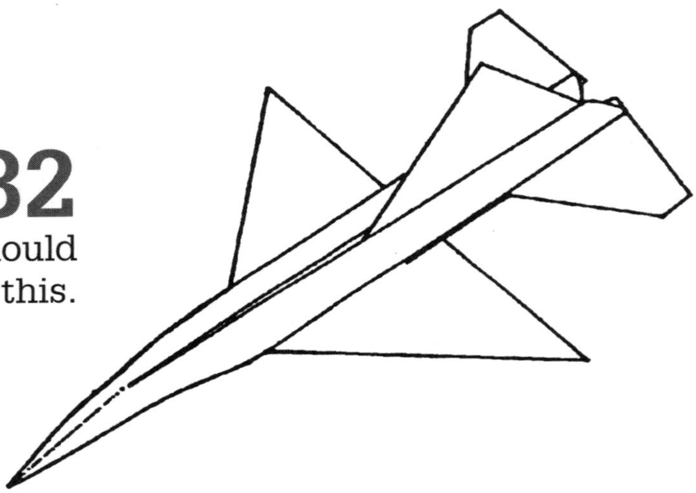

**33**

Curve the side of the nose for a nice, round, clean, front end like the one in Diagram B.

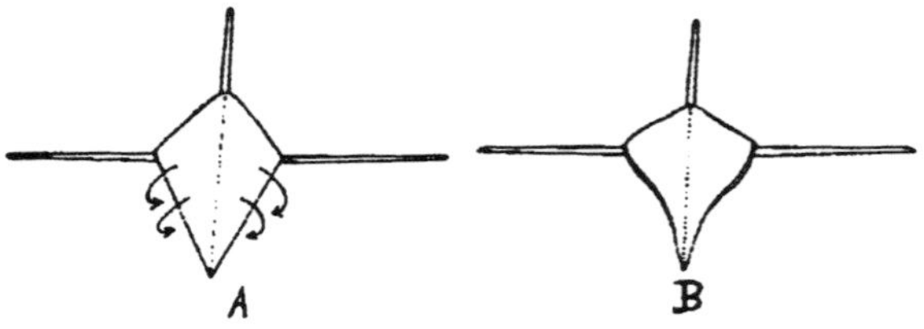

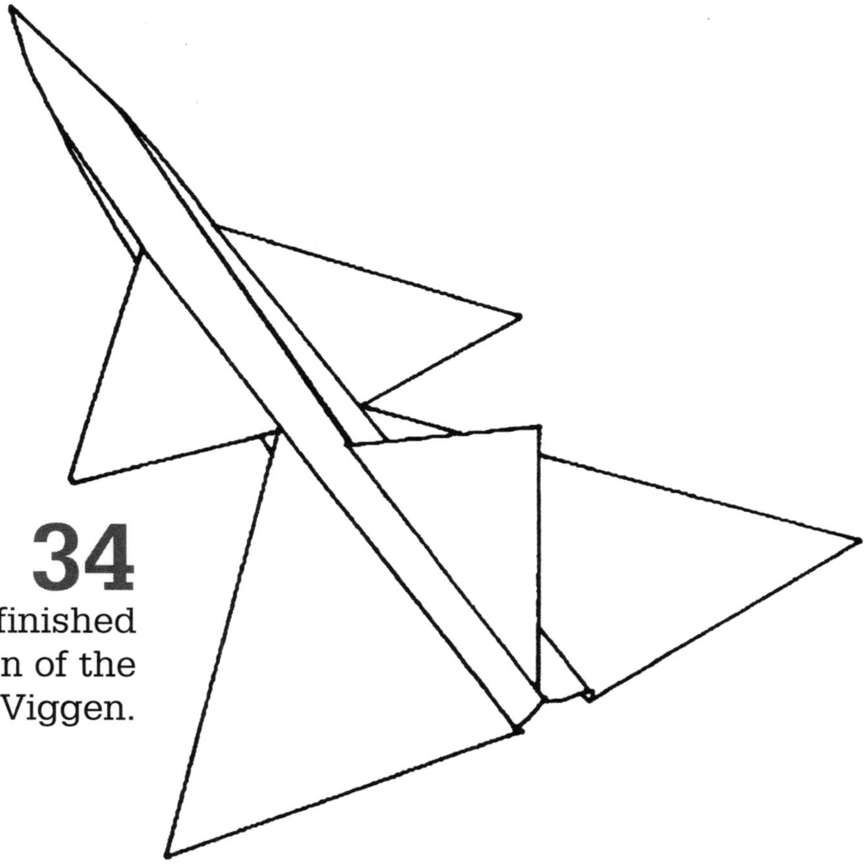

**34**
The finished version of the Viggen.

# SAAB 37 VIGGEN

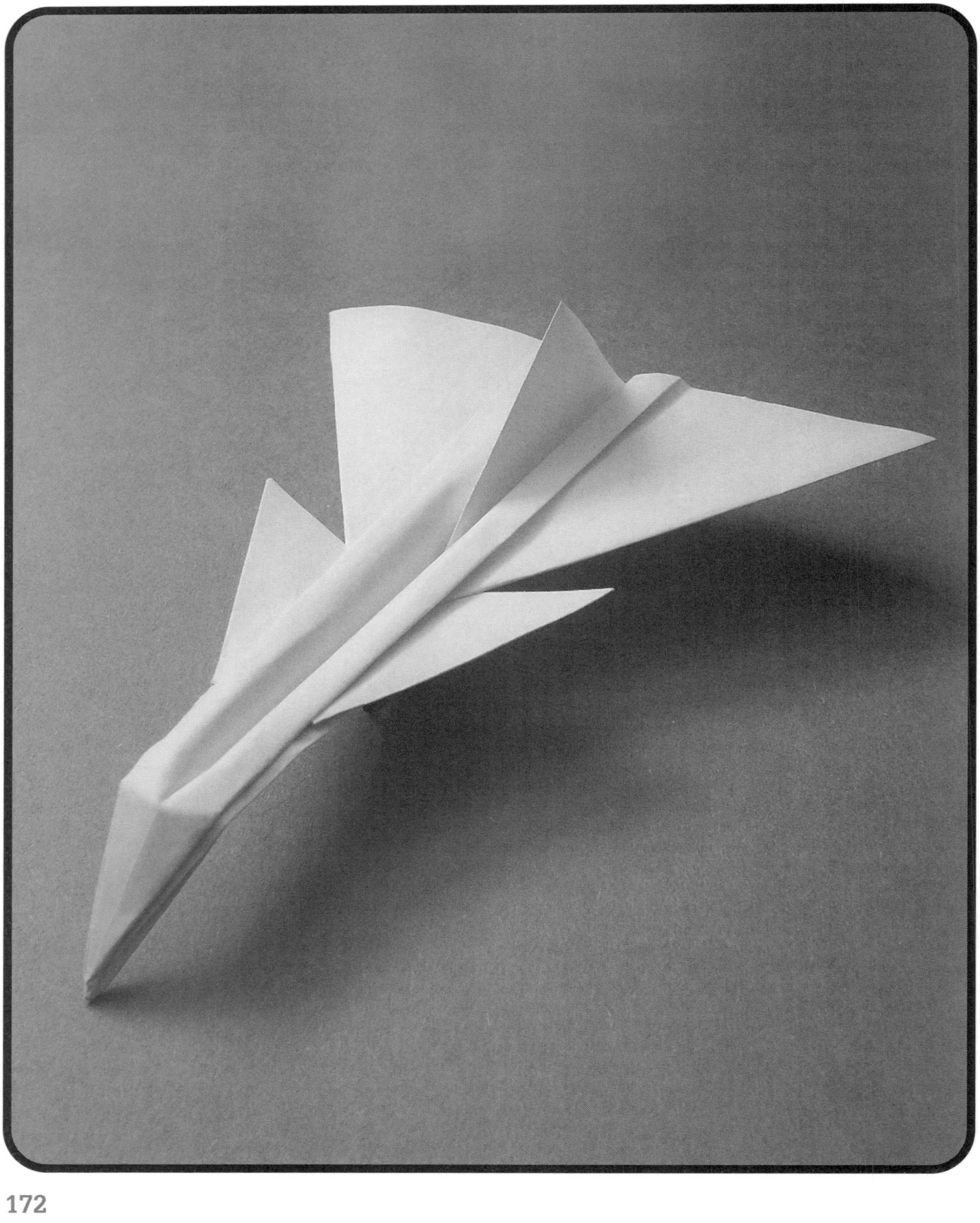

# F-18 HORNET

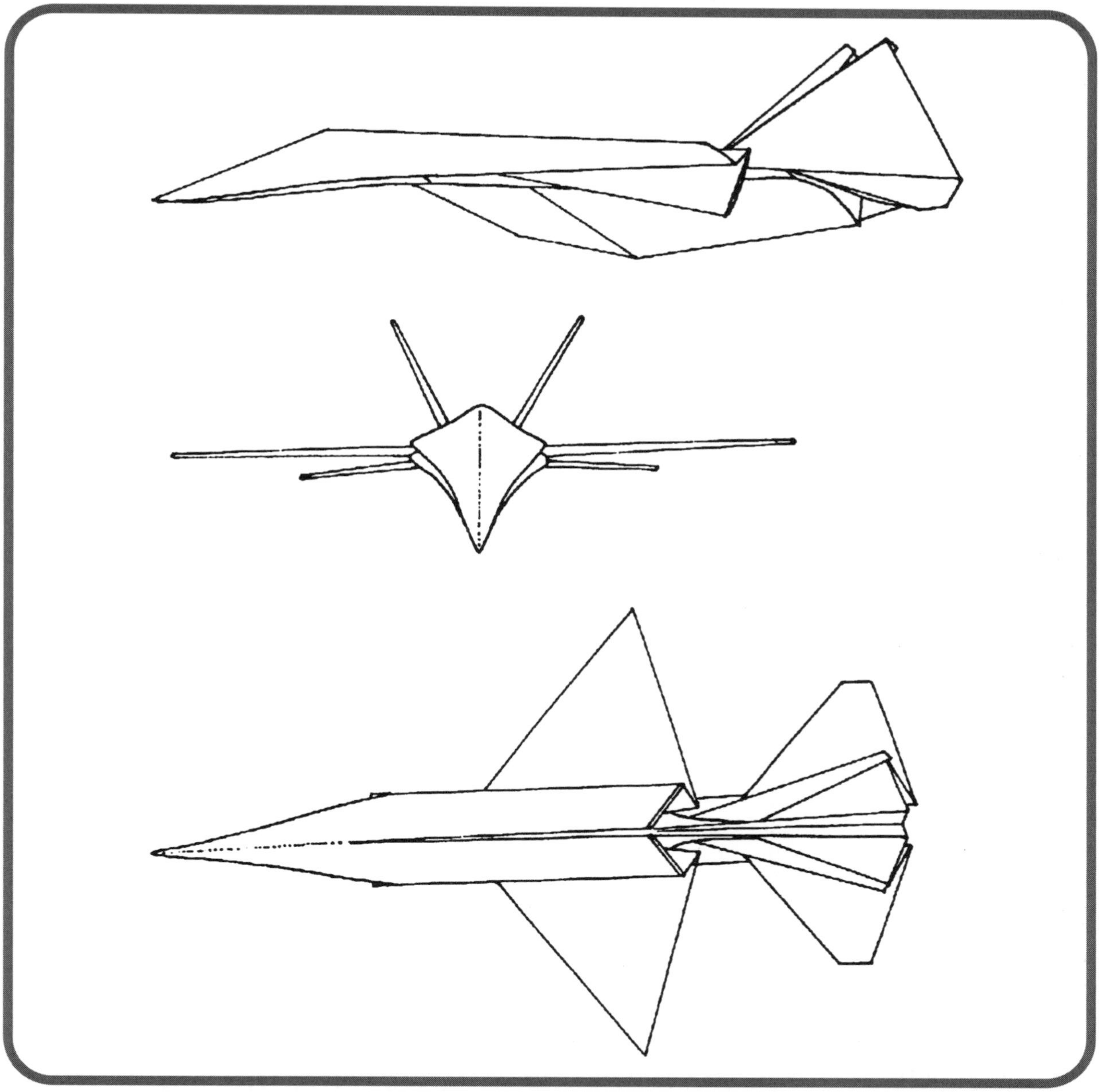

This is the U.S. F-18 Hornet, a unique fighter. The Hornet cannot be folded until you have mastered the Jet and the planes that follow. Like the real Hornet on which this plane is modeled, it will fly straight and fast. It's a tough plane, so be patient. You can ensure a compact and sturdy shape by making sure the folds are tight and accurate.

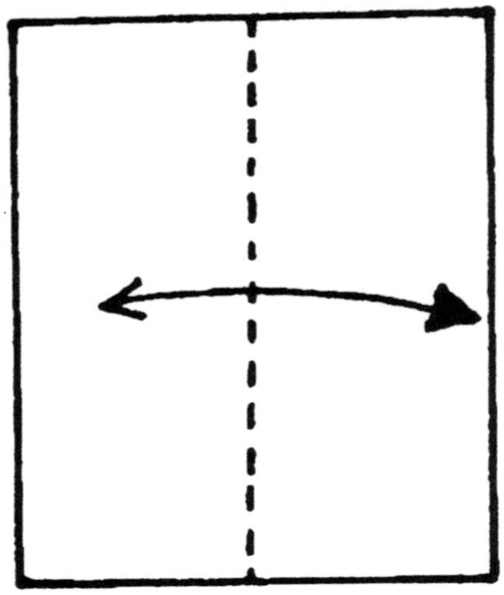

1

Fold paper in half, then unfold.

2

Fold diagonally at dotted lines, then unfold.

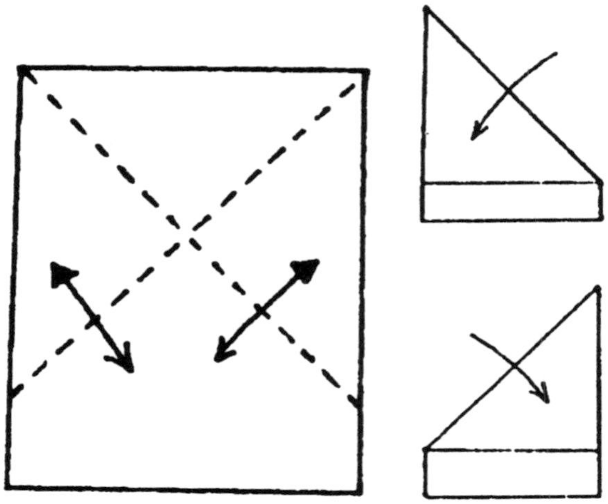

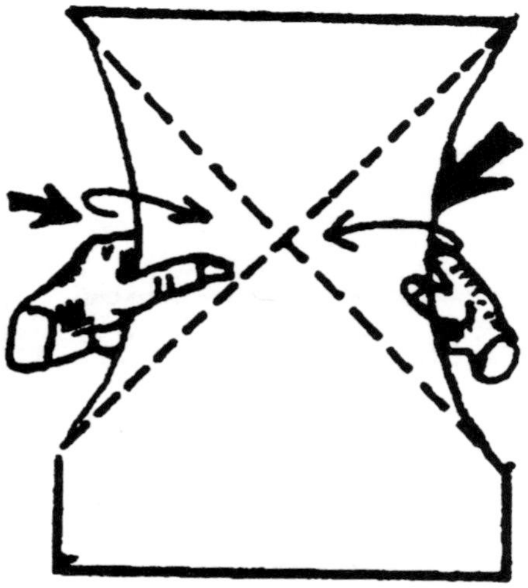

3

Now, use both hands and fold the paper up and in toward the middle.

## 4

This is how the paper should look. Gently press down from the top.

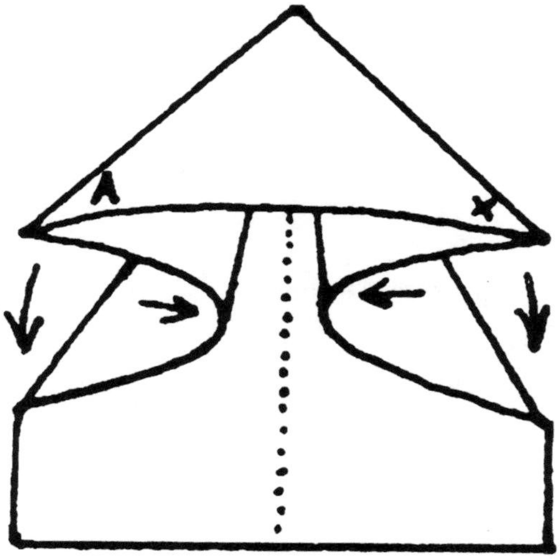


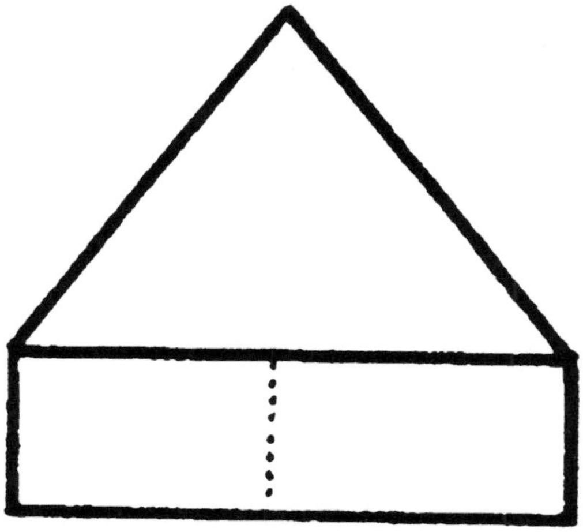

## 5

Now, it should look like this.

## 6

Slide your right hand under Flap X as shown here.

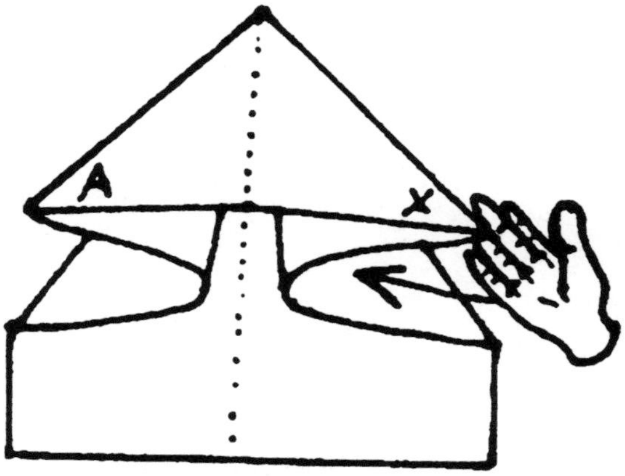

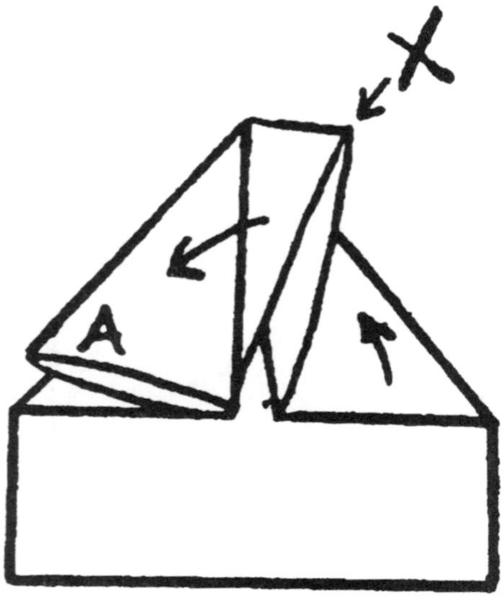


# 7

Flip Flap X over and onto Flap A.

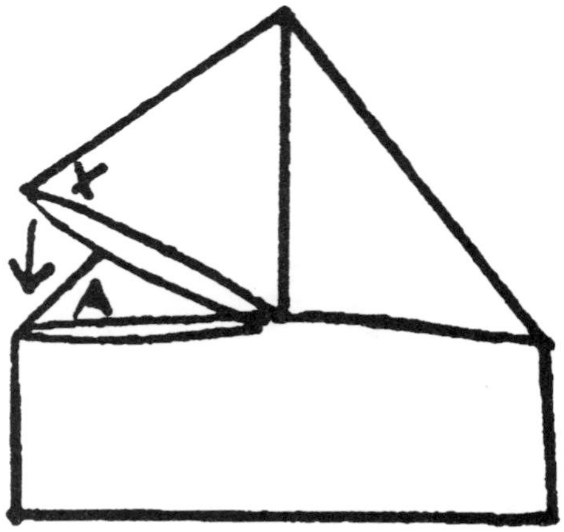


# 8

Flap X should line up evenly with Flap A on the left side.

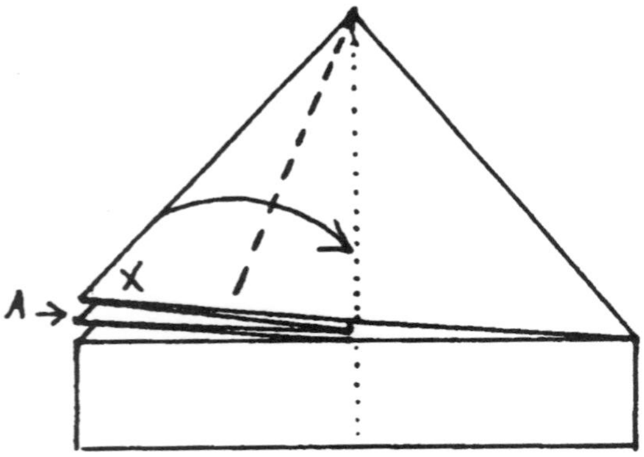


# 9

Now, fold Flap X on the dotted line toward the centerline.

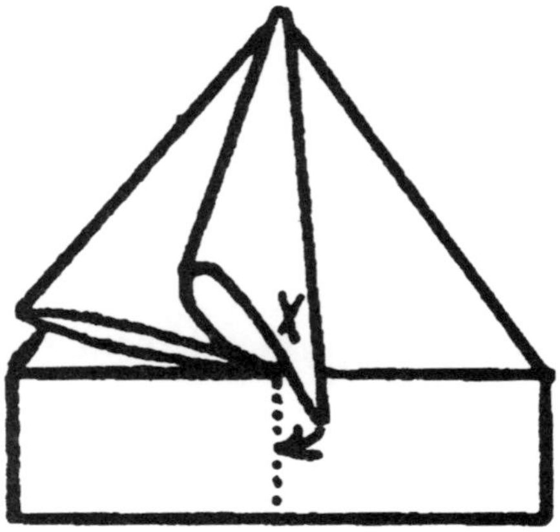


# 10

This is how your fold should look.

# 11

After you have folded Flap X toward the middle flap, flip it to the right side. Notice the B edge.

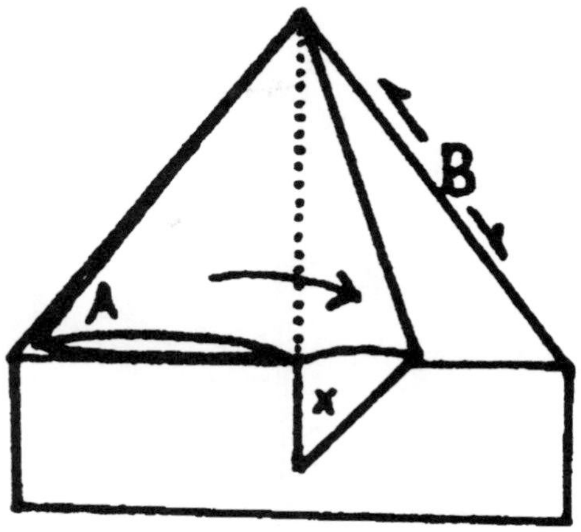


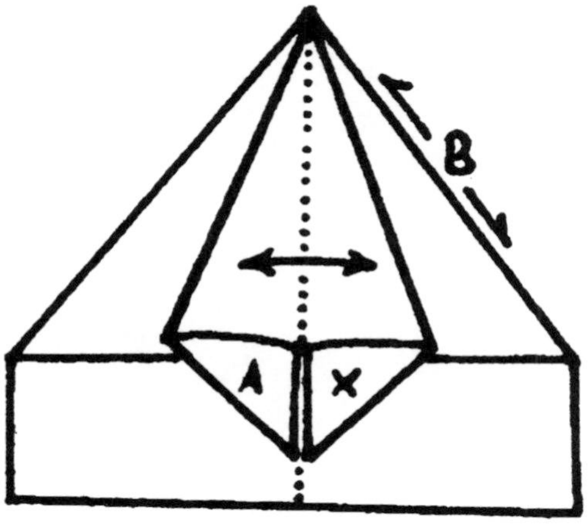


# 12

Now, repeat Steps 9–11 for the left side, and open the flaps to look like this.

# 13

Now, flip Flap X to the left, over Flap A again.

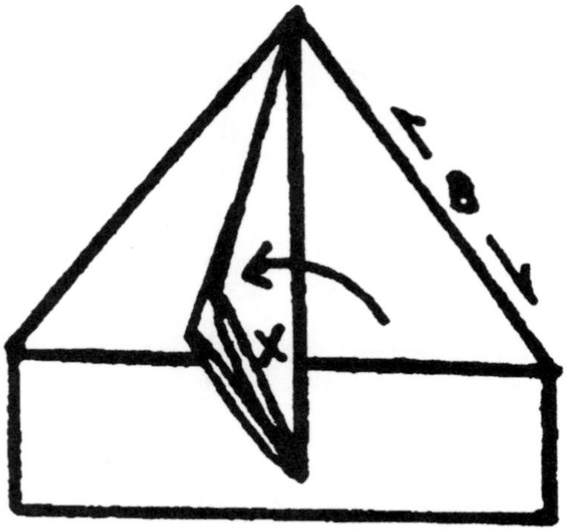


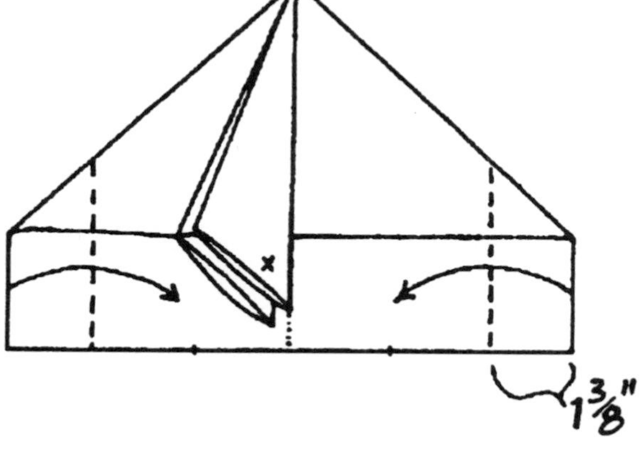


# 14

Measure about 1⅜ inches in at each side; fold toward the middle as indicated by the arrows.

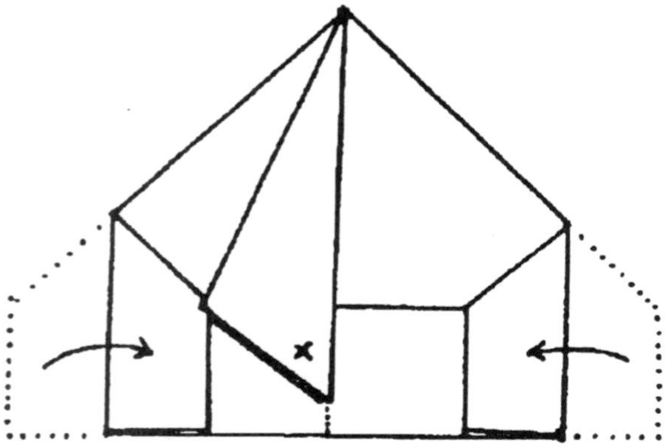

## 15

Your folds should look like this.

NOTE: Back sides are Wings A & X.

## 16

Turn the model over. Fold each side in toward the middle.

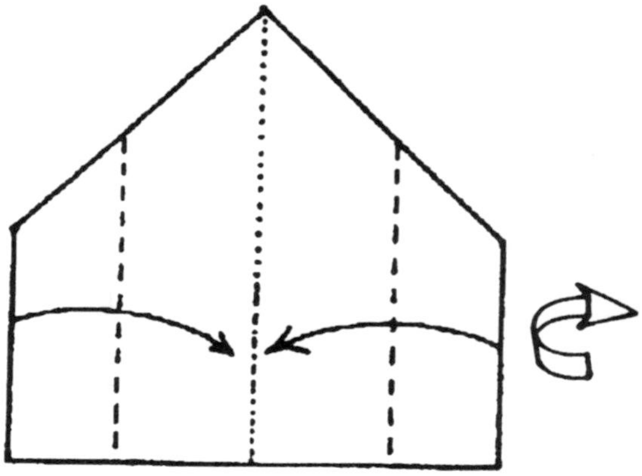

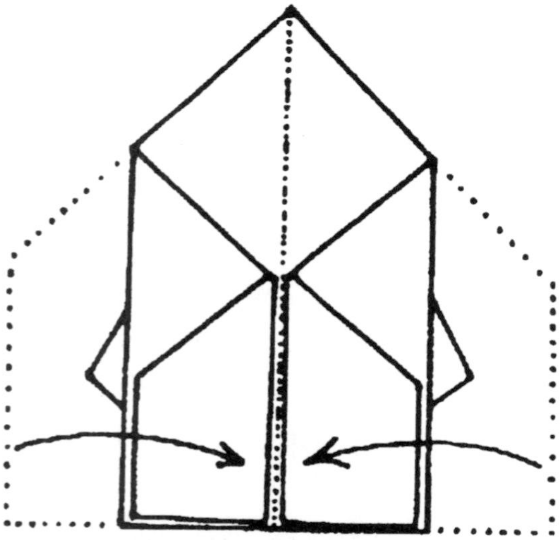

## 17

Your plane should look like this.

## 18

Turn the model over and flip the wings (A & X) onto the left side; fold Edge M toward the center.

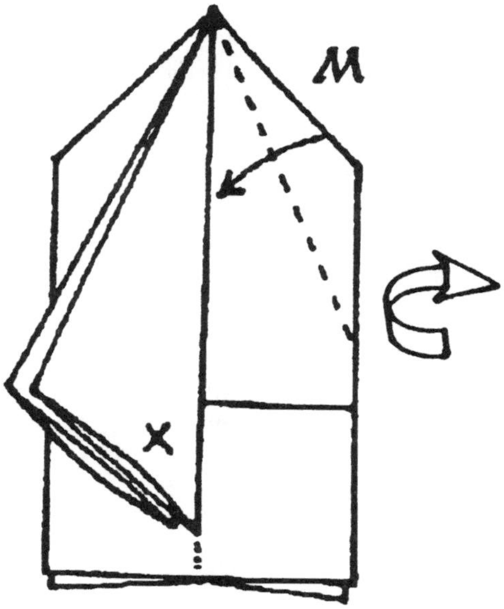


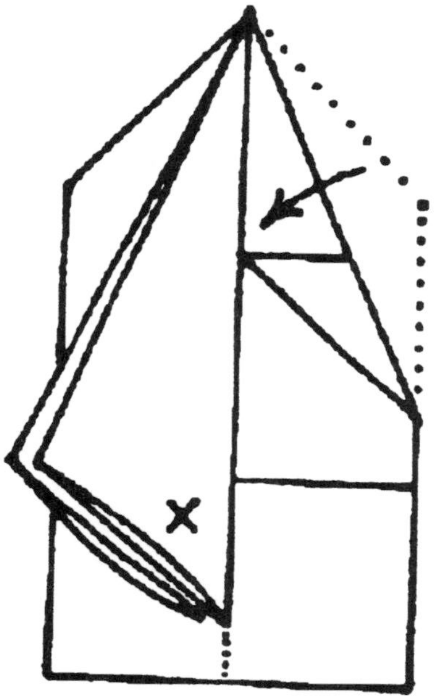


## 19

It should look like this. Do the same on the left side.

## 20

This is what you should have after completing Steps 18 & 19 and separating the two wings.

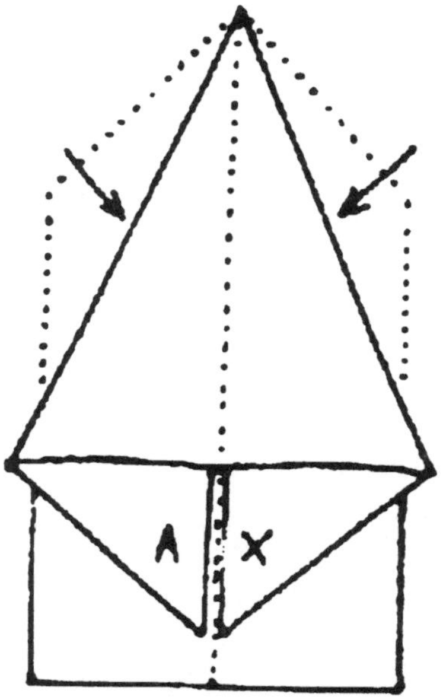

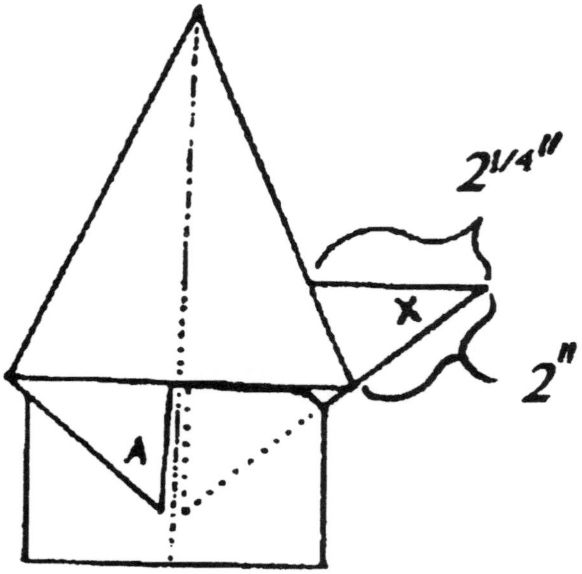


## 21

Pull the wings out (using the technique learned on earlier planes). Do the same to the left side.

## 22

Now your plane should look like this.

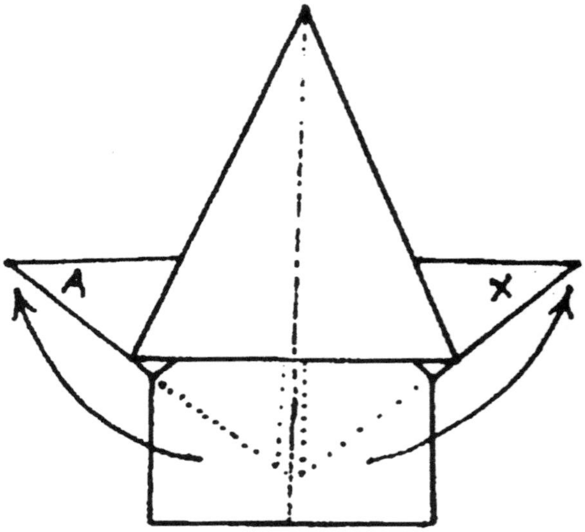


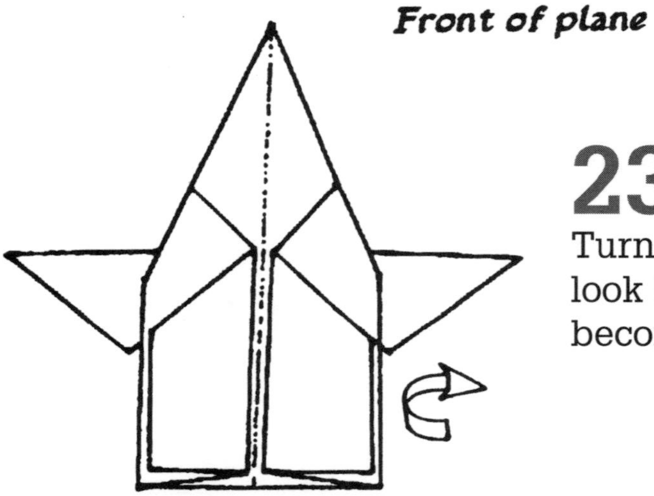


## 23

Turn the plane over; it will look like this. (The back now becomes the front.)

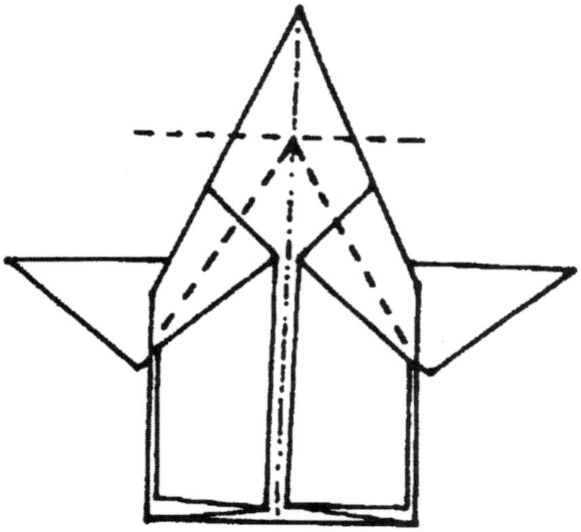

## 24

Fold the nose down and both sides of the body together. (You should remember how from previous planes.)

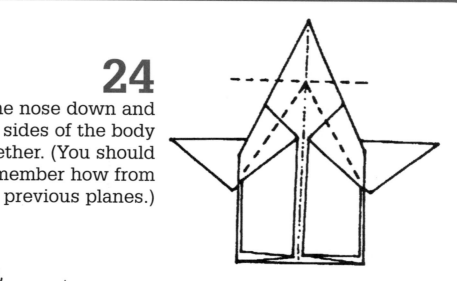

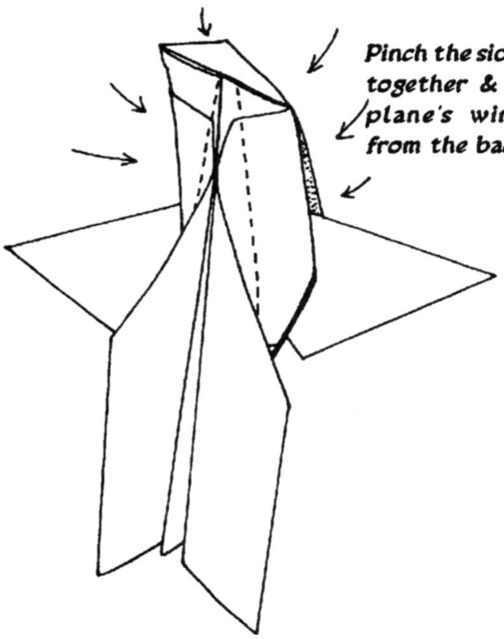

Pinch the sides tightly together & push the plane's wings open from the back.


## 25

Your plane should look like this.

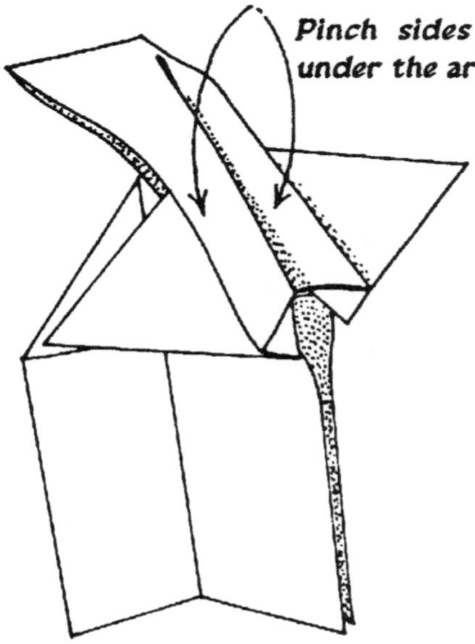

Pinch sides together under the arrows


## 26

Your plane should look like this.

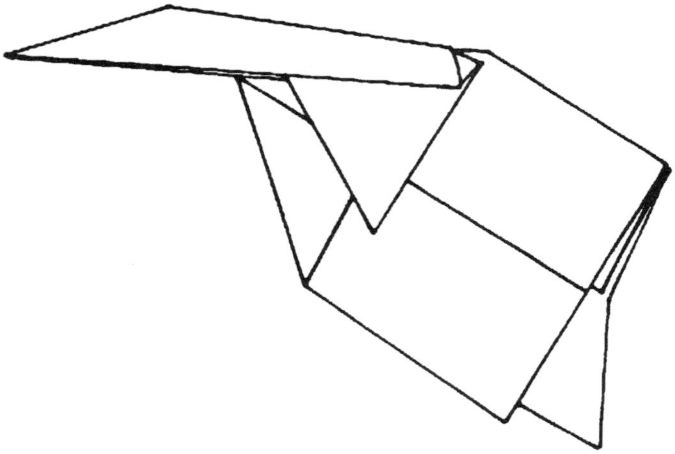

**27**
Side view.

**28**
Tail (back view). Push up, as you've done with the tail fins of previous planes.

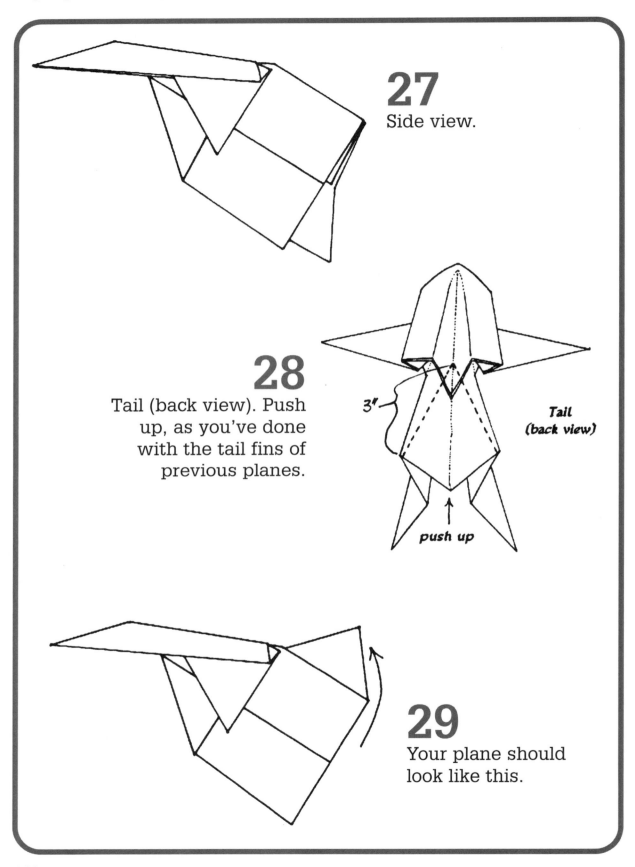

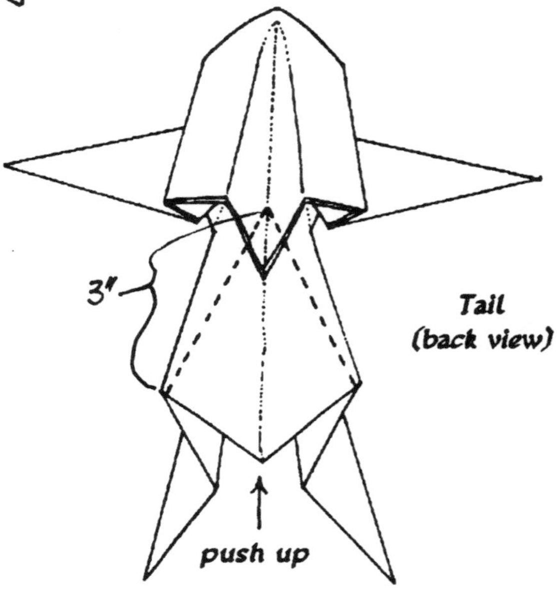


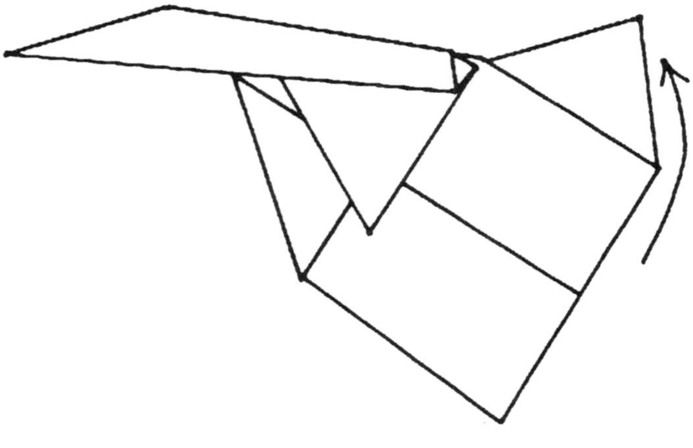

**29**
Your plane should look like this.

## 30

Now, open up the wings and fold as indicated. Do one side first, then the other.

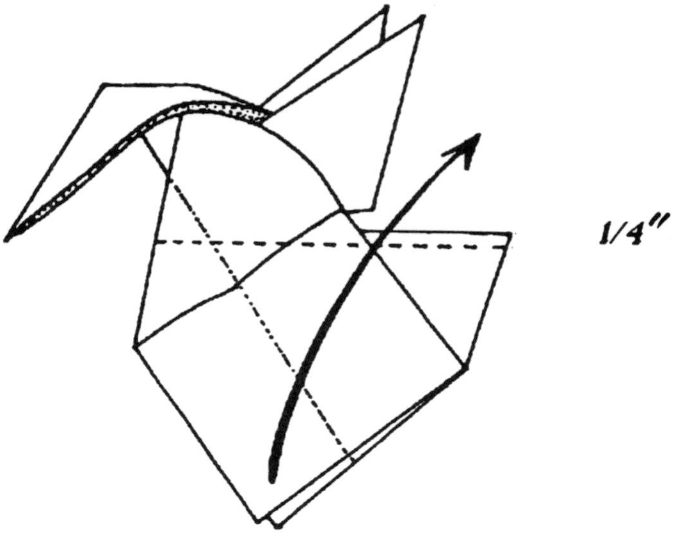


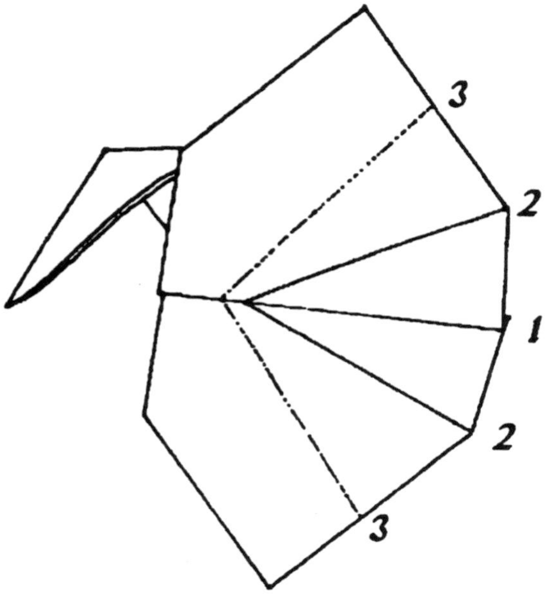


## 31

Your plane should look like this. Do the same on the other side. (Notice the 3 crease lines.)

## 32

Unfold and fold again, so that Crease Line 3 is directly on Crease Line 1.

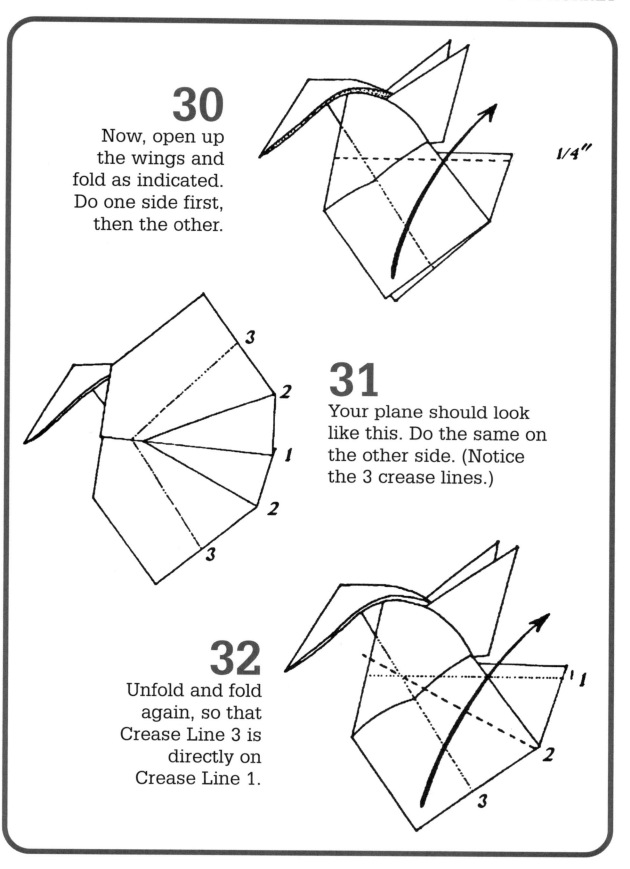

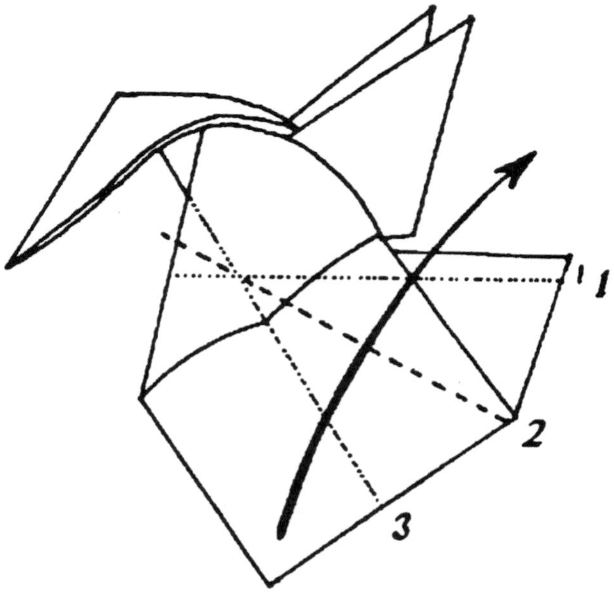

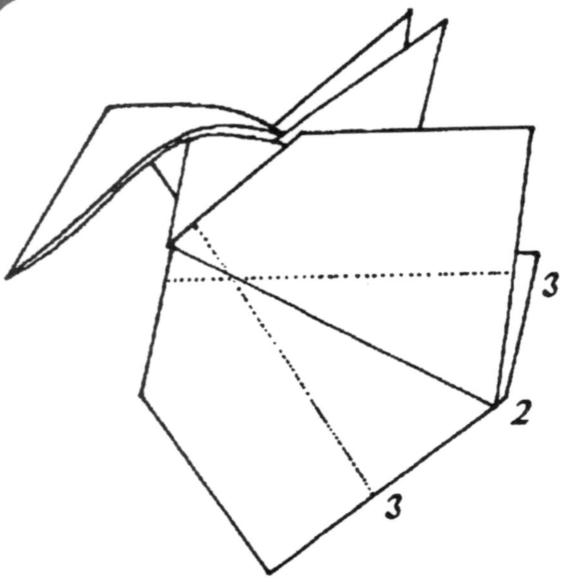


## 33

Your fold should look like this. Do the same on the other side.

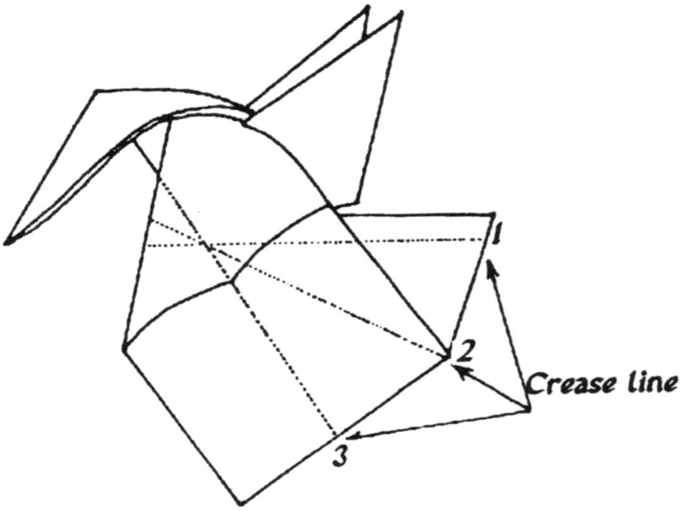


## 34

Unfold it and, as in step 31, you should have 3 crease lines.

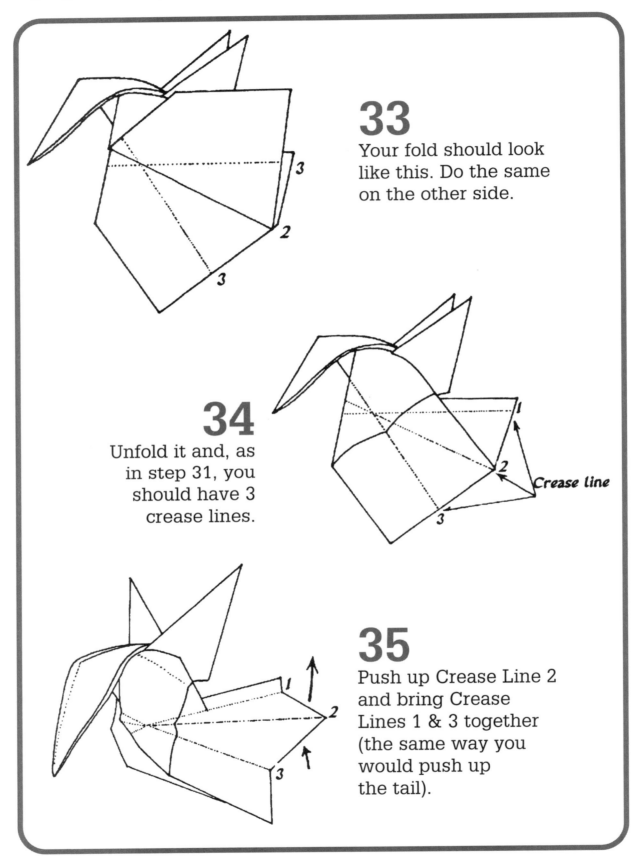

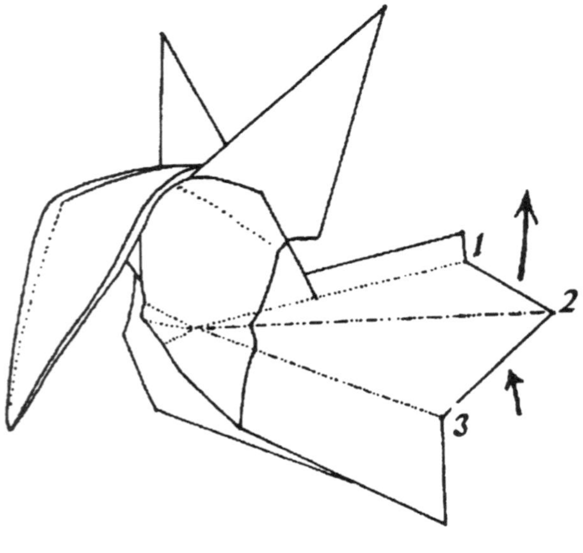


## 35

Push up Crease Line 2 and bring Crease Lines 1 & 3 together (the same way you would push up the tail).

## 36

Your plane should look like this. Repeat Steps 34 & 35 on the other side.

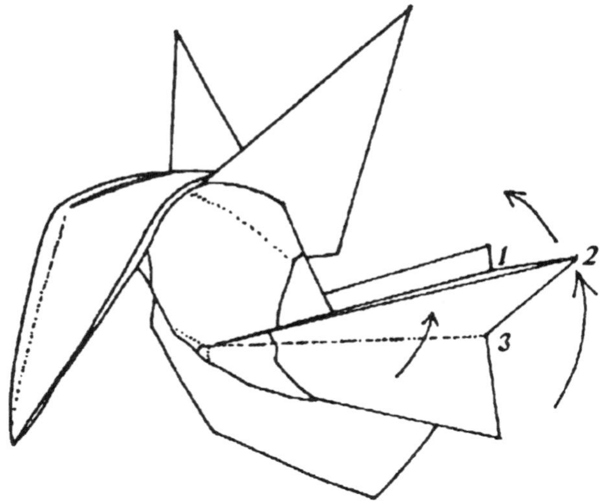


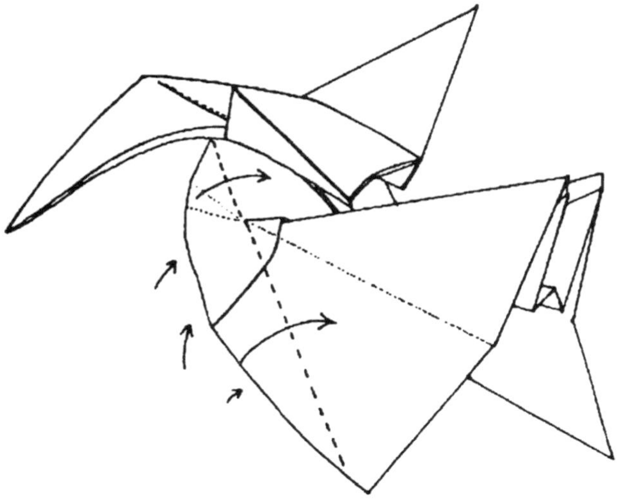

## 37

As you bring up the tail fin, the side shown here will collapse inward. Carefully fold it inward along the dotted line, as indicated by the arrows. Do the same to the other side.

## 38

Your plane should look exactly like this. Fold the stabilizers up. Make sure you duplicate this pattern on both sides.

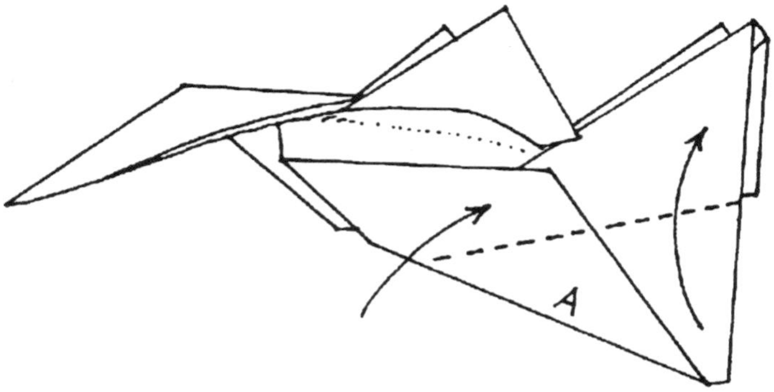

# 39

Now, fold the stabilizers down. Do the same on the other side.

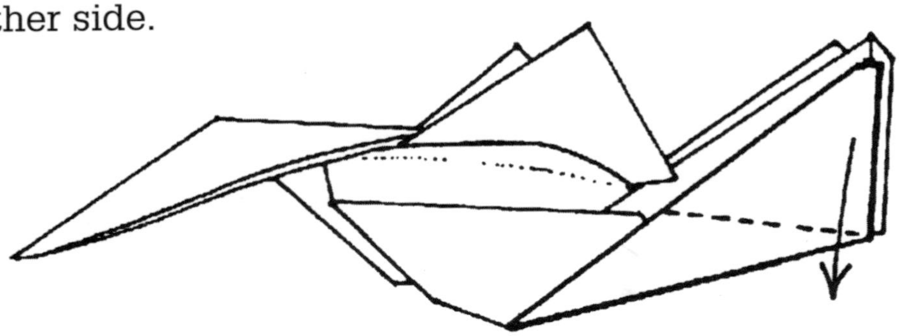

# 40

Open the stabilizers down completely.

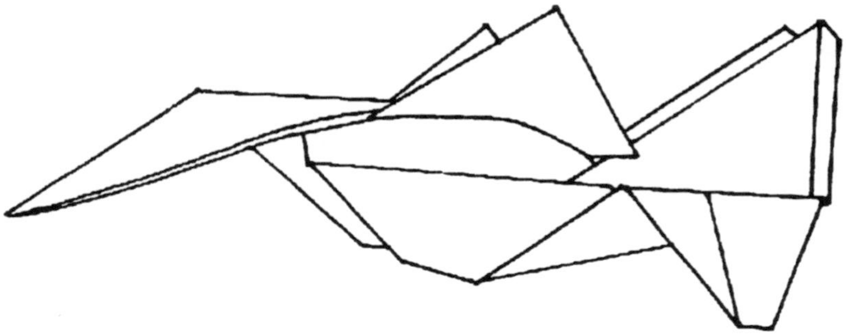

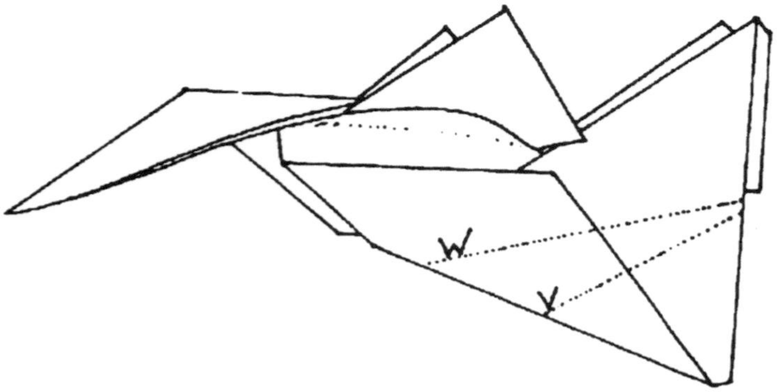


# 41

Your plane should look like this. Crease Lines V & W should be visible.

## 42

Using the inward-up folding techniques you learned when folding the jet's tail stabilizers and tail fins, fold the tail inward and up on Crease Line V.

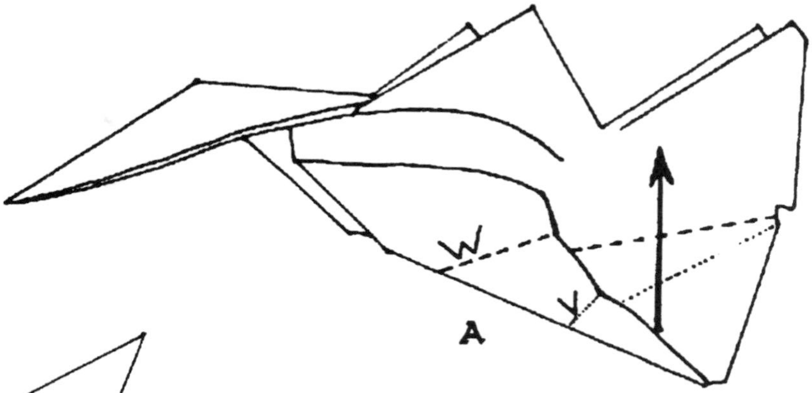

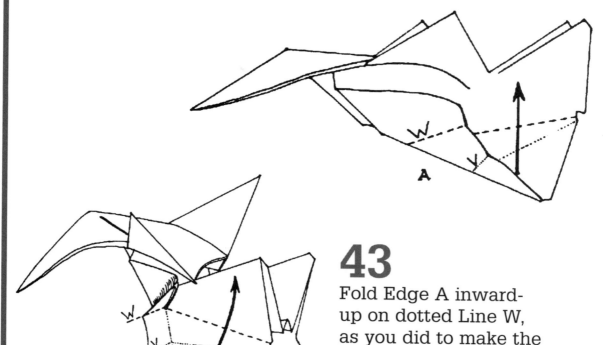

## 43

Fold Edge A inward-up on dotted Line W, as you did to make the tail fin.

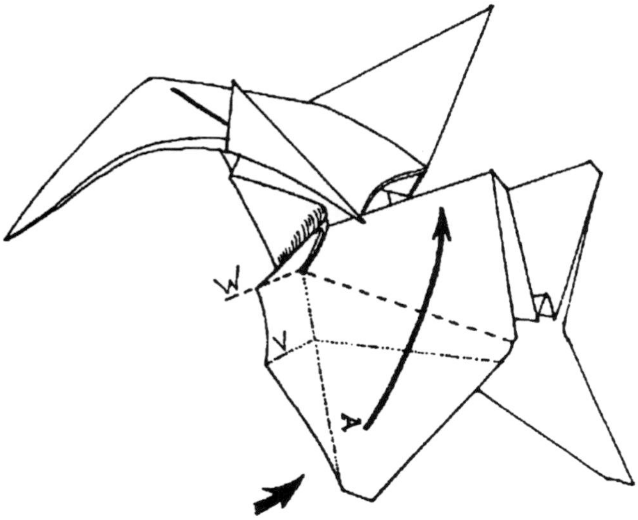

## 44

Your plane should look like this. Fold the stabilizers down. Repeat on the other side.

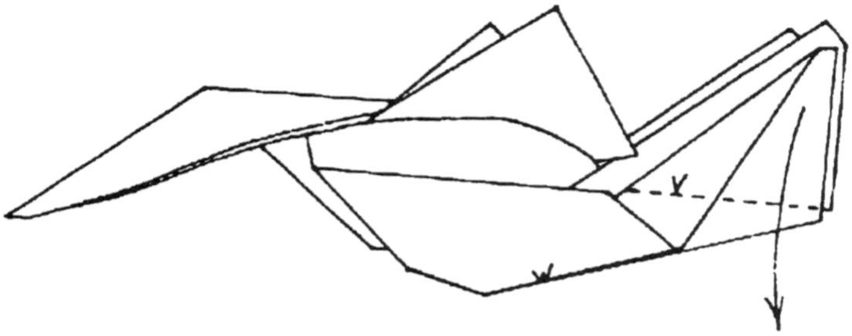

## 45

Your plane should look like this.

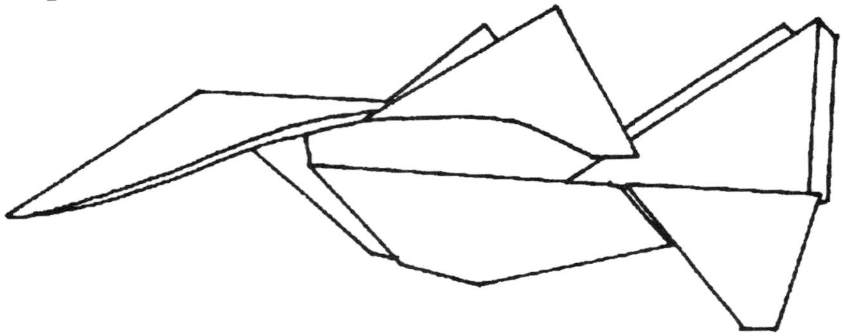

## 46

Press the body tightly together. Push down at the tail joint to separate the two tails.

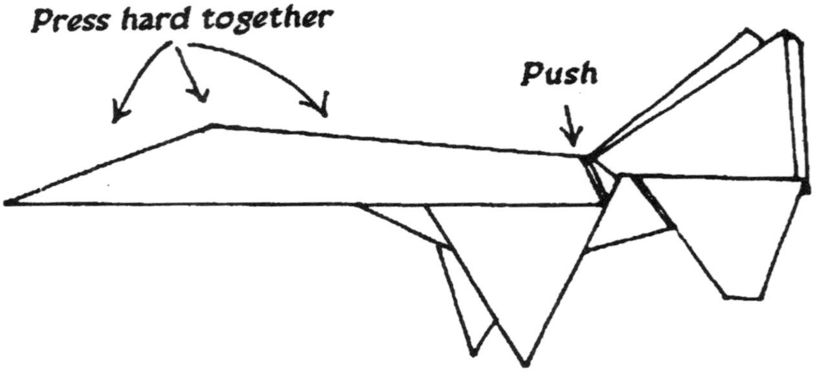


## 47

Fold the wings up.

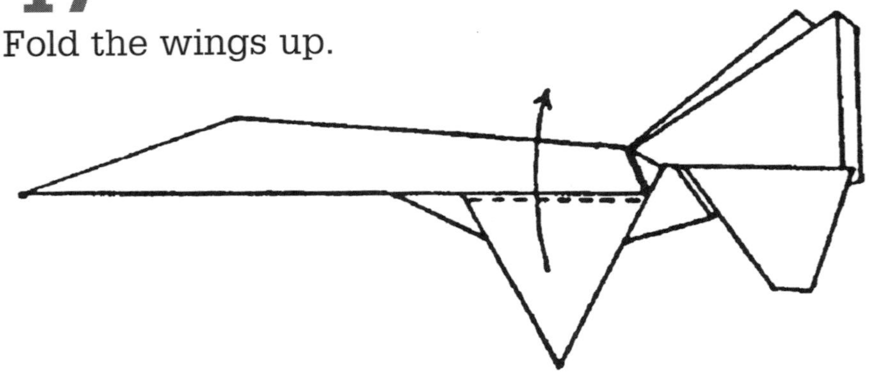

## 48

The finished version of the Hornet F-18!

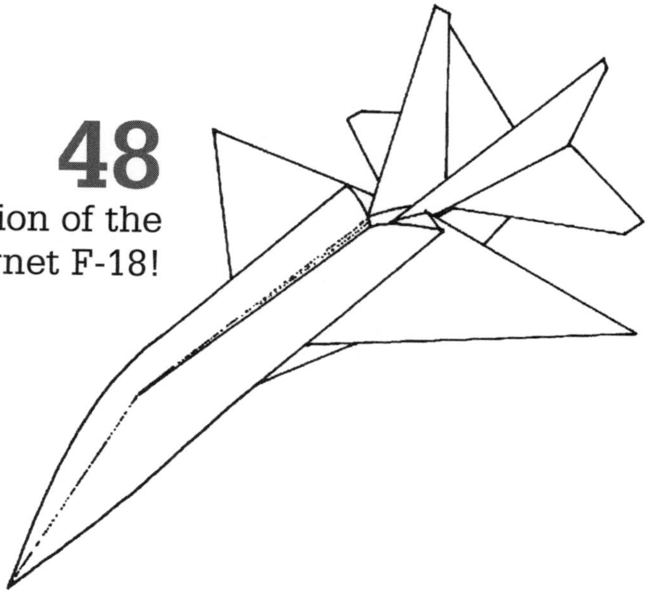

## 49

Curve the side of the nose for a nice, round, clean, front end like the one in Diagram B.

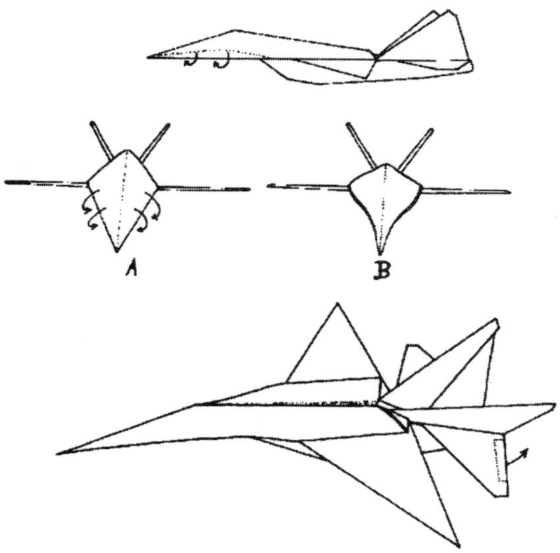

# F-18 HORNET

# F-14 TOMCAT

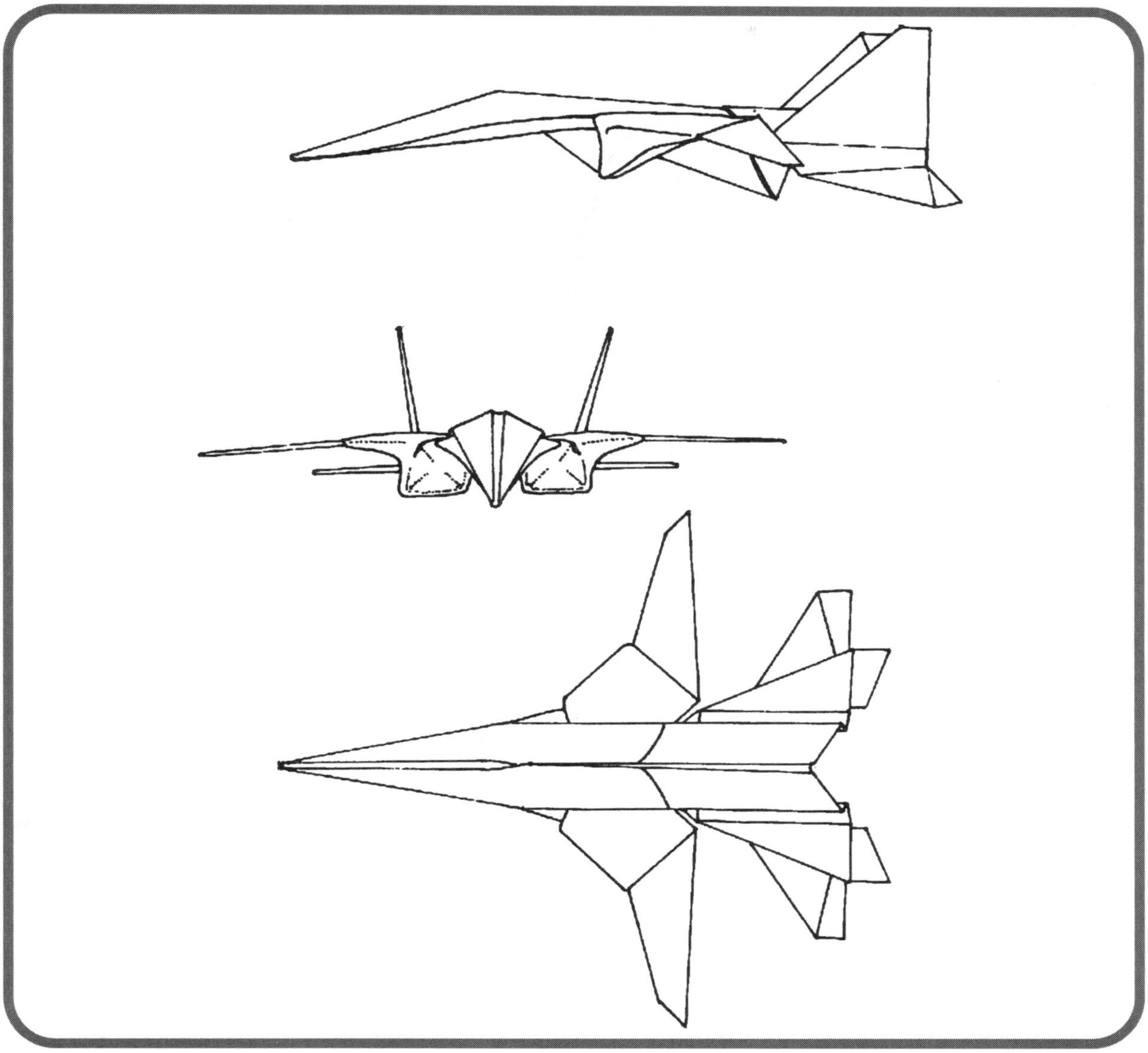

You're about to receive your "Top Gun U.S. F-14 Tomcat Trophy" for achieving the pinnacle in the art of paper airmanship. This plane will dazzle your eyes. Its structure is that of a real F-14 Tomcat and it will emulate the Tomcat's performance as well. You can fly it or treasure it, but make sure this plane is symmetrical & sturdy. For practice you may use an 8½ x 11 sheet of typing paper, but if you want the Tomcat to perform, use a 12½ X 15 or larger sheet of thin but strong paper.

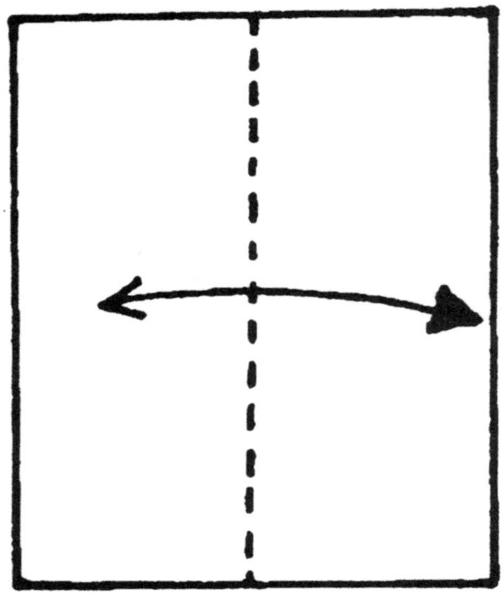

1

Fold paper in half, then unfold.

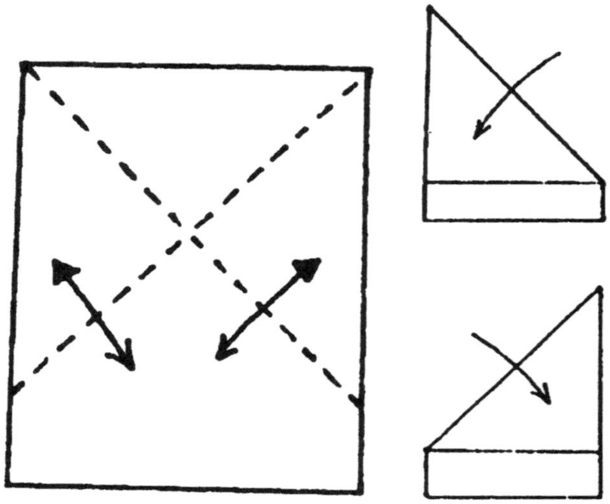

2

Fold diagonally at dotted lines, then unfold.

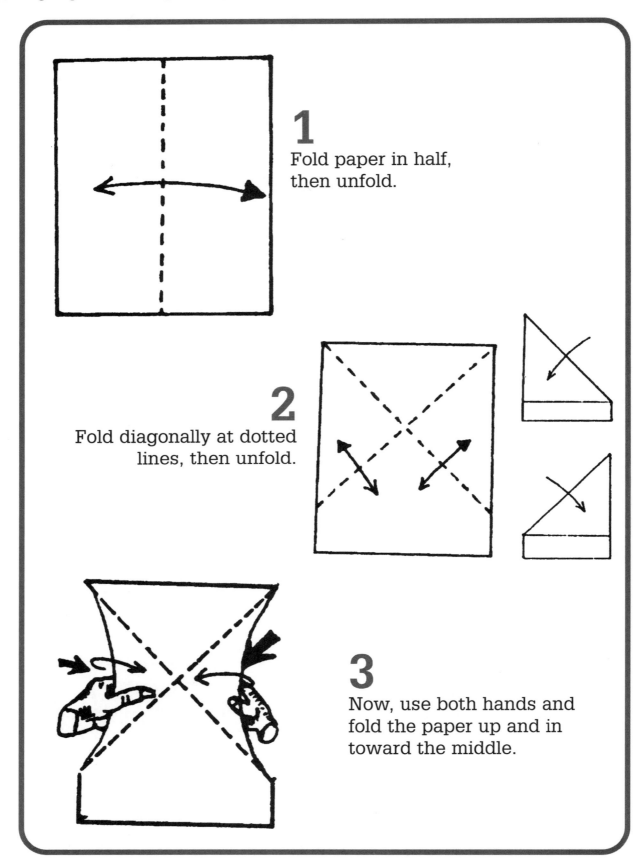

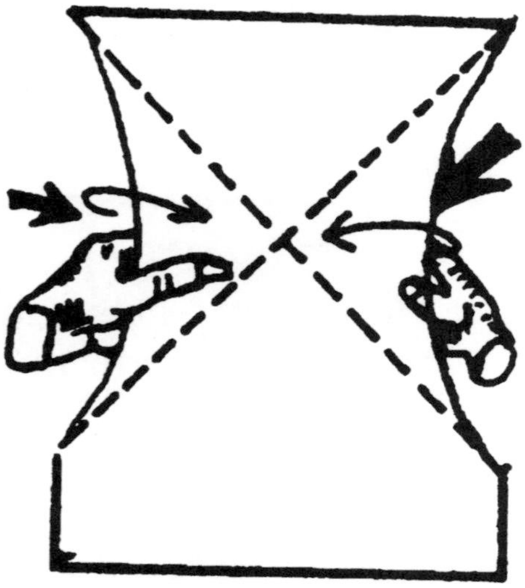

3

Now, use both hands and fold the paper up and in toward the middle.

## 4

This is how the paper should look. Gently press down from the top.

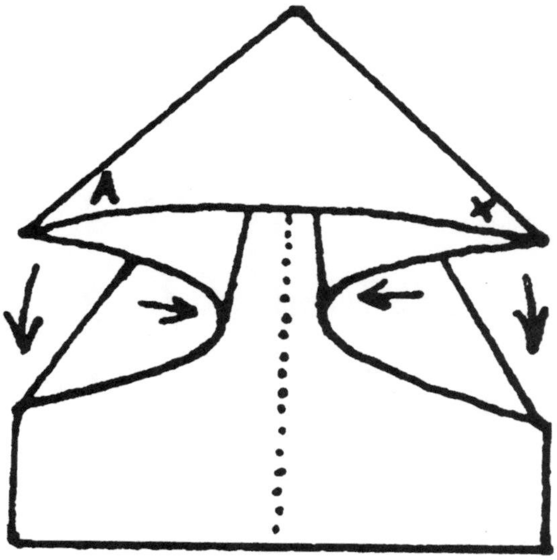


## 5

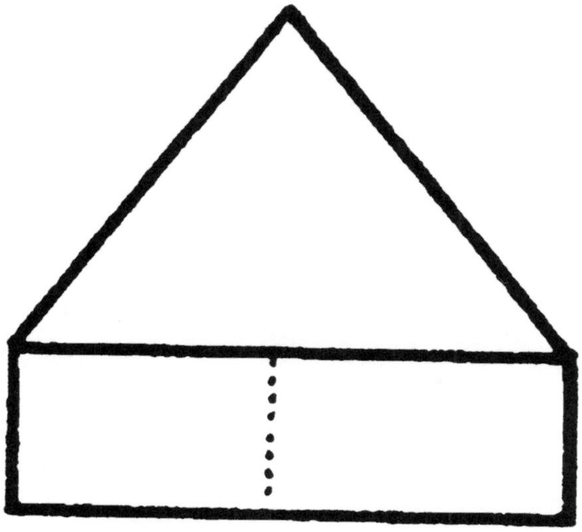

Now, it should look like this.

## 6

Slide your right hand under Flap X as shown here.

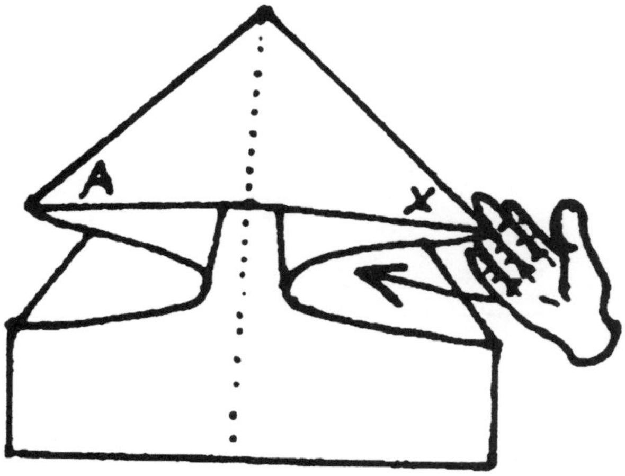

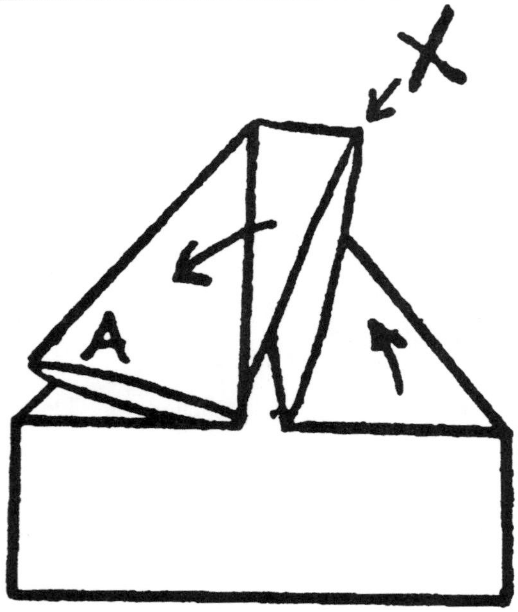


# 7

Flip Flap X over and onto Flap A.

# 8

Flap X should line up evenly with Flap A on the left side.

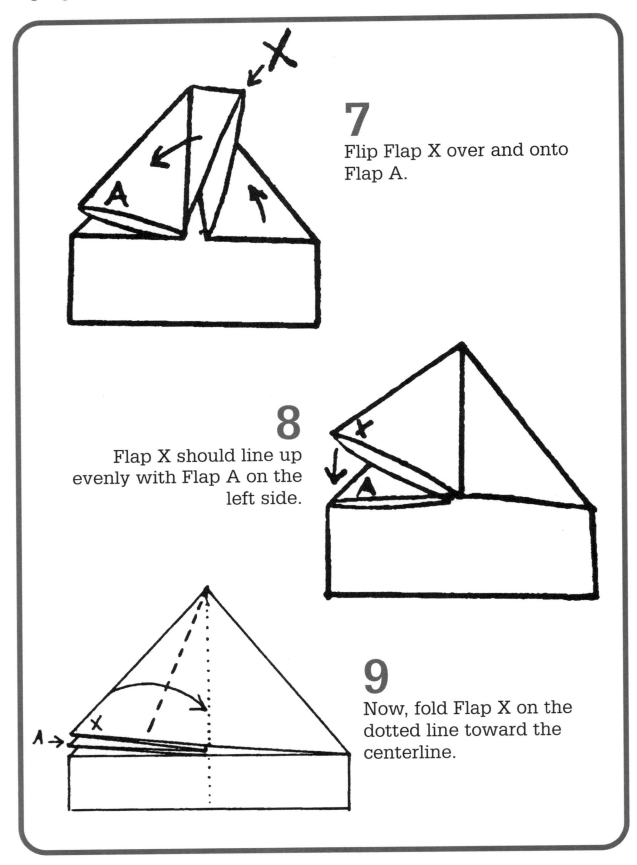

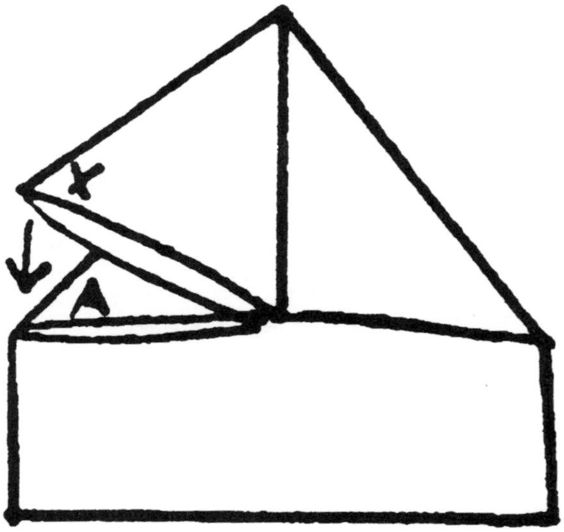


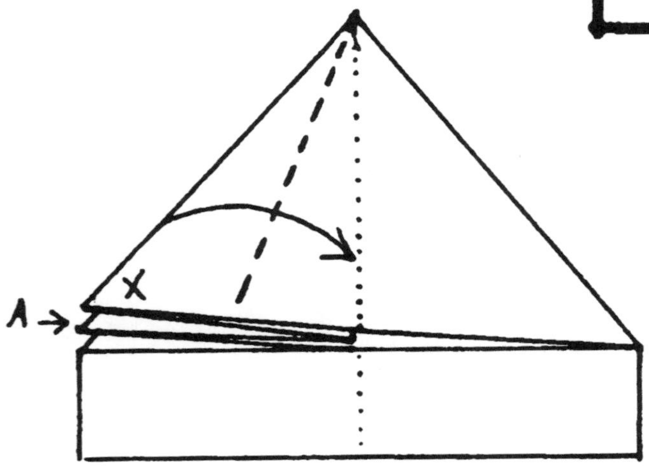


# 9

Now, fold Flap X on the dotted line toward the centerline.

## 10

This is how your fold should look.

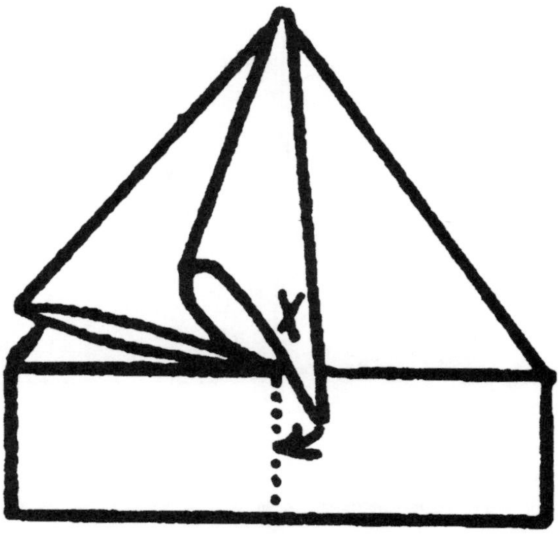


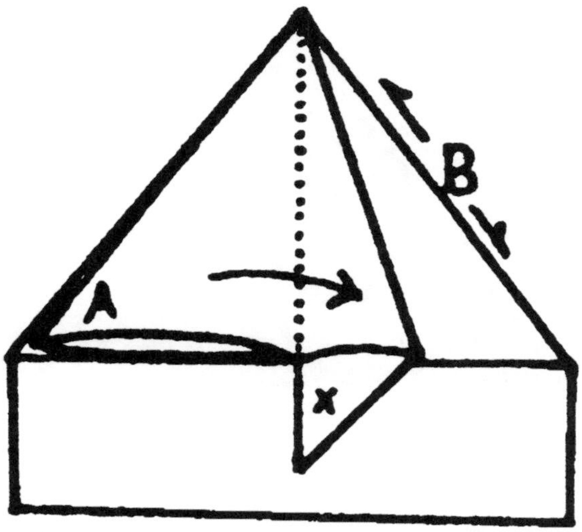


## 11

After you have folded Flap X toward the middle flap, flip it to the right side. Notice Edge B.

## 12

This is how your plane should look. Now, unfold & flip the right wing to the left side.

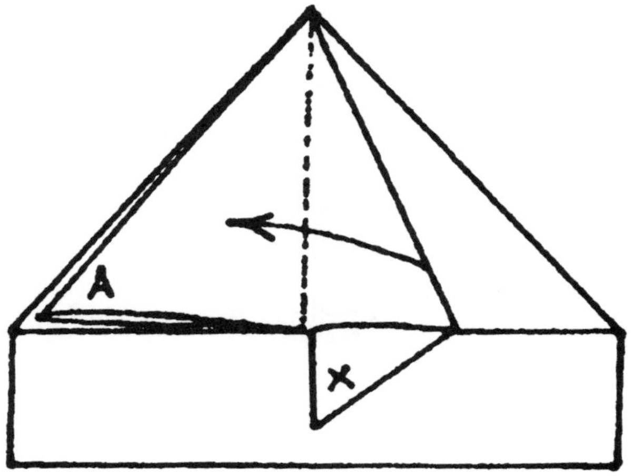

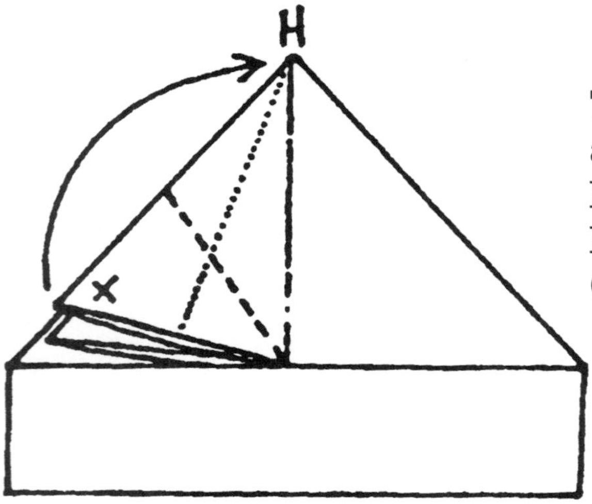


## 13

This is how it should look after you've flipped it to the left. Now fold on the dotted line so that Corner X meets Corner H.

## 14

This is how Step 13 should look. Repeat this fold on the left side.

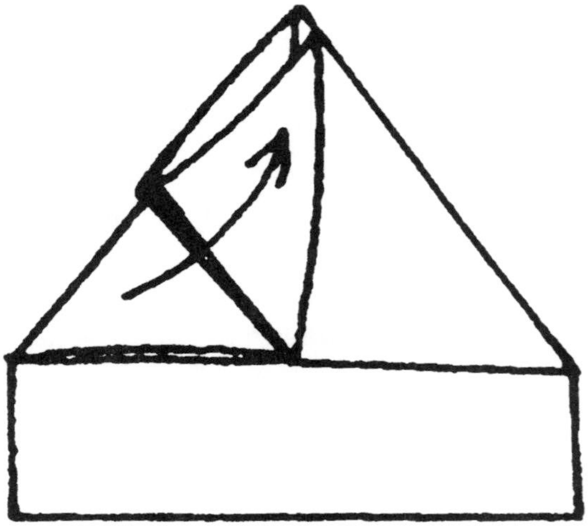

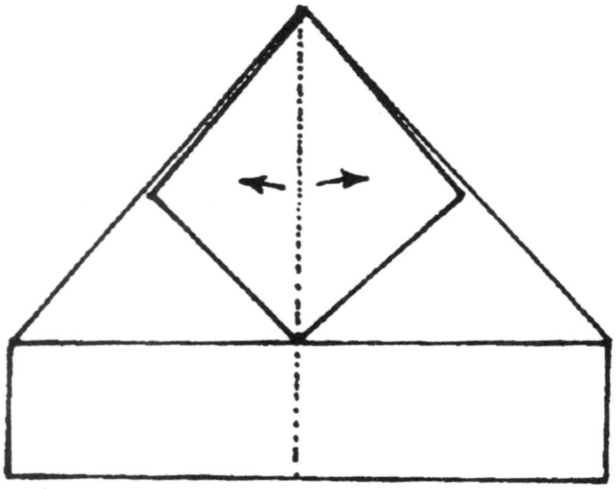

## 15

After you fold the left side, open both sides as indicated here.

## 16

Now open the wings further. The front wings now have two intersecting crease lines. Label them P and O.

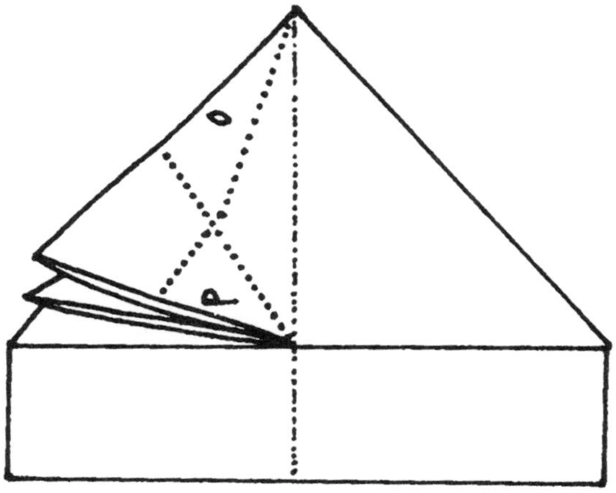


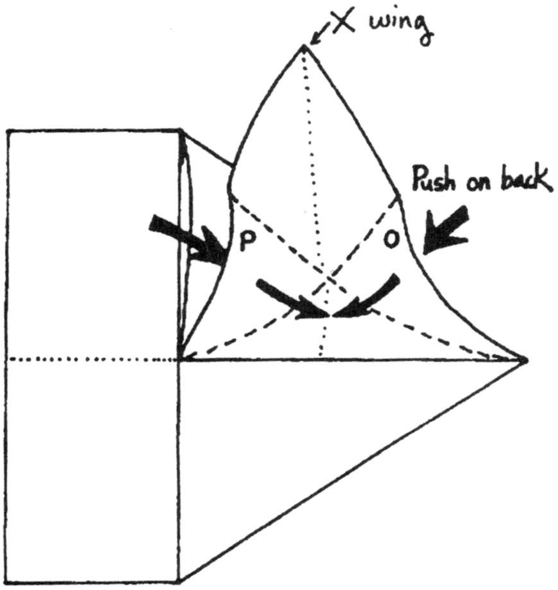


## 17

Rotate your paper ¼ turn to the right and fold P & O together and toward you on the crossing crease lines.

## 18

Your folds on P & O should look exactly as shown here. Put your hand behind the wing at M & N and press the two sides together.

NOTE: The fold here is similar to that used for the F-15 but it is shifted toward the M side instead of the N side.

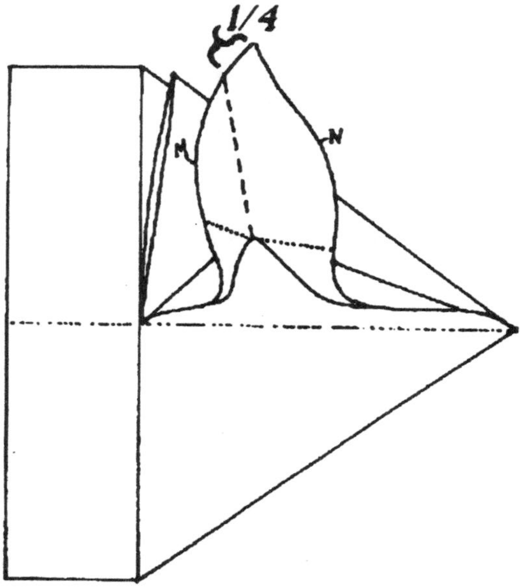

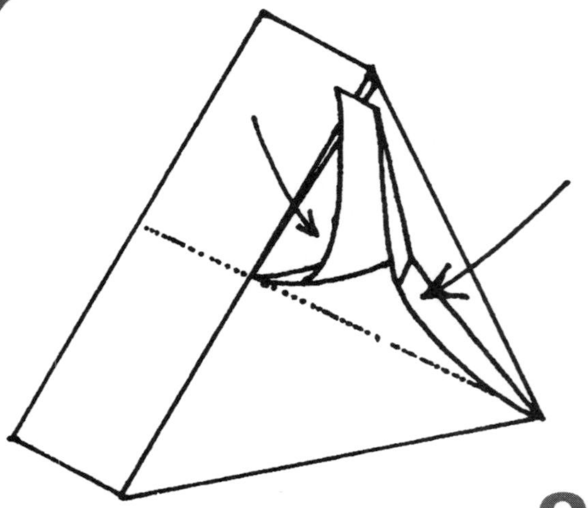

## 19

After pressing sides M & N together, this is how your plane should look. Do the same on the left side, beginning with Step 16, before going on.

## 20

Your finished folds of the wing should look like this. Fold the wing up toward the nose exactly as the arrow indicates.

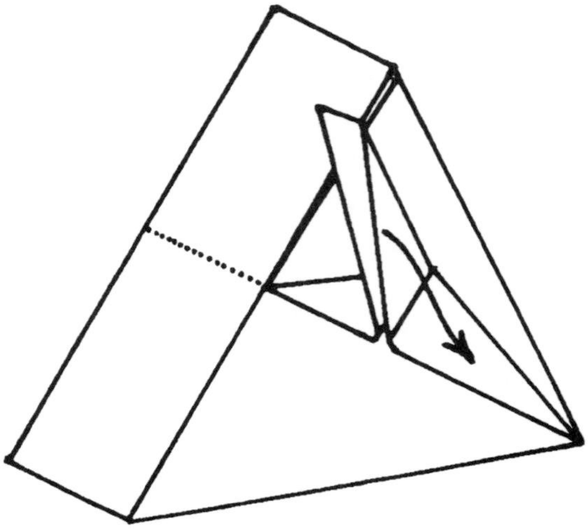

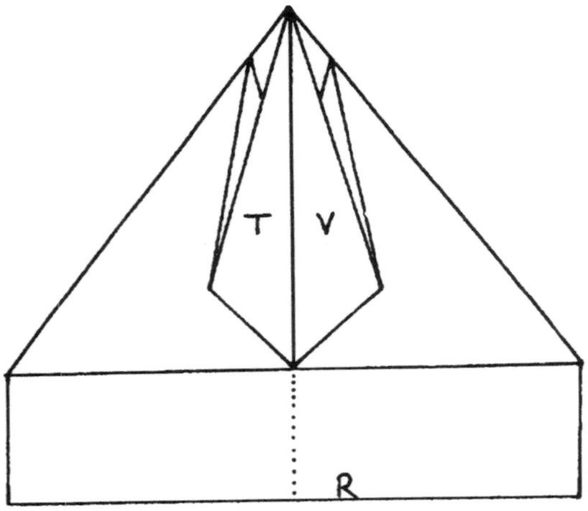


## 21

After you have finished with the other side, separate both sides as displayed. (Notice the R edge.)

## 22

Fold up the R edge at the midpoint, along the dotted line.

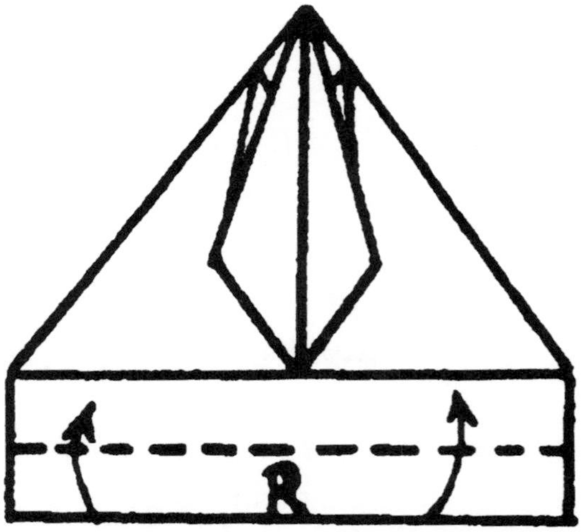

# 23

Now, fold back along the dotted line.

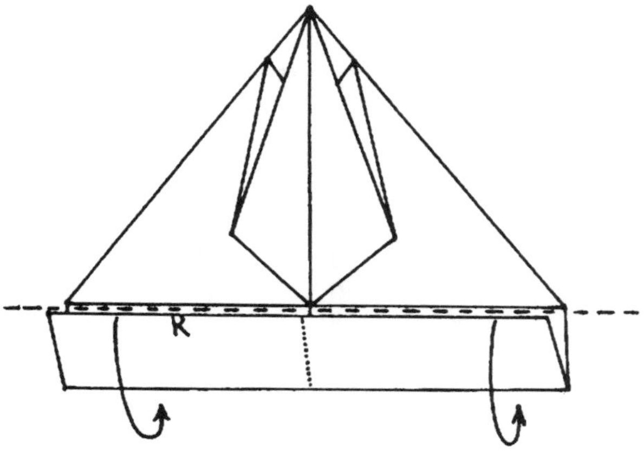


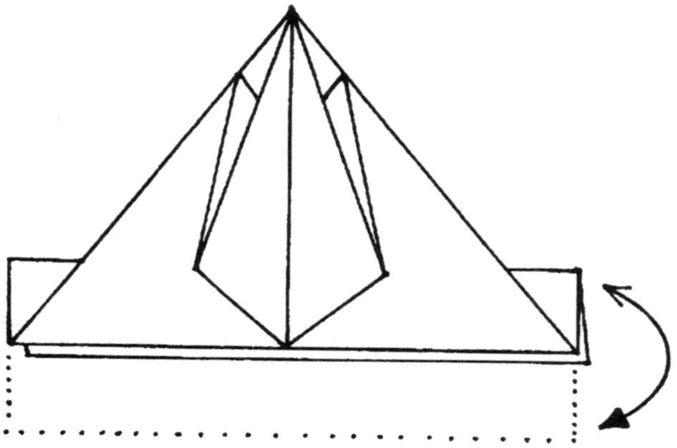

# 24

This is how your fold toward the back should look. Now unfold it as shown, so that it looks like the end of step 22.

# 25

Fold diagonally up, then back and forth at each corner, as shown here.

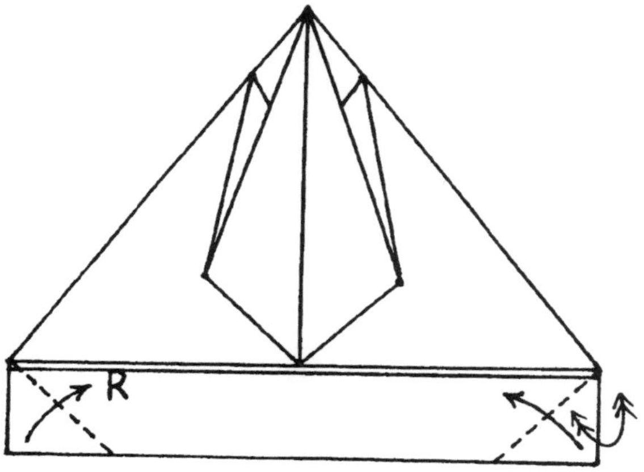


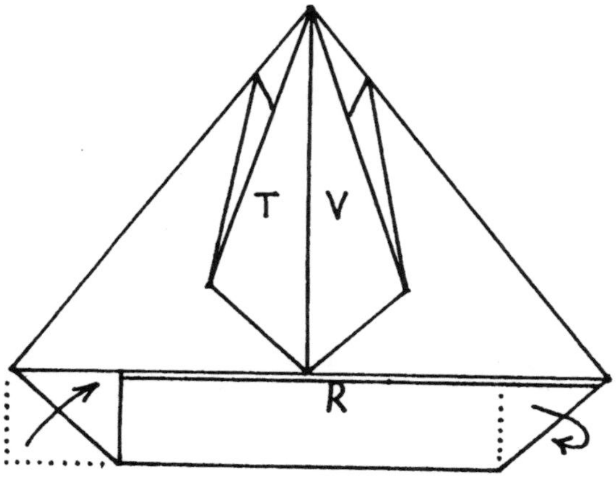


# 26

This is how the folds on step 25 should look. Fold back and forth five or six times.

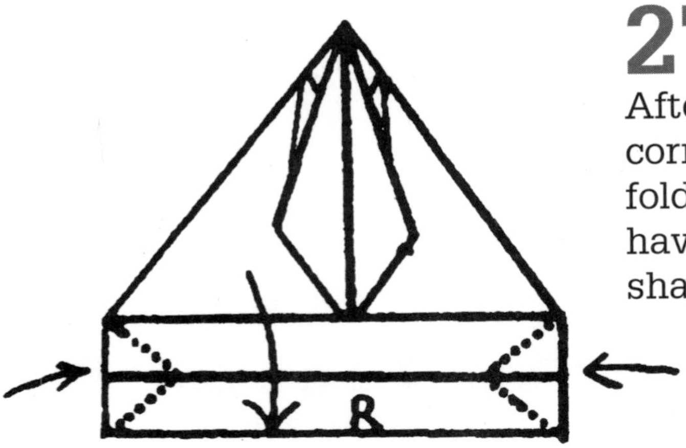


## 27

After you've folded the corners, unfold the R edge fold as shown. You should have two triangular shapes.

## 28

Push the two triangular sides inward as shown.

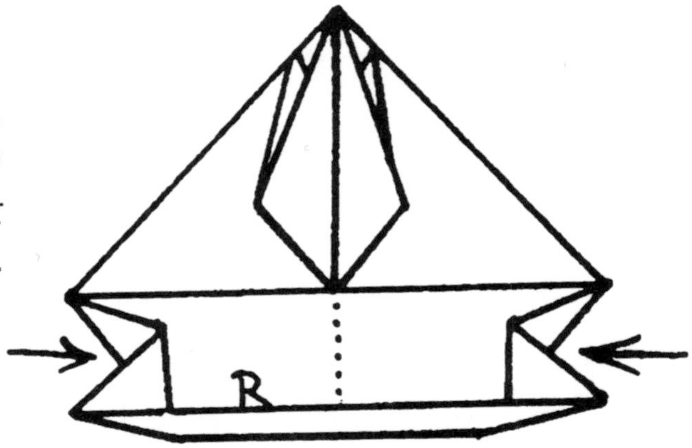


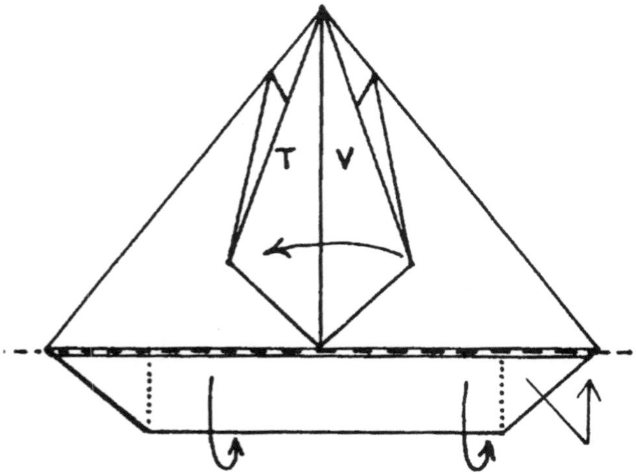


## 29

After you have pressed both triangular sides inward, it should look like this. Now, fold this part back on the dotted line. Next, flip the V wing to the T wing on the left side.

## 30

Now, fold Edge B to Centerline C on the dotted line. Do the same to the left side.

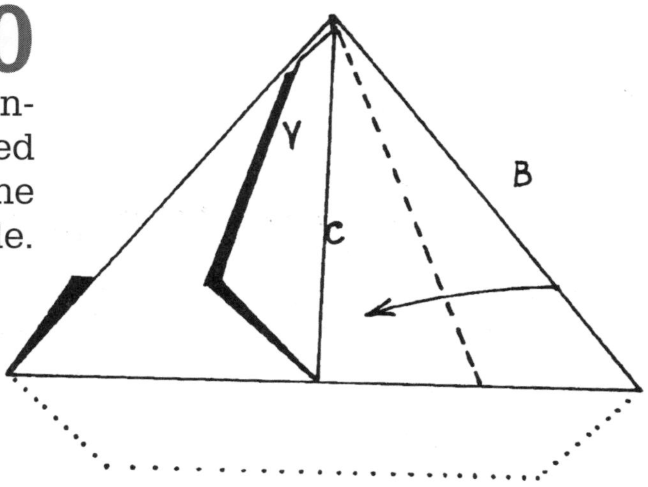


## 31

Fold Wing V to the left. Now your plane should look like this.

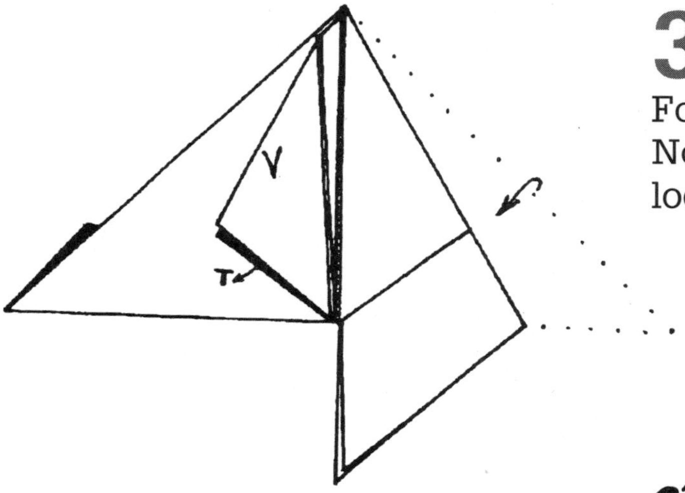


## 32

Fold Wing V down as shown here and align with the fuselage.

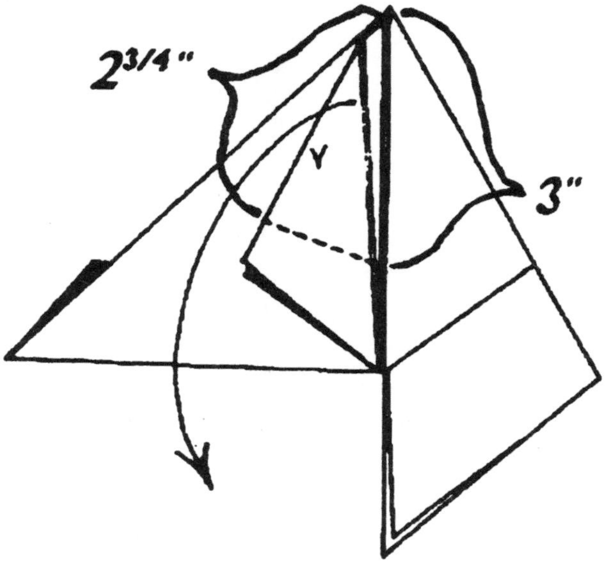

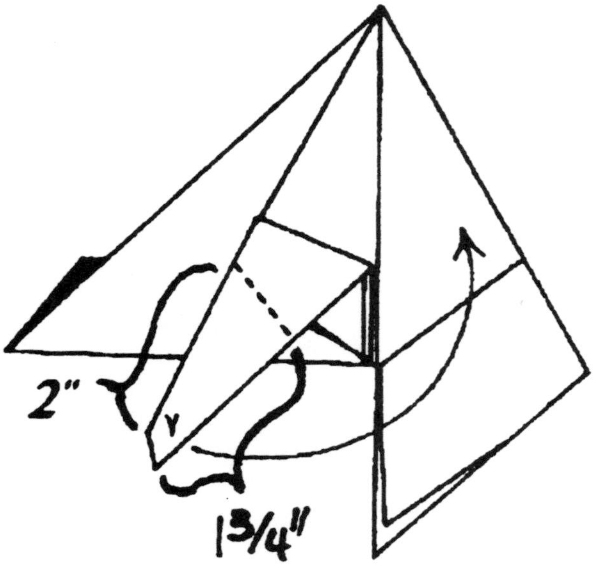


## 33

Your fold should look exactly like this. Now fold up toward the right. Remember to make crisp folds.

## 34

Your fold should look exactly like this. Now fold straight to the left.

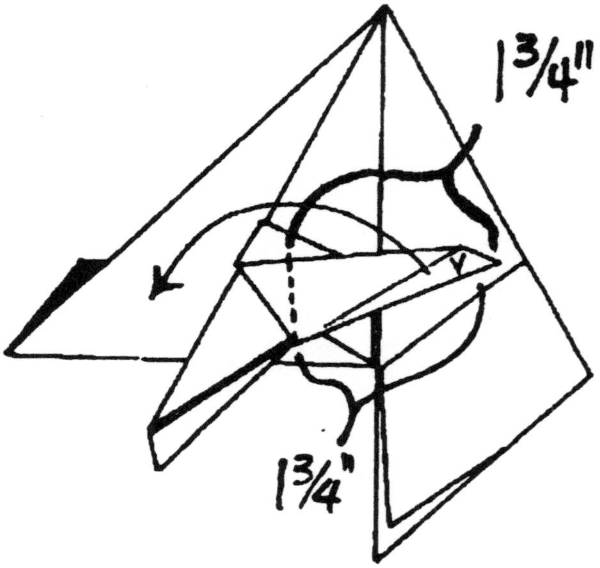


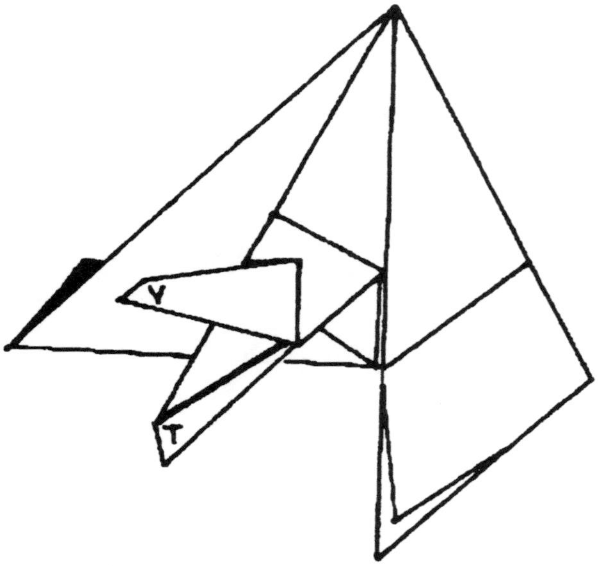


## 35

Your V wing should look like this. Make an even-opposite fold, following Steps 32-35, on the other side.

## 36

When the left side is finished, separate the sides and your plane should look like this. Look at the wings carefully now. You will be tucking the wings next but they will have this same definite appearance when finished.

NOTE: the purpose of this tuck is to make the wings more rigid and sturdy.

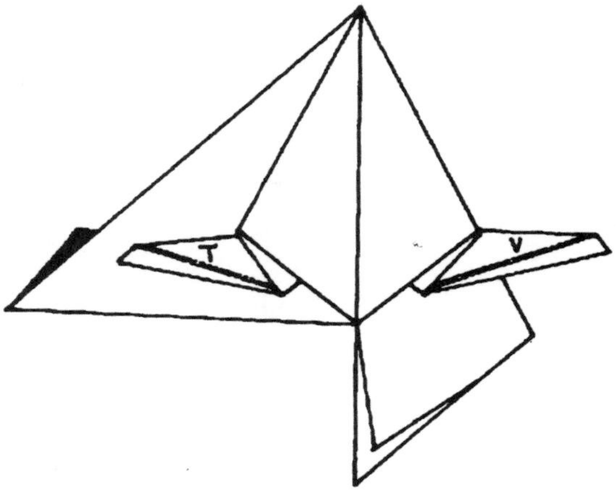


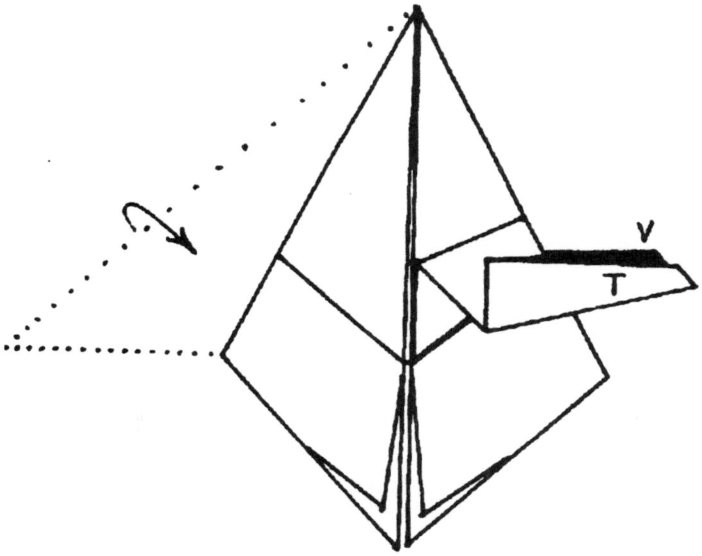


## 37

Flip the left Wing T over to the right and fold the left side to the middle. Your plane should look like this.

## 38

Unfold both wings, flip Wing V to the left and the plane should look like this. Crease Lines 1, 2 & 3 should be visible.

NOTE: You must know or mark the 3 crease lines.

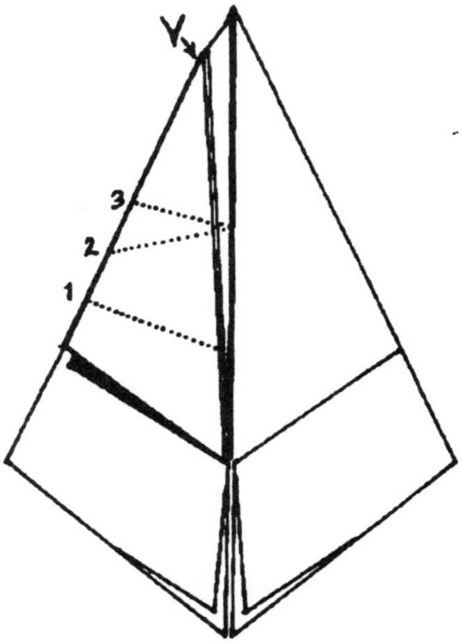

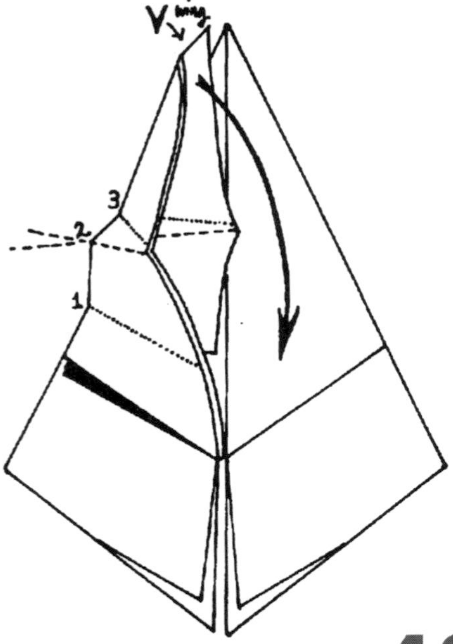


## 39

Very carefully open Wing V & fold down on Crease Line 2. (Simply tuck in the wing, downward, along dotted Crease Line 2.)

## 40

Fold it back up on Crease Line 3. Make sure Crease Line 3 is tucked in between Creases 1 & 2 exactly as shown here. Close the wing's side together so it looks like Step 36.

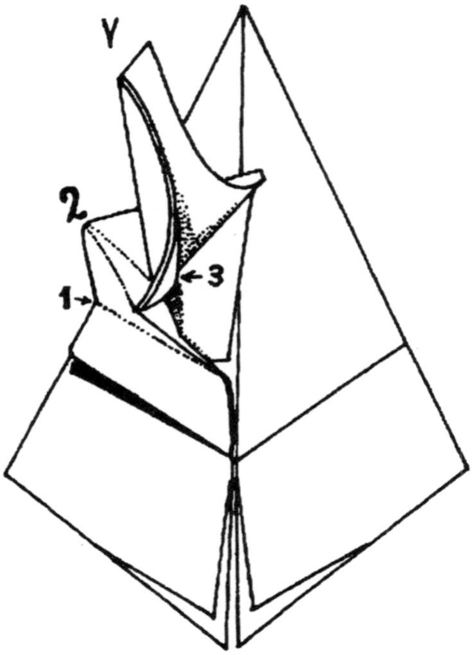


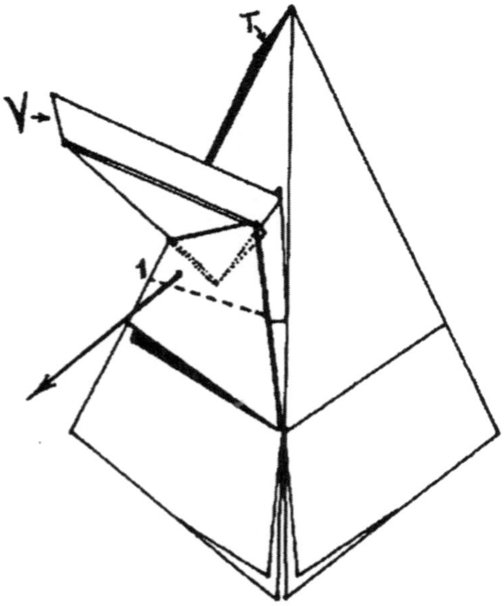


## 41

Your wing fold should look like this. Fold down on Crease Line 1.

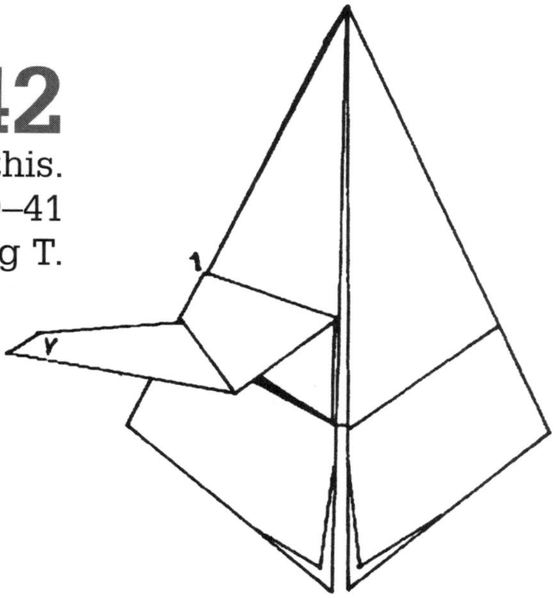

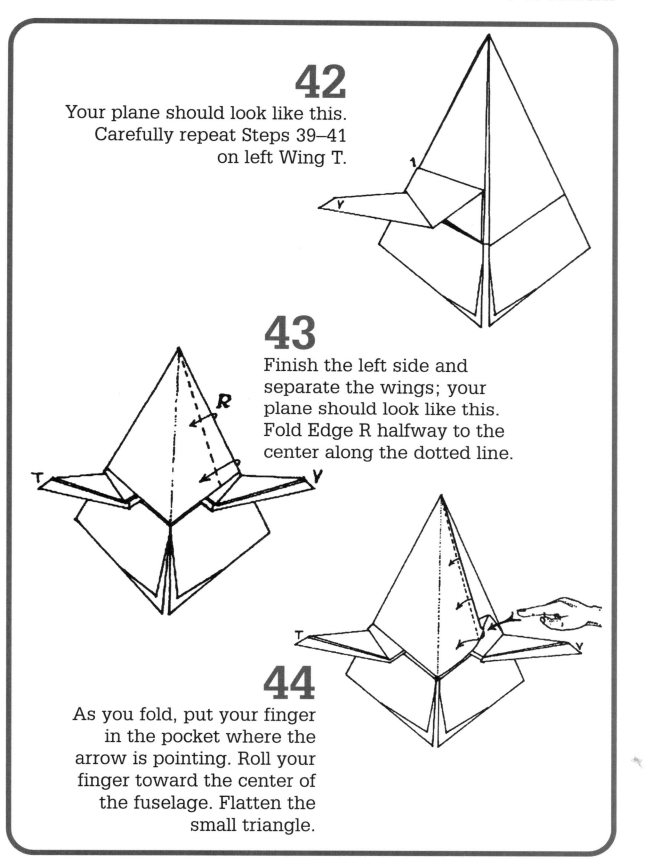

## 42

Your plane should look like this. Carefully repeat Steps 39–41 on left Wing T.

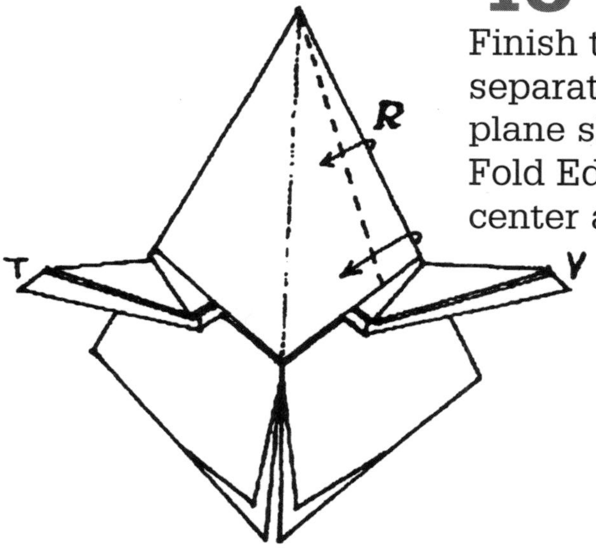


## 43

Finish the left side and separate the wings; your plane should look like this. Fold Edge R halfway to the center along the dotted line.

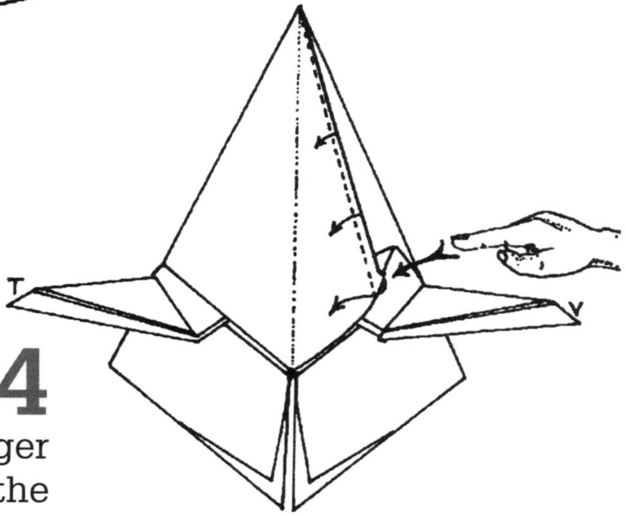


## 44

As you fold, put your finger in the pocket where the arrow is pointing. Roll your finger toward the center of the fuselage. Flatten the small triangle.

## 45

Your plane should look like this. Do the same on the left side.

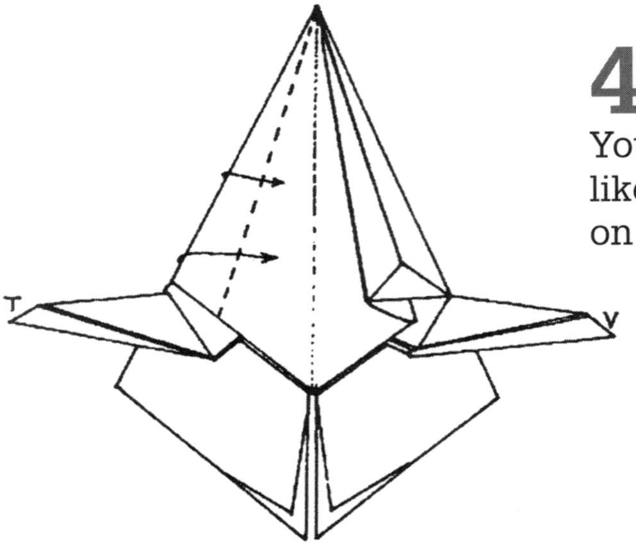


## 46

Turn the model over and your plane should look like this.

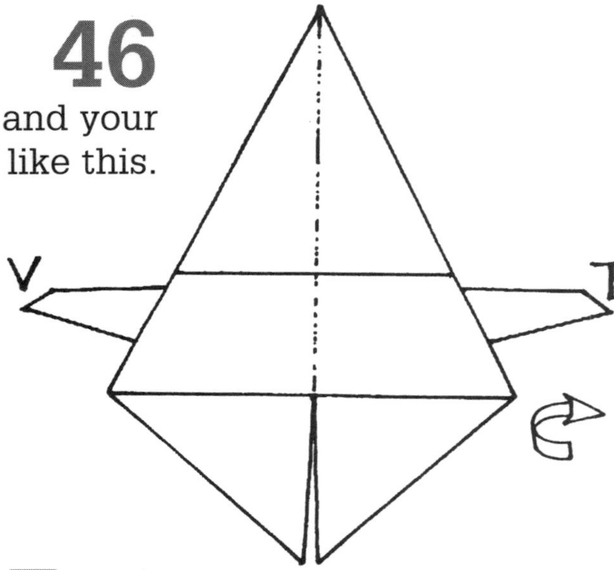


## 47

Fold the right side to the middle along the dotted line.

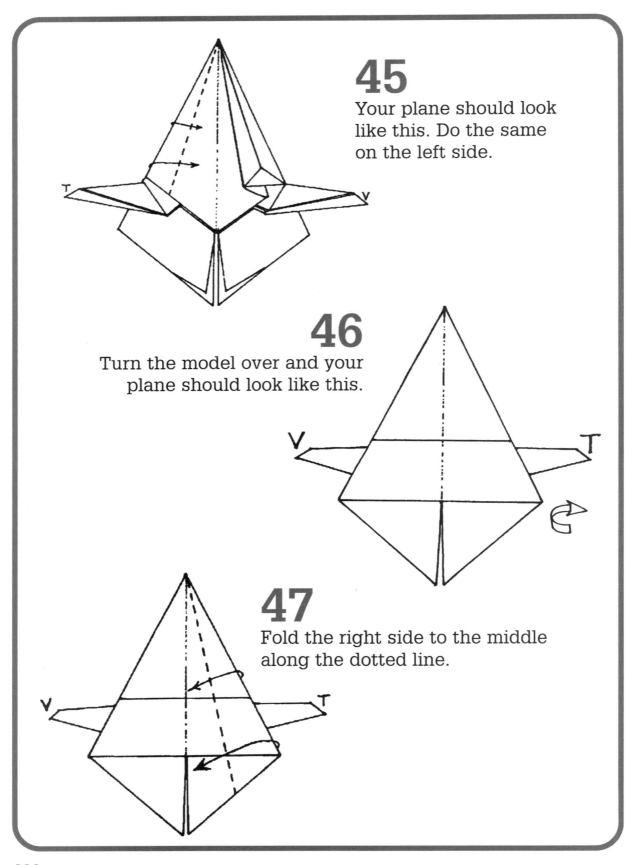

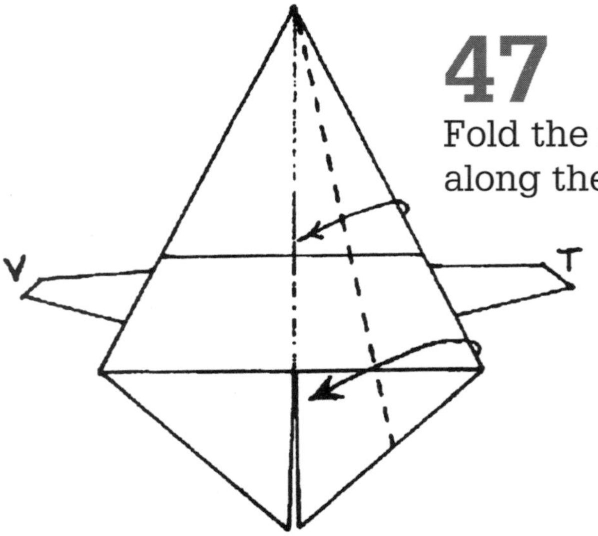

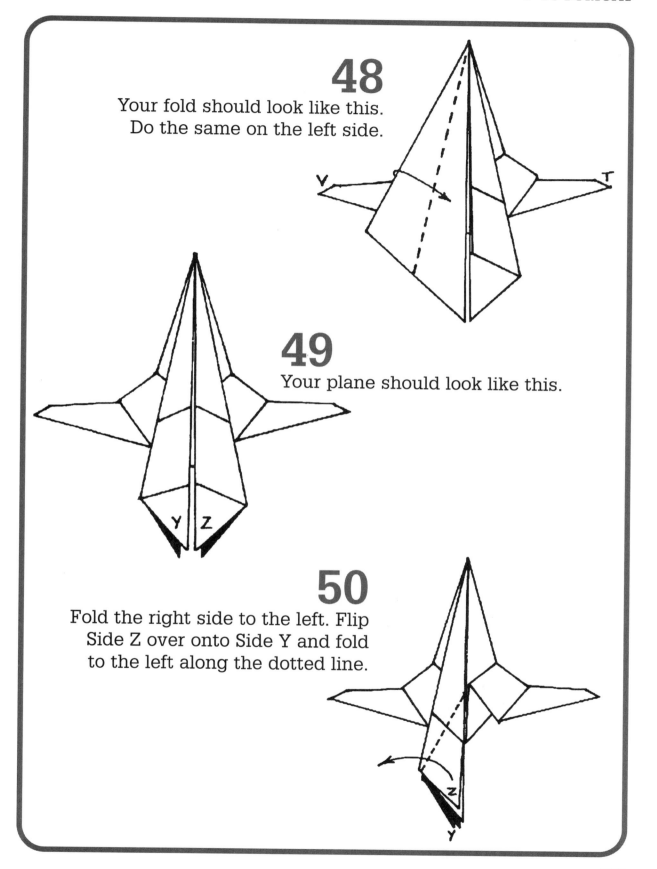

## 48

Your fold should look like this.
Do the same on the left side.

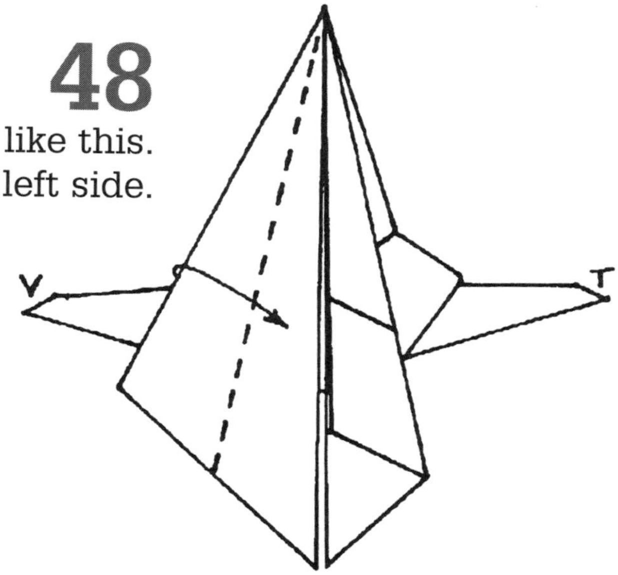


## 49

Your plane should look like this.

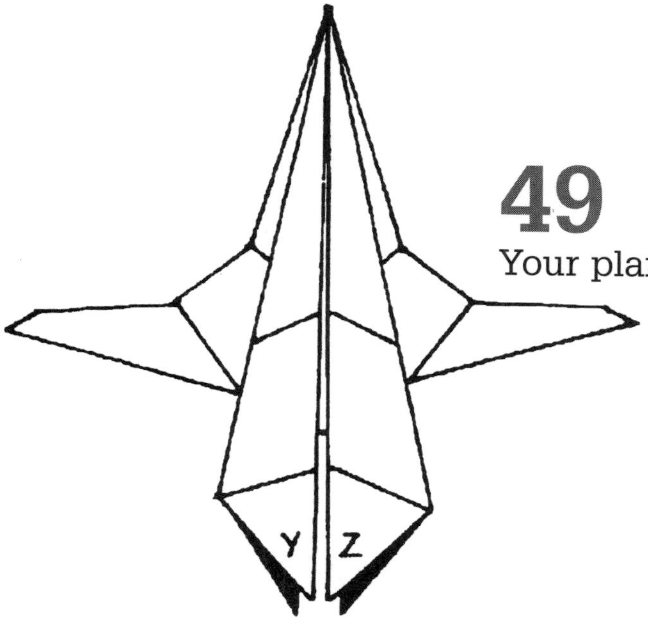


## 50

Fold the right side to the left. Flip Side Z over onto Side Y and fold to the left along the dotted line.

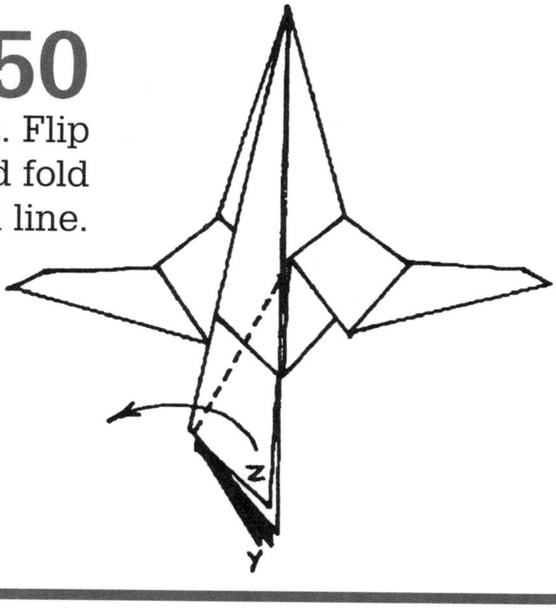

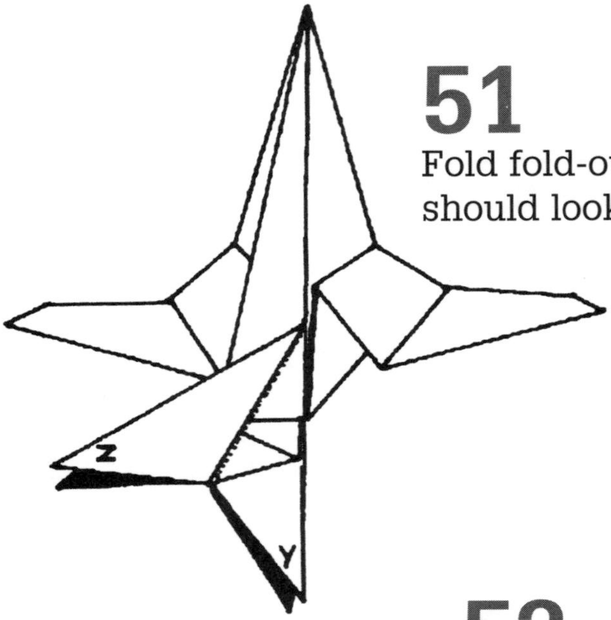


## 51

Fold fold-out to the left should look like this.

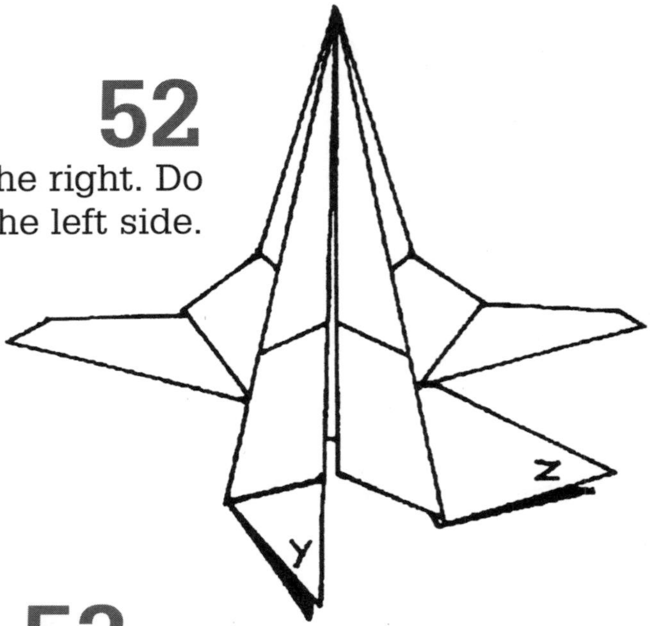


## 52

Flip Side Z back to the right. Do the same on the left side.

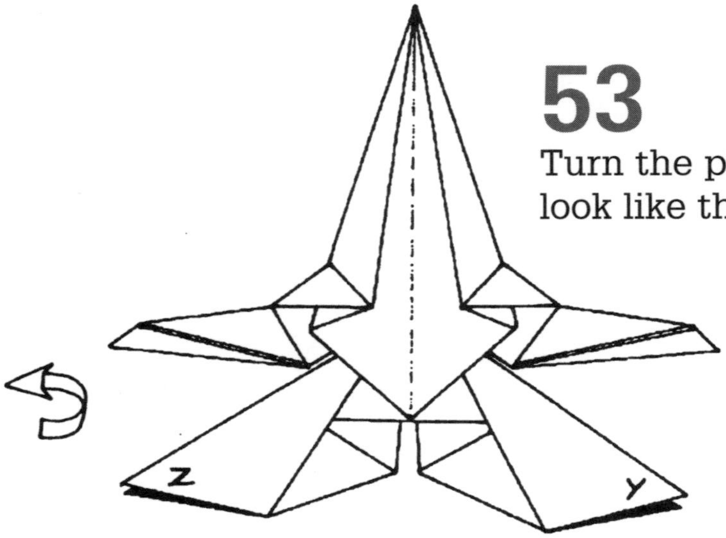


## 53

Turn the plane over and it should look like this.

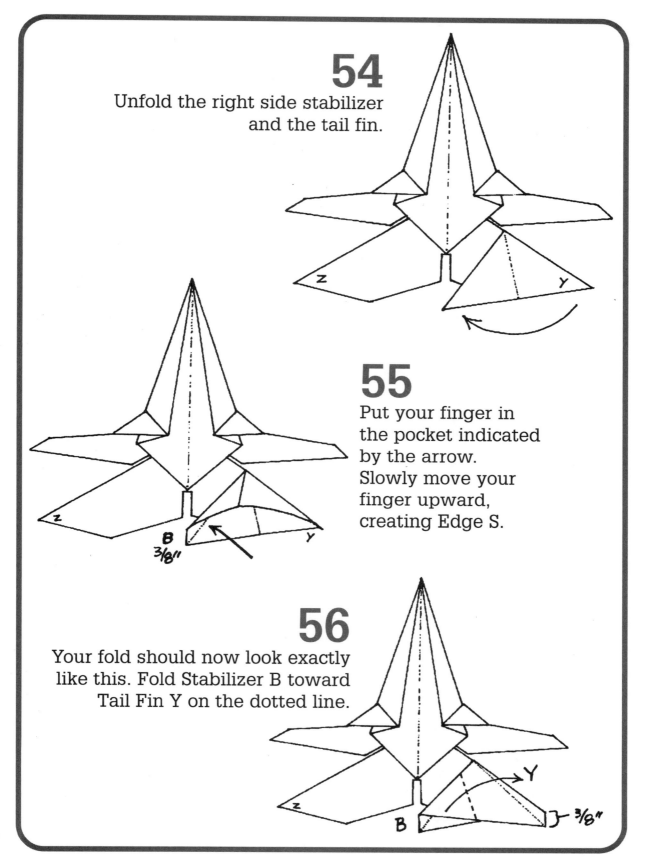

## 54

Unfold the right side stabilizer and the tail fin.

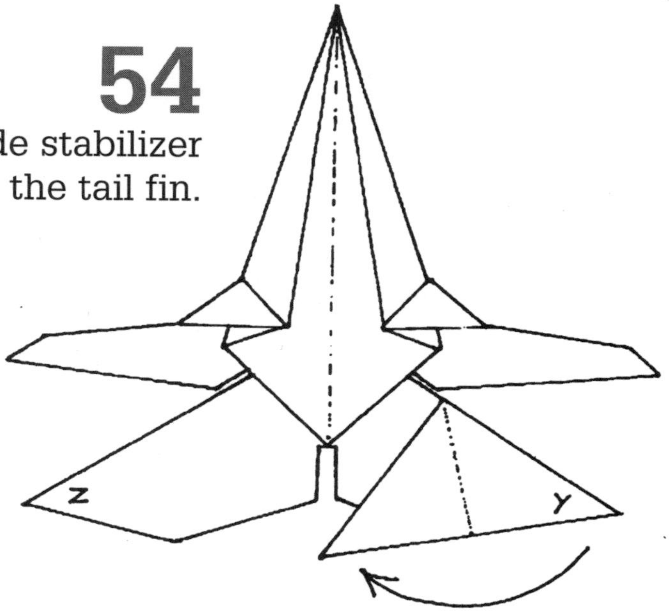


## 55

Put your finger in the pocket indicated by the arrow. Slowly move your finger upward, creating Edge S.

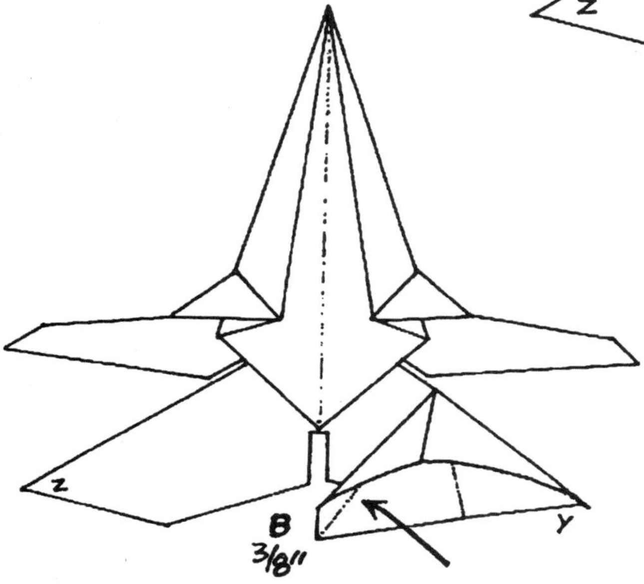


## 56

Your fold should now look exactly like this. Fold Stabilizer B toward Tail Fin Y on the dotted line.

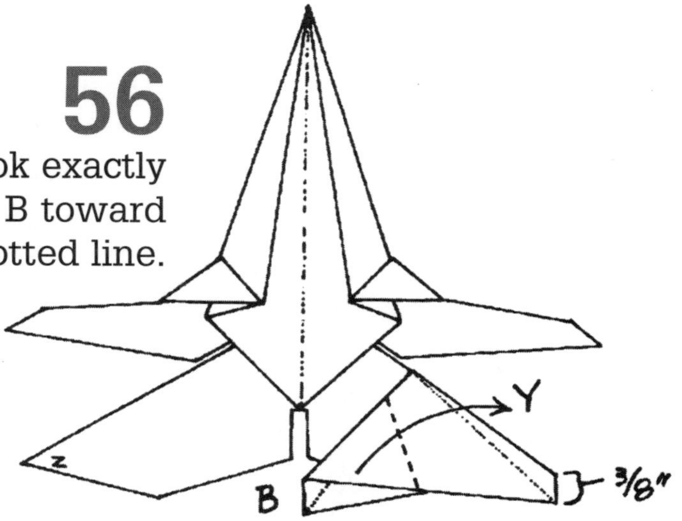

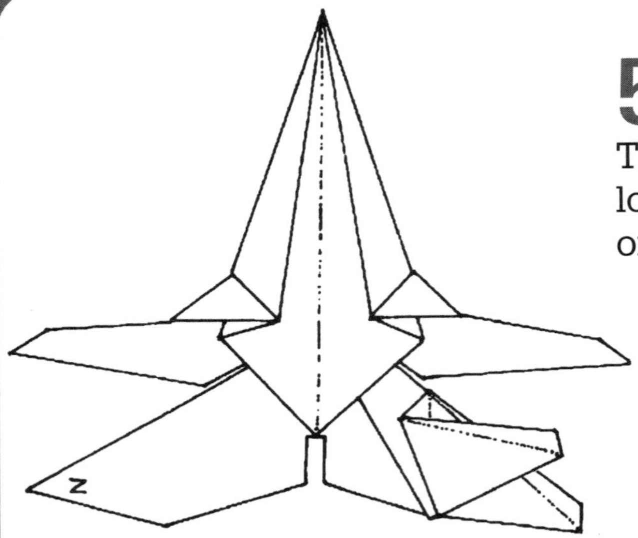

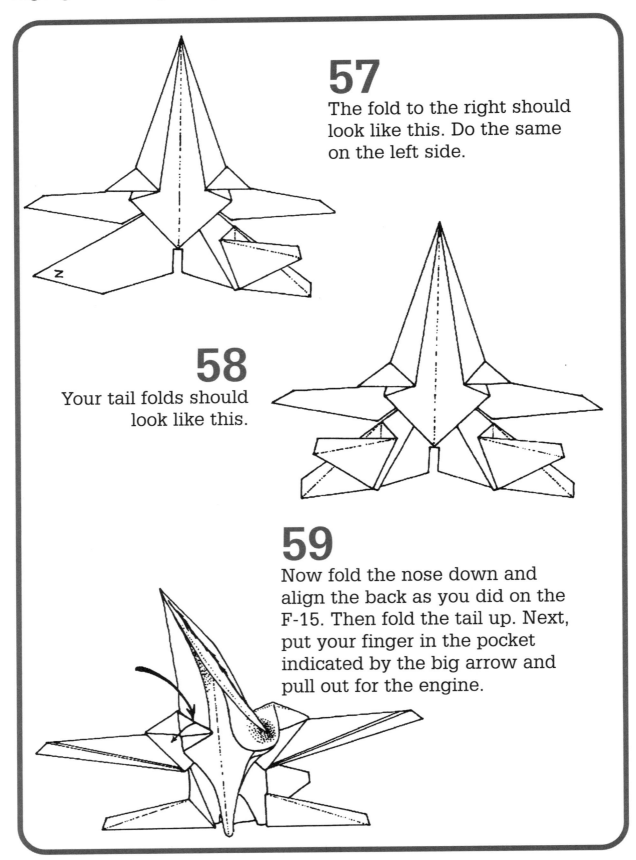

## 57

The fold to the right should look like this. Do the same on the left side.

## 58

Your tail folds should look like this.

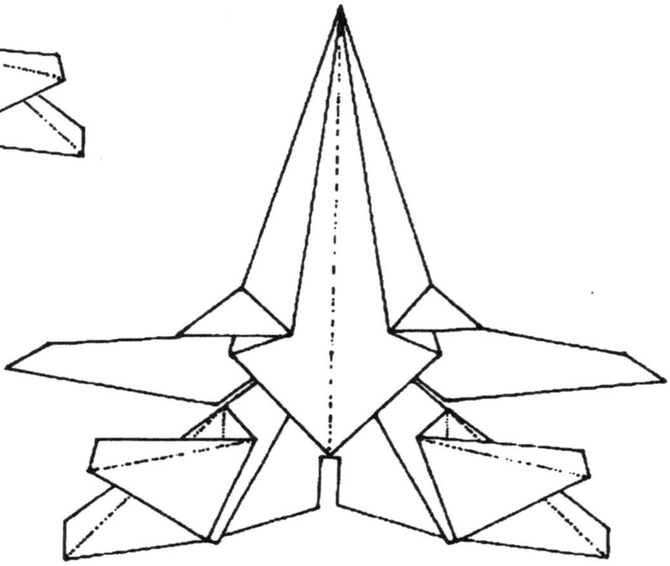

## 59

Now fold the nose down and align the back as you did on the F-15. Then fold the tail up. Next, put your finger in the pocket indicated by the big arrow and pull out for the engine.

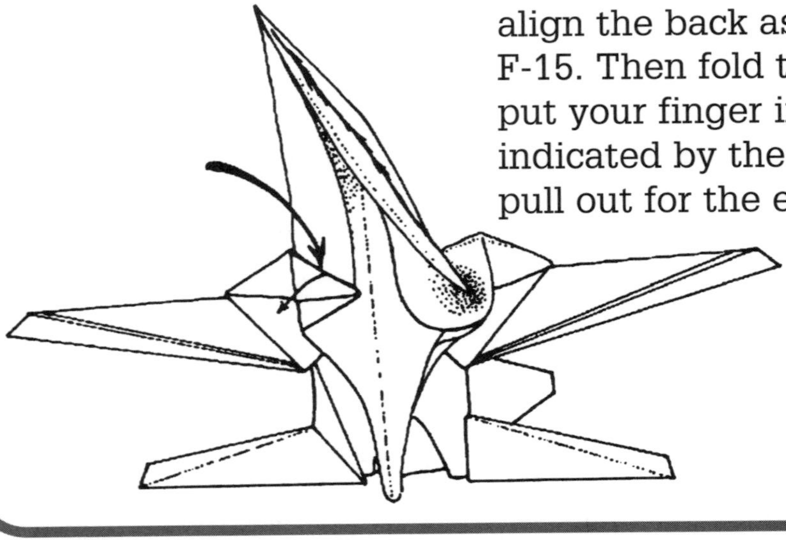

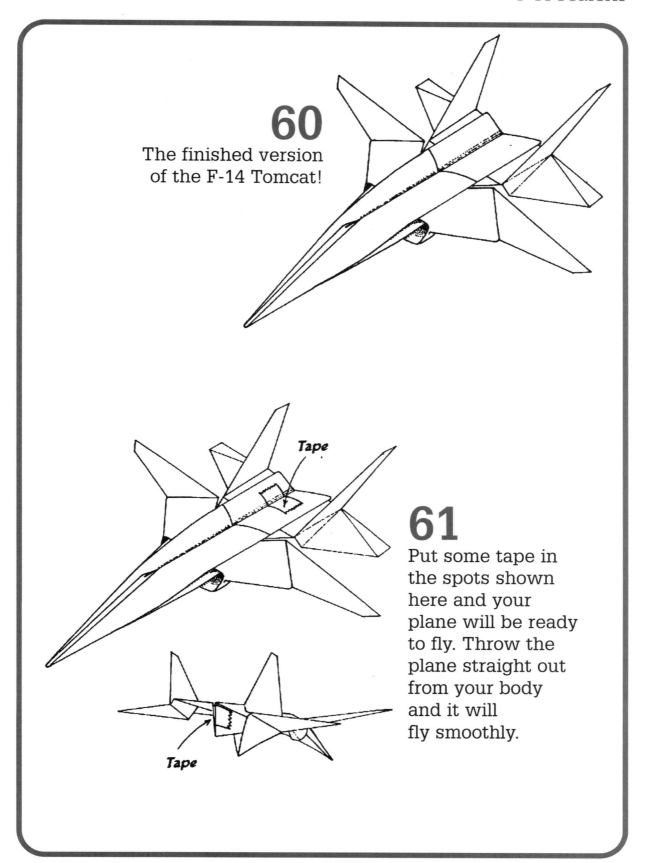

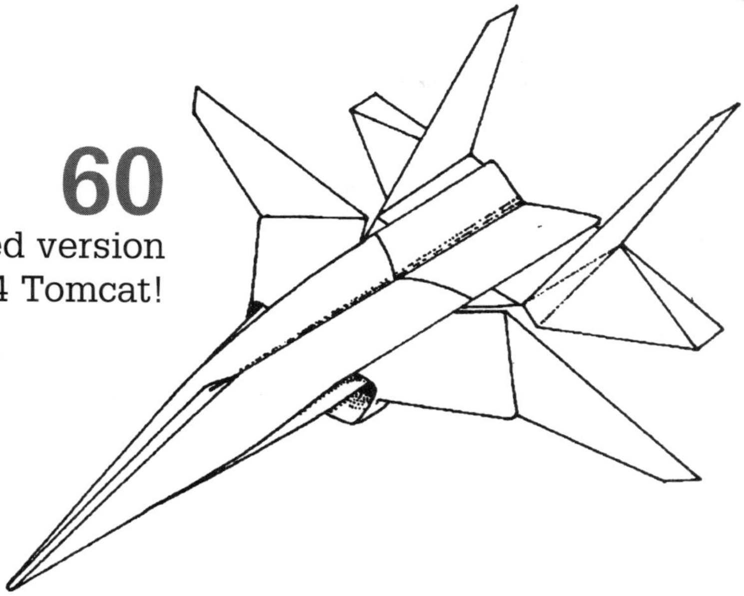

## 60

The finished version of the F-14 Tomcat!

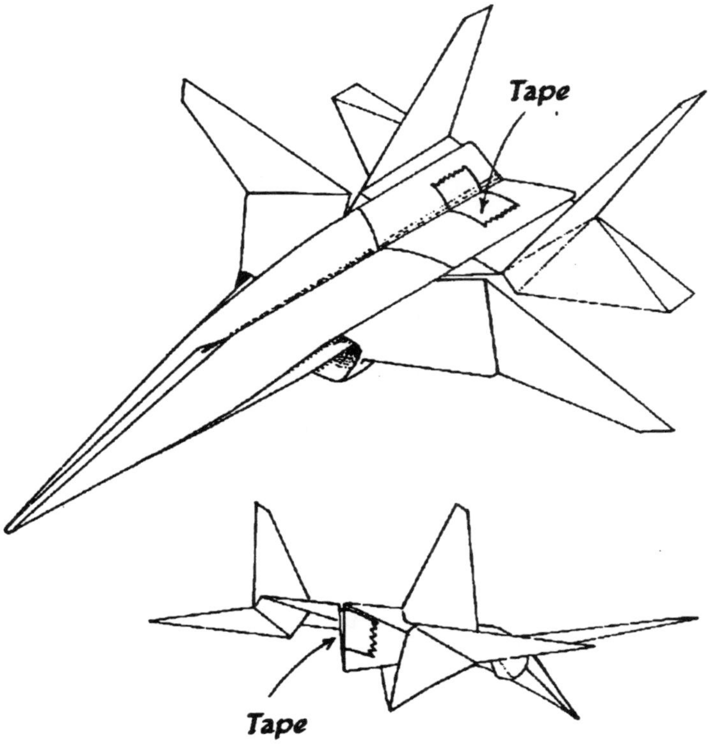


## 61

Put some tape in the spots shown here and your plane will be ready to fly. Throw the plane straight out from your body and it will fly smoothly.

# F-14 TOMCAT

# F-86 SABRE

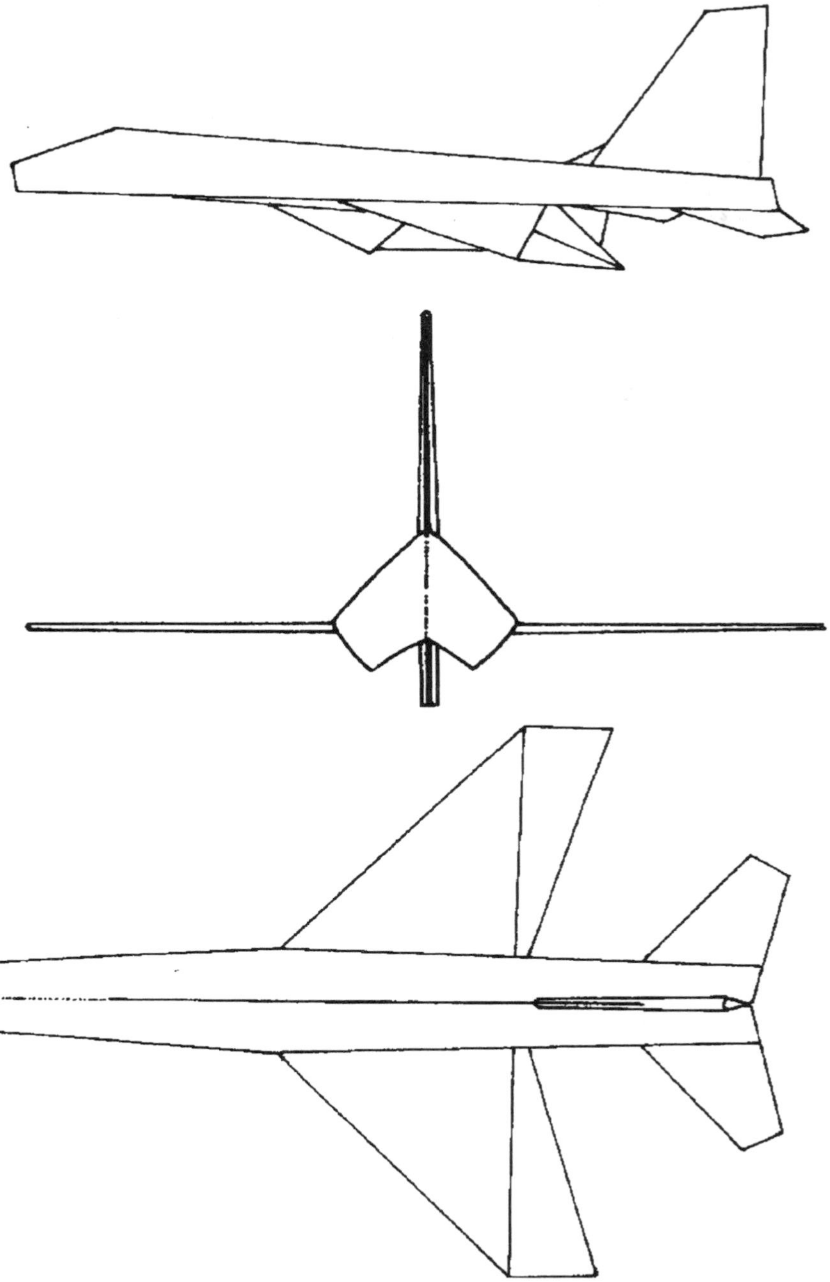

The F-86 uses more advanced folds than even the F-14 and it is recommended that you complete the other models before folding this plane.

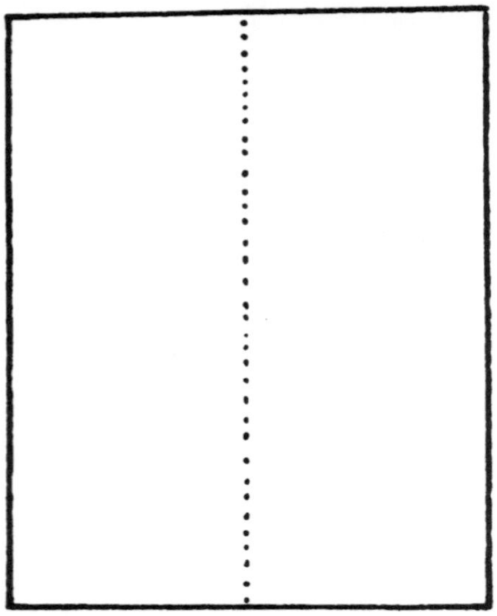

**1**

Book-fold paper in half,
then unfold it.

**2**

Fold paper down.

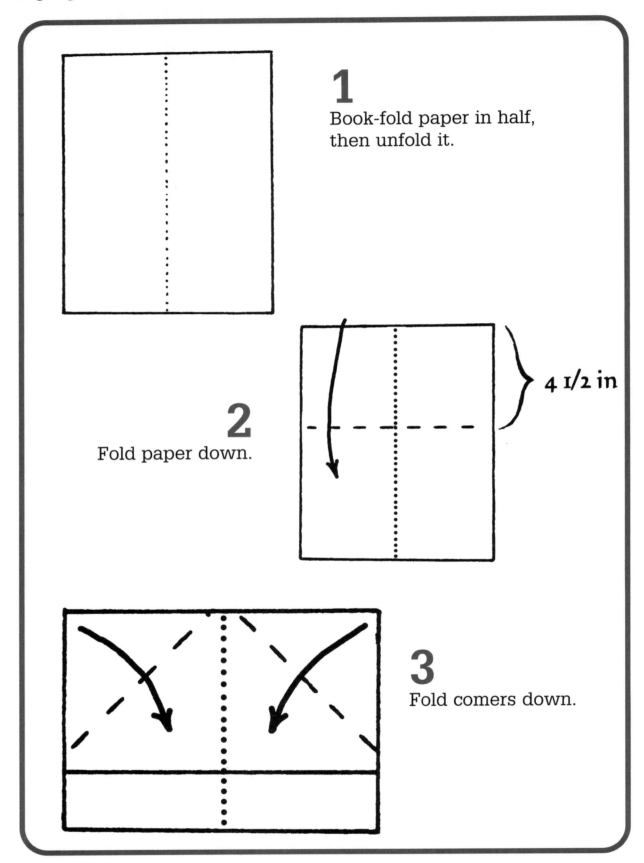

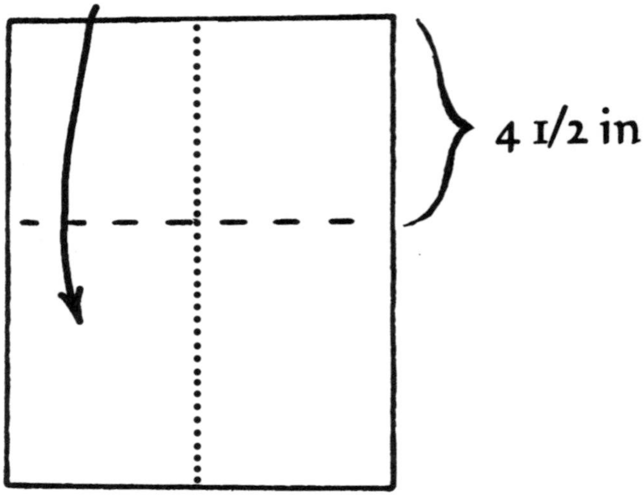


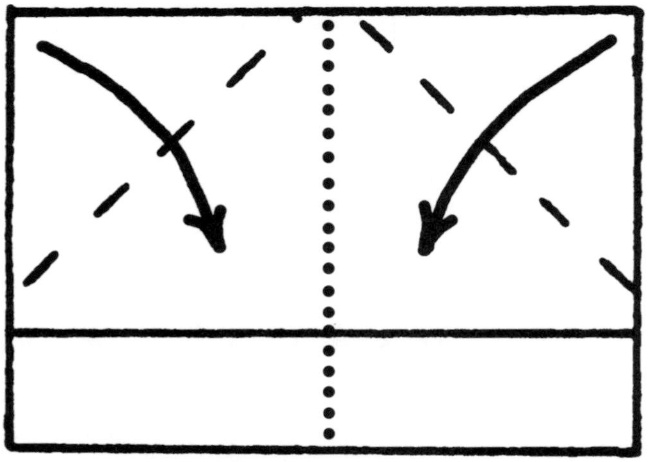

**3**

Fold comers down.

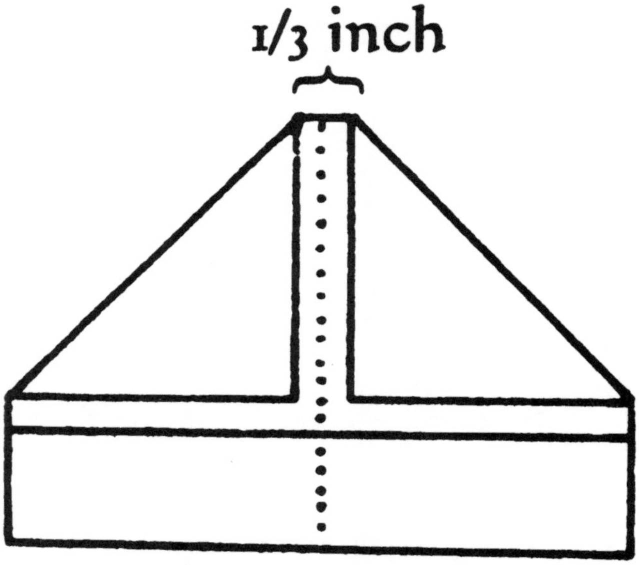


**4**
The fold should look like this.

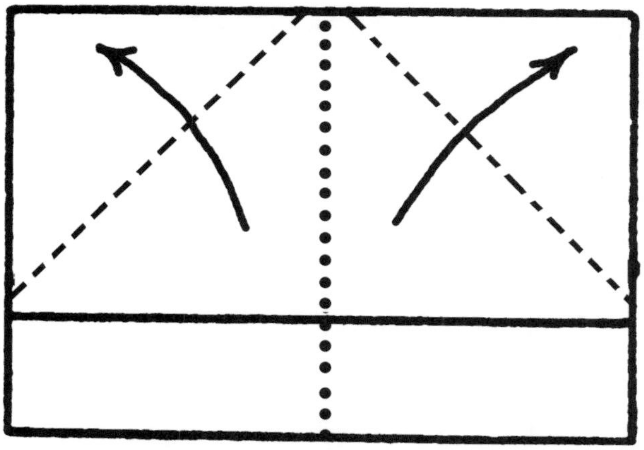

**5**
Unfold completely.

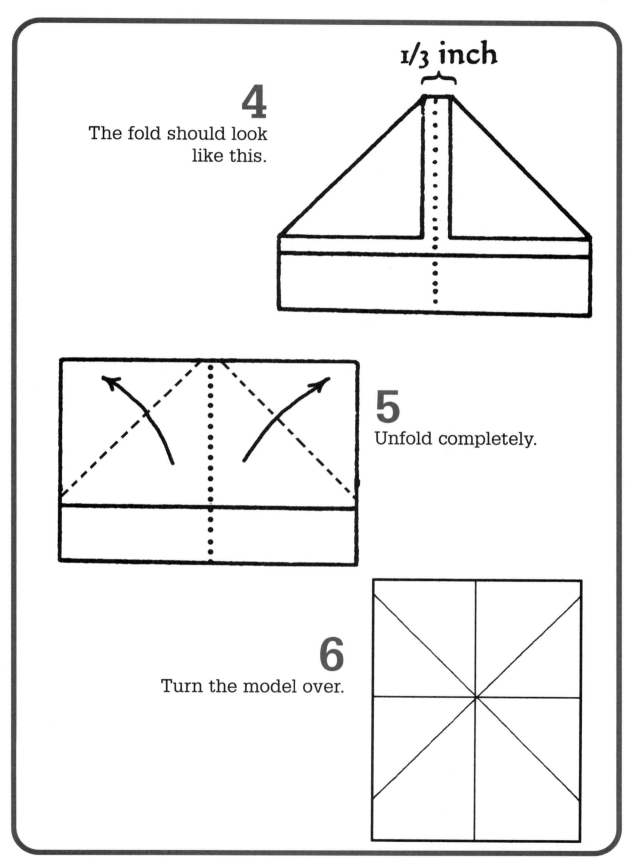

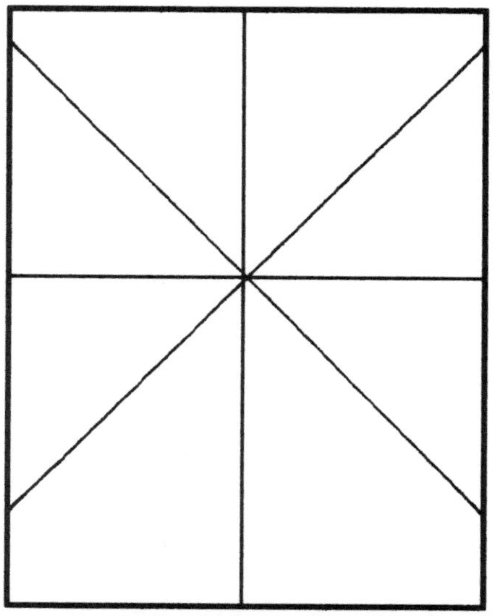

**6**
Turn the model over.

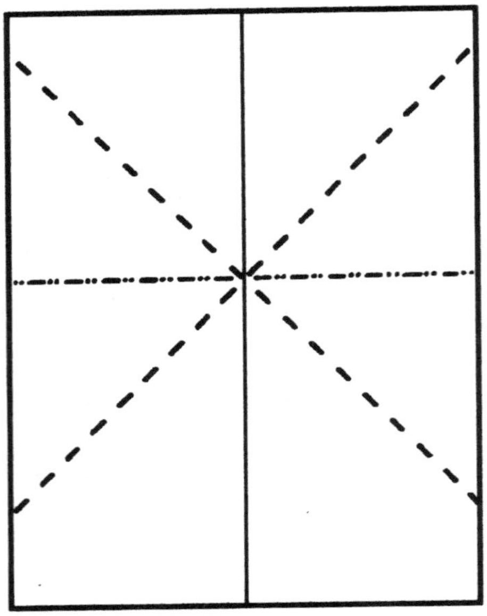

# 7

Press the center point with your finger, and the paper will fold upwards.

# 8

This is the folding diagram for the base. Fold the sides in and the top down.

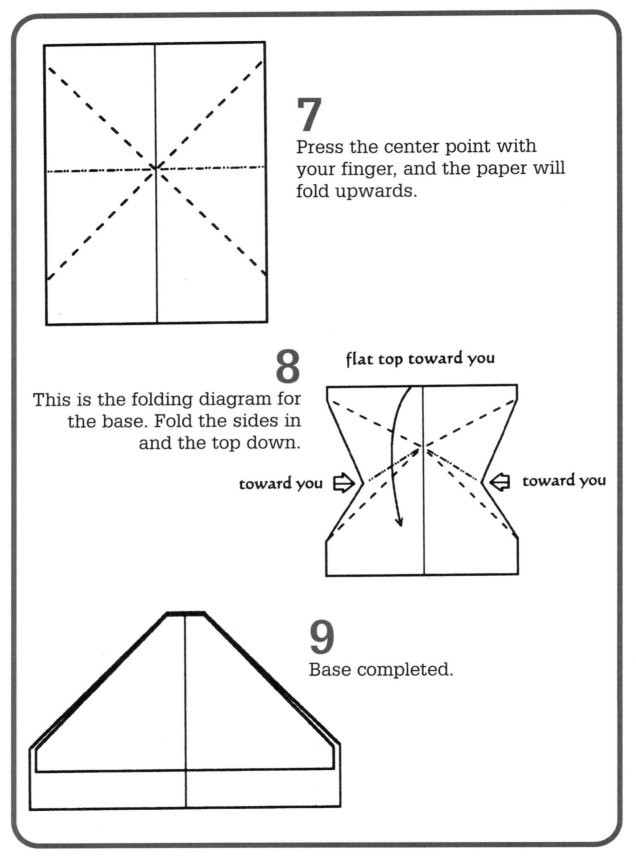

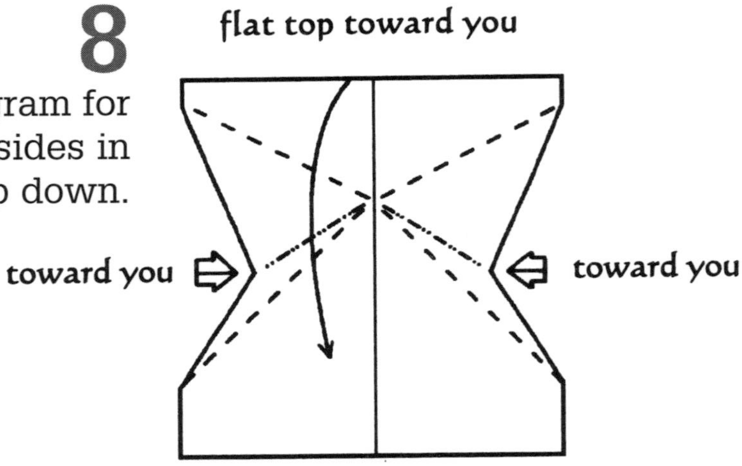


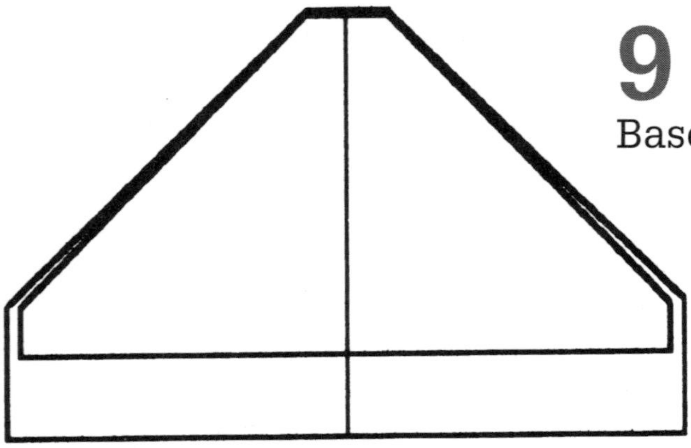

# 9

Base completed.

## 10

Fold towards center to look like the next diagram.

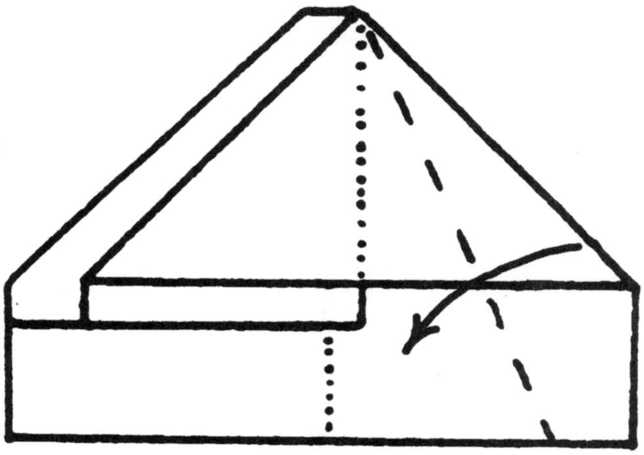

## 11

Make a matching fold for the left side.

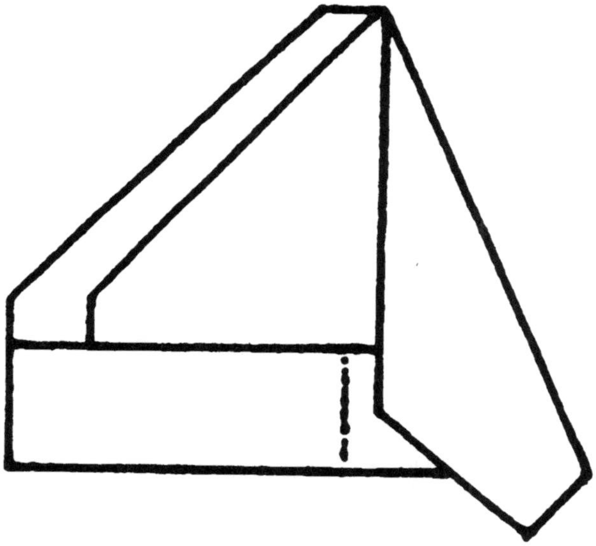

## 12

Flatten the plane so it looks like this.

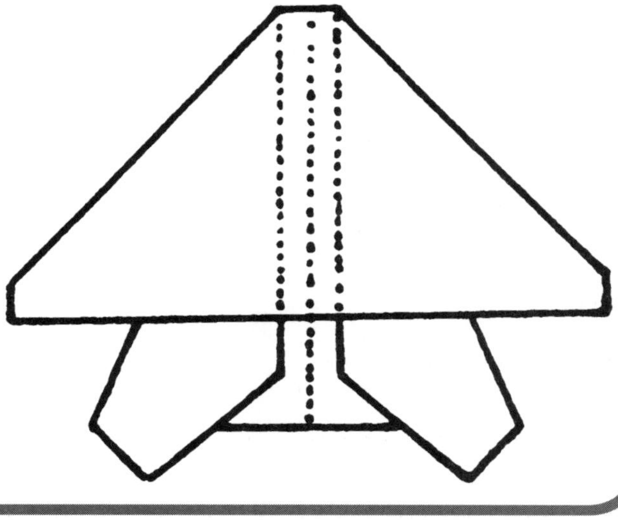

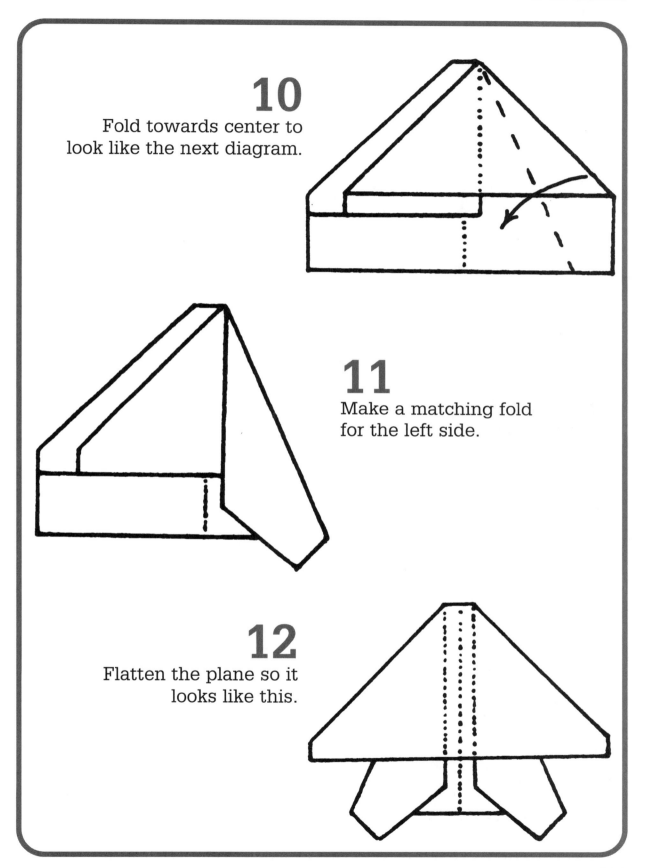

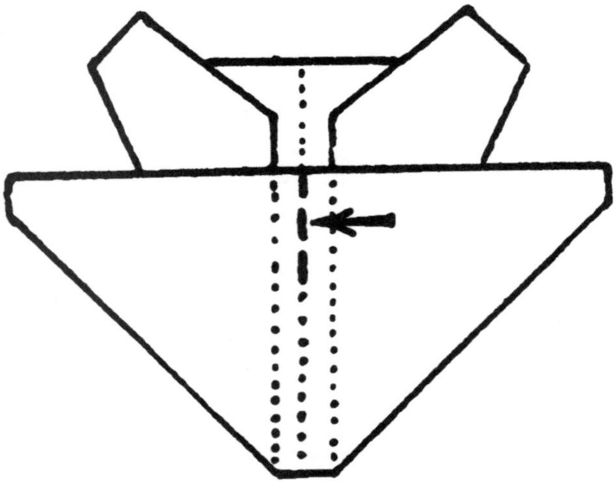

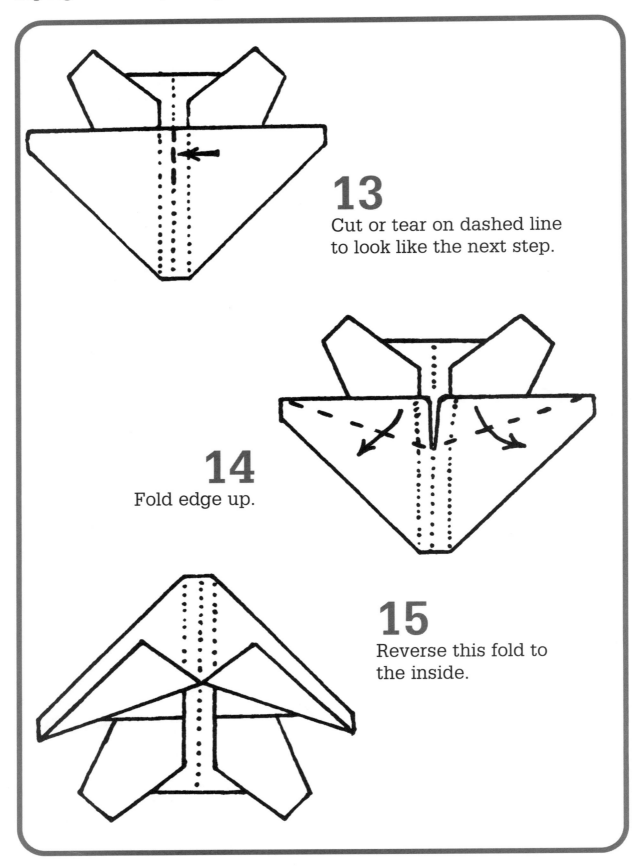

13
Cut or tear on dashed line to look like the next step.

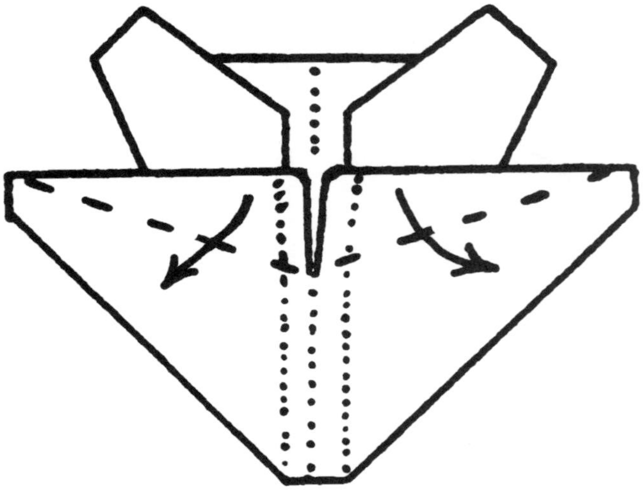

14
Fold edge up.

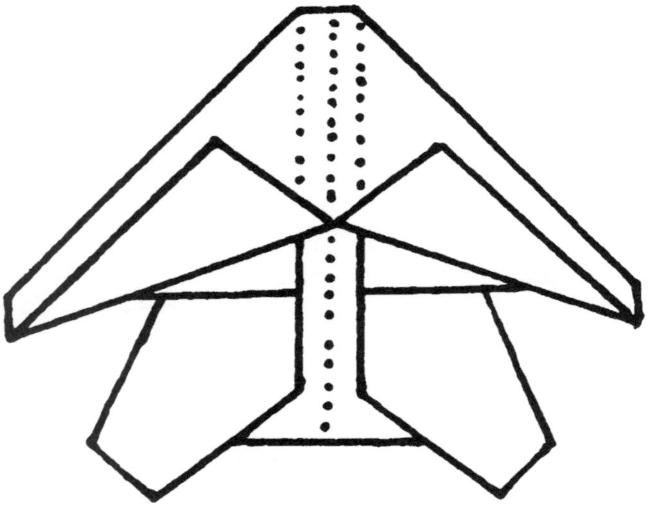

15
Reverse this fold to the inside.

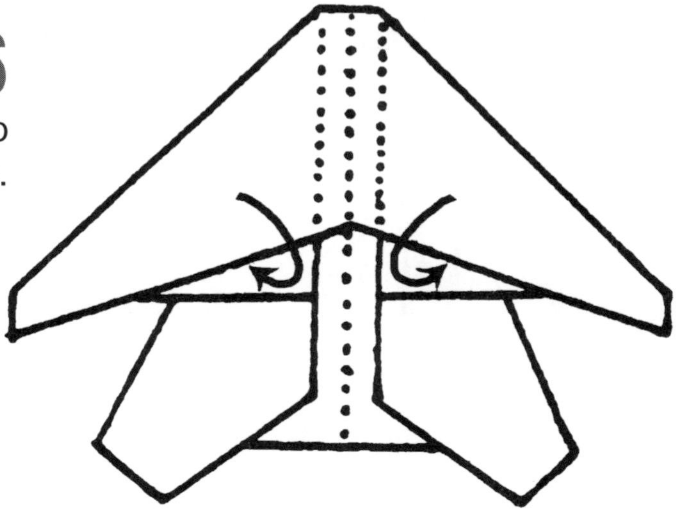

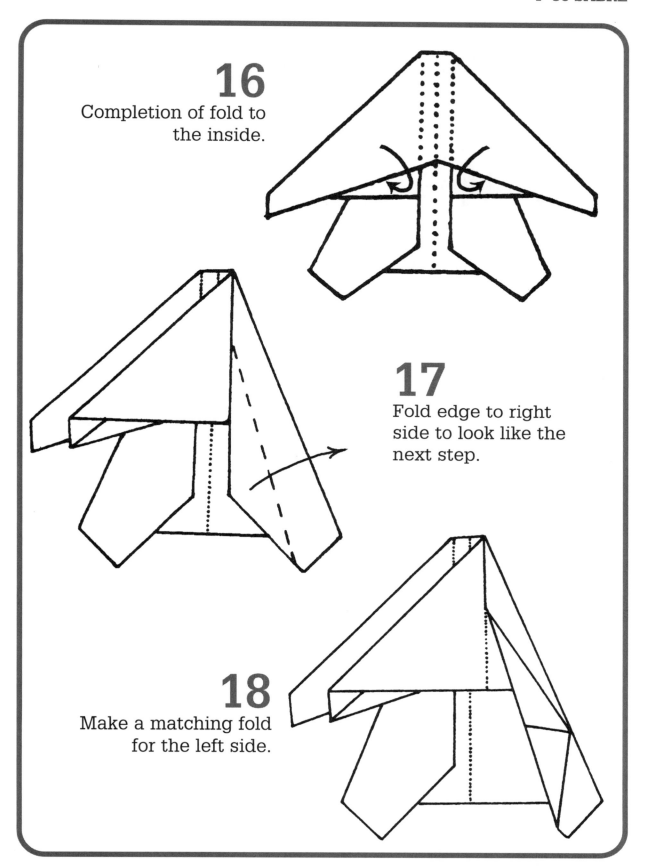

## 16

Completion of fold to the inside.

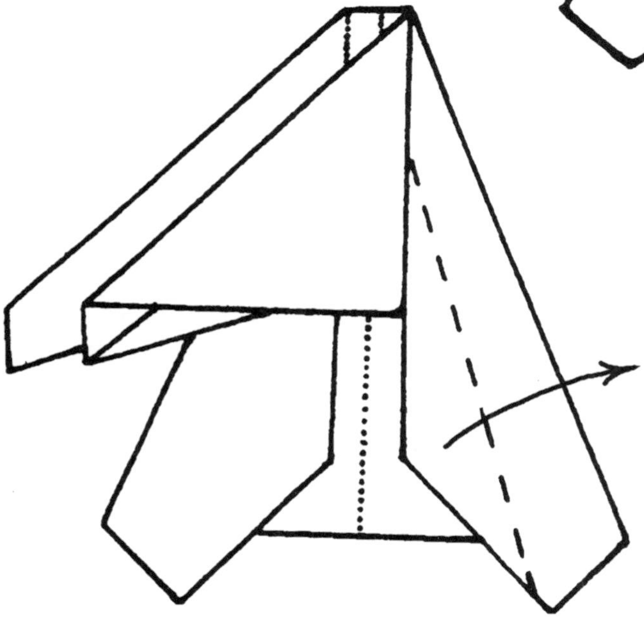

## 17

Fold edge to right side to look like the next step.

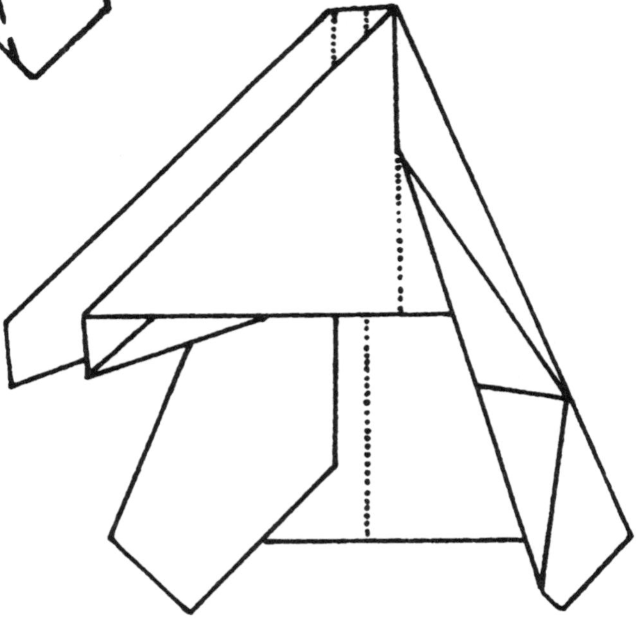

## 18

Make a matching fold for the left side.

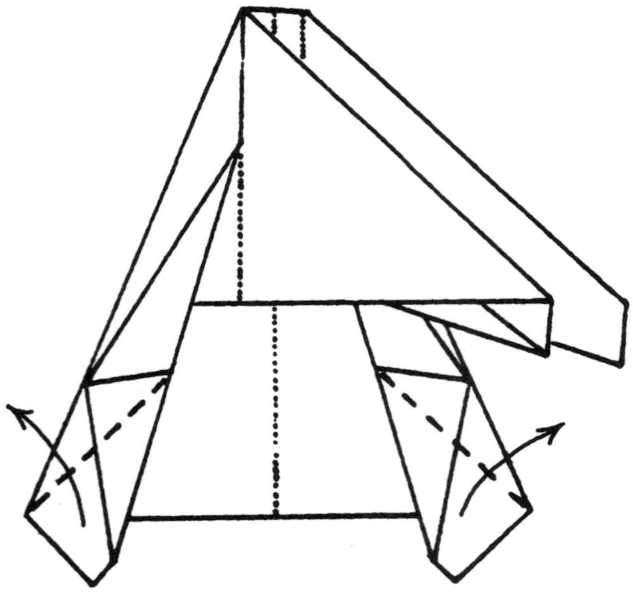

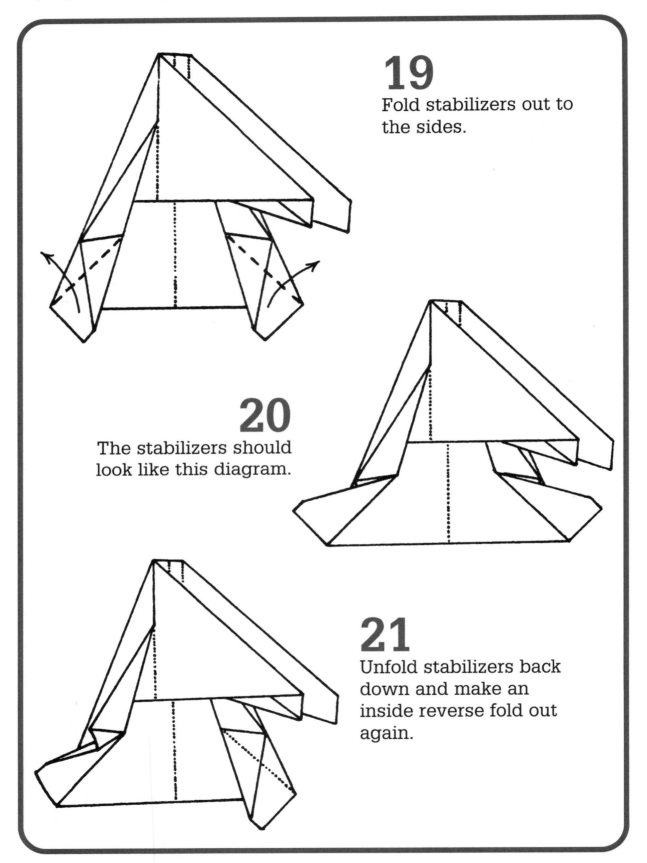

## 19

Fold stabilizers out to the sides.

## 20

The stabilizers should look like this diagram.

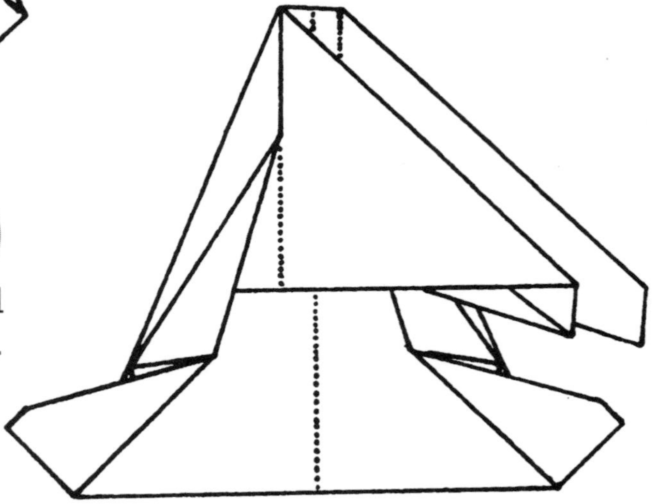

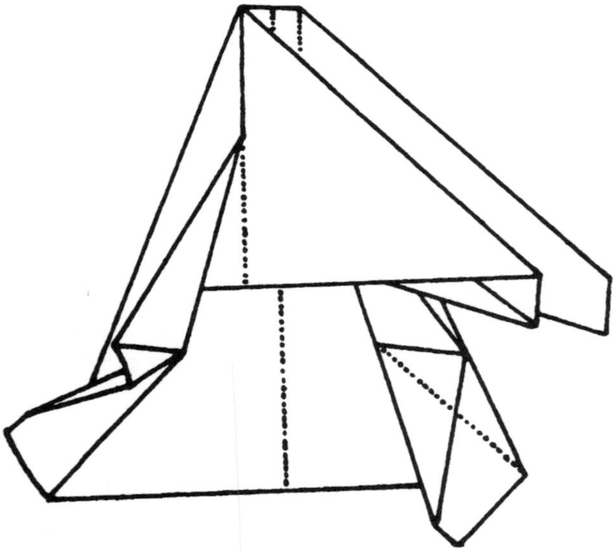

## 21

Unfold stabilizers back down and make an inside reverse fold out again.

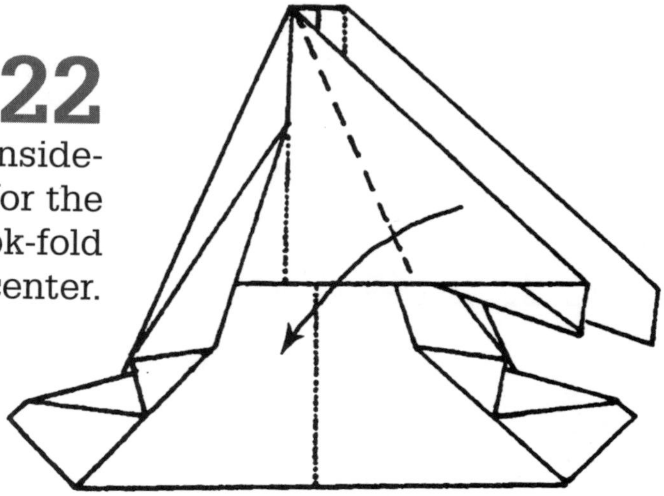

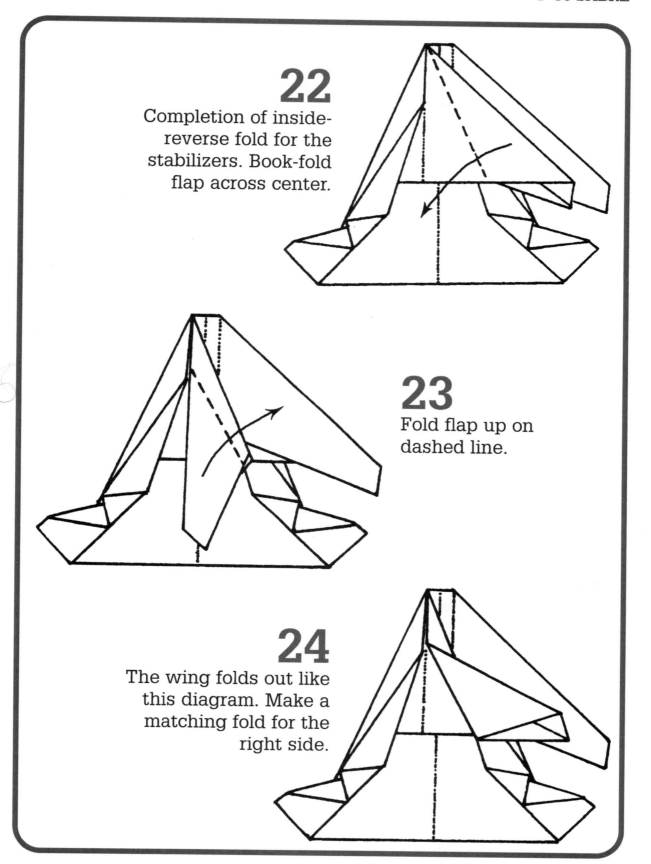

## 22

Completion of inside-reverse fold for the stabilizers. Book-fold flap across center.

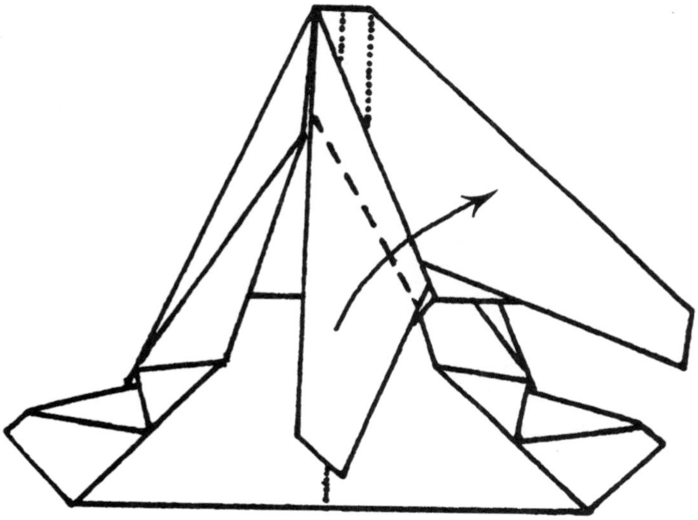

## 23

Fold flap up on dashed line.

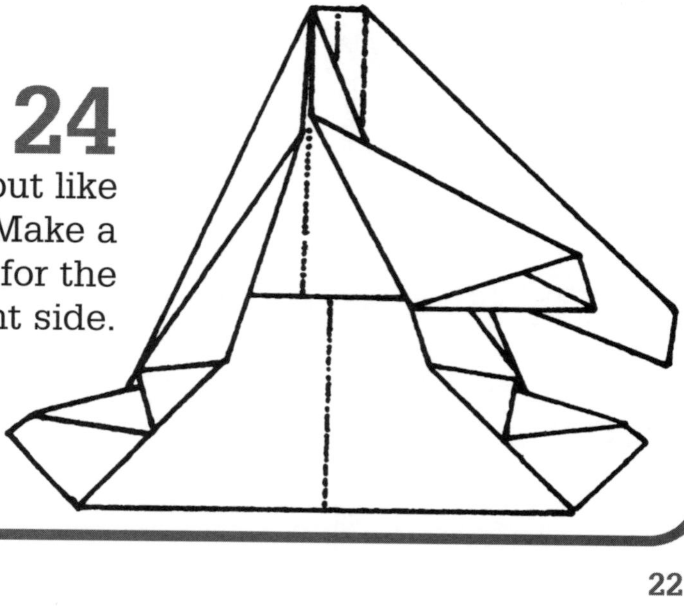

## 24

The wing folds out like this diagram. Make a matching fold for the right side.

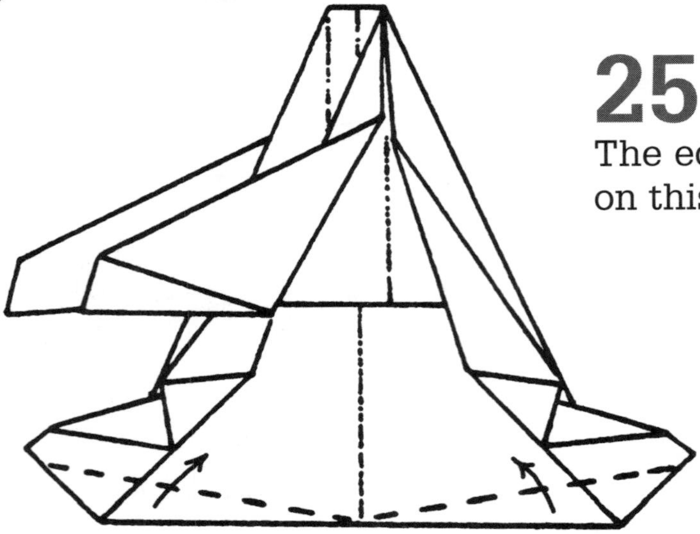

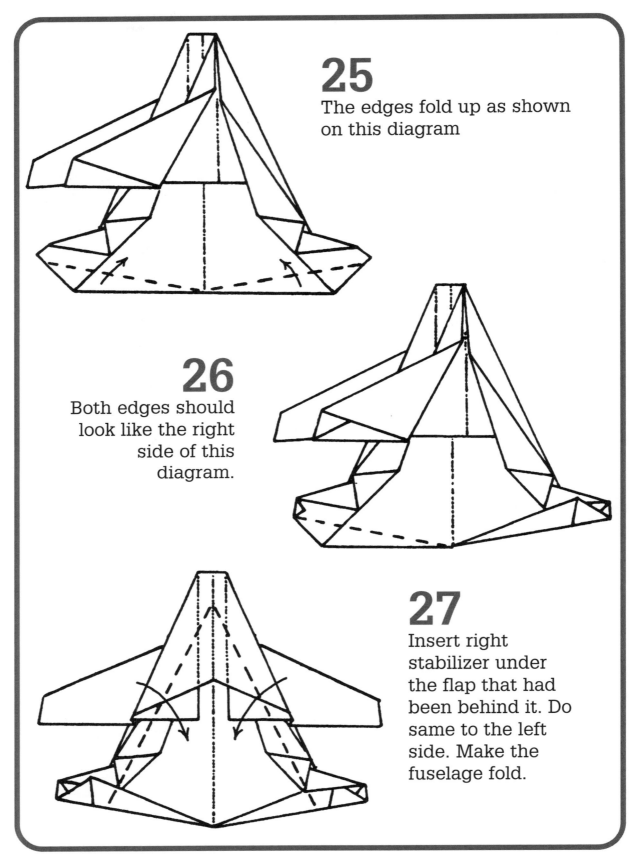

## 25

The edges fold up as shown on this diagram

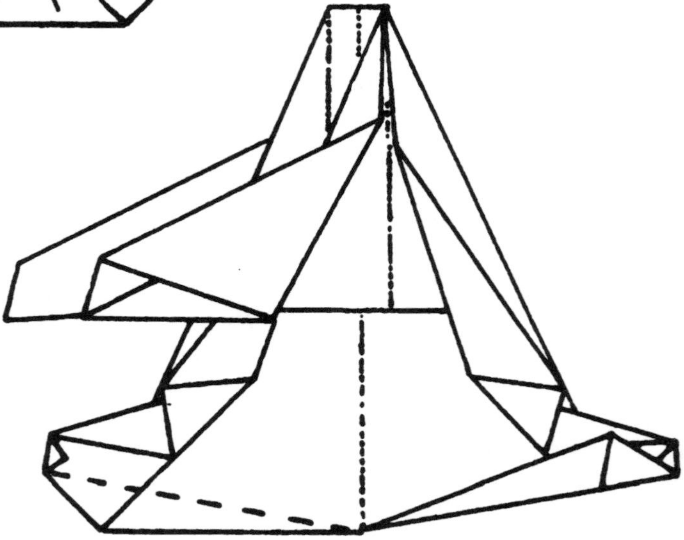

## 26

Both edges should look like the right side of this diagram.

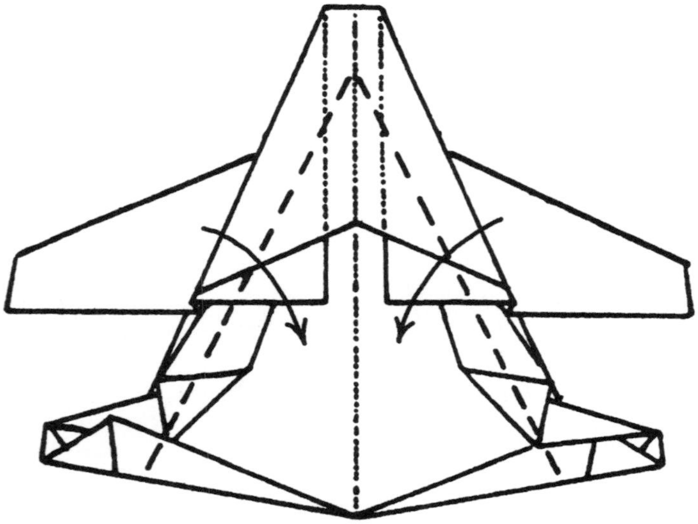

## 27

Insert right stabilizer under the flap that had been behind it. Do same to the left side. Make the fuselage fold.

## 28

Completion of fuselage fold. Fold wings and stabilizers up.

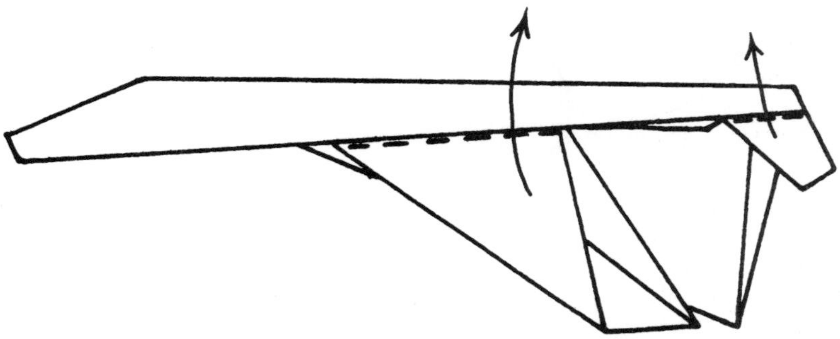

## 29

To create the tail, do an inside-reverse fold: fold the belly of the plane up between the wings to get a pointed tail, then fold the top of the tail back down into itself to give the tail its correct shape. (See Inside-Reverse Fold in the front of the book if you need help.)

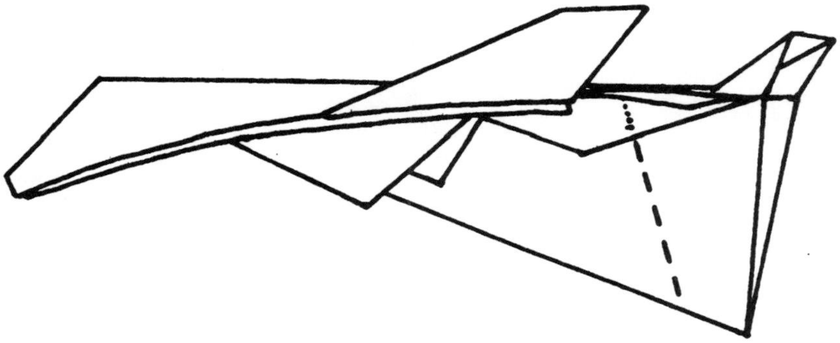

## 30

Completed F-86 Sabre!

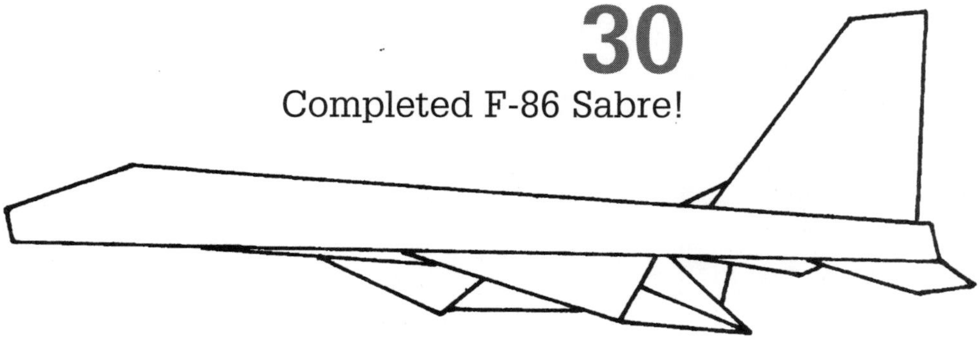

# F-86 SABRE

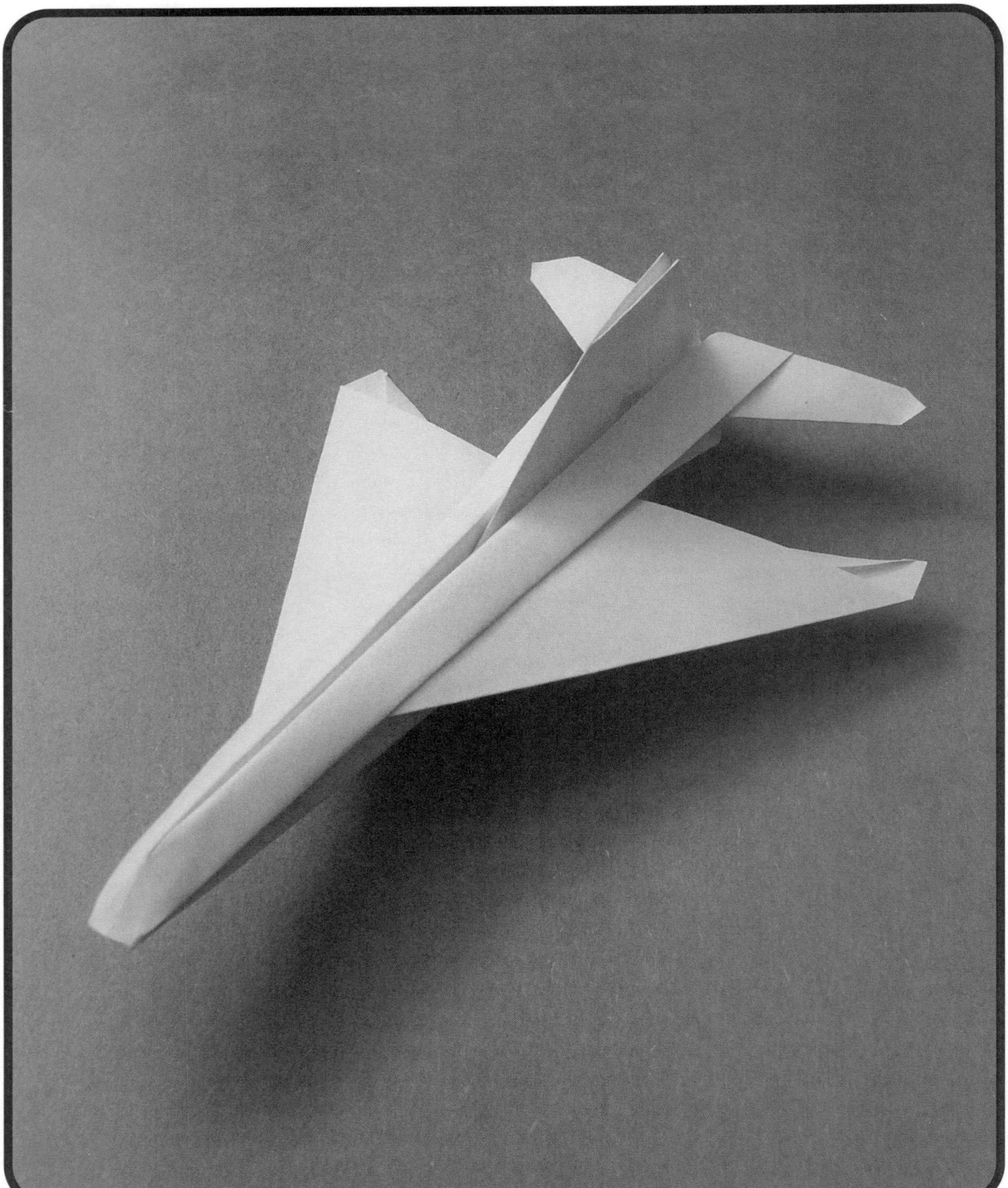